April 27, 1988

To: Lt. Governor
Evelyn F. Murphy

From: Your many friends at the
Worcester Area Chamber of Commerce

Please accept this as a token of our
appreciation for a most informative
day on Beacon Hill.

# WORCESTER

*This view of Worcester as it appeared in 1864 was done by lithographer John H. Bufford of Boston. Courtesy of the Worcester Historical Museum.*

# HEART OF THE COMMONWEALTH
# WORCESTER

## An Illustrated History
### by
### Margaret A. Erskine

Sponsored by the Worcester Historical Museum and the Worcester Area Chamber of Commerce

Windsor Publications, Inc.    Woodland Hills, California

Opposite

*The Washburn Iron Works circa 1860. This view of the rear of Nathan Washburn's factory shows how rural the land was near industrial areas of Worcester. Nathan Washburn made railroad wheels, rails, and tires. He was not related to Ichabod Washburn, the wire maker. This painting is attributed to William H. Titcomb (1824-1888) who taught painting and drawing in Boston. Courtesy of the Worcester Historical Museum.*

Editors: Lissa Sanders, Margaret Tropp
Picture Editor: Teri Davis Greenberg
Color Photographer: Ron White

Windsor Publications, Woodland Hills, California 91365

All antiques, works of art, maps, and historical documents reproduced in this book, except those appearing in Chapter IX and where otherwise noted, are from the collection of the Worcester Historical Museum.

First Edition

**Library of Congress Cataloging in Publication Data**

Erskine, Margaret A. (Margaret Ayres), 1925-
    Heart of the Commonwealth: Worcester.

    "Sponsored by the Worcester Historical Museum and the Worcester Area Chamber of Commerce."
    Includes index.
    1. Worcester (Mass.)—History. I. Worcester Historical Museum. II. Worcester Area Chamber of Commerce. III. Title.
F74.W9E77          974.4′3          80-54000
ISBN 0-89781-030-9          AACR2

# Contents

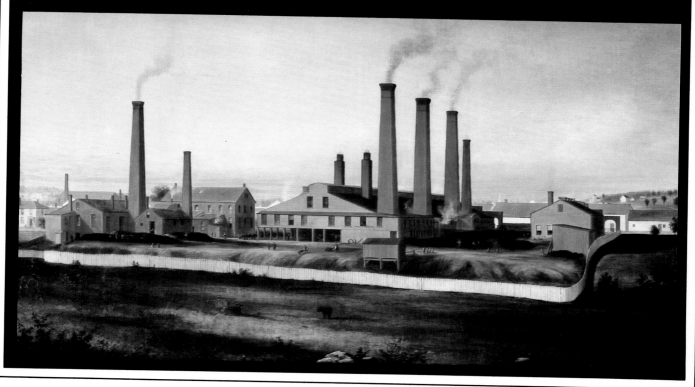

*The Ethan Allen mansion in Worcester was depicted by William O. Bemis in 1854. Ethan Allen (1806-1871) invented a self-cocking revolver called the "pepper box" which was much in demand at the time of the Mexican War and the California gold rush. He built this large mansion on Main Street. It had very elaborate gardens. To the left is Goat Hill with the romantic towers of the Oread Collegiate Institute on the top. The mansion was torn down in 1924. Courtesy of the Worcester Historical Museum.*

*This sign hung outside Stephen Salisbury's Store at Lincoln Square. Courtesy of the Worcester Historical Museum.*

"*May we realize that the true greatness of Worcester is not evidenced now and never will be evidenced by the number and length of its streets, its magnificent buildings, its extensive factories, or its great population, but it is found now, and ever will be found, if found at all, in the minds and hearts of the people.*"

From the address of Burton W. Potter at the dedication of the new City Hall, April 28, 1898

Chapter One

# "Like Lambs in a Large Place"

*The Jo Bill House, located on South Main Street in this 1886 photograph, had originally been located on Institute Road, called "Jo Bill Road." This house was undoubtedly typical of the type built by many early settlers. Courtesy of the Worcester Historical Museum.*

**I**t seemed an auspicious time to start a new settlement in the heart of the thriving colony of Massachusetts. Sir Joshua Child, in his *Discourse on Trade* (1667), had described the colony as "the most prejudicial plantation of Great Britain; the frugality, industry, and temperance of its people and the happiness of their laws and institutions, promise them long life, a wonderful increase of people, riches, and power."

In May 1667, the Massachusetts General Court appointed a committee to determine whether the place "called Quandsicamond ponds . . . was capable to make a plantation . . . and then to offer unto this court some meet expedient how the same may bee setled and improved for the public good."

Grants of land in the area known as Quinsigamond had already been made by the General Court in 1657, 1662, and 1664, on condition that the land be occupied and cultivated, that Christian worship be maintained, and that schools be established. None of the original grantees actually took up residence, however, and their rights were sold or passed on to others.

In October 1668, after a visit to that lonely, hilly region in the very center of the colony, Captain Daniel Gookin, Captain Edward Johnson, and Andrew Belcher presented their report to the General Court in Boston. By that time, the name Worcester was being used in connection with the proposed settlement, in honor of the English town where Cromwell had been victorious over King Charles I. Both names, Quinsigamond and Worcester, presented serious problems of spelling then, as they do to this day.

"For a plantation at Quansikamund now Called Wocester . . . we find it is a trract of very good Chestnut tree land . . . but of meadow wee find not so much." Meadowland, generally kept open by the Indians by cultivation or burning, was of prime interest to prospective settlers; other land would have to be cleared of deep forest before it could be cultivated. The best meadowland had been included in the 4700 acres granted earlier. "But not withstanding wee conceive therre may bee enough medow forr a plantation orr towne of about thirty families and if those farms be anexed to it, it may Supply about Sixty families."

The committee proposed that a town about eight miles square be laid out, that a new committee be appointed to oversee the organization of the town until it could be settled, and "that a good ministerr of God's word bee placed therre, as Soone as may be, that Such people as may therre be planted may not live like lambs in a large place."

The General Court approved the report and ordered that a new committee be formed to include Gookin plus Thomas Prentice, Daniel Henchman, and Richard Beers, or any two of the three. In June 1669, they drew up the proposed rules for "mannaging and orderring a new plantation ... near Quansitamund pond, now called Worcester."

Daniel Gookin was particularly well qualified to serve as the key member of the committee. Leaving Virginia when the Puritan mission was driven out of that colony, he had settled in Cambridge, where he became prominent in political and military affairs. He was a colleague of John Eliot, the "Apostle to the Indians." Historian George Bancroft wrote of Eliot, "his actions, his thoughts, his desires, all wore the hues of disinterested love. His uncontrollable charity welled out in a perpetual fountain."

Though Gookin did not share Eliot's personal magnetism, his general view of the Indians was charitable. "But this may on sure grounds be asserted, that they are Adam's posterity, and consequently children of wrath; and hence are not only objects of all Christians' pity and compassion, but subjects upon which our faith, prayers, and best endeavors should be put forth to reduce them from barbarism to civility; but especially to rescue them out of the bondage of Satan, and bring them to salvation by Our Lord Jesus Christ."

The local Indian tribe was called Nipmuck. Their main habitation was on Pakachoag Hill, though they hunted, fished, and cultivated land in various places throughout the area. Like the other tribes in the area, they had suffered enormous losses in a plague that swept through the region in 1612 and 1613. By the 1670s, their numbers were still relatively few. They seemed peaceful enough, and willing to sell their land to the new settlers.

Between 1673 and 1675, Gookin established seven towns of Praying Indians—Christian converts friendly toward whites—in the Worcester area. Both he and Eliot visited the local Nipmucks at their village on Pakachoag Hill. Gookin served as superintendent of the Praying Indians, appointing magistrates and generally watching over their affairs. Thus, he was familiar and friendly with the native population of the area.

On July 13, 1674, Hoorrawannonit, Sagamore, or local chief, of Pakachoag, and Woonaskochu, Sagamore of Tatassit, signed a deed to eight square miles of land in exchange for an initial payment of two coats and four yards of cloth. The total purchase price of the land was 12 pounds.

At least one white settler, Ephraim Curtis, had established himself in the area prior to the formal transfer of land. A native of Sudbury, he had bought the rights granted in 1664 to Thomas Noyes, who had never exercised them. Curtis later recalled that he often worked all day, until dusk

# HISTORICAL COLLECTIONS

### OF THE

# I N D I A N S

#### IN *NEW ENGLAND*.

OF THEIR SEVERAL NATIONS, NUMBERS, CUSTOMS, MANNERS, RELI-
GION AND GOVERNMENT, BEFORE THE ENGLISH PLANTED THERE.

Also a true and faithful Account of the present state and condition of the Praying
Indians (or those who have visibly received the gospel in New England) declaring
the number of that people, the situation and place of their Towns and Churches,
and their manner of worshipping God, and divers other matters appertaining
thereto.

Together with a brief Mention of the Instruments and Means, that God hath been
pleased to use for their Civilizing and Conversion, briefly declaring the prudent
and faithful endeavours of The Right Honourable the Corporation at London, for
promoting that affair.

Also suggesting some Expedients for their further Civilizing and propagating the
Christian faith among them.

## By DANIEL GOOKIN, Gentleman.

One of the Magistrates of Massachusetts Colony in New England, who hath been
for sundry years past, and is at present, betrusted and employed for the civil
government and conduct of the Indians in Massachusetts Colony, by order of the
General Court there.

Ps. ii. 8. *Ask of me, and I shall give thee, the heathen for thine inheritance, and the ut-
termost parts of the earth for thy possession.*

Ps. lxxii. 8, 9. *He shall have dominion also from sea to sea, and from the river unto
the ends of the earth. They that dwell in the wilderness shall bow before him ; and his
enemies shall lick the dust.*

Is. xlix. 6. *And he said, It is a light thing that thou shouldest be my servant to raise
up the tribes of Jacob, and to restore the preserved of Israel : I will also give thee for
a light to the gentiles, that thou mayest be my salvation unto the end of the earth.*

*First printed from the Original Manuscript.*
MDCCXCII.

English-born John Eliot
(1604-1690), a colleague of Daniel
Gookin's, preached to the Indians
in their own language and
published a translation of the Bible—the first Bible of any
language to be printed in America.
This engraving appeared in
Bancroft's History of the United
States. (WHM).

Left
Daniel Gookin wrote accounts of
the Indians in Massachusetts Colony for the Corporation in London.
Although Gookin never actually
lived in Worcester for any extended
period of time, he took an active interest in its affairs. (WHM)

forced him back into the house, where his loneliness, his utter solitude, brought tears to his eyes. But for all his work, his claim to much of the best land was challenged in court, and he was forced to relinquish part of his holdings.

The new settlers began arriving in 1674. In December of that year, a license was granted to Thomas Brown of Cambridge to keep an inn, or "ordinary," in his house in Worcester "to furnish travelers with wine and strong waters."

A total of 30 families were granted land in Worcester, on condition that they settle the land within three years or lose their claims. Most of these families, it may be assumed, took up residence sometime in 1674 or 1675.

The area to which they came was hilly and wooded. Its most notable feature was the lake, four miles long and half a mile wide, bearing the troublesome Indian name that eventually came to be spelled Quinsigamond. Deep waters at the northern end rose to muddy shallows at the southern end. The long, narrow lake gave the appearance of a mighty river, but had no current. Two other smaller lakes, known today as Indian Lake and Bell Pond, were the only other natural bodies of water.

From the level of Lake Quinsigamond, 356 feet above sea level, the land rose to a height of about 1000 feet at the western edge of the present city of Worcester. Beyond, just to the west, Mount Asnebumskit rose 1408 feet high. To the north the rounded dome of the monadnock called Mount Wachusett in the town of Princeton, 2108 feet high, dominated the landscape for miles around.

In between the wooded hillsides rose and fell. Among them ran a number of small brooks, not one of them worthy of the name river and not one of them navigable by any vessel larger than a small rowboat or canoe.

The terrain presented serious problems to travelers as the numerous hills exhausted men and horses alike. Other towns in the area were situated more conveniently along navigable rivers, providing easy access to other towns up- and downstream, as well as to the port cities where one might hope to sell the products of the local farms and small industries. Worcester undoubtedly seemed destined to remain a small, isolated rural settlement.

Still all seemed peaceful and pleasant enough in the newly formed settlement. Then in June of 1675, Philip of Pokanoket—son of Massasoit, the great chief who had befriended the Pilgrims at Plymouth—fled from his tribal headquarters at Mount Hope and took refuge among the Nipmucks. An able leader with a magnetic personality, he was bent on a war to drive the white man out of his land and reclaim the ancient rights of his people.

The Nipmucks joined him, and war spread throughout the colony. "They rose without hope," wrote Bancroft, "and, therefore, they fought without mercy. For them, as a nation, there was no tomorrow. ... The war, on the part of the Indians, was one of ambushes and surprises. . . . They were secret as beasts of prey, skillful marksmen, and in part provided with fire-arms, fleet of foot, conversant with all the paths of the forest, patient of fatigue, and mad with passion for rapine, vengeance, and destruction, retreating into swamps for their fastness, or hiding in the greenwood thickets, where the leaves muffled the eyes of the pursuer.''

Sometime during that summer of 1675, all the settlers left Worcester. Many of the men joined in the fight; Curtis, Gookin, Henchman, and Beers all distinguished themselves as officers. By the time the Indians passed by in December, the little settlement of Worcester was silent and empty. The deserted village was burned to the ground; not a single building remained.

When the war ended with the death of Philip in August 1676, the vengeance of the white man was swift. The Indians, especially those from areas near the seacoast, were rounded up in great numbers. Many were killed outright; others were sent off to die of starvation on Deer Island in Boston Harbor; still others were sold into slavery in Bermuda and the West Indies. Daniel Gookin and John Eliot tried to help those remaining, but the inflamed public sentiment against the Indian made their lives difficult.

No one returned to Worcester despite repeated urgings by the General Court which threatened to declare the land forfeit unless it was resettled. In 1678, the grant holders were ordered to go and "build together so as to defend themselves" before 1680. The committee reported, "There was no going by any of them or hope that they would do so; for divers of them being importuned to go would not."

In March of 1679, 19 families agreed to try to settle Worcester again but nothing came of it. In October 1682 the committee again received notice that the General Court would declare all the land rights forfeit unless some effort were made to resettle the place.

In the Commonplace Book of Samuel Sewall of Marlborough, an entry for April 23, 1683, notes that "Captain Daniel Henchman set out from Marlborough towards Quinsickamum with his Pack Horses in order to settle a plantation there." On April 1, 1684, the Middlesex County Court permitted the inhabitants of Worcester to hold Sabbath meeting in their town "in the best manner they can," rather than travel to the nearest town where there was a church—though the court warned that as soon as their numbers had increased, they were to "call and maintain a learned, pious, and orthodox minister as they will answer their neglect at their peril." Thus by the spring of 1684 there must have been a number of settlers at Worcester. Most likely they had built their houses during the summer of 1683 but the records have been lost.

In April 1684 Nathaniel Henchman, the 22-year-old son of Daniel, was licensed to run a tavern where he could sell rum and "strong waters." He

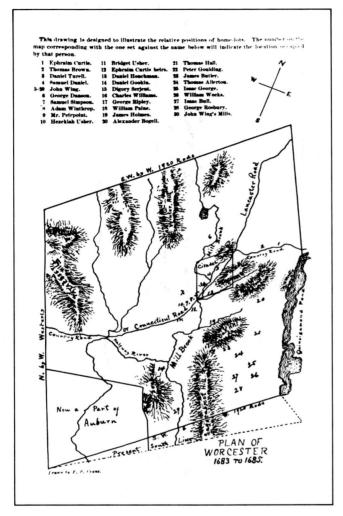

This drawing is designed to illustrate the relative positions of home-lots. The number on the map corresponding with the one set against the name below will indicate the location occupied by that person.

| | | | | | |
|---|---|---|---|---|---|
| 1 | Ephraim Curtis. | 11 | Bridget Usher. | 21 | Thomas Hall. |
| 2 | Thomas Brown. | 12 | Ephraim Curtis heirs. | 22 | Peter Goulding. |
| 3 | Daniel Turell. | 13 | Daniel Henchman. | 23 | James Butler. |
| 4 | Samuel Daniel. | 14 | Daniel Gookin. | 24 | Thomas Allerton. |
| 5-20 | John Wing. | 15 | Digory Serjent. | 25 | Isaac George. |
| 6 | George Danson. | 16 | Charles Williams. | 26 | William Weeks. |
| 7 | Samuel Simpson. | 17 | George Ripley. | 27 | Isaac Ball. |
| 8 | Adam Winthrop. | 18 | William Paine. | 28 | George Rosbury. |
| 9 | Mr. Peirpoint. | 19 | James Holmes. | 20 | John Wing's Mills. |
| 10 | Hezekiah Usher. | 20 | Alexander Bogell. | | |

PLAN OF WORCESTER 1683 TO 1685.

This "Plan of Worcester, 1683 to 1685" was made by Ellery B. Crane, a local historian, for the celebration of the bicentennial of the town's first settlement. Though earlier maps were lost, this is probably an accurate representation of the town's layout. (WHM)

was not to serve drinks in the house or "suffer tippling there."

The business of establishing a new town now proceeded apace—the marking out of boundaries, the official changing of the name from Quinsigamond to Worcester, the settling of earlier claims on the land, and the gradual establishment of a pattern of order.

There were a number of arguments and squabbles along the way, the most serious of which was a dispute over the water rights to Mill Brook, where John Wing was in the process of building a gristmill and a sawmill.

Wing owned land and water rights near what is now Lincoln Square, but George Danson claimed rights and land beyond Wing's to Indian Lake. The argument came to blows and eventually to a lawsuit, which Danson lost.

The whole affair is of interest today primarily because it produced two lists—one of witnesses, and one of those who signed petitions. From them we know the names of most of the families who were settled here at the time.

As the squabbles continued Gookin warned in June 1685 that the continuing arguments and lawsuits would hinder further settling of the area. "It is desired no interruption may be given to any man in their settlement of their lots, which will tend to discourage or hinder the settlement of the said place." Danson and Wing continued to argue, especially over the water rights, until Danson died, when Wing finally acquired both the land and the rights.

Mill Brook, like all the others in town, was only a small stream. The brooks flooded in the spring, overflowing the meadows, but were only small trickles in dry seasons. They would never provide great sources of power; a mill dam upstream would, in effect, shut down the mill downstream for much of the year.

From 1686 to 1713 no entries appear on the books of the proprietors of Worcester. It was a time of turmoil throughout the colony. The Massachusetts Charter was abrogated in 1684. Sir Edmund Andros was appointed governor of all the New England colonies in 1685, and his repressive measures did not encourage the growth of new towns. By 1687 economic restrictions threatened the whole colony with ruin. But complaints to the monopolists in England were met with the reply, "It is not for His Majesty's interest you should thrive."

A garrison house had been built on Captain Wing's land at the time of the resettlement. In addition to its role as a fortification, it had two rooms set aside for the accommodation of new settlers while their houses were being built, as well as for travelers. The man sent to command the garrison was Edward Downing. Worcester had had her share of heroes during King Philip's War, but Downing was an outsider, not a hero but a coachman, "an Irish stranger," and not much liked by the townspeople. In fact, he may have been one of the Scots Presbyterians settled in Ireland under James I who were just beginning to come to New England.

The local men refused to serve under him and set about building their own "citadel" at the southern end of town. Five soldiers were sent to strengthen the garrison, but even they did not want to serve under Downing, who was "very much resented by the inhabitants." Samuel Leonard was then appointed constable, and Downing's name is never mentioned again.

Meanwhile the troubled times continued. Indian tribes from the north were on the warpath again. From 1690 on there was continuous fighting, some of it close to Worcester.

In 1695, 12-year-old Samuel Leonard, Jr., the constable's son, was kidnapped from his home in Worcester by a traveling group of Indians. Young

Leonard became the slave of a brave named Bampico and learned many of the Indian ways. He was traveling with a raiding party that surprised Haverhill in March of 1697. They entered the house of Thomas Dustin, who fled with seven of his children. His wife, Hannah, a newborn infant, and a neighbor, Mrs. Mary Neff, who was helping attend the mother and child, were captured.   The infant's brains were dashed out, and the two women were forced to join young Leonard as prisoners. They journeyed for more than a month before Mrs. Dustin conceived the idea of killing their captors and escaping. Leonard had learned from Bampico how to kill with one blow of the tomahawk, and he showed Mrs. Dustin and Mrs. Neff how it was done.

They were camped on an island in the Merrimack River near Concord, New Hampshire, when the trio set upon the Indians as they slept after a hard day. Ten Indians were killed and their scalps taken as proof of the adventure. One wounded squaw escaped and one Indian boy was taken into a boat with Leonard and the two women. The other boats on the island were scuttled and the little party floated and paddled down the river ever fearful of being captured again until they reached Haverhill.

Samuel Leonard, along with the women, was given a hero's welcome and was reunited with his family in Connecticut. Like most of the other residents

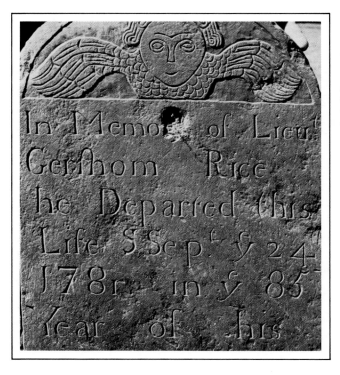

*Gershom Rice's gravestone carries the figure of a winged angel carved in a manner common to the work of many New England stonecutters. With her book,* Gravestones of Early New England, *Harriette Merrifield Forbes, a Worcester author, became the first to recognize this type of carving as an art. Photo by Daniel Farber.*

of Worcester the Leonards had left for safer places. On March 22, 1699, the name of Worcester was dropped from the list of frontier towns. By 1702 only one family remained.

Diggory Sergeant stayed when everyone else was gone in spite of all urgings to leave. He and his wife and their five children were the only people left in what must have been a terrifyingly lonely place.

During the winter a Captain Howe and 12 soldiers were sent to remove the family—by force if necessary. Delayed by a snowstorm about two miles from Sergeant's house, they arrived the next day to find Sergeant lying in a pool of blood and the rest of the family gone. They spent the night in the house and only later learned that six Indians had been hiding in the cellar below.

Mrs. Sergeant was killed as she struggled along the paths through the forest and so was the youngest child. Two other children remained with the Indians for the rest of their lives. The oldest girl and one of the boys later returned, but they never came back to Worcester.

The area was deserted, a wilderness again. The Treaty of Ryswick had officially ended King William's War in 1697 but in 1702 the War of the Spanish Succession, known in America as Queen Anne's War, broke out and the Massachusetts countryside was once again in turmoil.

In 1709 Joseph Sawyer and 15 others proposed to settle again in Worcester. However, the House of Deputies was unwilling to accept the provisions of their petition and the attempt failed.

The Treaty of Utrecht in 1713 brought peace at last and on October 21, 1713, Jonas Rice returned to his land on Union Hill. He and his family were the only settlers for miles around. There were three children in the family; a fourth, Adonijah, was born on November 7, 1714.

In June of 1714 a report was presented to the governor stating that 28 persons wished to settle in Worcester. Provisions were made for settlement of the claims of the earlier inhabitants. In the spring of 1715 Gershom Rice, the brother of Jonas, arrived with his wife and their six children. Shortly afterwards their sister Grace arrived with her husband, Nathaniel Moore, and their eight children. These three families were the first permanent settlers of Worcester.

They proved to be a hardy lot. At the time of their arrival Jonas Rice was 41, Gershom Rice was 48, and Nathaniel Moore was 37. Over the years they held many offices in the town and gained the respect of all who knew them. All three men lived to the age of 84 while Nathaniel's wife, Grace, reached 94. When Nathaniel Moore died in 1761, the *Massachusetts Spy* observed, "He saw this town rise from a state of uncultivated nature to its opulent improvement. . . . Thus has ended the life of an honest man, the noblest work of God."

*The gravestone of Jonas Rice was uncovered by workmen in 1973 when the common was being relandscaped as part of the renewal of the center of the city. The carving is thought to be by William Young, a stonecutter who worked in the Tatnuck section of Worcester. Photo by Daniel Farber. Gravestone is in the collection of the Worcester Historical Museum.*

By 1718 there were a total of 58 houses, four garrison houses, fortified in case of further Indian attacks, and about 600 people in the little village. In the beginning, all the inhabitants had slept in the garrisons, joining together in all the activities necessary for the successful establishment of a village on the frontier—raising the frames of new houses and barns, planting and harvesting, setting out orchards, and building a gristmill. Much of this activity was undoubtedly accompanied by social activities, eating and the drinking of "strong waters."

They met on the Sabbath for their worship services in private homes, most often that of Gershom Rice. Everyone came for they were all of one persuasion, and all were required to attend services. In 1717 a small meetinghouse was built at the corner of Franklin and Green streets. The population grew steadily, and soon more room was required. In 1719 a larger building was erected on the common near where City Hall stands today.

The church was the center of village life in Worcester, as it was in every other New England town and was supported by local taxes. Though everyone listened to the minister's sermons, they did not necessarily agree with him or with each other.

The people of Worcester had been admonished to "seek out, at the earliest opportunity, a good minister of God's word." The first man to be called was the Reverend Andrew Gardner. A native of Brookline, he had been graduated from Harvard in 1712. The new minister arrived in the fall of 1719, usually given as the date of the founding of the church.

Things did not go smoothly. The Reverend Gardner was fond of deer-hunting and practical jokes. Once he appeared in the pulpit in his stocking feet, having given away his shoes. The people did not like his sermons and they neglected to pay his salary. They petitioned the General Court for his removal; he petitioned for the payment of his salary. The dispute went on and on, with numerous petitions and orders traveling back and forth between Boston and Worcester.

Meanwhile, a new and disturbing element came to the village. A group of Presbyterians, originally driven out of Scotland by James I, had settled in Londonderry, Ireland, where they had struggled to keep their church together. But the burdens of excessive land rents and taxation to support the state church at last forced them to seek a new home in America. The first group of 100 families landed in Boston in 1718 and others soon followed.

Beginning in 1719 a number of Presbyterians arrived in Worcester and soon set about building a church of their own. The newcomers were perceived as foreign, a threat to the established order. A separate Presbyterian church meant that its members would ask to be excused from contributing taxes for the support of the established church.

The citizens of Worcester set upon the half-built little church and pulled it down. Many of the Presbyterians left to go further west where they founded the town of Pelham. But many others stayed. They continued to hold their services in private homes and were eventually absorbed into the mainstream of the community.

The village was now firmly established. More and more houses went up, generally built around a central chimney, with oiled paper in the windows or, more rarely, a window of diamond-shaped panes of glass set in lead. Great fires burned in the winter to ward off the bitter cold. In this respect at least, Worcester was better off than Boston because firewood was still plentiful on the nearby hillsides.

Land was cleared and crops planted. The problems of a severe climate and rocky terrain were compounded by the necessity of keeping an ever-watchful eye out for marauding Indians who still descended periodically from the north. But this time the settlers were definitely here to stay.

The Goddard-Winslow house on Chester Street was the oldest house still standing in Worcester when Harriette Merrifield Forbes photographed it in 1909. With its massive central chimney and rough clapboard siding, the house resembled many of the other early Worcester houses. By the time of this photograph the house had gone through many changes. It eventually collapsed. (WHM)

# Chapter Two

# The Town and the County Seat

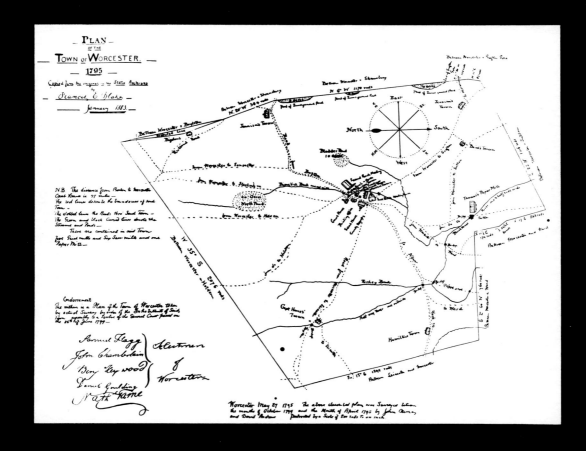

rom its beginning Worcester had been governed by committees and officers appointed by the General Court in Boston. By 1721 the townspeople wanted to govern their own affairs. Gershom and Jonas Rice drew up a petition to have Worcester made a town and entrusted it to John Houghton of Lancaster and Peter Rice of Marlborough who were requested to carry it to the General Assembly in Boston. They were uncertain when the petition could be presented because of "a contagious distemper now raging in Boston— smallpox brought in by the crew of a ship from the West Indies."

On September 7, 1722, Justice Francis Fullam signed a warrant ordering all qualified voters to meet on the last Wednesday in September to choose officers for the new town. These officers would serve for five months, when Worcester would adopt the pattern of all other Massachusetts towns and reelect town officers "as by Law accustomed for Towns to Do at their annual meetings in March."

Daniel Heywood was chosen "Modrator" and town treasurer, Jonas Rice was the town clerk; Nathaniel Moore was the "Clark of the Markit." All the other offices were filled by the sturdy men of the town.

Meanwhile Reverend Andrew Gardner was still trying to collect his wages. He was dismissed in October 1722 but it was not until August of 1723 that the town meeting appointed Daniel Heywood and Henry Lee a committee to settle with Mr. Gardner in order to prevent his suing the town. Consideration was then given to the need for a new minister, more agreeable to the congregation.

Meanwhile work was progressing on the meetinghouse, where a pulpit and a "Body of Seates" were being installed. In May 1724, the pews were assigned and in February 1725, the Reverend Mr. Isaac Burr was named minister. He proved to be satisfactory and served for 20 years. The townspeople were careful not only to pay his wages, but to adjust them "in Consideration of the Dearness of the necessaries of Life."

The Indians from Canada continued to be troublesome. They did not have the forces to attack whole towns, but they roamed through the woods, swooping down on people working in the fields or on an isolated house when the men were away. They killed and kidnapped, taking their captives back to be sold as slaves to the French in Canada. New settlers were afraid to come to frontier towns. Agriculture was neglected. The people of Worcester wanted soldiers to "scout out the woods . . . and guard our defensible places."

Other Massachusetts towns were in the same predicament, but very little aid was available. People kept to their houses, afraid to attend church or work in the fields except in large groups, with guns at the ready. The harvests were poor, the people hungry and afraid. A few soldiers experienced in the ways of the Indians were sent to "scout the woods," but they were never enough. Finally, in the spring of 1726 the ratification of a treaty with the Indians ended the raids for the time being.

*The house of the Reverend Isaac Burr was built in 1724. The following year Mr. Burr replaced the Reverend Andrew Gardner as minister. (WHM)*

The population of Worcester remained static for the next five years. The townspeople voted to complete the assigning of pews in the meetinghouse, a matter that evidently caused much dissension. They voted not to allow horses or cattle belonging to people who were not freeholders in the town to graze on the common. They voted "that the Selectmen forthwith take care and provide sufficient school for the education of youth." Jonas Rice became the town's first schoolmaster.

And they faced the problem of the way hymns should be sung in church, an issue that occupied much thought and argument for years. An article in the special town meeting warrant for September 1726 proposed that the question, "being of an Ecclesiastical nature . . . ought not to stand upon our book of town records." The article was defeated.

The musical abilities of the local deacons were nil, but they spoke each line of the hymn, which was then sung, more or less, by the congregation, who had no more musical talent than the deacons.

The warrant for the town meeting of March 3, 1728, contained an article "to see if the Toune will consider of what may be proper for the Toun to Do with reference to a New County as Lately Proposed." The town of Worcester was at that time part of Middlesex County, but the idea of creating a new county had been discussed for some time.

Other towns were considered to be better places for the county seat, notably Lancaster and Brookfield, both much larger than Worcester. Rutland was eager for the honor, and even built an extraordinarily wide main street in anticipation of being chosen. Rutland was the exact geographical center of the state, but the General Court may have had second thoughts about the long climb up the hills to that town, especially in the winter.

The discussions were long and complicated. Worcester was chosen eventually by an act of the General Court passed on April 2, 1731. Worcester County was made up of seven towns taken from Middlesex County and five towns taken from Suffolk County. Sutton, Mendon, and Brookfield were larger towns than Worcester, and more influential. Worcester lacked waterpower, and transportation over the hills was a problem. But now the little agricultural town's destiny was changed. A new pattern was established that would hold for 100 years.

In a time and place that did not permit theater, the presence of the court in town was a truly theatrical event. The justices arrived dressed in their white wigs and scarlet robes followed by an entourage of clerks, servants, and lawyers. They were often greeted at the town line by the local officials, sometimes heralded by a drum or trumpet. A procession formed and made its way to the court's meeting place.

Worcester's first courthouse was built in 1732. Until then, the court met in the meetinghouse. Court days brought great crowds to town. In 1756 John Adams, who was teaching in Worcester, wrote in his diary: "The week past was court week. I was interruped by company and the noisy bustle of the public occasion so that I have neither read nor wrote anything worth mentioning." (WHM)

Under English law there were several courts which held sessions at various times of the year: the Court of General Sessions of the Peace, the Inferior Court of Common Pleas, the Superior Court of Judicature, the Court of Assize, and the Superior Court. Court days not only involved the parade into town of the court officials, which was meant to impress the populace with the supreme authority of the king and the might and majesty of the law, but also meant a general influx of people into the town. Some had business at the court. Others came in hope of selling their wares or produce.

Some came to watch the punishments at pillory, stock, and whipping post, and to jeer at the prisoners. And some came just to have a rowdy good time.

They drank quantities of rum, whiskey, and hard cider at the local taverns. They gambled, traded, fought, and raced their horses up and down the main streets. No wonder Judge Joseph Wilder of Lancaster had insisted that the courts not hold session in his town lest this undesirable and obnoxious crowd corrupt the morals of the population.

For Worcester it not only meant this bedlam several times a year; it meant a future that could not have been imagined by the first settlers. New roads had to be laid out and old ones improved, to make journeys to the court safe and speedy. Worcester was beginning to be a center of transportation and people began to look upon the town as a trading center.

In the beginning the court met in the church. In February 1734 a new courthouse was opened, "so agreeable a house . . . a model of capaciousness, regularity, and workmanship," 26 feet by 36 feet, with a 13-foot ceiling. The rise of ground it stood upon was named Court Hill. The new building was paid for in part by "sundry worthy gentlemen, some of whom live in other parts of the province." It seems reasonable to assume that they hoped their generosity would not be overlooked by the judges.

Prisoners were housed at first in a cage in the house of Judge William Jennison, and then in a room at the home of Deacon Daniel Heywood. A jail was built in 1733. Part of the building was a residence for the jailer. Prisoners were housed in a cell of oak timbers, 18 feet square, with a stone dungeon underneath. Long jail terms were not common, however. Other forms of punishment, including banishment from the town, were considered preferable to keeping prisoners at the taxpayers' expense. The original jail continued to serve until 1753. A new stone jail, built in 1784, was used until 1819 when the Worcester County House of Correction was built on Summer Street.

A new population came to town, people associated with the courts—lawyers, judges, and court officers. Most of them were well paid in their profession. They had money to spend, and they soon attracted merchants who provided goods for them to buy.

The original settlers and their children remained—farmers rich in land, but struggling to raise crops in an inhospitable climate. But new families whose names would be important to the town for generations to come now began to settle in Worcester. John Chandler, who came from Woodstock, Connecticut (then a part of Massachusetts) was appointed Chief Justice of the Court of Common Pleas and the General Sessions of the Peace. He held 13 well-paying offices in all. Other lawyers and officers of the court made their homes here and the first doctors came to town. This new group of professionals built large comfortable houses and lived well.

In August of 1735 Governor Belcher and the Councillors of the Colony of Massachusetts paid a visit to Worcester. It was the occasion for much ceremony and speechmaking. The governor was on his way to Albany to hold a conference with the Indian tribes of the Six Nations, for the troubles with the French and Indians in Canada and upper New York State continued.

On October 14, 1740, the governor returned again; this time he was traveling with George Whitefield, the fiery English evangelist who was the spokesman for a movement known as the Great Awakening. Inspired by John Wesley and the writings of Jonathan Edwards, Whitefield toured throughout New England, preaching 130 sermons in 73 days.

Whitefield had an enormous voice which could be heard by as many as 20,000 people. He was what we would call today an old-fashioned revivalist preacher. He held a meeting on the common, and the people flocked from miles around to hear him.

Whitefield's performance reflected poorly on the Reverend Mr. Burr, who found his calmer style of preaching suddenly out of favor. A minister by the name of David Hall from Sutton began to preach in private houses using Whitefield's ideas and style. At first Burr did not object but finally he refused to allow him to continue. A struggle between the two factions in the church culminated in the dismissal of Burr in March 1745.

The Great Awakening led to a revival of interest in religion in many New England towns. As often as not it also led to a division of the established church into several smaller ones. Although the controversy continued in Worcester, it did not lead to the breakup of the congregation and the church on the common remained the only one in town.

In 1741, the town of Worcester was reduced in size when the area known as North Worcester was separated off to form the town of Holden.

War came again in 1745. King George's War was a reflection of the War of Austrian Succession in Europe. A group of Worcester men, including Adonijah Rice, joined the New England militia under the leadership of William Pepperell. This group of seemingly undisciplined farmers and fishermen succeeded in capturing the impregnable French fortress of Louisbourg in Cape Breton. Worcester men defended Fort Massachusetts in Williamstown, and 53 of them joined other Massachusetts men in driving the Indians back to Canada in the summer of 1748. Then the war ended.

In 1747 the Reverend Thaddeus Maccarty of Boston was installed as minister at Worcester. "As a preacher he was solemn, loud, searching, and rousing." He was tall and slender, with flashing black eyes. John Adams, a schoolteacher here from 1755 to 1758, was hired by Maccarty. "Mr. Maccarty, though a Calvinist, was no bigot," he recalled "but the town was the scene of disputes all the time I lived there." Nonetheless, Maccarty remained as minister for 37 years.

In 1751 a new, two-story courthouse was built. The lower floor held the county offices; the upper floor contained the courtroom with an arched ceiling and two fireplaces.

In 1754 the fighting began again, known this time as the Old French and Indian War. The French Acadians of Nova Scotia, considered a threat by the British, were forcibly removed and scattered to all parts of the American colonies. Twelve of them were sent to Worcester. The townspeople took them in, settled them on some land, permitted them to hunt deer at any time, and generally sympathized with their forlorn state. In 1767 the town meeting voted enough money and supplies to help those who were still living here to return to Canada.

Worcester men joined in the fighting and the town became a regimental headquarters. Military detachments came and went as the English forces struggled through the disastrous years of 1755 to 1757. On September 17, 1757, General Amherst halted for a few days with 4500 men, who camped out on the town's hills. The news was bad, with losses on all sides. By 1759 however, the tide had turned. Quebec fell to the English in September, and by the spring of 1760 the war was substantially over as far as Worcester was concerned.

The peace treaty was signed in 1763. A total of 435 Worcester men had seen service, many of them as officers. Names such as Curtis, Rice, Chandler, Flagg, and Willard appear on the rolls. The British now ruled the continent and it seemed that there would be peace at last.

The burden of taxation as a result of the war was enormous. Yet, Worcester prospered, mostly as a result of business generated by the court. By 1765 the population was about 1475. The towns that had scorned to be the county seat now looked on with envy, especially Lancaster, but the town officers successfully defended Worcester's claims before the General Court. This sort of maneuvering to divide the courts or the county would continue until the end of the 19th century, but always without success.

During this brief period of respite before the Revolution the town assumed a pleasant rural aspect. The houses were set quite far apart, surrounded by fields and gardens, carefully fenced to keep wandering animals out. Main Street had the courthouse at one end and the meetinghouse at the other. The old building was too small, and a new one was built in 1763. It was a handsome building with many panes of glass in the windows, a sounding board above the high pulpit, and the same old struggles over the music and the ownership of the pews. The sixth article of the town warrant for May 1769 moved that "the Elder Seat be used for Some Suitable persons to Lead the Congregation in Singing." It was voted down.

Animals still grazed on the common, and swine wandered about at large,

Above
*John Chandler was Worcester's leading citizen. Loyal to his king, he left the town at the time of the Revolution and never saw his wife or most of his children again. (WHM)*

Above Left
*Governor Jonathan Belcher visited Worcester in August of 1735 on his way to Albany to hold a conference with the Indian tribes of the Six Nations. Five years later, the governor returned with English evangelist George Whitefield. From Cirker,* Dictionary of American Portraits, *Dover, 1967.*

Bottom Left
*English evangelist George Whitefield was spokesman for the religious movement called "The Great Awakening." While touring New England preaching, White-*

*field stopped in Worcester on October 14, 1740 and held a meeting on the common. His enormous voice and fiery style of speaking attracted people from miles around. From Cirker,* Dictionary of American Portraits, *Dover, 1967.*

Top
*The courtroom of the second courthouse was located on the second floor. After the building was moved in 1900 the Trumbull sisters, who owned it, restored it to its original appearance except for the lighting fixtures. (WHM)*

Above
*Worcester's second courthouse was built in 1751. Here the men of Shays's army met their old commander General Artemas Ward when he was chief justice. They pressed their bayonets into his flesh, but could not bring themselves to harm the man who had commanded them during the Revolution. In 1802 the courthouse was moved to Trumbull Square where it stood until 1900 when it was moved to Massachusetts Avenue and restored as a residence. (WHM)*

"being yoked and ringed according to law." There was a bounty on wolves and rattlesnakes which were still found occasionally within the town limits. In 1760 nine "wild catts" were killed and fees collected. Disease was a problem. Smallpox made its rounds in 1762 but there were several doctors in town including Dr. John Green. He studied his profession with his father in Leicester and understood not only the accepted medical practice, but also the use of herbs which his father had learned from the Indians.

Much time and effort was devoted to laying out roads and improving them. The town's boundaries were "perambulated" annually and were gradually adjusted with the surrounding towns.

The town fathers were beginning to be concerned with the proper care of trees. They set out new trees on the common by the church and gave instructions that they were to be "boxed" with wooden frames to prevent them from being broken by passing animals or vehicles. What is more, the "Inhabitants be desired not to Tye the horses to them."

There were a number of hotels in town by this time. Captain John Curtis kept an inn on Lincoln Street which served as a general rendezvous for traveling clergy, whom he always entertained without charge. The Heywood family still kept a hotel on Main Street and Noah Jones had one on the road to Leicester. Thomas Stearn kept an inn known as the King's Arms.

The town was notoriously tightfisted about its schools. Teachers, both men and women, were paid only grudgingly and were expected to teach in private homes. Thus schools moved from place to place in the course of the year, and none of the children received a full year of instruction. The town would more than once be taken to task by grand juries and even fined for failing to provide proper education for the young.

There was plenty of commerce coming and going in and out of town and Worcester seemed a promising place for an enterprising merchant to settle. In 1767 young Stephen Salisbury arrived from Boston to establish a branch of his family's store. He boarded with Timothy Paine until he could set about building a mansion that would serve as both home and store.

In 1762 Judge John Chandler died. His son, also named John, inherited many of his father's offices. The younger John served as the colonel in charge of the Worcester Regiment in 1757, a selectman, town treasurer, town clerk, county treasurer, sheriff, judge of probate, and representative to the General Court. A loyal subject of the king, he left Worcester at the time of the Revolution, when his estate was confiscated. The court records of the time provide us with a clear picture of how Worcester's leading citizen lived in those days.

Chandler had 16 living children, though some were already grown and away from home in this period before the Revolution. The family home on Main Street, just north of the common, was large and comfortable with two barns. There were several servants: a good cook, a chambermaid, a girl to care for the youngest children, a black girl who served at the table, and a woman who cared for Mrs. Chandler's laces, fine clothes, and the household linens. The house was filled with comfortable furniture, the library shelves lined with valuable books, the tables set with silver, and the cellar well-stocked with fine wines.

Chandler not only collected revenues from the many offices he held, he also owned a store near his house, a farm near Lake Quinsigamond which supplied the provisions for his household, and numerous other farms and properties, all of which produced income. He was "possessed of as large property as any person in the County."

On the 22nd of March 1765, the Stamp Act was passed by the English Parliament. It was the first direct internal tax on the colonies other than customs duties. It taxed every type of document and paper and was offensive to everyone but most of all to a town whose main business involved legal documents of every kind. The town meeting of October 21 instructed Captain Ephraim Doolittle, their representative to the General Court, "to join in no measures countenancing the Stamp Act."

Mob action in Boston, New York, and other towns effectively made it impossible to enforce the act and it was repealed in March 1766.

The town was undoubtedly full of discussions about politics. The rumblings of discontent can be detected in the report of the town meeting of May 17, 1766. Ephraim Doolittle, again the town representative, was instructed to use his influence to prevent military officers, judges, and other officers of the court from being elected "to His Majesty's Council of this Province." He was to urge that "for the future the General Court of this Province be held in an open manner," that the fee table be made null and void, and that new fees be established so that no officer in the government would be paid "more nor less than you would be willing to Do the same Service for yourself." These fees were paid to every court official for almost every service and had become such an offensive burden that the ordinary person was prohibited from seeking justice in the courts by the huge expense entailed.

The town meeting also urged that no one person be permitted to hold several offices, and that representatives to the court be dismissed if they were appointed to other offices by the governor. In addition, they instructed their representative to seek repeal of the excise tax, the prevention of bribery and corruption in the choice of representatives, and repeal of the law that required the town to support a Latin grammar school. The townspeople were certain that a knowledge of reading, writing, and arithmetic was quite sufficient for the young people of Worcester.

Joshua Bigelow, elected representative the following year, was instructed to "use your influence to maintain and continue that harmony and good will between Great Britain and this province as may be most conductive to the prosperity of each,'' but not at the expense of "any encroachments on our charter rights.''

Bigelow's second instruction was quite extraordinary and reflected a concern that would occupy much of Worcester's energy in the next century. He was instructed to "use your Influence to obtain a law to put an End to that unchristian and Impolitick Practice of making Slaves of the Humane Species in this Province and that you give your vote to none to serve in his Majestys Council who you may have Reason to think will use their Influence against such a Law.''

He was again instructed to try to change the fee tables, to get rid of the law requiring those unnecessary Latin grammar schools, to "make Diligent Inquirey into the Cause of such General Neglect of the Militia,'' and to "take Special Care of the Liberty of the Press.'' He was to "have a watchful Eye over those who are seeking the Ruin of this Province and Indeavor to make this Province Reciprocally Happy with our Mother Country.''

Judge John Chandler was moderator, town clerk, and town treasurer during this period, besides being the holder of many high offices in the court. There is no evidence that he took the pronouncements of the town meeting seriously, but he may well have felt a certain chill at what they foretold.

In October of 1767 British troops were in Boston. By March of 1768 the town meeting was resolving not to buy British goods, in order to avoid paying the taxes imposed by the Townshend Act of 1767. They voted in particular to avoid using imported tea and to drink brews made from native plants, described as "more healthful.'' The ladies of the town met and voted to use only locally grown herbs, but rescinded the vote when the potions in their teapots proved undrinkable.

Imported goods were boycotted in local stores and the strong sentiment against Britain organized itself into the Whig party. The Loyalists, or Tories, however, remained in control of all important public offices.

The town records from 1768 to 1773 do not reflect the sharp division of the townspeople into two factions, but we can be sure it was there, and growing sharper on both sides. The only thing they did agree on was that Nathan Perry and Josiah Pierce should sit in the Elder's seat in the church to assist those already seated there in leading the singing.

Sometime before 1769 a private school was started in Worcester, apparently by a group of parents who wanted to give their children a more adequate education than the town was willing to provide. They erected a building on town land and the town eventually paid some tuitions as a way of escaping the burdensome requirement of maintaining a Latin grammar school. The school lasted only a few years.

In September of 1772 Governor Hutchinson announced that judges in

Above
In 1750 Gardner Chandler, the son of the first Judge John Chandler, built this house on Main Street. It was a favorite Tory meeting place before the Revolution. Judge Barton later owned the house and added a third story. In 1870 the building was torn down to make way for the commercial buildings that later held MacInnes' Store. The tall elm trees in the front formed part of the "arcade of verdure" along Main Street, the pride of the townspeople. (WHM)

Right
Timothy Paine built his house, "The Oaks," before the Revolution. His stepfather was the first Judge John Chandler and his wife was one of Chandler's seven daughters who were called "The Seven Stars." Paine held numerous local offices and was one of the hated Mandamus Councillors who had the power to order Americans to stand trial in England. Though he was made to run the gauntlet through the patriots, he remained in Worcester throughout the war. (WHM)

William Paine was the surgeon general of the British Army during the Revolution. (WHM)

Massachusetts would henceforth receive their salaries from the Crown, thus effectively removing them from local control.

At the town meeting of 1773 the 12th article was a petition by Othniel Taylor and 40 others to read the "Pamphlet drawn up by the town of Boston containing the grievances this Province labour under." After "some debate" the article was passed and a committee appointed to "take the same into consideration." William Young, Samuel Curtis, Stephen Salisbury, Timothy Bigelow, and David Bancroft were appointed to the committee, which presented its report in May.

"It is our opinion that mankind are by Nature free, and the End and Designe of forming Social compacts, and entering into civil Society, was that each member of that Society, might enjoy his liberty and property, and live in the free exercise of his Right, both civil and Religious, which God and Nature gave; except such as are expressly given up by compact."

The report affirmed that the English constitution was a noble system of government, asserting that the people of Massachusetts were entitled to all the rights and privileges of that constitution "as though we were born within the Realm of England." Their ancestors, the report continued, had had "the amazing enterprise" to leave their homes and journey 3000 miles to a "hideous wilderness" to enjoy liberty of conscience. They were not criminals and had made no attempt to overthrow the government or the church, but had come in "a laudable and peaceable manner."

The committee reminded the king of their past loyalty, their service in numerous wars, their affection for Great Britain and its sovereign. "We have ever called it our home, and always rejoice when they have rejoiced, weep when they have wept, and, whenever required, bleed when they have bled."

The report called for the appointment of a Committee of Correspondence to watch for further offenses against their "Natural and Constitutional rights." The town meeting named William Young, Timothy Bigelow, and John Smith to form such a committee.

The meeting then turned to other matters and voted that the people who had been leading the singing from the gallery of the church should now sit in the "two hind seats" of the men's section and lead the singing from there.

Committees of Correspondence were established in most of the other colonies by July. They served as an extralegal organization to be called into action by their radical leaders. Their proceedings were always secret.

In May of 1773 Parliament passed the Tea Act, allowing the East India Company to sell its vast surplus of tea in the colonies directly. The effect would be to ruin the local merchants. In December the Boston Tea Party dumped the offensive herb into the harbor. On December 27 the American Political Society was formed in Worcester, and the ruling Tories were faced with a new, organized opposition.

The society met at least monthly in public houses in the town. They decided how they would vote on the articles in the town warrant, presenting a united front that could not be manipulated or voted down by the town officers. There were 31 original members; during the two and a half years of the society's existence, its membership totaled 63.

By the time of the town meeting in March 1774 they were well organized. The fourth article in the warrant called for a discussion of the Tea Act and William Young, Josiah Pierce, and Timothy Bigelow were appointed a committee to present a report. Their report began by stating that "Affairs of the greatest consequence to ourselves and posterity are hastening to a crisis." In the strongest terms they declared that they would use no tea and buy no British goods. They complained bitterly of merchants who had sought to gouge the people by increasing their prices, accusing them of "extortion that is sufficient to put them to the blush, if they are not lost to every sentiment except that of self interest."

Twenty-six men voted to dissent and protest the report.

The American Political Society next decided on a bold move of protest. The men chosen as members of the grand jury for the Superior Court of Assize would refuse to serve under Judge Peter Oliver. Oliver had refused to go along with the other judges when the Assembly instructed them not to accept their salaries from the king—a form of intervention in local affairs that the Assembly considered an abridgement of the constitution of Massachusetts.

Joshua and Timothy Bigelow were chosen for the jury, and the society agreed to pay any fines they might incur for refusal to serve. The other jurors were warned in advance of the impending action. When the court convened, and while they were waiting for the sheriff to return from meeting the judge in the usual fashion, they presented a strong firm statement of "remonstrance." They would not serve under Judge Oliver and would consider any action taken by the court while he was presiding to be illegal. All the jurors concurred.

The sheriff returned without the judge, who had sensibly stayed in Boston, and the court continued with its work. No action was taken against the jurors.

On May 16 a new town meeting presented instructions to the town representative, Joshua Bigelow. By this time it was known that the port of Boston was to be closed in June and to remain closed until the East India Company had been paid for the tea they had lost in December.

Bigelow was told, "Whatever measures Britain may take to distress us that you be not in the least intimidated." And if the Assembly should be required to pay for the tea, "We hereby lay the strictest injunction on you not to comply.'' More generally, he was instructed, "Let the strict union of the Colonies be one of the first objects in your view." The Committees of Correspondence were to be the instrument of maintaining this union.

The Loyalists strenuously opposed these instructions, but they were voted down. Forty-three of them obtained a warrant for another town meeting which was held on June 20.

The Loyalists presented a statement in which they declared that the so-called "friends of liberty" were "spending their time in discoursing of matters they do not understand." They described these men as envious of their betters, evil-minded, ill-disposed, and deluded. The Committee of Correspondence, they declared, was an illegal body that refused to let the public see the records of its "past dark and pernicious proceedings."

The document ended with the declaration, "These and all such enormities, we detest and abhor, and the authors of them we esteem enemies of our king and country, violators of all law and civil liberty, the malevolent disturbers of the peace of society, subverters of the established constitution, and enemies of mankind."

A total of 52 men signed this document, at a time when the town had about 250 voters in all. The discussion was heated but the meeting refused to act on the warrant and that seemed to be the end of it.

The *Boston News Letter* of June 30 and the *Massachusetts Gazette* of July 4 printed copies of the Loyalist statement with the astonishing news that the warrant had been written into the town records by the town clerk, Clark Chandler, the son of the judge. The selectmen were then petitioned to call a new town meeting, which was held on August 22. A committee was appointed to study the matter and the meeting was adjourned to August 24. Meanwhile all but five of the original signers had recanted their positions.

The Committee of Correspondence summoned all the friends of liberty from the other towns to meet on the common on the 24th, early in the morning. They told the Loyalists that they would be obliged to recant publicly. The Sons of Liberty formed a double line, and the Loyalists were forced to run the gauntlet, reading their written apologies. These were some of the most respected, powerful, and honored men in the town.

The voters then removed to the town meeting, where the committee presented its report. It declared that the members of the Committee of Correspondence were not a "parcel of unprincipled knaves" and that the offensive description of the patriots in the earlier document should be blotted from the record by the clerk, who would stand admonished. The clerk was then required to stroke out the entry with his pen. When that seemed not enough, he dipped his finger in the inkwell and blotted out every word.

Some of the townspeople retired to their homes after this day's work, but others went to Rutland to seek out another Loyalist, Colonel Murray, and require him to repent. They were met by another group from surrounding towns. The colonel was not at home, however, and the crowd dispersed.

The Loyalists found these events so frightening that they gathered arms and provisions and barricaded themselves at Stone House Hill, beyond the Tatnuck area, over the Holden line. The place came to be known as the Tory Fort. They stayed a few weeks until they felt that calm had returned. The most ardent Loyalists then left town. John Chandler left for Boston with his son Rufus, carrying the silver and books, which they sold in order to support themselves.

The town selectmen were appointed a committee to receive goods for the poor of the blockaded town of Boston, and people were asked to sign a covenant promising to refuse to buy British goods.

On September 6 the doorway to the courthouse in Worcester was blocked by an armed force of patriots. It would be nearly two years before the courts would hold session again.

All the Committees of Correspondence in the county were convened in Worcester on the 21st of September. They assumed the legislative powers, as well as those of the suspended courts of justice, and they organized a military force that was to be ready at a minute's notice. The men armed themselves and the town ordered cannons, which were brought to town secretly and mounted.

The first Continental Congress was meeting in Philadelphia when Joshua Bigelow was appointed representative to the General Court, which was to be held in Salem. His cousin Timothy was chosen as the delegate to the Provincial Congress, to be held in Concord.

Timothy Bigelow was a blacksmith by trade; his house and forge were at Lincoln Square. A tall man with a commanding presence, he was a remarkably able soldier who had seen service in earlier wars. During the summer, he had organized the local militia, drilled them on the common, and made them into an effective fighting unit. They continued to drill almost every day throughout the winter. The town became a storage area for ammunition. Merchants were inspected to see that they were not carrying British goods.

By the fall of 1774 the Revolution had been accomplished in Worcester and the king's representatives ruled no more.

As winter came on, hard and severe, the town waited for word from Philadelphia. Town meetings on January 3 and January 24, 1775, elected Timothy Bigelow to be the delegate to the Provincial Congress to be held in Cambridge. "The fate of millions depends upon your wise, cool, and prudent conduct; you, we make no doubt, will be duly sensible of the great and important trust reposed in you by us, your constituents." His specific instructions were few, other than to be careful of "disposing of the public monies" in "extravagant grants."

Meanwhile, General Gage was waiting in Boston for the coming of spring. He knew that there was a great store of ammunition at Worcester, and he sent two officers to inspect the town secretly. The officers stayed at Jones' tavern, acting like casual visitors. As they left Worcester with sketches and plans of the area they were overtaken by a horseman, who looked them over carefully, as if he wanted to be sure of recognizing them again. It was Timothy Bigelow who had been alerted to the presence of two strangers with military bearing. General Gage then decided to try to capture the stores at Lexington instead.

Timothy Bigelow was also the man who traveled back and forth with news from the patriots in Boston. In the course of one of these trips, he persuaded Isaiah Thomas, publisher of the *Massachusetts Spy* in Boston, to publish a newspaper in Worcester, to be known as the *Worcester Gazette,* or the *American Oracle of Liberty.* As there was no printing press in Worcester, however, one would have to be set up before the paper could get started.

By April of 1775 Isaiah Thomas found his situation in Boston perilous in the extreme. His printing office was being called a "sedition factory" and threats against his life were becoming very ominous. On the 16th he packed

*Isaiah Thomas smuggled his printing press out of Boston with the help of Timothy Bigelow and began printing the* Massachusetts Spy *in Worcester. The first edition printed in Worcester carried the news of the battle of Lexington and Concord. (WHM)*

up his press and type and in the dark of night sent them off to Worcester in the capable hands of Timothy Bigelow and General Joseph Warren.

On the 19th of April a messenger on a white horse arrived in Worcester with the news of Lexington and Concord. His horse collapsed by the church, but a fresh mount was found and the man rode on. The church bell was rung and the cannon fired to sound the alarm. Before long 110 men had assembled and marched off toward Sudbury where they paused at Howe's tavern and then marched on to Cambridge. More volunteers followed in a few days and joined the army under General Artemas Ward of Shrewsbury.

By the 20th of April Isaiah Thomas was in town, setting up his press and searching for paper. On the 3rd of May the first news of the battle was printed.

Meanwhile the remaining Loyalists were rounded up at Stearn's tavern, where they were disarmed. Most were allowed to return to their farms. Some were required to promise either to serve in the army or to find substitutes. A few were arrested. It was the beginning of a period of constant harassment for them.

Refugees began to arrive from Boston. General Warren's daughters were here, as were Stephen Salisbury's relatives. This young bachelor made a home in his new mansion for his brother Samuel's wife and their three children. Before long his sister and his mother also arrived. By the time the war had ended Mrs. Samuel Salisbury had produced five more babies and the mansion was bursting its seams.

Early in May, 15 British prisoners were sent to Worcester and released on parole to work in the place of the absent men.

On May 22 David Bancroft was sent as a delegate to the Provincial Congress. His instructions from the town meeting referred to "this time when a corrupt and despotic ministry, with a wink or a nod, rules both the king and the parliament of Great Britain with such absolute sway that they are but a mere nose of wax, turned and moded any and every way to answer despotic purposes." Bancroft was instructed, above all, to "take proper measures for keeping up harmony and union with all our sister colonies."

By the fall of 1775 Timothy Bigelow had left to take part in Benedict Arnold's expedition against Quebec. He was taken prisoner and held for a year when he was exchanged.

In November two of the town's large cannons were sent to Gloucester. By March the courts were functioning again and jurors were appointed by the town meeting.

At the town meeting of May 23, 1776, a motion was made to support independence if it should be declared. By a unanimous vote all pledged their "lives and fortunes."

On Saturday, July 14, a messenger from Philadelphia passed through town carrying a copy of the Declaration of Independence. Isaiah Thomas read it from the porch over the side door of the church. It was read again on Sunday morning in the church after services.

On July 22 the whole town gathered for a celebration. The people of Worcester hoisted the flags of the 13 colonies, rang bells, beat drums, set bonfires, tore down the arms of the king from the courthouse and from Stearn's tavern, and drank numerous toasts to the new republic.

The fighting never again came near Worcester, but the town's efforts continued throughout the war. Most of the able-bodied men saw service. The town supplied blankets and clothing for the army at regular intervals, and no doubt every woman in the town did her share of spinning, knitting, and weaving. The townspeople contributed money, horses, and foodstuffs, especially beef, in remarkable quantities to support the army.

At last on the 7th of November 1781, they celebrated the surrender of Cornwallis, 19 days after the event. The last requisition of men in the town was in March 1782, when six men were drafted for a period of three years.

The town was exhausted from the years of effort. Some of its most able people had left, returning to the mother country or emigrating to Canada rather than desert their king. Some of these Loyalists now wanted to return, but there was strong feeling against them. Still more men had been lost in the fighting, dying far from home of injuries or disease. The economy was in a shambles. Money was worthless. Farm produce could not be sold. There was no employment to be had in any town. The burden of taxation was heavy, falling on rich and poor alike in the form of the poll tax. Court fees were enormous and were considered to be unfair.

Everyone was in debt, and the penalty for debt was prison. There were 2000 trials for debt in Worcester County in 1784, and another 1700 in 1785. The local storekeepers owed the merchants from towns such as Boston and Salem, who threatened them with court action. The storekeepers, in turn, tried to collect from the farmers who owed them. Other states made special provisions for payment of debts to relieve the situation, which was the same throughout the country. Massachusetts did not, and it appeared to the farmers that the wealthy merchants in the seacoast towns, who dominated the legislature, were out to buy up all the land in the interior at forced-sale prices, turning the independent farmer of Massachusetts into a dependent peasant as in Europe. The state legislature ignored all requests for redress and adjourned on July 8, 1786.

The farmers revolted, using the same means to gain their ends as had been used before. They marched on the courts to prevent them from sitting.

In August, the Worcester town meeting protested the laws pertaining to debt and the expense of the court. A convention of 50 towns from Hampshire County registered a similar protest, and on August 31, a group of armed men under the leadership of Daniel Shays prevented the court from sitting in Northampton.

On September 4, the day before the first session of the court, Captain Adam Wheeler of Hubbardston occupied the Worcester County courthouse with a force of 80 men. By morning, he had more than 100 men with him.

The court procession began in the morning. Although the king was gone, and the wigs and robes of the judges with him, the court officers still made their ritual procession, led by the sheriff dressed in a navy blue coat with brass buttons, a buff-colored vest, a tall beaver hat with a cockade in it, and carrying a cane.

The chief justice was Artemas Ward, the general who had led the army until Washington took over, and the officer in command of Massachusetts men throughout the war. He looked at the men who barred his way and ordered them to put up their arms. Unable to disobey their old commander, they let him pass.

When Ward reached the courthouse steps, he was met with bayonets. They pressed against his chest, cutting through his clothing, but he would not be moved. At last, he was allowed to address the crowd. But his arguments—that their action was treasonous, that it would lead to civil war, throwing away everything they had fought so long and hard to gain—were to no avail. The court retired to the tavern across the way where it adjourned until the next day.

The militia was called, but the local men would not respond. Their sympathies were all with the rebellion. The judges held firm in the tavern the next day, while the courthouse continued to be held by the rebels. Finally the court decided to hold all its cases over until the next session in November.

After a little more milling around the rebels dispersed. No harm had come to anyone, no shot had been fired, and no court business had been conducted.

On the 26th of September the court was prevented from sitting in Springfield. The militia was again ineffective. The Congress was so alarmed by this news that more than 1000 men were called to the ready in Connecticut and Massachusetts under the leadership of General Knox.

In November the court was ready to convene in Worcester, but again armed men barred the way. Once again the militia refused to act, and once again the court was adjourned, this time until January.

The governor put 4400 men into the field under the command of General Benjamin Lincoln to try to end this affair. Shays' men were all over the county, extending as far east as Concord. They assembled in Worcester on December 3; on the 4th, the local militia was called out to confront them. Men who had been comrades in arms now faced each other as enemies on the main street of Worcester. Shays' men had no heart for such bloodshed, and they retreated.

More men joined the rebels in the snowy weather. They effectively controlled the town, patrolling the streets. But they had no supplies, no food, and little organization. They camped with townspeople who would let them in.

Later in December, the rebels marched to Springfield, arriving there on the 26th, apparently in the hope of capturing the arsenal. On January 24, 1787, they attacked, but the plans went awry and the rebels retreated. General Lincoln was in hot pursuit, following them to Amherst and then to Petersham. On February 4, after a 30-mile march through mountainous snows, Lincoln caught Shays' men, capuring some and sending the rest fleeing. The rebellion was ended.

Shays' rebellion caused no real harm in Worcester, but it had a great influence on public opinion. It confirmed the opinion of the English Tories that the Americans would never be able to govern themselves. Its greatest effect was to reinforce the arguments in favor of a stronger federal government. When Massachusetts had asked for help from the other states, the Confederation had not been able to do anything.

In the end the rebels were pardoned or let off with mild punishments. Their cause was not without justification, and there was widespread sympathy for them.

We can rest assured that there was plenty of political discussion in Worcester while the problems of the new constitution were thrashed out, and as General Washington was inaugurated President in April of 1789. In October President Washington came to Worcester. The town was ecstatic. He was seen as the very embodiment of the ideal American: noble, strong, wise, and modest. The *Massachusetts Spy* could not decide what to call him—His Highness, President, or President General.

Forty of Worcester's leading men rode out to greet Washington at the Leicester line and escort him into town. When he came within sight of the meetinghouse the cannons fired salutes. The troops passed in review. He ate breakfast in the tavern appropriately called the United States Arms. Then, to please the waiting crowds, he rode slowly along Main Street in his open carriage pulled by thoroughbred Virginia horses, quite unlike the local animals. The cannons roared again as he rode on toward Shrewsbury.

Among those in the crowd which greeted him was Colonel Timothy Bigelow, his old comrade in arms, now returned to his forge at Lincoln Square. On February 15, 1790, Bigelow was put into jail for debt. On March 3 he was carried to a nearby house where he died—alone, forsaken, and heartbroken. The jail records read, "discharged by death." His friend Isaiah Thomas gave notice of his passing in a single line.

The Jedediah Healy house was built in 1789 on Main Street. (WHM)

Nathan Patch built the United States Arms hotel opposite the courthouse in 1784. Here George Washington breakfasted when he visited Worcester. Later it was called the Exchange Hotel and gave its name to Exchange Street. (WHM)

Above
Artemas Ward, the general who led the American troops in the early part of the Revolution, was the judge at the time of Shays's Rebellion. (WHM)

Everything was changing. The Reverend Mr. Maccarty died in 1784 and church members were divided over the choice of a new minister. Eventually a new church was formed with the Reverend Aaron Bancroft as its minister. The church on the common continued to be supported by taxes until 1787, while the new one had to raise its own funds.

Daniel Waldo, whose wife was Stephen Salisbury's sister, came to town in 1782 and opened a hardware store. He took his son Daniel Jr., into partnership. In 1804 the elder Waldo was named the first president of the Worcester Bank. A year later, he was succeeded by his son. The bank hired the well-known architect Charles Bulfinch to design a "Superb Rich Edifice" on Main Street to house the bank and its president. The new building had "two kitchens, two parlors, and thirteen chambers," in addition to a well, a woodhouse, a garden, and a carriage house. The older Daniel Waldo amazed the town by riding about in the first one-horse chaise ever seen here.

Worcester had postal service beginning in 1775. The mail went out to the west one day a week, and to the east another day. The town's first postmaster was Isaiah Thomas, and the post office was in his printing house, near the courthouse. In 1782 Thomas built a mansion nearby, which he painted yellow.

By this time, several people in town were producing potash and pearl ash, used in the manufacture of glass and soap. Potash and pearl ash were derived from wood ashes and great clouds of smoke rose from the burning piles of logs. There was also a small mill weaving cotton cloth on School Street. Isaiah Thomas owned a paper mill at the southern end of Lake Quinsigamond and was always advertising for linen rags. Thomas employed a total of 150 people.

Abel Stowell was making clocks, and John Smith was making hats, advertising that he would pay one shilling for each cat skin. The Gouldings were starting another hat manufactory and advertising for an apprentice. Abraham Lincoln had a trip-hammer and a gristmill at Lincoln Square.

These industries supplied local wants, but if they were to grow, two problems would have to be solved: the lack of water for power, and the lack of cheap transportation to carry the finished goods to market.

Isaiah Thomas believed that the transportation problem could be solved by a turnpike going in a straight line to Boston, and he laid the road out in 1804. It required a bridge over Lake Quinsigamond, but the engineering skills to build such a structure were not available. Instead, a bridge was made by floating hewn timbers covered with planks across from one shore to the other. The road was finished in 1807 and collected tolls until 1841.

Others thought that a canal cut through either to Boston or to Providence would solve the problem. Proposals were made in 1796 for both canals, but they were not acted on, and horses or oxen and wagons remained the only available mode of transportation. Stagecoaches began making regular runs to many other New England towns in 1783.

The wounds of war were healing, and some of the Loyalists who had left town during the Revolution were returning and were forgiven for their failings.

The most prominent lawyers in town had been Loyalists; by the end of the Revolution, only two were still practising in Worcester. In 1775 Levi Lincoln came to town, fresh from Harvard and the battle of Lexington. He filled the vacuum ably, married Martha Waldo, and thus allied himself with the most powerful families in town.

It was Levi Lincoln who argued the case of Quork Walker of Barre, a slave owned by Nathaniel Jennison. The outcome of that case led to the decision by the Massachusetts Supreme Court that "there can be no such thing as perpetual servitude by a rational creature." Thus, slavery was outlawed in Massachusetts in 1783.

Soon a whole new generation of lawyers arrived, and the courthouse was becoming too crowded and small. In 1801 Isaiah Thomas gave the county a piece of land near the old courthouse. The older building was jacked up on wheels and, pulled by 20 yoke of oxen, was moved to Trumbull Square. A handsome new brick courthouse (also designed by Bulfinch) took its place.

The Worcester Fire Society was organized in 1793, ostensibly to assist in putting out local fires, but it soon became an exclusive club of the town's best citizens, much given to amusing themselves by listening to orations. The Worcester Light Infantry was organized in 1803, and not only became a colorful addition to every parade and public occasion but covered itself with glory in military encounters.

By 1810 Worcester had more than 2500 inhabitants—more than any other town in the county—and was beginning to take on the appearance of a very fashionable place. Everyone in town suddenly discovered music. They studied instruments. They learned to sing, taking lessons from a singing teacher who had come to town, and even reformed the singing in the church on the common. It was the beginning of an interest that blossomed into the Harmonic Society in the 1820s, leading in turn to the Sacred Music Society, the Mozart Society, the Beethoven Society, and on down to the Music Association and the Music Festival, which continue to this day.

War with France was threatened in 1798, and seemed so imminent that the Worcester Volunteer Cadet Infantry was organized and ready to march. The ladies of the town made them a magnificent banner, but it never flew in battle.

By 1800 the town had built several schoolhouses—square buildings, small in size and quite inadequate, but more to the purpose than rooms in private houses. The children began having regular periods of education, and by 1808, the custom of having teachers move from one part of town to the other on a rotating basis was ended.

In November of 1812, Isaiah Thomas called a meeting in Boston for the purpose of establishing a new institution to be known as the American Antiquarian Society. The purpose of the society was to collect the history of America, and he intended to begin this great collection with his own library. Common sense dictated that the collection remain in Worcester, where it

*Governor Levi Lincoln lived in this house on Main Street at Federal Square from 1812 to 1835. He then built a house on Elm Street and the older house became a hotel. (WHM)*

would be safe from the British, who were already blockading American ports to the south. In the event of bombardment the collection would be safer inland. It has remained in Worcester ever since.

The War of 1812 with England was not a popular cause. Governor Strong condemned the war, refused to raise militia for the federal government, and even threatened to have Massachusetts leave the Union. But the Worcester town meeting authorized a payment of $10 to each man who was mustered and ready to march, if it should prove necessary.

British officers were jailed in Worcester in 1813, held as hostages with the threat that if American prisoners were harmed in England, British officers would suffer the same fate here. Isaiah Thomas entertained the officers by sending them meals, and even dined with them in jail.

The officers escaped one night. Four made their way to Canada, and five others were caught. A short time later, they were paroled.

The British hoped to exploit the feeling in New England against the war. The blockade of southern ports, reaching as far north as New York, did not apply to New England. By April of 1814, however, it was obvious that the New Englanders were not going to come over to the British side, and all New England harbors were shut off by a very tight blockade.

The effect on Worcester was dramatic. All sorts of people came inland from Boston, bringing with them money, goods, and talents. Money poured into the local bank from Boston and Salem banks. One million dollars in specie was secreted in Worcester vaults. A considerable volume of illegal trade continued through Canada, but the price of farm produce fell.

The lack of imports from abroad served as a tremendous stimulus to American industries which had been actively discouraged throughout the colonial period by the British who wanted their American colonies to remain suppliers of raw materials.

If industry was thriving, farm products were a drug on the market. The dreadful monetary upheavals of the Revolutionary period were repeated all over again, and the Massachusetts farmer felt there was no hope for him.

There was an extraordinary reservoir of talent in these farm communities. A New England farmer had to be clever to stay alive. He had to tinker about with all sorts of primitive machinery to make it run. A young man growing up on such a farm, if he had any mechanical ability at all, had plenty of opportunity to make things go, and to develop that patient persistence in the face of repeated failure that was to characterise the Yankee inventor and make the world call him a genius.

Many of these talented young men would come to Worcester, looking for opportunities. There they would find other people of energy and imagination willing to make a place for them, as together they began the process of turning the town into a city.

# Chapter Three

# Transformation by Steam

*The second engine house in Worcester was built by the Boston and Albany Railroad near the Bloomingdale switching yards. (WHM)*

One day in the autumn of 1818, in the quietest way, one of the most dramatic events in the history of Worcester took place. A young blacksmith named Ichabod Washburn walked from Millbury to Worcester and asked to see Daniel Waldo, the banker. The young man had finished his apprenticeship and now wanted to set up shop for himself making plows, but he needed a modest amount of capital to buy supplies. He had no one to recommend him, only his own appealing earnestness.

Daniel Waldo lent him the money and Washburn returned to Millbury. Then, in the summer of 1819 he was offered a job in Worcester working with William Hovey making hay cutters in a small shop on Summer Street. He moved to Worcester, as he later said, "the next day."

Ten years later Ichabod Washburn began manufacturing wire, founding an industry that would do much to transform the town into a city, and to endow it with many of the institutions that still enrich the city's life today.

The town Washburn came to in 1819 was changing rapidly. The court was still the center of drama in the town's life, but strong efforts were being made to control the more raucous aspects of its presence. The whipping post, pillory, and stocks were gone and the town had firm rules about the racing of horses, or any other animals, on the main streets, or rolling "whoops" down the new sidewalks, or setting off firecrackers or strings of fireworks known as "serpents."

People were busy planting ornamental trees and shrubs on the common, in the burying ground, and along the town streets. Although these plantings were undertaken at private expense, the town levied severe fines if the trees were willfully injured. Main Street was described as an "arcade of verdure," shaded by tall, overarching elm trees.

Each family was permitted to have not more than one milch cow wandering at large. The cows served to keep the sides of the roads mowed down; at the end of the day they would return of their own accord to be milked. The streets in the center of town were given names, and the names were painted on wooden posts at the corners.

Almon Hodges, a visitor to Worcester at the time, wrote, "This is a flourishing village. All the buildings are in excellent repair; I did not see an old house in the place. I was told that the Society lines were drawn sharply—one must be aquainted with Daniel Waldo to ride in the troop with the big bugs.''

The town had a new poorhouse where the indigent could live, instead of being boarded out in private homes. The town tried to find occupations for them, such as spinning wool. A grove of mulberry trees was planted on the poorhouse land in anticipation of starting a silk industry, but that idea came to nothing.

Worcester had a fire engine, and the men of the town were organized into brigades. The leaders of the brigades carried poles with brass twists on the top to identify themselves in the confusion of a fire.

The town also had a hearse that was available as required, along with a pall and other furnishings; funerals were very elaborate affairs. The town hearse was not good enough for Daniel Waldo and the "big bugs," and a group of them had a much finer one of their own.

In 1812 the first Baptist church in Worcester was organized. In 1820 a Calvinist church was formed, with Daniel Waldo among its members. In 1823, the Calvinists moved into a new building built for them by Waldo on land next to his store. The old church on the common soon found itself only one among many congregations. Church affiliation was a deadly serious issue in those days. Many friends and families split over the founding of these new churches, and ended up not even speaking to each other. The Fire Society and other organizations split into two groups over the issue of church membership.

Oratory was becoming an art. At first, the pulpit was the center of discussion. The minister preached a sermon, and the townspeople discussed it. Political debate revolved around the town meeting, even though property owners were the only ones allowed to vote. There never was a better training ground for enthusiastic oratory than that open meeting. And in the course of the 19th century, the people of Worcester would find plenty of opportunity to put their oratory to good use in promoting causes of every kind.

In 1819 the first Worcester County Cattle Show was held, presenting an array of improved breeds of livestock which, it was hoped, would increase the farmer's income. Also on display were the various industrial products of the local mills. The fair soon became an annual tradition. Planned to take place just before election time, it rapidly became a favorite event for politicians. Not only those running for local office, but candidates for state and national positions as well, came to present their views. Men such as John Quincy Adams, Edward Everett, and Daniel Webster addressed the crowds, which literally jammed the town.

The "best" people then attended the Agricultural Ball, which was the climax of the fair. Held in the Central Tavern, the ball was the greatest social event of the season. The Light Infantry and the Rifle Corps marched

These prize bulls were the pride of farmer W.R. Wesson of Worcester. G.A. Johnson drew the animals and their owner in 1848. (WHM)

Above
Ichabod Washburn used the blacksmith's motto "By hammer and hand all arts must stand." He was proud of his mechanical skills, but usually left the management problems of his factory to others. (WHM)

Top
The town hall and church, shown in this photo circa 1885, were the center of all activity in Worcester. The town hall was originally square and had two halls on the upper floor. In 1841 a 50-foot addition was added to the rear. The entire second floor was converted into one room that seated 400. In 1848, at the invitation of Alexander Bullock, Abraham Lincoln attended a Whig convention here. (WHM)

This relief portrait of Ichabod Washburn by Benjamin Harris Kinney, a Worcester artist, was a gift to Washburn's twin brother Charles. Because Charles was born without a right hand he was kept at home and sent to college rather than being "put out to live" as Ichabod was at the age of nine. Charles came to Worcester to manage his brother's factory and later he went into the wire business for himself. (WHM)

in their colorful uniforms. The governor and numerous other worthy dignitaries attended. The ladies of the town arranged the decorations, and wore their best gowns. Great quantities of food were consumed, and many speeches made. In 1822 the enthusiasm for music had progressed so far that the Handel and Haydn Society of Boston presented an oratorio in the church on the common before the opening of the fair.

Small mills began to spring up along every available stream of water in town. Little villages, each with a separate name, though still within the town limits, grew up around them. Places such as Northville, Trowbridgeville, and New Worcester were all separate little centers of activity. But in the absense of any large river, the most common source of power was the horse on a treadmill. If a manufacturer wanted to know how many horsepower he was using, all he had to do was go out to the shed and count!

Stagecoaches carried passengers, newspapers, and mail in and out of town; as many as 20 at a time, painted brilliant colors and drawn by teams of horses, passed through the center of town. Many of these vehicles were manufactured by Osgood Bradley at his factory on Summer Street. The coachman was the greatest hero to all the boys in town. Meanwhile, great heavy wagons drawn by teams of draft horses or oxen moved goods in and out of town. They wore out the roads, and maintenance was a continual problem.

The twin problems of transportation and power, which had plagued the town from the beginning, were now seen as serious obstacles to growth. There were enormous amounts of money to be made as the Industrial Revolution changed every aspect of New England life, and the people of Worcester wanted their share. The idea of building a canal was revived, and even a railroad with horsedrawn cars was proposed.

By 1822, a canal was being seriously discussed. There were those who wanted it to come from Boston and continue west to the Connecticut River. But the design for a canal from Worcester following the Blackstone River to tidewater in Providence, Rhode Island, won out. The canal idea was given further impetus by the discovery of a rich vein of anthracite coal at the north end of Lake Quinsigamond. It seemed there would be no end to Worcester's riches as soon as it could be mined and shipped. The coal proved ultimately to be of poor quality, leaving almost as much waste in the furnace as the amount of coal originally put in. But in the meantime, plans for the canal proceeded.

Surveys for the canal were made in 1822, the charter was granted in March of 1823, and in 1824 construction began at the Providence end. Hopes were high and many people invested in the Blackstone Canal Company.

The town decided to build a town hall. It opened in 1825. A big building by local standards, it was 54 feet square and two stories high. The building was shared with the Masonic Lodge and the Agricultural Society, who had halls on the second floor. The first floor held the town offices, while the basement housed a meat market and other shops.

From the earliest days of settlement, it had been the custom for everyone to consume large amounts of alcohol. The "strong waters" of the early settlers were rum, hard cider, or beer. "West India Goods" on a shop sign meant rum and nothing else. Whiskey was considered a healthful drink because it was made from good grain. As new lands were settled to the west, there was a glut of grain, and the easiest way to store it was by distilling. Whiskey was plentiful and cheap.

People felt extremely hard pressed if they were reduced to drinking water. There was a certain logic in this attitude, as many wells and streams were contaminated, especially as the town grew and people began living closer together. Men who engaged in hard labor drank as they worked. Every building ever built in Worcester was raised with the aid of "strong waters." The account books for the building of the town hall list sums for "labor and grog."

By 1826 the canal construction was underway in Worcester, bringing to town a population of Irish workmen. They were, for the most part, men who were alone, without families. The work they did was brutal and hard. Richard O'Flynn, who kept notebooks about the Irish in Worcester, recalled, "It was the rule to give a dollar a day and sixteen 'Jiggers', or glasses, of new rum, thus keeping the men continually half drunk and at the utmost strain of work, from dawn to dusk. It is true a little money might be made in this questionable manner, but is the loss of body and soul, caused by such proceedings ever taken into account? Well, that is a question no mortal can pass judgement on. God only is the infallible Judge."

In another passage O'Flynn remarked, "It is painful and sickening to see our young men, the hope and pride of the future, staggering along our streets, swearing and smoking, blasphemous and obscene. Oh, the sight and thoughts evoked are painful."

The canal was completed in 1828. On October 7 the barge *Lady Carrington* arrived loaded with slate, grain, and dignitaries. The towns all along the canal turned out in force to cheer the event, and Worcester's population was delighted.

The canal was beset by problems. It iced up in winter. The banks eroded in the spring thaws. Mills along the way drew off too much water. In dry summers, the flow of water was shut off entirely. As a major mode of freight transportation, the canal was simply too unreliable. Also without a reliable source of waterpower, Worcester was unable to support the large textile mills, with their endless rows of spinning and weaving machines, that were becoming so much a part of other New England towns. Worcester's smaller mills specialized instead in making the tools and the machines required by others, and for this they needed highly skilled and reliable workers. With sober workers at a premium, there was a growing reaction to the abuse of alcohol at all levels. The temperance movement was beginning to find its cause.

By May of 1829 Ichabod Washburn had married and built himself a house. The frame of the house was raised without serving any alcohol for the first time in the history of Worcester. The temperance movement was growing, and Washburn was one of its most ardent supporters.

At the town meeting of March 23, 1835, the temperance advocates prevailed, and all liquor licenses were revoked. The innkeepers responded by closing their doors; only the Temperance House remained open. Travelers arrived in Worcester to find no accommodations.

The advocates of both sides were anything but temperate, and some of the most distinguished people in town got into fights that came to blows. C.C. Baldwin remarked in his diary, "The friends of temperance are as intemperate as their opponents. Everybody is getting mad, and what is the cause of especial madness with me is that I am already as mad as the maddest."

Those on the middle ground favored strict licensing and punishment for public drunkenness, while the advocates of prohibition and the spokesmen for the liquor interests stood at opposite poles. The citizens of Worcester were to wage this battle, back and forth, in the political arena and the churches, for another 100 years. But they voted to reconsider their initial act of prohibition on April 13, 1835.

Fashions were changing. The new fashion in houses was the Greek Revival style, with its great columns supporting the front porches of large square houses. Elias Carter, an architect and builder in the Connecticut Valley for many years, came to town, and Daniel Waldo hired him to design a house of great elegance. Soon everyone wanted one like it, and the whole center of town was turned into a precinct of Greek temples. The area of Main Street opposite the common, which stood on a rise of ground, became known as Nobility Hill.

There was a growing desire to understand how things worked and to explore the entire world of knowledge, which seemed to be expanding daily. Because of the longstanding neglect of the schools, young people in Worcester found that their education was sadly lacking. Eight or 12 weeks of school a year was not enough to prepare them for the new world of industry. Only the lucky few were able to attend a good academy or boarding school, and possibly go on to college. There were a few small private schools for young children. One of these was taught by Dorothea Dix from 1816 to 1818, beginning when she was only 14 years old. Her students remembered her as an extraordinarily severe teacher.

Dorothea Dix was born in Maine in 1802. Her grandfather, Dr. Elijah

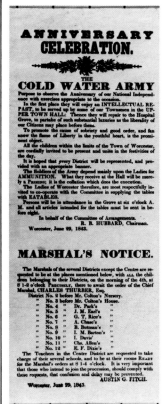

Temperance was one of the great
causes occupying Worcester's attention for most of the 19th century. This rally was held at the
town hall with a picnic to follow in
the gardens of the lunatic asylum.
(WHM)

This closeup of the Butman-
Sargent house porch shows the
masterful handling of the
fashionable neoclassical details by
Carter and Studley. (WHM)

Top
The Salisbury House circa 1900.
This house on Highland Street was
the last house Elias Carter
designed in Worcester. It was built
in 1836 on a rise of ground behind
the earlier Salisbury Mansion. The
house still stands and is the headquarters for the Red Cross, but the
lawns and gardens have been
replaced by a forest of parking
meters. (WHM)

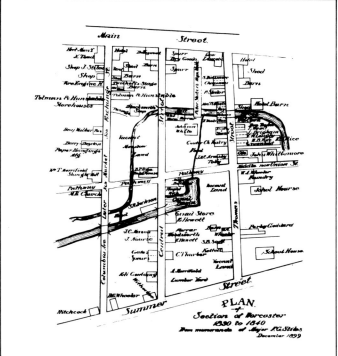

On this map of Worcester as it appeared during the 1830s, one can
see that the canal came into the
very heart of town. William
Wheeler's foundry and William T.
Merrifield's shingle-making mill
were located nearby. Merrifield's
father, Alpheus, had his lumber-
yard at the corner of Summer and
Central streets. Many of the streets
were still only pathways and most
of them were unpaved. (WHM)

Dix, had lived in Worcester from 1770 to 1795, and she came here to teach in 1816. Two years later, she moved to Boston to live with her widowed grandmother. She became the nation's best-known advocate of adequate facilities and humane treatment for the mentally ill.

In 1830 the state legislature resolved to build a hospital for the insane—a "lunatic asylum," as it was called in those days. It was the first time that public money had ever been appropriated for such an institution. There were private asylums for the mentally ill, but these institutions were only for those who could pay. Poorer patients were boarded out at town expense and were frequently kept in the most dreadful conditions—chained, caged, abused, and never given any treatment for their illness.

Worcester, characteristically, welcomed the idea of the new institution when other towns looked askance at it. Horace Mann was one of the committee appointed by the legislature to work out the design of the new hospital. Studies of existing hospitals in Europe and America showed that there was no real consensus of opinion regarding such facilities. The committee chose Elias Carter as the architect and evidently attached great importance to his work. "Architectural fitness . . . promotes humane and compassionate treatment, gives additional efficacy to medical skill and often disarms the rage of a spirit intent upon the destruction of the body in which it dwells."

The building was enormous, and provided a great deal of work for Worcester builders. It opened on January 19, 1833. Dr. Samuel Woodward came to Worcester to be its first superintendent. He was a man of towering height and enormous enthusiasm for his work. The insane were brought from towns all over Massachusetts, some in the most wretched state imaginable. To them, this doctor who struck off their chains and treated them with kindness seemed a godlike figure. Within two years the hospital was full and plans were made for an addition.

In 1826 Josiah Holbrook wrote an article for the *American Journal of Education* in which he proposed the formation of Lyceums—self-help study groups designed to benefit the community as a whole. Holbrook traveled about the country advocating the Lyceum idea and was present at the first meeting in Leicester of the American Lyceum of Science and Arts for Worcester County. From the Worcester Lyceum, founded in 1827, the Lyceum movement spread throughout the United States.

The local newspapers were not yet the sources of information and opinion they would become later in the century. Worcester was fortunate to have the Antiquarian Society library in town, but there were no other libraries open to the public. Public addresses at events such as the Cattle Fair and Fourth of July, as well as talks before groups such as the Lyceum, were a principal means of education. The debate was a highly popular form of entertainment and the art of golden-voiced oratory flourished. Worcester had its share of great speakers, many of whom found politics to their liking and made great reputations for themselves—among them, Levi Lincoln, governor of the state from 1825 to 1834, Isaac Davis, a famous lawyer and politician, and Elihu Burritt, known as the "Learned Blacksmith."

In December 1820 Christopher Columbus Baldwin, a lawyer and later the librarian of the American Antiquarian Society, gave a lecture before the Lyceum on the subject of the steam engine. He had no way of knowing how close Worcester was to making use of that marvelous invention.

In 1829 the legislature appointed a Board of Directors of Internal Improvements with Governor Levi Lincoln as chairman. Nathan Hale, the editor of the *Boston Advertiser* and a great advocate of railroads, was its most

*Dorothea Dix lived in Worcester with her grandfather, Dr. Elijah Dix, when she was fourteen to sixteen years old. She taught in a school for young children. Later she lived in Boston and made her life's work the crusade for the humane treatment of the insane. Later on she visited the Worcester Asylum during an inspection tour, but found nothing to criticize. From Cirker,* Dictionary of American Portraits, *Dover, 1967.*

active member. The board was to study a proposal for a railway to the west. There was some debate about the route for the proposed road. The northern route would have gone through West Boylston, Rutland, and Palmer, to the Connecticut River at South Hadley. But a route around the southern end of Lake Quinsigamond to Worcester, and then on to Springfield, proved less expensive.

By March 1831, subscriptions were being taken at banks in Worcester and Boston for the Boston and Worcester Railroad Company. Worcester investors were wary. They had found Isaiah Thomas's turnpike to be a poor investment, and the canal was losing money because of enormous maintenance costs. Boston investors were more enthusiastic. They had looked with dismay at the canal which threatened to draw all the trade from central Massachusetts away from Boston, and they believed the railroad might be the answer.

The tracks were laid, employing many gangs of workmen, including some of those who had come to build the canal. By April 16, 1834, the line was running as far as West Newton. On July 4, 1835, a single locomotive arrived in Worcester, a wonderful and awesome sight. On July 6 the first train pulled in. People gathered on the hills and along the tracks to watch it.

The locomotive was made in England. The boiler and engine were mounted on a wooden platform which rested on a metal frame with four wheels. A tender behind it carried the wood that was used for fuel. The engine belched forth smoke, cinders, live coals, and steam. The passenger cars were stagecoach bodies mounted on four-wheeled metal frames. Built by Osgood Bradley, they had been hauled over the turnpike to Boston to begin their run. The ride was dangerous and not comfortable, but wonderfully exciting.

The town welcomed the train enthusiastically. At a banquet held in the town hall the best orators waxed eloquent over its wonders and the new future that lay ahead for Worcester. This time, everything they said was true, and more. The steam engine was the answer to Worcester's greatest problems, power and transportation.

The railroad was a huge financial success from the beginning. It was not to end at Worcester, but to continue on to Springfield and Albany, where passengers and goods could transfer to the Erie Canal and continue on to the West. The route to Springfield presented more difficult terrain but it seemed that nothing was impossible for good practical Yankee engineers. The Western Railroad Company sent its first train into Springfield on October 1, 1839.

The Norwich and Worcester Railroad was chartered in March of 1833. This road carried passengers to New London where they could board paddle-wheel steamers that would carry them along Long Island Sound to New York and New Jersey. The line was opened on March 9, 1840. Its tracks crossed the common to reach the Foster Street station.

Financial interests in Providence organized a third railroad, the Providence and Worcester. That line opened in October of 1847, and a year later the canal collected its last toll.

Worcester now found itself in the wonderfully advantageous position of being at the center of a network of railroads and stagecoach lines, for the stages still ran to all the towns that had no rail service.

In 1837 Osgood Bradley sold his coach business and began making only railroad carriages. Soon more and more businesses in Worcester were making iron and steel parts for the railroads.

The first locomotive to come to Worcester arrived in 1835. It was made in Lancaster, England, and was called The Lion. The engine ran for 33 years and logged over 700,000 miles. (WHM)

Elihu Burritt, known as the "Learned Blacksmith," moved to Worcester in 1837 from New Britain, Connecticut. He entertained the residents of the city with his public lectures on various subjects and was an internationally known orator and scholar. From Cirker, Directory of American Portraits, Dover, 1967.

Below
The Worcester Lunatic Asylum received its first patient on January 19, 1833. Dr. Samuel Woodward was the superintendent. Many patients arrived chained in cages and Dr. Woodward's first order was to remove the chains. He would not permit walls or fences to be built around the fields and gardens that surrounded the hospital. Patients walked outdoors with staff members who were to act as "companions and guides" rather than keepers "with the object" that the patient's "self respect is awakened." (WHM)

*Old Eddy Engine No. 39 was one of the engines that steamed into Worcester. George Green, in the derby hat, was the yardmaster and Lyman Davis, in the cab, was the local engineer. (WHM)*

When Stephen Salisbury died in 1829 his only son, also named Stephen, inherited his commercial interests and large tracts of land in Worcester. The second Stephen Salisbury decided to build a factory on some of his land at Lincoln Square and to lease the building to manufacturers of farm implements.

This building and others like it that he built nearby came to be known as the Court Mills, because of their proximity to the courthouse. They made a profound impact on Worcester. Now it was possible for a man with an idea for manufacturing to go into business without having to find the capital to construct his own building. He could start small in the hopes of growing big.

Meanwhile, Ichabod Washburn was making screws at a factory in Northville, on Mill Brook, using machinery brought here by canal from Providence. Washburn was experimenting with wire, trying to improve methods of manufacture so that longer and longer lengths could be drawn at one time. He patented a block that permitted the continuous drawing of wire, which became the basic device for the whole wire industry. In 1834 Stephen Salisbury built a new factory to house Washburn's growing wire business. It was a huge building, 80 feet long and 40 feet wide. Washburn occupied one half, and the Phelps and Bickford loom works occupied the other.

Mill Brook was dammed to provide a head of water for the new factory.

*Foster Street Station was built in 1835. The building on the right ran along Foster Street for 229 feet. The ticket offices were housed in a connecting building that faced Norwich Street. On the left is the roundhouse. Trains from Boston, Norwich, and Nashua arrived here. (WHM)*

One of Salisbury's meadows was dug out, destroying a shallow pool overhung by a grove of willows, a favorite swimming place. This bit of the rural past survived only in the name given to the street that the factory faced, which was called Grove Street.

The factory belched forth smoke and steam and was considered a great addition to the landscape. Nothing was more pleasing to the eye of a Worcester man of enterprise than the sight of black smoke rising from a chimney. It meant that business was good and the town would prosper.

While the second Stephen Salisbury was transforming Worcester, his boyhood friend and Harvard College classmate, George Bancroft, was beginning to give the people of the new nation a sense of their own history. The first volume of his *History of the United States* was published in 1834. It would be another 40 years before the final volume appeared.

Bancroft was the son of Aaron Bancroft, the first minister of the Unitarian Church. His mother was the daughter of Loyalist Judge John Chandler. The eighth of 13 children, George grew up in a much freer household than his friend Salisbury, who was the only surviving child in his family. Mrs. Salisbury considered Bancroft to be a "wild bad boy" and scolded when the two went off on frequent larks together. But the two remained firm friends all their lives.

About the time that the first trains came to Worcester a young man named William T. Merrifield purchased some land on Union Street and built a building where he made sashes, shutters, and blinds in connection with his contracting business. To obtain lumber, he set up a steam-driven sawmill in Princeton, where he was cutting trees on the mountain. It seemed logical to him to bring the sawmill operation to the logging site, rather than drag the logs to a source of waterpower for milling. Merrifield was awarded the contract to build the Lancaster Mills in the newly formed town of Clinton, the largest textile mills in New England at the time.

Much of the profits from this lucrative contract were invested in more land and buildings on Union and Exchange streets in Worcester. Merrifield decided to enlarge on Stephen Salisbury's idea. He would not only lease space for manufacturing, he would supply the power, and the power source would be a steam engine. In 1840 he put in an engine of from four to six horsepower.

The first steam engine in Worcester had actually been installed by William A. Wheeler in his foundry near Lincoln Square. This early engine did not work very well, however, and Wheeler soon tired of it and went back to horsepower. In 1842 Wheeler was commissioned by Merrifield to build a new, larger steam engine—and a new era was born.

The steam engine drove overhead shafting in the Merrifield buildings. All a young man with an idea had to do was find enough money to buy supplies, to pay the rent for small quarters, and to hook his machinery to overhead belting from the main drive shaft. He paid only for the power he used. With only a modest capital investment he was in business.

The effect of these buildings on Worcester was profound. As Merrifield enlarged his buildings and replaced his engines with ever larger ones, almost on a yearly basis, more and more manufacturers were attracted to Worcester. They made a bewildering array of products. If they were successful in a small way in the Merrifield buildings, they tended to stay in Worcester as they expanded into larger quarters.

The population of Irish immigrants was growing. Most of them were men who had worked as laborers on the canal and then the railroad, and most of them did not have families with them. In 1834 Bishop Joseph Fenwick of Boston appointed Father James Fitton, then pastor of a church in Hartford, to come to Worcester once a month to hold services. He had a problem finding a place to meet, but finally was allowed to use a private house.

About 60 men, plus a small number of women and children, attended the first Mass on April 7, 1834. Some of them came from outlying towns, including Millbury and Clappville. They immediately subscribed $500 toward the building of a church.

During the summer Masses were said at various places around the town, even on a rocky knoll by the railroad track where the altar was decorated with wild flowers and sheltered by evergreen boughs.

A suitable lot was found for the church at the corner of Salem and Franklin streets, but the owner tore up the deed when he realized the purpose for which the lot would be used. William Lincoln, Francis P. Blake, and Harvey Price intervened and bought part of a pasture near the canal, then turned the deed over to Father Fitton. Temple Street was laid out along an old wagon path. The deed was dated July 7, 1834, and work began immediately on the foundations of Christ Church.

There were plenty of strong laborers to work on the new church, and the building went up quickly. By May of 1836, it was finished and free of debt,

Top Left

*William T. Merrifield was born in Worcester in 1806. Many Worcester businesses began in his industrial buildings. When the buildings burned in 1854 he began rebuilding the next day. The new Civic Center now occupies that location. (WHM)*

Top Right

*George Bancroft, the son of the minister of the Unitarian Church, graduated from Harvard with his friend, the second Stephen Salisbury. In 1834 he published the first volume of his* History of the United States. *While Secretary of the Navy, he established the Naval Academy at Annapolis. He was ambassador to England in 1846 and to Germany in the 1860s and 1870s. (WHM)*

Above

*In this 1855 woodcut of Lincoln Square the tower on the left belongs to the Unitarian Church and beside it is the 1802 courthouse with the statue of Justice atop its cupola. The square house with the balustrade around the roof is the Salisbury Mansion and beside it is the building used as a storehouse for the Salisbury shop. Up the hill is the house of the second Stephen Salisbury. (WHM)*

and Father Fitton came to Worcester to live.

In the summer, a delegation of Penobscot Indians came to Worcester to visit. Father Fitton had been their pastor in Maine. They pitched their tents near the church and, after Mass was said, kneeled in a circle waiting for their priest to lay his hand on each of their heads as a benediction. Then they packed up and started the journey back to Maine. The people of Worcester were amazed. It was an annual ritual as long as Father Fitton remained in Worcester.

Father Fitton traveled far and wide in Worcester County, saying Masses in many towns. He purchased land on Pakachoag Hill and founded the Seminary of Mount St. James. Students were to be admitted at the age of eight and to have two terms a year, from September to March and March to August, with only three weeks of vacation.

In 1842 the seminary was deeded to Bishop Fenwick, who founded the College of the Holy Cross there. A new building, started in June of 1843, was ready for use in January of 1844.

Father Fitton left Worcester in 1843. By 1845 his church was too small for the growing congregation and it was moved away to a new foundation and renamed the Catholic Institute. A new church was begun on May 11, 1845, and was finished in June of 1846. It was named St. John's.

There was considerable opposition to the founding of a Catholic Church in Worcester. The dislike of the church sprang from the same roots as the dislike of the Masons and the strong anti-Masonic party that flourished for a time in Worcester. Secret societies, or churches that professed a loyalty to a power outside the United States, were thought to be pernicious and anti-American. All feelings in this period seemed to run at a fever pitch; C.C. Baldwin described the anti-Masonists as "furious as a windmill in a tornado." Strong emotions, it may be recalled, had also been aroused at the founding of the Calvinist Church in Worcester by a group led by Daniel Waldo, and even earlier by the coming of the Presbyterians. Opposition to new church denominations was not confined to the Catholics.

During the campaign to have Missouri admitted to the Union as a free state in 1819, a convention of those who opposed the extension of slavery met in Worcester; the secretary of the convention was the younger Levi Lincoln. In 1838, a convention of 80 ministers under the leadership of the Reverend George Allen declared themselves against slavery, and two antislavery societies were formed. Among the officers was Ichabod Washburn.

In 1839 the women of the town formed the Worcester Anti-Slavery Sewing Circle. They sold linens, wax flowers, and fancy work at fairs in both Worcester and Boston, raising money to distribute William Lloyd Garrison's abolitionist paper, *The Liberator,* and to support the underground railway, a network of people helping slaves escape to Canada. The Sewing Circle

*St. John's Church on Temple Street was built in 1846. It replaced the earlier building that proved to be too small. (WHM)*

continued its work for many years.

On May 6, 1844, another political convention in Worcester protested the admission of Texas as a slaveholding state. In September of 1847 the caucus of the Whig party elected delegates to the state convention which in turn elected delegates to the national convention. Strong resolutions opposing slavery were written by Charles Allen of Worcester, but no stand was taken by the convention.

Members of the convention then offered to nominate a Massachusetts man for vice-president if the Massachusetts delegation would support Zachary Taylor for president. At this point, Allen rose and declared, "You have put one ounce too much on the strong back of northern endurance. You have even presumed that the state which led the first revolution for liberty will now desert that cause for the miserable boon of the vice presidency. Sir, Massachusetts scorns the bribe!"

The population of the town was growing and so were the problems. The fire department had been functioning since 1835, but there was no regular police force, only the constables. Crowds of new immigrants and rowdy workmen made parts of the town dangerous. In addition, there were all the problems of new roads, water supplies, streetlights, and rights of way. The town-meeting form of government was unable to cope effectively with these complicated problems; it was time for Worcester to become a city.

The town had a population of more than 10,000 when the petition for a city charter was presented to the state legislature in 1847. On March 18, 1848, the charter was accepted by the town meeting. Worcester had long been called "The Heart of the Commonwealth." Now that motto became official and the heart was placed at the center of the city seal. Before long there would be a new motto for Worcester: "The City of Diversified Industries." The variety and diversity of her manufacturers would bring Worcester prosperity in good times and save her from disaster in bad.

The elections for the first mayor took place in a setting of rapid change. For more than a century, Worcester had been dominated by the interests of the court and the legal profession. But now their power, wealth, and influence over politics were being challenged by a rapidly rising new group who called themselves "mechanics." These were the men who were developing new industries and giving Worcester an entirely new financial and political base.

Levi Lincoln campaigned for the office of mayor. A distinguished lawyer and former governor of the state, he was noted for the elegant hospitality of his home and for his abilities as an orator. It might have been assumed that he would win the office with ease.

He was opposed by the Reverend Rodney A. Miller, a temperance advocate whose ideas were "more in accord with the opinions held by intelligent mechanics." The Reverend Mr. Miller had been the minister of the church on the common, now called "Old South," from 1827 until his dismissal in 1843, and was the first president of the Temperance Association. He was defeated, but only by a narrow margin. With a total of 1534 votes cast, Lincoln won by a plurality of 138.

The new government inherited 23 schoolhouses, a fire department, a debt of $99,677, and a host of problems. The eight aldermen and 24 members of the Common Council labored hard that year to get the new city off to a good start.

In June of 1848 two meetings were called in Worcester. One was to ratify the nomination of the Taylor-Fillmore ticket for the presidency. The meeting was supported by all the prominent Whigs of the city—a list of names that reads like a *Who's Who* of Worcester.

The other was an open meeting addressed by Charles Allen. Allen, a lawyer and a judge, had been a loyal Whig until the national convention earlier in the year. The meeting he addressed was overflowing with "mechanics." For the first time, the city came to realize that these men were about to take over the destiny of Worcester.

Allen addressed the meeting at length, and the crowd responded with enthusiasm. Charles Allen's brother, the Reverend George Allen, rose and declared, "Resolved, that Massachusetts goes now and will ever go for free soil and free men, for free lips and a free press, for a free land and a free world." The Free Soil party was born that night in Worcester's City Hall.

While the Free Soil party organized that summer, the Whigs were actively campaigning. Daniel Webster came to address a crowd at City Hall in support of Taylor and Fillmore. As he spoke, the Free Soil group marched in a huge torchlight parade down Main Street to the railroad station, where they held a mass rally. Henry Chapin, a lawyer, addressed the crowd. Emotions were at a fever pitch.

By the time of the next election, the Free Soil party had become domi-

*George L. Brown, who had a studio in Brinley Row, made a drawing of the great fire on School Street in August of 1838. The drawing was made into an engraving for the Worcester Fire Department's membership certificate. (WHM)*

nant. Free Soilers won a majority of local offices, Chapin was elected mayor of the city, and the Whig party was on its way out.

Meanwhile Ichabod Washburn's factory was producing wire in ever-increasing quantities. The fashion among ladies who lived in neoclassical houses was to wear hoopskirts. Washburn's crinoline wire began to replace the old-fashioned and expensive whalebone. The wire was lighter, more flexible, and cheaper, and soon everyone was wearing hoops. The factory was capable of turning out 60,000 pounds of crinoline wire a week.

The newly invented telegraph began sending messages all over the United States, and the demand for wire increased dramatically. In 1840 Washburn's firm built a new factory south of Lake Quinsigamond to produce telegraph wire and larger-gauge wire for industrial use. Washburn also experimented with piano wire, and his product soon replaced imported English wire. The prosperity of the Washburn mills was the economic cornerstone of the new Worcester, now a full-fledged industrial city.

# Chapter Four

# The Union Forever

*Preparations began in May for the grand celebration of July 4, 1865. Decorative arches made by the city government and private citizens decorated the main streets. (WHM)*

For many years, local industries had exhibited their wares at the annual Cattle Show. In 1841, the Mechanics Association was formed, and in September of 1848, the first Mechanics Fair was held.

The fair was a huge success. Originally scheduled to be held at the city hall, it had to be moved to the railroad station to accommodate all the products offered for display. Day and night the crowds came, and the Mechanics Association was so well pleased with the response that they held fairs again in 1849 and 1851, using space in the Merrifield Buildings. Among the highlights of the second fair was the new gas lighting on the city's streets. The success of the fairs led the Mechanics Association to construct a building of its own, completed in 1857.

For years a majority of the people of Worcester had disapproved of slavery, but they did not always agree on what to do about it. In the 1830s, there was a movement known as the Colonization Society that sought to return blacks to Africa. C.C. Baldwin remarked in his diary on September 2, 1832, "I have from the beginning entertained a very poor opinion of the Colonization and its objects. Slavery is too great an evil to be trifled with. Nothing should be done which may increase it. This society proposes to remove to Africa all Free blacks and the only object which the Slave holding States in accomplishing this can have, is that there may be no one to incite the slaves to insurrection, and to remove the blacks from the Northern States is rank oppression. The black population of Worcester (there are about fifty) is temperate and industrious and they are as much attached to the soil of New England as any descendant of the Puritans." The Colonization Society had few supporters in Worcester.

Many did support William Lloyd Garrison and his newspaper, *The Liberator,* though there were some who found him too emotional, too much given to telling pathetic, heartwringing stories of the abuses of the slaves.

Abby Kelley Foster and her husband Stephen Foster were crusaders for abolition. In 1849, they moved to a farmhouse on Mower Street in Worcester and called it Liberty Farm. Both of them by this time had national reputations. Stephen Foster had published his antislavery tract, *The Brotherhood of Thieves, or, A True Picture of the American Church and Clergy,* in which he condemned churches that permitted proslavery ministers and members

*An aging Eli Thayer sits in one of the tower rooms of the Oread Col- legiate Institute where he lived for many years. (WHM)*

to remain in their congregations. He would often rise up in the middle of a church service to preach his views to a startled audience. Their house was part of the underground railway which was active in Worcester County, particularly in the small towns.

Abby's interests extended also to the rights of women. Nominated to the business committee of the American Anti-Slavery Society, she was asked to withdraw, not because she was incompetent, but because she was a woman. "I rise to speak because I am not a slave," she replied, arguing that to have women always represented by men was also a form of slavery.

In 1834, a school called the Worcester County Manual Training School was founded as an institution where poor boys could get a good education. The officers of the school were of the Baptist denomination, and the boys were given the opportunity to earn their tuition by working on the farm connected with the school on South Main Street.

One of the students was a young man named Eli Thayer. He went on to Brown University in Providence, Rhode Island, graduating in 1845. Thayer returned to teach at the school, which had changed its name to Worcester Academy, and soon became its principal.

In 1848 he began building on Goat Hill, near the academy, an enormous round building of a very curious design. In 1849 he announced that this medieval tower was to be the Oread Collegiate Institute—a college for women with a four-year academic curriculum closely modeled after the one at Brown University. The new college opened on May 14, 1849.

Thayer taught at the school for the first three years, while a second tower and connecting building were being constructed. As the only school in existence that offered women the same academic training as men had traditionally received in their universities, the new college attracted young women from all over the country.

Once the school's financial success was assured, Thayer turned the administration over to others and devoted his attention to another method of dealing with the slavery issue—the settling of "Bleeding Kansas" by immigrants from the Northeast.

New Englanders were settling in the new territory in order to vote in the coming plebiscite that would determine whether Kansas would enter the Union as a free state or a slave state. On May 11, 1854, Thayer announced his plans for the Emigrant Aid Society. A practical businessman, Thayer believed that the Southern economy, based on slave labor, would collapse of its own weight in time. The free worker was so much more productive that he was certain the industrial North would soon surpass the South and overwhelm it. The Emigrant Aid Society was originally conceived of as a profit-making organization, selling shares, but Thayer was forced to reorganize it on less ambitious lines. Plans were soon underway to gather a group of settlers to move to Kansas, which they called "Eden of the West."

The people were to go in groups. The Society would build sawmills, establish boardinghouses, set up printing presses, and, in effect, start small towns. On July 17, 1854, 20 young men from Worcester boarded the train taking the first group. In all, 2000 settlers from New England cast their votes and helped bring Kansas into the Union as a free state in 1861.

Since 1840 the Worcester County Horticultural Society had been collecting books and presenting shows. In 1852, the society opened its new hall on Front Street. The building had stores on the ground floor and a magnificent exhibition hall and library on the upper floors.

A year later the Agricultural Society bought 20 acres of land on Highland Street, fenced it, and built exhibition buildings. The annual fair became a two-day affair beginning in 1854.

The year 1854 was one of considerable turmoil in Worcester. John S.C. Knowlton, a Democrat, was the mayor, succeeding two mayors of the Free Soil party. Knowlton was the editor of a newspaper called the *Worcester Palladium,* which he had started in 1834.

After years of putting up with the constant problems of mud in wet seasons and clouds of dust in the dry summers, the city was paving Main Street with cobblestones. It was also rebuilding Southbridge Street, which had collapsed into a swampy area during a rainy season. A new poorhouse and a new school on Sycamore Street were under construction. The old burying ground on the common was being leveled, with the old stones buried under the sod.

In March the city purchased land for Elm Park—the first time any city in the United States had purchased land for such a use. It was to be called the New Common, while the old common was to be called Central Park. At the time, the New Common was a swamp with a small hayfield and a few apple trees on the edges. The city paid Levi Lincoln and John Hammond $11,257 for it and plenty of people in town were furious about wasting the taxpayers' money on that dreary bit of land at the edge of the city.

The Know-Nothing party, with its anti-immigrant, anti-Catholic, and anti-Masonic platform, was active in the city. In May, one of the most colorful characters in Worcester history turned up. His name was John Orr. Described as "a Scotchman with more impudence than brains," he wore a three-cornered hat with a cockade and an old brass horn suspended from his neck by a leather strap. Calling himself "the Angel Gabriel," he would chalk "Gabriel" in large letters along the sidewalks, blow his horn at intervals, and harangue the crowds that gathered with his anti-Catholic preachings.

He was arrested by the police for stirring up an unruly mob, but was released after he promised to leave Worcester and not return.

On May 18 he reappeared, and a mob soon gathered around him. When he was arrested, the mob grew angry and milled about the police station demanding his release. The mayor addressed the crowd, appealing for calm and reason, but he was shouted down. The sheriff, George Richardson, was hit by a rock, and the station-house windows were broken by stones pulled up from the newly paved street.

The City Guard was called out, as the mayor read the riot act to the crowd. The loaded muskets of the militia soon brought order. The Guard, under Captain George Ward, then marched to the armory and deposited their guns, and the mayor took them all to the American Temperance House for a "collation."

All was calm the next morning. The Angel Gabriel was sent packing. The only problem that remained was that all the muskets were still loaded and had to be discharged. The Guard marched off to Institute Road, which was then just a cart path called Jo Bill Road, and did a little target shooting.

The Angel Gabriel took his message to other places, ending up in San Domingo where he died in prison.

On June 4 the Merrifield Buildings caught fire, and before the day was over they were totally destroyed. Fifty businesses were completely lost and others suffered damage. It was an overwhelming blow to the new city. The

Top
*The Oread Collegiate Institute, opened on May 14, 1849, was the first college for women to offer a four year liberal arts curriculum. Eli Thayer built the school and served as its principal until 1857. Oread functioned until 1881 and later became a school of domestic science. The area is now called Castle Park. (WHM)*

Above
*On June 4, 1854, the Merrifield Buildings on Union Street burned to the ground with a loss of 50 businesses. This very early daguerreotype shows the blaze as it broke through the fourth floor. The following day Merrifield ordered a new steam engine and began to rebuild. (WHM)*

next day the businessmen of Worcester marshaled their forces to see what could be salvaged. Money was offered by Stephen Salisbury, bankers, and others, and space was found in other buildings so that shops could get reestablished.

H.H. Houghton later recalled that his company, Thayer, Houghton, and Company, manufacturers of machinists' tools, had lost $25,000. "And yet while the fire was burning this firm secured new quarters, and while the ashes were yet hot located themselves, purchased new machinery, and began anew." Merrifield announced that he would rebuild immediately, a better building with a bigger engine. He was as good as his word and the buildings reopened in February.

In July another political convention in town formed the Massachusetts Republican party, following the lead of a coalition of Whigs, Free Soilers, and antislavery Democrats which had met in Ripon, Wisconsin, in February.

In October the town was the scene of turmoil once again.

In 1843 the state of Massachusetts had passed a statute forbidding the arrest of fugitive slaves by the police. And on April 7, 1851, Mayor Bacon had made it clear that the local police were not to enforce the provisions of the federal Fugitive Slave Act, under penalty of dismissal from the force.

In May of 1854, three slaves were arrested in Boston, and 900 people from the Worcester area went to that city to protest the action. Worcester's church bells tolled, stores were draped in black, and the flag flew at half-mast. Several Worcester men were arrested, including Stephen Foster, Martin Stowell, and Thomas Higginson, a minister.

On October 29 Deputy United States Marshal Asa Butman, the same man who had arrested the slaves in Boston, came to Worcester looking for another escaped slave. He and another officer stayed at the American Temperance House, under assumed names. They were soon found out. The *Spy* issued an "extra," warning, "Look Out for Kidnappers." All the blacks in town were warned, especially those who had come here through the underground railway.

A "vigilant committee" took up stations around the Temperance House and soon an angry mob joined them, calling for the "Human Bloodhound" within. In the middle of the night Butman was frightened enough to produce a pistol, which gave the police an excuse to arrest him. At first light, he was taken to the police court and arraigned before Judge Howe on a complaint of carrying a dangerous weapon.

The mob outside was ugly and getting worse. City Marshal Baker put Butman in his office while he addressed the crowd. A group of blacks burst into the office and started beating Butman. The marshal rescued him, but the men escaped.

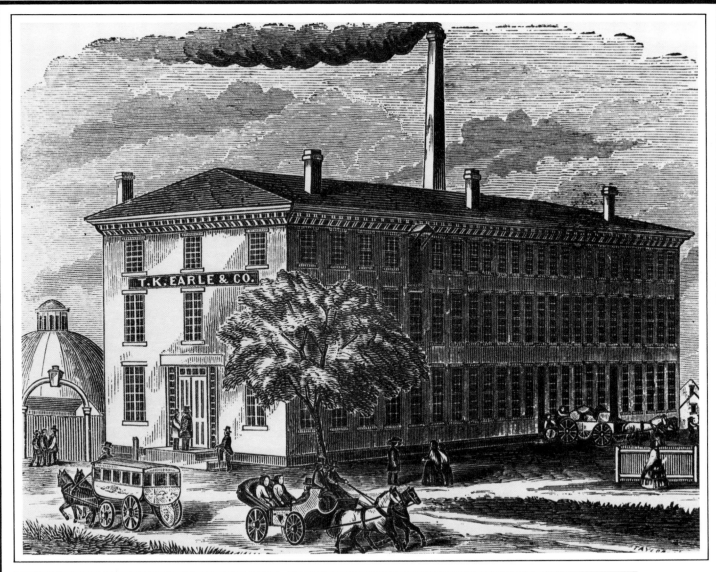

WORCESTER CITY GUARDS.

Above
*The Worcester City Guards were always ready to cope with emergencies such as the riot that occurred over the "Angel Gabriel." (WHM)*

Left
*The Reverend Thomas Wentworth Higginson was among the Wor-* *cester men arrested while protesting the unlawful arrest of three slaves in Boston in May of 1854. (WHM)*

Top
*T.K. Earle and Company built this factory on Grafton Street in 1857. It housed the largest card clothing factory in America. (WHM)*

A respected young lawyer named George Hoar pleaded with the crowd, and they listened. But the sight of Butman being escorted out of the building roused them again, and they charged at him.

George Hoar, Stephen Foster, Martin Stowell, and the Reverend Mr. Higginson surrounded Butman. They were the staunchest abolitionists in Worcester and were well known to everyone in the crowd. They were also determined that Worcester would not be disgraced by a lynching. They formed a guard and led Butman to the railroad station.

Unfortunately, the train was gone. The city marshal ordered a carriage to be brought. Butman left, accompanied by Higginson, and calm returned to Worcester.

At the end of the year, not surprisingly, Mayor Knowlton declined to run for reelection and went back to editing his paper. The next mayor was George Richardson, who ran on the Know-Nothing ticket, but a year later Isaac Davis, a Democrat, was elected.

Yearly elections presented problems. City departments were run by personnel whose jobs depended on patronage. A new mayor would dismiss the members of the police force and hire new ones. It meant little or no continuity for many departments.

And yet the city continued to grow. By 1855, one quarter of the population was foreign-born. The Know-Nothings appealed to those who found these newcomers a disturbing element. Richardson was returned to office in 1857, but Davis won again in 1858.

In 1857, the new Mechanics Hall opened on Main Street, replacing Daniel Waldo's neoclassical house, which had been moved away and turned into a hotel. It was the largest building on Main Street, an impressive monument to the pride of the manufacturers of Worcester. It was only 17 years after Merrifield's first steam engine was installed.

The new hall emphasized the profound changes that had taken place on Main Street. The beautiful Greek temples on Nobility Hill now stood in the midst of a noisy, dirty, industrial area. Crowds of people filled the streets, speaking a babble of strange languages. Traffic passed back and forth all day, clattering carriages and carts. The steam engines made noise and sent clouds of smoke into the air.

The wood planer at Merrifield's factory gave a shriek that could be heard for miles every time a board went through. With the movement for a 10-hour workday only beginning to have effect, all this noise and dirt was produced from early morning until 9:00 at night, six days a week.

The houses of the new industrialists were of a completely different style from those of an earlier era. Many of them were designed by Elbridge Boyden, the designer of Mechanics Hall. The new elite built their homes away from the very center of town. Merrifield built a house on Harvard

This house at 32 Cedar Street was built for Roswell P. Angier in 1849. The cast-iron fence was added in 1860 by Charles Anthony. This 1870 photo shows the third owner, William Clark, standing on the sidewalk while his coachman waits with the carriage and a matched pair of horses. The building was torn down in 1966 to make way for a modern apartment building. (WHM)

Left
The somber offices of the City National Bank were situated on the second floor of the building at 404 Main Street. The building was torn down in 1975 to make way for a drive-in bank. (WHM)

Above
Taken in 1855, this is the earliest known panoramic photograph of Worcester. The level flat area on the left is the overflow from the Blackstone Canal. In the foreground is the William Fox Woolen Mill. The photograph, found between the pages of an old book, was given to the Historical Museum by Alden Johnson. (WHM)

Street. When that area became too crowded for him, he built a new house on Highland Street, between West and Park Avenue. His wife was in tears because she would have to live so far out in the country.

The magnificent achievement of Mechanics Hall was overshadowed by the collapse of the economy in 1857. Worcester had survived bad times before, but this year was certainly one of the worst. The country still had no uniform currency. Worcester was now sending goods by railroad all over the United States. Payment was often in bills issued by state banks in the West which had no value in the East. Many were counterfeit. The manufacturers were reduced to a system of barter. Forbush and Crompton took bolts of cloth in return for repairs on looms; the cloth was exchanged with Thayer and Houghton for machine tools; Thayer and Houghton then gave the cloth to their employees instead of cash wages.

Thayer and Houghton also found themselves the owners of a railroad carload of flour from a milling company in the Midwest. They were hard put to know what to do with it, but finally managed to exchange it with a wholesale grocery concern in return for provisions for their employees. It was hard times for all concerned.

Things did not improve much as the ominous events in the rest of the country made the people of Worcester apprehensive about the possibility of war.

There were a few bright notes for the city. One was the offer by Dr. John Green and the Lyceum and Library Association to present the city with all of their books to form the nucleus of a library that would be open to the public. The offer, consisting of a total of about 12,000 books, was made in the fall of 1859. The cornerstone of the new building was laid on July 4, 1860.

The other bright note was the beginning of the annual music festival in the fall of 1858. It was called a musical convention, and all the performers were volunteers. They presented a cantata called *The Burning Ship,* written by the conductor, Benjamin Baker, as well as selections from *The Messiah* and *The Creation.*

That same year, the city purchased land in Leicester for a new reservoir to supply water to the ever-growing population and bought a new steam fire engine to replace the old hand pumpers. Work began on the new street railway system; the cars would be drawn by horses along iron rails.

The economy of Worcester was near collapse when the news of the bombing of Fort Sumter arrived. The fort was bombed on Friday, April 12, 1861. The news reached Worcester on Sunday. On Monday, the local militia companies gathered to arrange their gear for war, and on Wednesday evening, the Light Infantry left town to join the Sixth Massachusetts Regiment. They arrived in Washington on April 20, where they were quartered in the Senate chamber, sleeping in blankets on the floor.

The Worcester City Guards, the Emmet Guard, and the Holden Rifles were joined into the Third Battalion of Rifles and left for New York on April 20. The Emmet Guard was an entirely Irish organization formed in June of 1859. Their quick response to the call for soldiers ended permanently the unpleasant name-calling of the Know-Nothings.

As the soldiers marched away, a new monument was unveiled on the common, a marble memorial to Timothy Bigelow, hero of the French and Indian War and the Revolution.

With unemployment still a serious problem, the city undertook the public-works project of building a causeway over Lake Quinsigamond. The city paid 60 cents a day for laborers, giving work to a large number of people. Construction was begun in the fall of 1861 and completed on June 27, 1862. The first person to drive his carriage across the new causeway was Dr. John Green.

News of the war was of the greatest importance to the city. Tales of heroic deeds, deaths, defeats, and then victories appeared in the newspapers daily, and Worcester's men played an honorable part throughout. In all, 3972 Worcester men served in the army for various periods of enlistment. Those at home supported them by making supplies and raising money. Worcester was spared the draft riots that occurred in other cities because there were always enough volunteers.

*Colonel Pickett and his horse "Old Bill." This watercolor was done in 1863 in Newburn, North Carolina, by Volaire Combe, a bugler with the Company B, 3rd N.Y. Volunteer Cavalry. Pickett, who was born in 1822, came to Worcester in 1855 and joined the Worcester City Guards. In 1862 he was made colonel of the 25th Massachusetts Infantry. A contemporary declared that "His control over his men was somewhat wonderful." In January 1866 he was mustered out because of wounds, but lived to be a very old man who was greatly respected in the city. (WHM)*

*Every store was decorated for the grand parade of 1865. Here Barnard's Dry Goods Store, next to Mechanics Hall, displays its signs and bunting. (WHM)*

Clara Barton, who was born in Oxford in 1821, organized the nursing services for the sick and wounded. Several Worcester women joined her work. Dorothea Dix was appointed superintendent of women nurses by the surgeon general of the Union Army.

Business in the area began to prosper. Cloth, guns, wire, leather goods, all types of materiel needed to supply the army poured out of Worcester factories. New groups of immigrants arrived. The city grew. The new Worcester Horse Railroad Company began operations, but it was not a financial success. Three men were appointed Commissioners of Shade Trees and Public Grounds. And the city began building the Lynde dam in Leicester and laying pipe. On November 14, 1864, the first water flowed through the pipes, and in 1865 the Worcester Water Works became an official city department.

The building on Union Hill originally built as the Botanico-Medical College, which later served briefly as a woman's seminary, was renamed the Dale Hospital and used as a convalescent hospital for wounded soldiers.

The news of the assassination of President Lincoln reached Worcester at 8:00 A.M. on April 15. All the church bells began to toll. The people of the city gathered in Mechanics Hall, where several choirs sang hymns and ministers said prayers. No speeches were made. The solemn silence of the audience was more eloquent than words.

On the day of the funeral, the city was draped in black, schools were closed, flags were at half-mast, and every church was open for services. On June 1, another memorial service was held in Mechanics Hall. On the Fourth of July, the returning troops were welcomed home in a glorious parade down a gaily decorated Main Street lined with crowds of people and thousands of children each carrying an American flag.

AMATEUR THEATRICALS

IN AID OF

The National Sanitary Commission,

AT BRINLEY HALL,

Friday Evening, Nov. 28th, 1862.

PROGRAMME.

## The Dowager.

Lord Alfred Lindsay ;          The Dowager,
Sir Frederick Chasemore ;      (Countess of Tresilian ;)
Edgar Beauchamp ;              Lady Bloomer ;
Servant ;                      Margaret Beauchamp.

To be followed by the Farce of

"THE TWO BUZZARDS."

Mr. Benjamin Buzzard ;         Miss Lucretia Buzzard ;
Mr. Glimmer ;                  Sally ;
              John Small.

## Tickets, 50 CENTS each,

May be procured only at the Bookstores of Edward Mellen, Jr., 289, and Wm. H. Sanford, 184 Main Street.

The Hall will be open at 7 o'clock.    Curtain rises at 7 1-2.

Tyler & Seagrave, Printers, Spy Job Office, 212 Main-st., Worcester.

Above
*Architect Elbridge Boyden and builder William T. Merrifield designed and constructed this building in a style some have called "upside down billiard table." The central part was constructed in 1845 to house the Botanico-Medical College. In 1853 the Ladies Collegiate Institute purchased the building and added the wings. Sponsored by the Baptist Church, it existed only briefly. The building then became the Dale Hospital and in 1869 Isaac Davis bought the building for Worcester Academy. (WHM)*

Left
*Handsome young Willie Grout, a graduate of the Highland Military Academy, was the first Worcester man to be killed in the Civil War. He fell at Ball's Bluff on October 21, 1861. His father wrote the lyrics to a favorite Civil War song "There Will Be One Vacant Chair." (WHM)*

Far Left
*The National Sanitary Commission was organized as an auxiliary to the Army Medical Corps to outfit hospital units and keep them supplied. (WHM)*

## Chapter Five
# A City of Overflowing Prosperity

*Every device of the builder's art was lavished on this handsome house and barn designed by the Worcester architectural firm of Fuller and Delano. The steep pitch of the slate roof was to carry off the snow. Frederick A. Lapham bought* this house from William Burns, who built it, in 1894. Mr. Lapham lost the house when he declared bankruptcy. The house, which still stands on Cedar Street, is now a dormitory for Becker College. (WHM)

he countryside around Worcester was changing rapidly. The passage of the Homestead Act in 1862 drew settlers to the West. There, they could get 160 acres of land without cost if they settled on it for five years, or, after six months' residence, they could buy it for $1.25 an acre. What's more, the land could not be attached for debt. New England farmers left in great numbers. The pastures and fields of Worcester County began to grow up to brush and woods, and agriculture in the region began its long, slow decline.

In 1865 John Boynton of Templeton left money to found a new school to be called the Worcester County Free Institute of Industrial Science. Ichabod Washburn added another gift of money and a building to house industrial shops where the students could learn industrial skills and earn money.

The process of establishing this school brought into focus the profound problems faced by the new industrialists. Ichabod Washburn, like so many of his contemporaries, was brought up under the old apprentice system. He was "put out to live" with a harnessmaker at the age of nine, then served his apprenticeship to a blacksmith until the age of 21, when, on one "never to be forgotten day," he became a free man.

His childhood was hard. His first master was a cruel man, as mean as a character out of a Dickens novel. Washburn always felt very keenly his lack of formal education. He wanted the new generation to have different lives. He could see that the growing industries in Worcester would provide great opportunities for young men with mechanical skills. He felt, as did many others brought up in similar circumstances, that the apprentice system could not provide the technical training the new generation would have to have, and that it too often permitted the abuse of young boys by unscrupulous masters.

Washburn supported many schools during his prosperous years in Worcester; he was instrumental in founding the school that became Worcester Academy. But all these schools somehow turned away from the mechanical arts and adopted more traditional academic curriculums. Washburn had hoped that the Mechanics Association would found a school, but the financial disaster of 1857 and the Civil War ended that idea.

John Boynton's original gift was added to by others. His cousin David

Whitcomb, who ran a hardware store in Worcester and then developed the technique of making envelopes by machinery, joined with the second Stephen Salisbury and others in working out the philosophy of the new school. Washburn commissioned Elbridge Boyden to design and build the mechanical shops, which were to play an essential part in the curriculum. The shops "placed on the basis of intellectual education provided by Mr. Boynton, a superstructure for the practical application of mechanical science, in training the accurate eye and the skillful hand."

The school opened in 1870 and soon changed its name to Worcester Polytechnic Institute.

New factories were being built and old ones expanded at a rapid pace. The industrial areas were concentrated in the valleys, close to the railroad tracks. The largest and most important industry was the manufacture of wire. By 1880, the firm of Washburn and Moen was producing 58 percent of all the wire made in the United States, and its payroll supported one sixth of the city's population. Other factories made woven or highly specialized types of wire.

New improvements in the steam engine were being made by Jerome Wheelock at his factory on Union Street. The Wheelock engines were internationally famous. Wheelock once described himself as a firm believer in the doctrine that "sixteen ounces make a pound, and one hundred cents a dollar." .

The Osgood Bradley Company was manufacturing railroad cars of all kinds, and several other factories produced iron and steel parts for the railroads.

Manufacturers of looms came to Worcester to start with limited capital in the Merrifield Buildings. There was a foundry here to make the large parts of the looms, and skilled workers to make the intricate parts of the mechanisms. George Crompton was manufacturing his broad fancy loom, and the Knowles brothers were developing the 30- and 40-harness looms that were to transform the textile industry. Matthew Whittall was beginning his business of manufacturing carpets.

Another large business associated with the textile industry was the manufacture of card clothing, used on machines that combed wool and cotton fibers to prepare them for spinning.

Toolmakers of all kinds were established in Worcester, producing machinists' tools, woodworking tools, and wood planers.

Rice, Barton, and Fales were making machinery to manufacture paper. Dr. Russel Hawes invented a machine to automatically cut and fold envelopes in 1853. By 1870, there were two envelope companies in town: Hill, Devoe, and Company, the successor to Hawes, and the Whitcomb Envelope Company. Both factories employed many women.

Above
*George Crompton developed a loom that revolutionized the textile industry throughout the world. It was wider, faster, and more versatile than other looms made at the time. (WHM)*

Top
*The English High graduating class of 1895. The school had the most difficult curriculum of any school in the city and it was considered to be a great honor to graduate from English High. (WHM)*

Above
*When English High School was built in 1870 the students were so proud of their new building that they left their shoes at the door and wore slippers so that they would not scuff the floors. (WHM)*

In 1861, David H. Fanning began making hoopskirts. Then, as women's fashions changed, the corset became an essential part of every woman's wardrobe. The Royal Worcester Corset Company was to become the largest employer of women in Worcester. In an era when the garment industry in other cities was notorious for the appalling sweatshop conditions of its factories, Fanning's mill was a model of good working conditions. The buildings were clean, comfortable, full of light and air. When he built his new factory on Wyman Street, it had a dining room, a nurse in attendance, and a large garden next to the building.

Churches in Worcester went up almost as fast as factories. The majority of people in town had some strong religious affiliation which found expression in beautiful buildings in all parts of the city. Some of the new congregations were formed as a result of squabbles in the older churches, for people were not noticeably calmer about church affiliation than they had been earlier in the century.

For some, the churches were a continuation of the religion and language they had brought with them from another land. Their churches offered them comfort, friendship, and help in getting established in a strange new world. As the Catholic population grew, so did the number of their churches, and the city's first convents and parochial schools were started.

In 1869, work began on St. Paul's Church, an elaborate building in the Gothic style designed by Elbridge Boyden. The new church stood on the rise of ground known in an earlier era as Nobility Hill. At the foot of the hill was the original town church, now the least fashionable of the churches, in spite of its new pointed windows with tinted glass. The symbolism of it all was not lost on the city of Worcester.

It is impossible to underestimate the influence these churches had on the city. They were a strong influence on the character of many of Worcester's citizens. They provided active social organizations and supported many worthy causes that improved life for Worcester's citizens. Churches of all denominations supported the cause of temperance.

The churches developed a great interest in music. Many of them had excellent choirs, magnificent organs, and group of instrumentalists, and presented concerts of all sorts.

It is close to impossible to keep track of the number of church buildings that have been constructed in Worcester. Those that were originally built along Main Street and around the common have almost all been replaced by buildings farther away from the center of town. It seemed that congregations would just about get used to a building when they would begin another of a more fashionable design, or in a more convenient place. The older buildings were sometimes taken over by newer congregations.

Mayor James Blake was elected for five consecutive terms beginning in

Left
*Stephen Earle's design for the interior of Chestnut Street Church is an adaptation of the gothic style using great wooden beams. (WHM)*

Above
*Stephen C. Earle designed this house for G. Henry Whitcomb. Construction finished in 1880. Whitcomb, who developed a machine that made envelopes, went into business in 1864. Twenty years later the business was incorporated as the Whitcomb Envelope Company. It was sold to the United States Envelope Company in 1898. (WHM)*

1865. He was so popular that opposition to his candidacy almost vanished. In December of 1870 he was killed by an explosion at the gasworks. The city felt his loss deeply.

In 1871 City Hospital was opened in a private house, and the fire department had a new telegraph alarm system installed. A year later, George Jaques presented the city with four acres of land as a site for a new hospital building. At his death, in August of 1872, he left a fund of $200,000 for its maintenance.

In 1860 Edward Winslow Lincoln was named executive secretary of the Horticultural Society. Son of the second Levi Lincoln, he had been Worcester's postmaster, the editor of a newspaper named the *Aegis,* and later editor of another, short-lived paper called the *Bay State.*

*During the Women's Suffrage Convention held in Worcester in 1850 women complained they would never be free until they changed their cumbersome mode of dress. After World War I, women bobbed their hair, shortened their skirts, and threw away their corsets. The changing styles brought an end to one of Worcester's most prosperous industries, corset manufacturing. (WHM)*

*A display model of a Royal Worcester corset from the collection of the Worcester Historical Museum. Stitchers disliked the black corsets because it was so difficult to see black thread on black fabric. (WHM)*

Lincoln believed that one of Worcester's greatest needs was a system of public parks. At the time, the citizens of Worcester knew little and cared less about the subject, and the Commissioners of Shade Trees and Public Grounds still regretted the purchase of that unimproved swamp called the New Common. But in 1870, Lincoln was appointed chairman of the commission, whose name was subsequently changed to the Parks Commission. Obadiah Hadwen and the third Stephen Salisbury were two of the other members.

Lincoln had grand ideas. He thought the old common should be made into a real park, that the railroad tracks should be removed, vendors and pitchmen kept from peddling their wares on it, and grass encouraged to grow. He wanted a circumferential carriage road to go around the outskirts of the city. Mayor Jillson, strongly opposed to the idea, used his veto power for the first time in the city's history. The veto was overridden by the city council, and work on the road, which was named Park Avenue, was begun.

Lincoln ran the Parks Commission for 25 years, until his death in 1895. He was never paid a salary. After his death, Obadiah Hadwen remarked that the city would now have to pay a superintendent "to do the work his predecessor had done for no other reward than the privilege of expressing his mind in the annual report." Lincoln was a forceful and expressive writer, and his reports are as interesting and amusing to read today as they were when written.

In 1874 work began on Lincoln's favorite project, the transformation of the swamp in the New Common into Elm Park. Lincoln raised young trees and shrubs in his own nursery, many of them rare and unusual, to be planted out as the design for the park advanced. He badgered the city council to buy Newton Hill and add it to Elm Park. It was an open field at the

*The common was cleared of its sheds and railroad tracks to present this view of a true park in the center of town. The trees provide delightful shade in summer. In the foreground is the Civil War memorial which was dedicated in 1874. Behind it stands the old church and town hall. (WHM)*

top of a small hill. Lincoln envisioned the lower part as an area of formal gardens, and the hill as open space where one could walk about and enjoy the view. In 1888, the council gave in and authorized the Park Loan to purchase the hill and by 1890 the park was famous throughout the country. A magazine called the *Cultivator and Country Gentleman* wrote, "Elm Park is unquestionably one of the most perfect examples of landscape gardening in the country."

Other parks grew under his hands. North Park was developed out of another area of swale and swamp. The people of the city responded to these parks with enormous enthusiasm. They walked in the gardens, fished and skated on the ponds, and watched the view from the hills. Then, one by one, gifts of land, often accompanied by money, were presented to the city. H.H. Bigelow gave the city land at Lake Quinsigamond, the first time that the city had owned any land for public use along the shores of the lake. Edward L. Davis added to that land, then Bigelow added another piece, and Lake Park was developed. The third Stephen Salisbury gave the land for Institute Park, then developed it from a rough field into a well-landscaped park.

Worcester was affected by economic depressions, including the one of 1873, but they did not affect every business, and Worcester's people began to realize the great saving grace of their diversified industries. For one-industry towns, the economic problems were devastating, but when times were bad for some of Worcester's industries, they were better for others. Skilled workers laid off by one plant often found work in another.

In general, times were good and continually getting better. The city was growing at a rapid pace and the hills of the city were gradually being covered by the curious architectural phenomenon called the three-decker.

There were those who loathed the sight of them."This particular form of architectural monstrosity was conceived in avarice and born in rapacity. It is a blot on any landscape and, as it towers, an enormous dry goods box, on our sightly hills, it goes far to wipe away the goodly impressions made by beautiful churches, schoolhouses, and other public edifices."

But the people who disliked them the most were usually those who never lived in one. They were three-story buildings, each floor being a separate apartment identical with the other two. Relatively inexpensive to build, they provided the privacy of separate entrances and porches, both front and back, for each family. They offered a secure investment for many of Worcester's workers, with the owner living in one apartment and renting out the other two. Usually they were built within walking distance of the factory where the tenants worked.

People in the field of public health believed that these buildings did much to account for the general good health of Worcester's population. Each

Above
*This three decker on Shrewsbury Street lacks the refinement of shutters and a tree in the front. The vine growing up over the porches is probably "Dutchman's Pipe," (aristolochia durior). In the summer, the large round leaves of the vine would provide a deep shade for the porches and the odd, pipe-shaped blossoms would provide amusement for the children who "smoked" them. (WHM)*

Left
*The view from Newton Hill was an essential part of the design of Elm Park as Parks Commissioner Lincoln envisioned it. There Worcester's citizens could look out over the rolling hills of their comfortable and prosperous city. (WHM)*

apartment received sunshine and fresh air from all sides. People, young and old, took their daily airings on the comfortable porches, where they could enjoy some of the best views in Worcester. Each back porch held a clothes reel where the laundry could hang to dry in the beneficial sunshine, and one of the delights of living on the upper stories was to hang sheets and curtains full length so they dried without a fold. These buildings were in sharp contrast to the crowded, dark, airless factory tenements of other cities.

The health of the city was a special concern of Ichabod Washburn. At his death in 1868 he left money to found a hospital. Washburn's first wife, two

*Worcester native Maude Alice Ames lived in a house at 10 Preston Street almost all her life. This photograph of her was taken in 1897 by E.B. Luce, a company that still operates a photographic business in Worcester. (WHM)*

daughters, and only grandchild had all died within a three-year period, and the hospital was to be called The Memorial Hospital in remembrance of them.

A long dispute over the terms of Washburn's will delayed the opening of the new hospital. In 1874 the Washburn Free Dispensary opened at the corner of Front and Church streets in the building originally used by City Hospital. In 1888, The Memorial Hospital opened its doors at last, in the former Samuel Davis mansion on Belmont Street.

It was a hospital for women and children, staffed by women, except for the physicians, who were men. Because it was one of the few hospitals in the United States that accepted women as interns, in fact preferred them, it became a training ground for many excellent female doctors.

The hospital pioneered in social work, treating not only the patient's obvious physical problems, but attempting to help with domestic or job-related difficulties. Most of the hospital's services were free, although nominal fees were charged those who could afford to pay.

From the beginning the Memorial Hospital Aid Society raised money to support the hospital. The Society, consisting only of women, also supported the first teaching program for young children who were hospitalized for long periods of time.

The people of Worcester loved their city and its big lake. Jesse J. Coburn saw the possibilities that the lake presented. He bought land along the shore, laid out streets, encouraged the building of summer homes, built a hotel on one of the islands, and ran side-wheel steamers up and down it in the summers. In 1872, he organized a narrow-gauge railroad company to run between Worcester and Shrewsbury, which came to be known as the "Dummy Railroad." He had a flotilla of small boats that could be rented by the day. For very modest fees, the people of Worcester could spend pleasant summer days down by the water.

The Foster Street Station was known as "Le Depot du Pere Cote." French-speaking people arriving from Canada were greeted by Godfroi Cote who worked as an interpreter for the Worcester and Nashua Railroad for more than a quarter of a century. (WHM)

The lake's length and lack of current made it the perfect place for rowing. Several boat clubs were formed, and after the success of the first college regatta in 1859, rowing contests became an annual event.

In 1876 the city celebrated the nation's centennial along with the rest of the country. The American Antiquarian Society was still flourishing, still diligently collecting all sorts of material about the history of the United

States, particularly newspapers. The Worcester Society of Antiquity was formed, and one of its first undertakings was to transcribe and publish all of Worcester's early records.

During these fast-changing years, however, preserving the city's heritage held little interest for Worcester's citizens. Buildings were pushed down or pulled away to make way for new ones. Beautiful mansions became commercial buildings. It was only the new and fashionable that was interesting and exciting.

The Foster Street railroad station was closed and in 1882 the land was sold to Horace H. Bigelow. He had originally intended to put up a large office building on the land, but, unable to find enough investors, he decided to build a large exhibition hall and roller-skating rink instead. On the grounds around the building he installed fountains, gardens, and other amusements. All sorts of entertaining attractions were brought to Bigelow's Gardens.

In 1883, Bigelow bought out Coburn's interests near Lake Quinsigamond, including the Dummy Railroad. He gave land by the lake to the city for a public park, and his railroad began catering to the general public, not just those who belonged to private clubs or owned summer houses on the lake.

People rode bicycles. Dedicated cyclists, "whose enthusiasm was far in advance of their judgement," thought nothing of riding the old, high-wheeled "bone breakers" all over the county, or even to Boston and back. But the invention of the modern bicycle, with its two equal wheels and chain drive, made bicycling a popular sport.

The first bicycle made in the United States was manufactured in the Merrifield Buildings by William H. Pierce in 1878 for Hill and Tolman, a company that became one of the largest bicycle dealers in the area. A year later, the Worcester Bicycle Club was formed, then the Aeolus and the Bay State clubs, followed by the Columbus, the YMCA Wheelmen, and the YWCA Hickory Club.

Each club had its own uniform, and the city watched bicycle parades, sometimes in connection with holidays such as the Fourth of July, and sometimes just for the enjoyment of it all. Evening parades with the cyclists carrying torches were the most spectacular. Cycling tournaments gave the "scorchers" a chance to prove their strength on Worcester's hills. Cyclists from all over New England came to the annual spring meet of the League of American Wheelmen.

Ice skating was also a favorite sport. As the city's parks were developed, the ponds were kept clear of snow in winter for the enjoyment of skaters. In 1857 Seth and Samuel Winslow made 25 pairs of skates in their machine shop in the Merrifield Buildings. A year later they made and sold 2500 pairs.

# BIGELOW'S GARDEN.

## Thursday Evening, September 27, 1883,

# BAND CONCERT

By WORCESTER BRASS BAND, from 7.15 to 9 o'clock.

### GRAND DISPLAY OF

# FIREWORKS,

BY THE

### New England Fireworks Laboratory,

### MASTON & WELLS, Pyrotechnists, BOSTON.

OPENING WITH A

**GRAND ILLUMINATION on the WATER,**

In Red, Green and Blue Lights.

No. 2. Device, Revolving Sun. A Revolving Wheel in Emerald Fire, attached to a Shield of Fire in Crimson and Gold, rapidly changing to a Revolving Sun with sparkling Fire and terminating in a loud report.

No. 3. Flights of Colored Shells and Aerial Bombs.

No. 4. Water-wheels Revolving on the surface of the Water.

No. 5. Japanese Brilliants.

No. 6. Discharge of Colored Batteries.

No. 7. On the water hissing Serpents, darting here and there and exploding with loud reports.

No. 8. Epicycloid. Device, a Revolving Zone.

No. 9. Flight of Colored Courants.

No. 10. Flights of Colored Tourbillions.

No. 11. Device, illuminated Cypress formed of Sunfires illuminated with highly ornamented Rosettes, terminating with a Grand Explosion.

No. 12. Display of Water Fountain, Serpents and Marine Illuminations.

No. 13. Fairies Frolic.

No. 14. Flights of Streamer Shells and Marine Bombs.

No. 15. Device, the Kaleidoscope.

No. 16. Water Displays, Fountains and Serpents.

No. 17. Device, a revolving Globe representing the two motions of the earth.

No. 18. Grand discharge of large Shells filling the air with thousands of Colored gerbs. No. 19. The Grand Finial.

GEN. BUTLER on his Second triumphal march to the STATE HOUSE. At a distance is seen the State House Dome, and Flag. Approaching is a Life-like Figure of his Excellency

# GEN. B. F. BUTLER,

In living Fire, who on entering for his Second Term of Office, is received by a GRAND SALUTE OF MAROONED SHELLS.

ADMISSION: ADULTS 25 Cents, CHILDREN 15 Cents.
DOORS OPEN AT 6.45.        FIREWORKS AT 8 O'CLOCK.

Chas. Hamilton, Printer, 311 Main Street, Worcester.

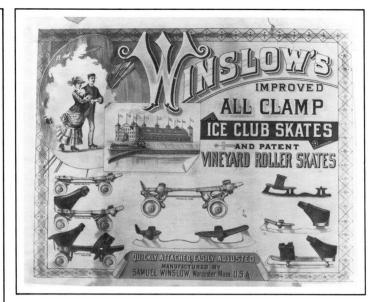

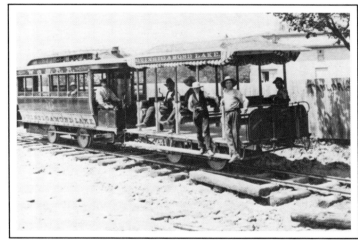

Above
*Band concerts and fireworks were favorite forms of entertainment in the 1880s. This extravaganza ended with a grand finale with political overtones. A "Life-like Figure" of General Benjamin Franklin Butler in "living Fire" capped the evening. (WHM)*

Upper Right
*The brothers Samuel and Seth Winslow made 25 pairs of ice skates in their shop in the Merrifield Buildings as an experiment in 1857. A year later they made 2500 pairs. After Seth's death in 1871, Samuel continued the business, making both ice and roller skates to be sold worldwide. The company also manufactured a very popular bicycle. Samuel went on to become the mayor of Worcester in 1886 and president of the first electric street railway lines to reach to suburban towns. (WHM)*

Center
*The Dummy Railroad ran between the center of the city and the lake on narrow gauge tracks. It provided cheap transportation to all the delights offered by the parks and regattas. (WHM)*

Above
*Small paddle-wheel steamers plied their way up and down Lake Quinsigamond in the summer, stopping at the steamboat landing in Lincoln Park. Edward Winslow Lincoln envisioned the whole lake as a "water park" where the working people of Worcester would find inexpensive recreation. (WHM)*

*The third Stephen Salisbury gave*       *This view shows cyclists traveling*
*some of his father's land to the city*  *along Salisbury Street. The band-*
*for a park and then spent years*        *stand and boathouse are behind*
*developing the plantings and*           *them and in the distance is the wire*
*building ornamental buildings.*         *mill. (WHM)*

In 1872 Samuel Winslow began to manufacture roller skates. In 1880 he developed the Vineyard roller skate, which became popular throughout the United States and was sold all over the world. Skaters rolled about all the streets and sidewalks, and in halls such as Bigelow's Gardens.

In 1884 the second Stephen Salisbury died. He had inherited his father's business interests and land holdings in Worcester at the age of 31 and managed them so successfully that at the time of his death he was one of the wealthiest men in the United States. He also served on committees and governing boards of many organizations in the city, giving them direction and encouragement. His main interests were in Worcester, and he was responsible for much of the city's development.

His estate was inherited by his only son, the third Stephen Salisbury. He was the last of the line, for he never married—a circumstance that was to prove an enormous boon to the city of Worcester. He began to give away his vast inheritance in a manner so judicious that it did much to transform Worcester from just another industrial city into an attractive center of culture and learning.

The third Stephen Salisbury was, like many of the children of the earlier builders of industrial Worcester, a well-educated, sophisticated man who had traveled extensively. He inherited his father's elegant home, filled it with books, works of art, and music. He believed in public service, but most of all he believed in Worcester. He was described as "our most generous townsman," a man who "never does things by halves."

In 1887 he gave the city the land surrounding the pond that had been dammed up by his father to make a head of water for Ichabod Washburn's factory. He then proceeded to develop the area, at his own expense, into beautiful Institute Park. In the Salisbury Street area, beyond Park Avenue, he began a real-estate development of beautiful homes. In the center was a hill, which was kept as a park. At the crown of the hill he built a stone tower as a memorial to his father's boyhood friend, George Bancroft.

In 1896 he organized a new group which developed the Worcester Art Museum and built its new building. The museum was opened to the public in 1898 with an exhibition of paintings loaned by members of the Worcester Art Society. The museum also conducted a school, "not intended for the dilettante, but for those desirous of employing art in some form toward financial gain."

Salisbury also donated land to the Worcester Society of Antiquity for a new building, and gave the lot next door to the Worcester Woman's Club. The list of his gifts to local institutions is almost endless.

At his death in 1905, Salisbury left the bulk of his remaining fortune to two institutions, the Art Museum and the Antiquarian Society. The museum began the long process of collecting objects of the highest quality, and the Antiquarian Society was able to construct a new, modern library building at the corner of Park Avenue and Salisbury Street. The Antiquarian Society made the decision to become a research library devoted primarily to the history of America up to 1876, disposing of most of its collection of objects. The great plaster copy of Michelangelo's Moses which stands in the entrance hall of the courthouse is one reminder of the diversity, not to mention the clutter, of that original collection.

In 1896 Worcester Tech made the fateful decision to discontinue the manufacturing operations of the Washburn Shops. The mechanics' shops had become so successful that they threatened to overshadow the school completely.

Milton Higgins and George Alden left the school. Higgins had run the shops from the beginning, having been brought to Worcester by Ichabod Washburn, and Alden was the professor of mechanical engineering. The two men then concentrated their efforts on the hydraulic-elevator company that had been the source of their embarrassing success, and on the small Norton Company factory at Barber's Crossing where they made grinding wheels.

Worcester celebrated its 50th anniversary as a city in 1898. The centerpiece of the celebration was the new city hall on the common. It was the supreme expression of the pride of the city's builders. Coupled with that pride was a considerable measure of amazement and wonder at all that had happened. Worcester was now a city of more than 100,000 people, overflowing with prosperity.

The old church on the common was gone, torn down with a minimum of regret. The location of the new city hall, however, was a matter of some debate. Stephen Salisbury offered land at Lincoln Square, where the Boys' Club now stands, plus $100,000 in cash if the hall was built there. He envisioned Main Street as a long boulevard with the city hall at one end and the federal building at the other. But he was outvoted, and the common was chosen instead.

Standing beside the new hall was the old one, painted barn red during one of the attempts to make it look more respectable. "It is not a pretentious edifice and makes no claim to architectural beauty, but it has been the governmental home of a free people for three quarters of a century." It would soon be cleared away. All that would remain on the common were the three monuments: the memorial to Timothy Bigelow, the Civil War Memorial, and the great new center of municipal government.

In May of 1898 Worcester men marched away to war again. The Worcester Light Infantry, the Worcester City Guards, and the Wellington Rifles all joined in the Spanish-American War. By August the men were home again, and the city was stunned by their appearance, for they were wracked with disease, pitiful shadows of the brave young men who had left in the spring.

As the new century began the city was still growing. More and more of the streets were lighted by electricity, and electric trolley lines made it possible for people to live farther and farther away from the places where they worked. Telephones made communications easier. Automobiles were becoming more common, but the majority of the city's traffic was still horse-drawn.

Clark University opened in 1889. Jonas Clark picked Worcester as the ideal setting for what he hoped would be a great research institution, patterned after European models. In 1903, President G. Stanley Hall announced a series of Saturday lectures, covering no less than 33 subjects, each one having a practical bearing on the work of teachers in the Worcester school system. Everything from educational psychology to school hygiene was covered.

Clark cooperated with the State Normal School in conducting classes for young children where the most advanced teaching methods were used. The children loved the romantic French castle that housed the school, with its special rooms full of stuffed birds, its collections of rocks and seashells, all used to stimulate the young imagination.

Above
*Worcester residents lined Main Street during the city's semi-centennial parade in 1898. On the left can be seen the State Mutual Life Assurance building. It was built in 1896 and was considered the first modern office building in Worcester. (WHM)*

Above Right
*The network of rail lines coming into the center of Worcester made the city a commercial center for all of Worcester County. Special trains came and went to the outlying towns for all sorts of events such as P.T. Barnum's extravaganza. (WHM)*

*The founders of the Worcester Society of Antiquity were Samuel E. Staples, Franklin P. Rice, Richard O'Flynn, and J.E. Smith. The Society collected historical treasures and published material about Worcester from its beginning in 1875. It was renamed the Worcester Historical Museum in 1978. It maintains a museum, library, and the Salisbury Mansion and concerns itself only with the history of the city of Worcester. (WHM)*

*Two Worcester policemen wait at the corner of Pleasant and Main streets for the arrival of a parade during the campaign of 1892 when Harrison and Reid ran against Cleveland and Stevenson. (WHM)*

Meanwhile, Holy Cross College, originally founded in 1843, offered a strictly classical course of study, including Greek. By the early years of the 20th century, the college had an enrollment of more than 300 boarding students plus about 60 day students.

In 1907 Albert A. Michelson, chairman of the physics department at Clark, became the first American to receive the Nobel Prize. In 1909, Sigmund Freud and Carl Jung came to Clark at the invitation of President G. Stanley Hall. More and more, Worcester's colleges were doing exciting things, bringing to Worcester a new population—not the lawyers and judges of the early days, not the "mechanics" and industrialists of the 19th century, but people with artistic and intellectual interests who would eventually change Worcester again.

In 1905 the city had an opportunity to acquire Green Hill and to make it the jewel of the parks system. The estate of more than 500 acres had been

Above
*Granville Stanley Hall, the founder and first president of the American Psychological Association, was chosen as the first president of Clark University in 1888. At Clark, Hall established the country's first institute of child psychology and formulated a curriculum of graduate studies in education and psychology. He died in Worcester in 1924. From Cirker,* Dictionary of American Portraits, *Dover, 1967.*

Top
*This 1889 photo of the Clark building at Clark University was taken at the time it was dedicated. The science building is shown in the background. (WHM)*

Above
*Fenwick Hall of the College of the Holy Cross was built after the fire of 1852 destroyed the college's earlier buildings. (WHM)*

developed by Andrew Haswell Green and his brother Martin out of a farm that had originally belonged to the first Dr. John Green.

It was somewhere on this farm that the family had secretly buried Bathsheba Spooner after she was hanged for the murder of her husband in 1778. Her sister had married into the Green family. Only members of the family ever knew where the grave was, and none of them ever told.

Andrew lived in New York and served as parks commissioner and comptroller of that city. His ideas for developing the family estate in Worcester were influenced by his close contact with Frederick Law Olmsted and Calvert Vaux as they developed Central Park in New York. Andrew acquired one piece of land after another, until at last he owned the whole hilltop.

His brother Martin, a retired civil engineer, developed the water system, a plant for making illuminating gas, the dams to make the ponds, the roads, and the farm, and supervised the remodeling of the house, which eventually had 42 rooms. Most of the wood for the mansion was cut on the hill. Carpenters of great skill installed the elaborate woodwork and inlaid floors.

The other Green children were scattered all over the world. One was a missionary in Ceylon; another was a medical missionary in Africa and later Chile. The house was full of fascinating curiosities.

Everyone in Worcester loved to go and see the great estate as it developed. It was opened to the public frequently, and great crowds came to admire the buildings, the gardens, and the glorious view.

After Andrew's death in 1905, the family offered the estate to the city for the assessed valuation of $104,000, and furthermore offered to contribute $50,000 toward the purchase price. In December of 1905, the city accepted the offer.

The mansion was used as a clubhouse, with rooms of various sizes which anyone could rent for modest fees. It was so popular that reservations had to be made months in advance. The farm had fields with buffalo, deer, and elk. Near the mansion, golden pheasants, peacocks, and other birds roamed about among rose arbors and gardens and under the huge locust tree planted by the first Dr. John Green.

On the eastern part of the hill, the city developed a golf course which soon became very popular. Worcester's park system was considered to be ideal, in perfect proportion to the city's population and beautifully maintained. A clear distinction was maintained between the uses of a park and a recreation area, as certain recreational uses would cause maintenance problems with the plantings in a park. Worcester was the envy of the nation.

At the same time, the Worcester Board of Trade was telling the world, "Send on your orders. Worcester will oil them, grind them, wrench them, shape them, drill them and envelope them." But, the 1909 brochure added,

Left
*The streets leading to Union Station were smokey and congested. As the trains pulled in and out, nauseating smoke filled the station. (WHM)*

Below
*Frederick W. Rice photographed the Classical High School orchestra in 1909. (WHM)*

"Never order poor goods in Worcester County. They are not made here."
In 1917, the city mobilized for war. Soldiers were encamped on Green Hill in July, and on July 31 had their final review at Worcester Tech's playing fields.

As the winter came, there was an acute shortage of coal. Factories closed for five days in January, and then every Monday for ten weeks. Some facto-

*The Green family posed for this portrait in 1861 during a family reunion. The whole group had not been together for 21 years. William Green, the father of this large family, is fifth from the left. Second from right is Andrew Haswell Green and sixth from right is Martin Green. (WHM)*

ries were burning sawdust. Men went out into the woods to cut trees as fuel for the poor, to be distributed through the Associated Charities. Many people shut up large parts of their houses and lived in the kitchen, the only warm place.

Wages in the city rose. Riveters were getting $50 a day. Many women left domestic service to go to work in factories, and many a housewife was appalled to find that she had to pay 25 to 30 cents an hour for any sort of help.

As the summer passed, an epidemic of the flu swept the country. By September almost all public gatherings ceased, churches were closed, and people dreaded to read the paper to see the lists of those dead from war or disease.

By the time of the Armistice on November 11, the epidemic had abated, and the city looked forward once again to an era of peace.

Above
*Clockmaker Abel Stowell made this cherrywood-encased clock in 1783. Stowell manufactured clocks and watches in his shop south of the meetinghouse.*

Left
*This portrait of Elizabeth Stone Denny (1811-1899) was painted in 1840 by Augustus Fuller, a classmate of Mrs. Denny and her husband Edwards Whipple Denny at the American Asylum in West Brookfield, Connecticut. All three were deaf mutes.*

Far Left
*Dr. Samuel Woodward (1787-1850) was the first superintendent of the Lunatic Asylum and a pioneer in the humane treatment of the insane. This ivory miniature of him was done by Sarah Goodridge. It was given to the Worcester Historical Museum by Dr. Woodward's grandson whose name was also Dr. Samuel Woodward.*

Left
*This Hepplewhite sewing table was constructed of mahogany with satinwood inlay by Jeremiah Healy in 1817. Healy ran a pattern shop in Worcester.*

*The first Stephen Salisbury built this house in 1772. His store was in the right hand section.*

*The building is now maintained by the Worcester Historical Museum and is open to the public.*

*Daniel Waldo (1763-1845) was the president of the Worcester Bank and ran a successful hardware business in Worcester. His mother was a Salisbury and one sister married Levi Lincoln. He never married, but lived with his two unmarried sisters on Main Street. Waldo was the man who lent money to the young Ichabod Washburn. This portrait is from the collection of the Worcester County Horticultural Society.*

*The second Stephen Salisbury, the only child of the first Stephen Salisbury to survive, managed the property he inherited from his father so astutely that he became one of the wealthiest men in the United States. This portrait is from the collection of the Worcester County Horticultural Society.*

*The third Stephen Salisbury inherited his father's vast fortune and proceeded to give it to the citizens of Worcester, endowing institutions that have made the city a cultural center. This portrait is from the collection of the Worcester County Horticultural Society.*

Top Left and Right
*Shown here are two of the delightful valentines made by Esther Howland. After graduating from Mount Holyoke College in 1847, Miss Howland tried making and selling valentines. Her father, a Worcester bookseller, arranged to buy imported supplies for her and the business soon amounted to $100,000 a year. The company was eventually sold to the Whitney Valentine Company.*

Above Left
*Benjamin Harris Kinney (1821-1888) was a Worcester sculptor and cameo cutter who did the portraits of many of Worcester's people. This painting is by William O. Bemis (1819-1883) who worked in the Worcester area.*

Above
*Frank B. Norton made a variety of ceramic objects, both practical and decorative. In 1876 he took out a patent on a formula to make an emery wheel that Swen Pulson had developed. Today the Norton Company is the world's largest manufacturer of abrasives.*

This memorial on the common was dedicated to Timothy Bigelow by the Bigelow family while Worcester's young men were marching away to the Civil War. The gravestones in the foreground were in the old cemetery.

Left
Daniel Wesson, the Springfield gun manufacturer, gave this house to his daughter as a wedding present when she married Dr. George Bull of Worcester in 1876. It was designed by Calvert Vaux and cost $125,000. It was used for many years by the GAR, an organization of veterans of the Civil War. It is now owned by the City of Worcester and is used by several veterans organizations. The attractive garden in the foreground is in the courtyard of the Freedom Federal Savings Bank.

## Above
The Mechanic Street Burying Ground was opened in 1795 at the corner of Mechanic and Foster streets. In 1878 it was closed and the bodies were moved to other cemeteries. This painting of the burying ground as it appeared in 1845 was done by Henry Woodward, once a teacher at the Oread Institute, who spent most of his life working as the treasurer of the Mechanics Savings Bank. He was the organizer of the Worcester Art Students Club.

## Left
The gilded pine statue of Justice once stood on top of the 1802 courthouse. It has been attributed to Jeremiah Stiles (1771-1826) who came to Worcester in 1791 and worked in Major Healy's pattern shop.

## Right
This dove-colored silk satin dress belonged to the first Mrs. Stephen Salisbury, Elizabeth Tuckerman of Boston. The dress is lined with blue silk. It is from the collection of the Worcester Historical Museum.

Left
*St. Paul's Cathedral. The church became a cathedral when the Diocese of Worcester was created in 1950.*

Bottom Left
*This rooster weathervane was perched atop the steeple of the church on the common in Worcester where it could be seen from all the surrounding hills.*

Bottom Right
*The Reverend Alonzo Hill came to Worcester to assist Dr. Aaron Bancroft in 1827. In 1839 he became pastor of the Unitarian Church and remained until his death in 1871. A contemporary said, "His face was a benediction." From the collection of the Worcester Historical Museum.*

Above
*This house on Mower Street in the Tatnuck section of Worcester was one of the stops on the underground railway.*

Left
*Levi Lincoln (1782-1868) was the son of Martha Waldo and the first Levi Lincoln, one of Worcester's most distinguished citizens. This Levi was governor of the state from 1825 to 1834. Lincoln Square was named for the family. This portrait is from the collection of the Worcester County Horticultural Society.*

Right
*The Civil War memorial was designed by Randolph Rogers. This figure of a sailor is actually a portrait of George Crompton, the founder of the Crompton Loom Works. He just happened to be chairman of the committee in charge of building the monument, and gave a generous donation to pay for it.*

# Chapter Six

# The Mature City

*Horticultural Hall, at the corner of Elm and Chestnut streets. The old Horticultural Hall on Front Street was made over into a commercial building when this new building was opened in 1929. All of the Horticultural Society's exhibitions are held here. Photo by Ron White.*

**O**n Monday January 12, 1920, front-page headlines across the nation announced, "Modern Jules Verne Invents Rocket to Reach Moon." Robert Goddard's monograph called, "A Method of Reaching Extreme Altitudes," had just been released by the Smithsonian Institution.

It was only nine years since Goddard had watched, along with 40,000 others, as the first airplane flew over Worcester in 1911. An army biplane and a Bleriot monoplane raced each other to the delight of everyone. The Bleriot won.

Goddard studied at Worcester Tech and then at Clark. In 1914 he took out the basic patents on his rockets. His health was precarious, and he had turned down offers from Columbia and Princeton, preferring to stay at Clark, where he had a light teaching load, time for research, and a sympathetic administration.

Jonas Clark's vision of a school primarily devoted to research had produced an absolutely startling result. The whole world was soon to be transformed by this invention, but Worcester took very little notice of it all, considering Goddard to be something of a dreamer, sending his toys up into the sky by Coe's Pond.

In 1924 the Planning Board presented a city plan for Worcester, the result of several years of study. The population had continued to grow, from 116,000 in 1900 to 180,000 in 1920, and it seemed reasonable to assume it would reach 300,000 by 1970.

It was a diverse population. Many descendants of the early settlers still lived in the city. The second and third generations descended from the industrialists who had transformed Worcester in the middle of the 19th century still made Worcester their home. They had married and intermarried, so that it was just as well to be discreet in one's conversation, for one never knew who was related to whom. Much of the capital realized from those thriving industries remained in Worcester.

The Irish population was well settled and represented the largest distinct ethnic group. They had their churches, their clubs, their festivals. Holy Cross was their college, Saint Vincent's was their hospital, their beautiful churches and parochial schools were spread throughout the city, and Worcester was fast becoming politically theirs.

Almost equal in size was the French-Canadian group, which began coming to Worcester during the Civil War period. In neighborhoods on Grafton Hill and near University Park, French was the first language, *Le Travailleur* and *L'Opinion Publique* were the favorite newspapers, and the Academy of the Assumption, where classes were conducted in French from kindergarten through college, was the school where they preferred to send their children. The last church standing near the common today is called Notre Dame des Canadiens.

About 1890, a group of Italians came to Worcester, primarily from the area of Bisceglia and Abruzzi. They soon settled along Shrewsbury and Plantation streets, built a church where sermons were preached in Italian, Our Lady of Mount Carmel, and established their own banks, stores, and restaurants.

The immigrants came in search of better economic conditions. Many of them left lives of extreme poverty behind them and arrived here with no skills. They found work in many industries, often being introduced to the foreman by a relative. Such a variety of people was employed by Washburn and Moen that the management boasted it had its own League of Nations.

Scandinavians, especially Swedes, comprised about a fifth of the population in 1920. Many of them were attracted by deliberate recruiting campaigns conducted by Worcester industries seeking skilled workers, especially in the iron and steel industries. Some were paid a premium to come here and had jobs and living quarters waiting for them.

In 1868, the pottery firm of Franklin Norton and Frederick Hancock employed four skilled Swedish potters; by the 1920s, the Norton Company was well established as a manufacturer of abrasives and expanding rapidly. The Swedes preferred Lutheran churches, where Swedish was spoken, and used Fairlawn Hospital. They put their money in the Skandia Credit Union, buried their dead in the Swedish cemetery, and formed a little Swedish town within the city called Quinsigamond Village.

There were small groups of Finns, Norwegians, and Danes in Worcester, and another small group of Germans. They had churches and social groups, but their numbers were never great.

By the 1920s, there was large Lithuanian population. The first Lithuanian church was St. Casimir's, followed by Our Lady of Vilna. St. Casimir's school conducted classes in Lithuanian, and more than 30 social and charitable organizations were almost exclusively Lithuanian.

The newly arriving Polish population shared St. Casimir's Church for many years. Its pastor, Father Jakstys, preached in both Lithuanian and Polish at alternate services. Our Lady of Czestochowa was built in 1906 and St. Mary's School opened in 1915.

A portion of both the Lithuanian and Polish populations was Jewish. The

Jews formed close-knit communities centered around their synagogues, both Orthodox and Reform. S.N. Berham's book *The Worcester Account,* published in 1954, gives a vivid account of his boyhood within the Jewish community of Worcester.

The Jews established many services for their people, including loan societies, free milk stations, societies that helped the sick and the poor, and groups to provide education and entertainment among their own people.

By 1923, the Worcester Modern Congregation had moved its community house to the old Bancroft School building on Elm Street and had begun using English in most of its services.

The Armenians formed another close-knit group. They began arriving in the 1870s, fleeing the terrible troubles in the Turkish Empire. Worcester had already established some connections with the Near East. Several residents of Worcester had taught at Robert College in Constantinople and at the American University in Beirut and could provide help in interpreting the new and strange city these people had come to.

Other groups—Assyrian, Syrian, Lebanese—came, too, founding small communities, always centered around their churches. They found jobs, established homes, and became a part of Worcester.

Meanwhile, the black community was a long-established part of the city. Many local blacks were descended from people who had been here since the time of the Revolution; many others came from families that arrived in the days of the underground railway.

The Greeks, destined to form a large and strong group later in the century, had just begun to arrive. In 1925, they moved into St. Spyridon's Church on Orange Street.

The towns around the city were almost entirely rural, depending on Worcester as a commercial center where people did their important banking and shopping. The court was still in Worcester, and the city still had its share of lawyers.

The center of the city was crowded. Almost half the population lived within walking distance of city hall. As many as 25,000 were employed in the retail trade, and that trade was almost entirely in the Main Street area. Worcester was a "rapidly growing city," stated the Planning Board report of 1924, "and yet it is a one street village."

Mayor Logan had declared in 1910 that the motor car was here to stay, but the city had not yet faced up to its implications. The congestion in the center of town was unbelievable. Cars were parked on the common behind the city hall. The junction of Pleasant, Front, and Main streets was a hopeless tangle. Pleasant Street had a little jog where it entered Main, rather than crossing directly. Twenty-eight trolley lines crossed that junction. There was no room for the cars to pass the trolleys. The sidewalks were narrow and jammed with people waiting for rides. On days when all that confusion was compounded by bad weather, it seemed as though no one would ever find his way home.

Lincoln Square was worse than Main Street. Roads and trolley lines poured into that area where the railroad lines had a grade crossing. In any 12-hour period, the gates would be closed for an hour and 20 minutes. As many as 300 vehicles would be stopped at once.

It was frustrating, but most of Worcester's people were philosophical about it as they watched the long lines of freight cars rumble past, bearing the products of Worcester's genius to the rest of the world, then hailed with relief the long-awaited red caboose. Police struggled to unscramble the mess and get everyone on their way before the next train came. As traffic moved away from the center of town, it had to pass through narrow streets, half of them less than 50 feet wide.

Worcester had 600 principal industries in 1922 employing 42,000 people, 9000 of them women, in addition to the 25,000 employed in the retail trade.

But the character of the city was changing. "The city has a distinct personality which is unfortunately rapidly disappearing through the unwarranted diffusion of factories and the spread of unattractive houses. In the creation of a city plan there is a real opportunity to save the city from itself by conserving good residential areas where they will count the most in assuring the appearance of the city and by keeping the factories along the valleys in the neighborhood of the railroads where they belong even in their own interest." Worcester's hillsides were covered with houses, churches, and hospitals, away from the dirt and noise, but the growing use of trucks for transportation meant that commercial interests were encroaching on residential areas.

People were having a good time in spite of the traffic problems. They enjoyed 19 parks and eight playgrounds. Plans were underway for a system of parkways that would provide "pleasing, broad, smoothly paved thoroughfares" going in and out of town. These parkways would be protected from becoming "tawdry semi-business districts" and, it was hoped, would eventually connect all the larger parks so that one could walk, ride, or bicycle all about the city without ever going through "sordid streets."

There were other problems connected with the rapid growth of the city, which had now been going on for 75 years. The only means of garbage disposal was still the town piggery at the Home Farm, the successor to the Poor Farm, near the northern end of Lake Quinsigamond. The runoff from that operation did cause a certain amount of scum to float along the surface of the lake and, as the 1924 report put it, "It is a fact that on hazy days in the summer, when the wind is right, the odors from the city pig farm are somewhat troublesome."

*The city's young ladies participated in Doll Day at the South Worcester Playground in 1928. (WHM)*

Right
*Senator George Frisbee Hoar, one of Worcester's most prominent politicians, entertained Teddy Roosevelt at his home on September 2, 1902. Mrs. Hoar is on the right. The two children at left center are the senator's grandchildren. The two at right center are Sophie and Walter Raad, two Syrian children who were refused admittance to the United States at Ellis Island because Sophie had an eye infection. With the President's help the senator intervened on the children's behalf so they could join their father in Worcester. (WHM)*

Right
*Trolleys, horse-drawn vehicles, cars, and pedestrians all made a glorious tangle of traffic on Main Street in front of city hall in 1914. All this activity was looked upon as a sign of prosperity. Ten years later the city planners began to realize that the traffic was beginning to choke the heart of the city. (WHM)*

Below
*The pigs at the Home Farm served as Worcester's early garbage disposal system. (WHM)*

There was also the perennial problem of sewage. The city had no great waterway to carry it off. When the canal was built, the people of the town found it a convenient place to dump all sorts of trash, from ashes to dead horses. Strict town ordinances on the subject were not well enforced. In 1867, the city started using Mill Brook as a common sewer. The complaints from downstream were heard immediately, as the little mill ponds filled with foul-smelling sludge. Time after time, the city was taken to court. In 1878 Charles A. Allen was named city engineer, and he developed a chemical disposal plant that was the largest in the world at the time. But still it was not enough. In 1882 Worcester's pollution of the Blackstone River was declared to be the worst in the nation. The city has struggled with the problem ever since, gradually laying sewer lines and improving the sewage-disposal plant.

Even so, the city's population was healthier than that of many cities, with a low rate of tuberculosis. Seven hospitals and five dispensaries tended to the needs of the sick. Pioneering work was being done in the fields of mental health, the prevention of contagious diseases, and the treatment of children.

More than 100 churches were flourishing, often acting as magnets for ethnic groups who formed both religious and political units in distinct areas of the city. Much of Worcester's social life centered around its private clubs. There were 33 different organizations of some size, plus an untold number of smaller groups. Many of them supported worthy causes, while others were just for fun, providing a delightful round of suppers, dances, plays, musicals, and sporting events.

Legitimate theaters were still being patronized, but movies were now the great favorites. The Music Festival continued its yearly presentations, but Mechanics Hall seemed woefully old-fashioned and much too small. The city needed a new auditorium seating 6000 to 10,000 people to provide a center for conventions of all kinds. The common was the preferred site, and that suggestion precipitated one more battle and round of petitions to save what was left of the common for open space in the heart of the city.

Public education, dreadfully neglected in the 18th and early 19th centuries—so much so that the town was constantly being called to account by the courts and fined for its lack of attention to its schools—became a central concern of the city during its period of rapid development. "Schools are cheaper than prisons" became the motto of the town fathers, who viewed the schools as a way to keep troublesome children off the streets.

Parents and teachers had other views. For them, education was the key to advancement. Many teachers were women, many of them graduates of the State Normal School. By 1924, the city had 80 grammar schools, 4 high schools, 8 special schools, and 11 parochial schools, with a total enrollment of 25,000 students. As many as 6000 children were attending double sessions, and most of the classrooms had 36 to 40 students. Most of the schools had no playgrounds, a matter of much concern. Yet in spite of these problems, the students did well. Many took their education so seriously that they filled the night classes given in some schools, in the local YW and YMCAs, and at local colleges.

Worcester was a pioneer in developing the concept of trade schools. Ichabod Washburn had urged the Mechanics Association to start one, and Milton Higgins had pressed for the idea. Worcester industries needed skilled workers. The Boys' Trade School opened in 1910 in a building at Lincoln Square, and the Girls' Trade School soon followed, eventually to be

*The Buckley Lunch Wagons delighted both the eye and the stomach. They were wonderfully decorated with paintings and colored-glass windows. The interior had an amazing assortment of bric-a-brac. The vents in the ceiling carried off the fumes from the kerosene lamps, and spittoons were placed in strategic locations. The company was founded in 1899 by Thomas H. Buckley. One wagon took first prize at the Chicago World's Fair. Its selling price was $5,000. (WHM)*

housed in a handsome building on Chatham Street donated to the city by David Hale Fanning.

It was common practice in most New England industrial towns throughout the 19th century for mills and factories to build housing for their workers. Rows and rows of identical buildings lined the streets, all rented out to mill hands. This type of housing was almost unheard of in Worcester. Most workers either owned their own homes or rented from a landlord who was someone other than their employer. It was a great innovation when the Norton Company began developing a 16-acre area near its factory for the benefit of its workers in 1915 and 1916. A total of 58 single-family houses with six rooms each were built. Soon another tract with 100 houses was added. The rent paid for the houses was eventually applied to the purchase price.

Two of the causes that had occupied much thought and attention in Worcester throughout the 19th century were brought to successful conclusions at last. The advocates of temperance finally had their way, and national prohibition was instituted on January 20, 1920. And with the ratification of the 19th Amendment in 1921, American women at last had the right to vote.

Prohibition cleared the streets of the rowdy drunks who were so common and so upsetting in the previous century. It was some time before the evils that accompanied this enforced sobriety became clear. Worcester was no different from any other city. Its speakeasies and bootleggers preferred not to have their histories written.

The women's suffrage movement began early in the 19th century with people like Abby Kelly Foster. In 1850, a women's suffrage convention was held in Worcester. Another was held in 1851. Susan B. Anthony, Lucy Stone, Lucretia Mott, and Elizabeth Cady Stanton were among those who attended. They solemnly declared, "A fearful and momentous responsibility rests upon the few who now act as pioneers in a reform to accomplish so gigantic a work." Lucy Stone urged, "Instead of asking 'Give us this, or give us that' let us just get up and take it." But it was not to be that easy.

Over the years, great numbers of speakers advocated that women be allowed to vote. In 1917 the women of Worcester rented what they called "suffrage rooms" in the center of the city, where they sought to convey their message to the men. The women frequently marched and demonstrated. On February 15, 1919, they held another convention at the Bancroft Hotel; two years later, they voted for the first time.

Worcester's schools were beginning to mean more and more to the city, both intellectually and economically. The Bancroft School, a private day school, was founded in 1900; in 1923, it moved into a new building on Sever Street. Worcester Academy, well established in its home on Vernon Hill, was thriving, with both day and boarding students.

Assumption College, founded in 1904, moved into new quarters in 1911. Holy Cross College still occupied its hilltop, still offered the classical curriculum, and was constantly adding buildings and athletic facilities. Worcester Tech, following some lean years, was now entering a new building phase, and its laboratories were experimenting with aerodynamics. For those who were not students, perhaps no school meant more to Worcester than Clark University, thanks in part to the fine-arts course run by English professor Dr. Loring Holmes Dodd. It began in 1922 and, for those lucky enough to hold tickets, provided a constant diet of fascinating lecturers and performers of every type of theatrical art for the next 34 years.

Above
*These second grade students attended the State Normal School in Worcester in 1903. By 1924, 25,000 children attended Worcester's 80 grammar schools, 4 high schools, 8 special schools, and 11 parochial schools. (WHM)*

Left
*The Bancroft Hotel, opened in September of 1913 on Franklin Street, was the site of a 1919 women's suffrage convention. The hotel was considered to be the most modern and elegant one in New England. Though its rooftop garden and dance pavilion were favorite spots for the fashionable people of the city, a change in the fire laws forced them to close. (WHM)*

Right
*Waiting on tables was one of the skills taught at the Girl's Trade School. This tea room was run by the students. (WHM)*

# Chapter Seven
# Troubled Times

*Exhausted winners of a Worcester dance marathon pose in the 1930s. One way to temporarily forget the Depression and possibly win some cash was to participate in the dance marathon craze sweeping the country. (WHM)*

At the end of October 1929, the stock market collapsed. In Worcester, as in the rest of the country, many people were totally wiped out financially. But the city had weathered other bad times, and it hardly seemed possible that it would not do so again.

There were 527 manufacturing firms in the city, several of them the largest concerns of their kind in the country. The Osgood Bradley Car Company was the largest maker of railroad cars, and the Samuel Winslow Skate Company was making more ice skates and roller skates than anyone in the world. Allen Higgins Company was the largest manufacturer of wallpaper. Graton and Knight made more leather belting than anyone, and Wyman Gordon made 90 percent of the automobile crankshafts produced in the United States. Baldwin Chain made 75 percent of the bicycle and automobile chains. Crompton and Knowles had the largest loom manufacturing plant in the world, while the Whittall plant was one of the largest rug and carpet mills.

The Norton Company was making abrasives and planning to open a new plant in England. American Steel and Wire, the successor to the Washburn Company, was producing steel and springs. The Whitney Company was making valentines. There were several envelope manufacturers. The Royal Worcester Corset Company was still functioning, in spite of changing styles, and the William H. Burns Company was a large manufacturer of muslin underwear. The city was still a center for banking, and the banks were sound and optimistic.

But little by little the city lost its greatest asset, the bursting enthusiasm and optimism that had carried it from success to success. The population stopped growing. Banks found themselves in trouble, as people lost confidence in them, withdrew deposits, and began to hoard gold and coins. Unemployment became a problem.

The city instituted a program of public works, spending $500,000 on paving new roads in 1930; Burncoat was one street paved at this time. In December, the Worcester County Extension Service was asked to cooperate by providing apples to sell on street corners. The enforcement of prohibition became less and less effective.

Still, there were things to be cheerful about. The Art Museum, principal beneficiary of Stephen Salisbury's will in 1905, had husbanded this great bequest carefully, and the museum survived the stock-market crash with its funds still in good order. Francis Henry Taylor, who became its new director in 1931, believed that the purpose of the museum was to serve every interested Worcester citizen, and that it ought to display fine examples of as many periods of art as possible. The museum made plans for a new building, which opened in 1933.

By 1932, one quarter of Worcester's work force was unemployed. Those who did have jobs were working at greatly reduced wages, usually on short hours. The financial problems of the city were acute. Municipal employees returned $300,737 out of their wages to the treasury.

Three mornings each week, about 2000 unemployed men checked in at the Boys' Club building. They were assigned work at City Hospital, doing painting and carpentry, or at one of the parks or Hope Cemetery, doing tree pruning and raking, or working on the roads.

One of the new roads that was built cut across Green Hill Park, destroying the design so carefully thought out by the Greens and making the park a short cut from Lincoln Street to Belmont. Still, the park provided the hard-pressed city with some income from the rental of the mansion and fees from the golf course, a total of about $16,500 in 1932.

The Home Farm was producing meat, poultry, milk, eggs, and vegetables, but in November it was decided to close the piggery and end the problems it caused.

On March 4, 1933, Franklin Roosevelt was inaugurated President and immediately closed the banks. On March 6, the commercial banks reopened for limited business; on the 8th, payrolls of not more than $25 per employee could be drawn from Worcester banks. People were short of cash. Some grocery stores would not give credit. When some of the banks reopened, others did not. For some people, it meant the loss of nearly everything and the depths of discouragement.

In April, 3.2 beer and wine went on sale. Meanwhile, work was progressing on the new auditorium and war memorial at Lincoln Square, providing work for some lucky people. The new building was designed to seat 3500, a great reduction from the 10,000 originally proposed in 1924, and an earlier plan to provide parking near the building was abandoned.

In July, the Heald Machine Company instituted the first 40-hour work-week for its employees, and seven Worcester firms reported an increase in their payrolls. The Norton Company began to produce diamond wheels, an important new product.

The discouraging economic picture did not prevent the city from holding a parade to celebrate the opening of the new auditorium. The building was dedicated on September 25. On the 27th, a military parade wound through the streets. On the 28th, a civic parade passed in review. On the 29th, a

*The White City Amusement Park was located just across the Lake Quinsigamond Bridge in Shrewsbury. Generations of Worcester people found inexpensive entertainment on its many rides. The park closed in 1960. (WHM)*

footrace and pageant took place. And on the 2nd of October, a capacity audience listened to the first concert of the 74th Worcester Music Festival.

In November of 1933, the city dedicated the war memorial at Lincoln Square. The Salisbury mansion was gone, moved away to a new location. The Salisbury factories still stood across the square, and the traffic still got snarled when the trains passed, but the lines of freight cars were shorter. The depression deepened.

In 1934, the mansion at Green Hill was closed, and the toboggan slide, which had been a great favorite, was dismantled—all in the name of economy. The Oread Castle was torn down to save having to pay taxes on it. The population was smaller and so was the number of schoolchildren. The one cheerful note was an announcement by President Wallace Atwood of Clark University that the school was about to begin a $2-million dollar building program.

In the midst of all the gloom, there were those who struggled to keep people's spirits up. Neighbors helped each other. Church groups pulled together to help the less fortunate. Doctors and hospitals performed their services without thought of payment.

In the summer of 1934 the Worcester Rosebuds of the Northeastern League played baseball on the "exceptionally fast and smooth" diamond at Whittall Field, and in the fall, Ted Lewis and his Happiness Follies played at the Elm Street Theater.

The city controlled less of its own destiny as the federal government took on new authority. Ways of doing business changed. The automobile was assuming new importance. Small towns around Worcester began to grow.

The city struggled to maintain its position as a retail center by holding "Worcester Days," when most of the stores in town had special sales.

By 1937 business seemed better, but 1938 was worse. A gauge of the economy was the sight of houses in the fashionable area the third Stephen Salisbury had developed along Salisbury Street, empty and deserted, with their doors swinging in the wind.

Companies with foreign affiliations were becoming nervous. Norton Company employees in England and Italy were brought home, as the ominous rumblings of Hitler and Mussolini grew bolder.

In September it rained a lot. By September 17 the rivers were high and the low areas saturated. Another 17 inches of rain fell by the 21st, when the wind began to blow.

Worcester had seen hurricanes before, most notably the ones of 1815 and

*The mast of the S.S. Constitution was brought to the war memorial at Lincoln Square on October 19, 1933. Before it could be put in place it broke, killing one woman. (WHM)*

1877, but this one was the worst ever. Trees and power lines went down everywhere. The beautiful plantings in the parks and on the streets were devastated. The destruction was widespread throughout New England, not only from the wind, but from the great floods that swept down the valleys, washing out dams, destroying factories, houses, roads, everything.

The city tackled the huge job of cleaning up. The railroad, after the tracks were repaired, brought power-company crews from as far away as Georgia and Michigan to help with the repair work. In parts of Worcester County, the damage could still be seen 30 years later.

The city found itself welcoming a new wave of immigrants as war swept Europe, and the economy began to revive as the preparations for war brought new orders to Worcester factories. Banks that had struggled to survive for 10 years suddenly were on a sound footing again. Companies began to call themselves "defense plants" and to worry about security.

The younger men of the city were obliged to register for the draft at the end of October 1940 and soon began to leave for the service. The next year, in August, their terms of enlistment were extended. Jobs were plentiful now; finding the skilled people to fill them became the problem. More and more women came into the work force, in jobs that had traditionally belonged to men.

After Pearl Harbor, the war began to have its effect in earnest. Worcester's industries produced a curious variety of wartime products, many of them absolutely vital to the war effort. Defense-related factories stepped up production to their utmost capacity. Other companies, forbidden to produce what were considered luxury products, found work for their employees by subcontracting from larger firms. The flag with the big E, for excellence and

*The Unitarian Church on Court Hill was destroyed when the steeple collapsed during the 1938 hurricane. Fortunately, measured drawings of the original building had been made earlier and the church was rebuilt. (WHM)*

efficiency of manufacturing operations, flew over several plants.

The shortage of skilled workers was a constant problem. In one week, the Norton Company hired 105 men; that same week, 101 were drafted. Gasoline and oil were rationed. People who had moved outside the city came back to where the jobs were. Housing became a problem. Trains and buses were crowded. Equipment broke down. Older men did not retire but stayed on in their jobs. Retired men returned to work, often struggling to the limits of their physical capacities.

Worcester was once again a town full of energy and optimism, with plenty of work to be had and fortunes to be made.

When the war ended and the young men came home, the city was still thriving. But now it had to face the fact that it was a 20th-century city in a 19th-century setting.

# Chapter Eight

# The Old City Renews Itself

*This Jewish Community Center on Salisbury Street is an outgrowth of the early self-help groups started by Worcester's Jews. Nearby is the Jewish Home for the Aged and the Jewish Family Service Organization. Courtesy of the Jewish Community Center.*

he end of World War II brought Worcester into a period of change as profound as that which occurred during the 1840s and 1850s. As the automobile became the principal mode of transportation, more and more people began moving to the suburbs. Industry soon followed. No longer a city surrounded by a rural population, Worcester had become the center of an extended metropolitan area that covered the whole of Worcester County.

One by one, the industries that had been the cornerstone of Worcester's economy in the 19th century either moved away or went out of business. The big wire mills closed, leaving behind empty buildings. The railroad car factory begun by Osgood Bradley, and later acquired by Pullman Standard, closed. So did the great mills associated with the textile industry, including the Crompton and Knowles Loom Works and the Whittall Carpet Company.

Use of the railroads sharply declined, and in 1958 old Union Station was demolished. Even the newer station was neglected, then closed, then abandoned, leaving only an endless legal wrangle over its actual ownership. Trolleys were long out of use and the tracks were pulled up or paved over. Every spring certain sections of track reappear among the potholes dotting the streets—the sole reminders of the network of rails that once crisscrossed the city.

Worcester was struggling into the second half of the 20th century, but it was still a 19th-century city in many ways. It was time for many changes, and one of the first was a change in the political structure.

On November 4, 1947, the city manager form of government was adopted, replacing the mayor and alderman form that had served Worcester for a century. While the nine-member city council, six-member school committee, city auditor, and city clerk were all elected by proportional representation, the council appointed the city manager.

Everett Merrill, the first city manager, was succeeded by Francis McGrath in April of 1951. He has held the office ever since. This form of government, although it has not been without its controversies, has provided the city with a long period of political stability. Undoubtedly, this has had much to do with the stability of its economic climate.

Three great problems faced the city: inadequate water resources, aging schools, and poor streets. The traffic trying to make its way in and out of the city worsened as the city's industries turned more and more to trucks to move their goods.

The process of urban renewal was begun. It involved the relocation of streets, highways and railroads, and, eventually, the rebuilding of the center of the city. The process, which continues even today, completely disrupted the retail trade in the city, changing its character entirely.

Because Worcester was still a city of diversified industry the postwar period of adjustment was less devastating than it might have been. If the largest wire mill was gone, there were still others that drew miles and miles of wire. New industries began, reflecting the computer age. The Norton Company and the Wyman Gordon Company grew and flourished.

Worcester's insurance business also grew after the war. The State Mutual Life Assurance Company and the Paul Revere Life Insurance Company expanded, built new buildings in the city, and employed more people.

Worcester is still the county seat, the center of court activity for a large geographical area. This means that the city still has a good share of lawyers and court officers, although they never entertain the town with colorful parades as in former times. Worcester has also remained a center of banking activity, with both savings and commercial banks.

The Worcester Housing Authority, formed in 1938, had not functioned during the war. In 1946, however, it was reactivated and 300 temporary apartments were built at Lincolnwood. At Lakeside, 204 more were built to accommodate veterans and relieve the city's acute housing shortage. The Curtis Apartments were completed in 1951 and Great Brook Valley in 1952.

In the new era, a discovery came out of Worcester which was as profound in its effect as Robert Goddard's rockets. In 1931, Hudson Hoagland arrived at Clark University and soon became head of the physiology department. Seven years later, Gregory Pincus joined him. In 1944, the pair formed the Worcester Foundation for Experimental Biology. Through the fundraising efforts of Worcester people, the Foundation became a leading independent research institution. There Hoagland and Pincus developed the world's first oral contraceptive.

Immigrants continued to arrive in the city, notably Lithuanian and Polish people. A new innovation was the preaching of a sermon in English at Our Lady of Czestochowa for the first time in 1950.

That change reflected the arrival in Worcester of the Reverend John Wright, who came to be the first Bishop in the newly formed Diocese of Worcester. The city welcomed him with open arms. He was hailed as its new leading citizen. On March 13, 1950, 12,000 people gathered at the Auditorium to greet him. St. Paul's Church became a cathedral and the interior was remodeled to suit its new function.

One by one the improvements that enable a modern city to function well

Top
*Nothing speaks more eloquently of the loss of the railroads in Worcester than this 1978 photograph of deteriorated, empty Union Station. Photo by Ron White.*

Above
*The gradual phasing out of wire-making operations at Ichabod Washburn's Grove Street factory was one of the most profound effects of the postwar period. This*

*photo, taken in the 1940s, reminds us of the amount of pollution emitted from the antiquated factory. (WHM)*

were made. A new sewage treatment plant, begun in 1946, relieved the disgraceful pollution of the Blackstone River. Miles and miles of new sewers, water mains, streets, and highways were laid. One after another modern structure replaced the old school buildings.

In April 1953, the Mechanics Association voted to admit women as members. Its hall, once a Worcester showpiece, was dirty and gloomy, used principally as a place for wrestling matches, and later as a roller skating rink. Negotiations were under way for its sale.

On June 9, 1953, a tornado swept through the northern part of the city, and within an hour's time destroyed more than $55 million worth of property and left 91 people dead and 1350 seriously injured. It was a stunning blow. The Lincolnwood apartments were destroyed, as was the old Home Farm. Assumption College's main building was seriously damaged. The Norton Company's new building had its roof torn off. Hundreds of private homes were utterly demolished. Thousands of people were injured.

If ever the city knew the mettle of her citizens it was in the days that followed the tornado. In a great outpouring of sympathy and help, everyone turned to the task of recovery. Organizations, large and small, came to the aid of the stricken. Individuals offered places to stay, food, and comfort. Worcester's industries contributed, and Worcester's hospitals were strained to the utmost to care for the thousands of injured.

In 1954 the new airport was dedicated to the memory of James O'Brien, a former mayor. That fall two hurricanes swept through the city, one in August, another in September. A year later another hurricane hit. It seemed that the city was in a pattern of annual disasters, with all their accompanying winds, floods, and devastation.

In 1955 the massive task of relocating the railroad tracks at Lincoln Square went forward. Most of Stephen Salisbury's factories were removed. The last vestiges of Mill Brook vanished into underground culverts and the tracks were placed through an underpass. Never again would the city's automobiles have to wait for the long lines of freight trains to pass.

The impact of the Korean and Vietnam wars was felt in Worcester as the city's young men left for war. At home restlessness and threats of violence filled the air. In all its long history the city has known very little mob violence, somehow managing to avoid situations of confrontation.

New immigrants arrived, many Spanish speaking, and the city's black population increased dramatically. The city set about absorbing the new arrivals, as it had done with so many others. The process was smoother than in the 19th century, but not without its problems.

In 1958 the old Union Station at Washington Square was demolished, leaving behind only the stone lions which once guarded the entrance. They were moved down Shrewsbury Street to East Park. This event symbolized

This gothic hall was built inside the office building of the Worcester Pressed Steel Company to house John W. Higgins's collection of ar-mor. Today the armory is open as a museum. Courtesy of the John Woodman Higgins Armory.

the beginnings of the renewal of the city's center. One by one the buildings that were the pride of the 19th-century industrialists were demolished. The Merrifield buildings became a parking lot. MacInnes Store closed and was torn down. Worcester Center was designed, and demolition got under way. The city came to resemble a place devastated by war. New modern buildings, towers of glass, steel, and concrete, were erected.

As the bicentennial approached, the residents began to take an interest in their past. A series of publications sponsored by the Bicentennial Commission reminded them of their almost-forgotten history.

The Barnard, Sumner, and Putnam department store on Main Street was demolished. When that structure went down, it weakened the support for one of the side walls of Mechanics Hall. The decision had to be made either to repair the wall or tear down the building.

The trustees of the Mechanics Association decided to try to raise enough money to save the building. Foundations, businesses, industries, and thousands of individuals immediately and enthusiastically responded to their appeal. It was a signal that Worcester had seen enough of the wrecker's ball and now wanted to appreciate her past.

The great building, which was the pride of Worcester's earlier industrialists, never had any major alterations to its original design or ornamentation. It is the only remaining concert hall of its type and period in the United States. The restoration effort involved repairs to the elaborate cast iron facade and redecoration of the interior, returning it to its original colors. All the mechanical systems of the building were modernized without any visible changes to the original structure. An imaginative new glass-enclosed addition on the rear houses the elevators and reveals the original exterior.

In November 1977, the hall was reopened to the public, a place of extraordinary beauty with superb acoustics. The people of Worcester now mount the red-carpeted grand staircases and sit in happy comfort, listening to concerts and programs in a building which is uniquely their own.

The City of Worcester stands today, spread out among her rolling hills and valleys. It is perhaps a bit too cold in the winter, and hotter than the ideal in the summer, but her crystal-clear days fill one with energy, and the infinite variability of the climate makes her citizens both philosophical and hardy.

The basis of the city's economy today is a bewildering variety of industries, most of them considerably lighter, and therefore cleaner, than those of the 19th century. The city's colleges and schools, both public and private, play a significant part in her prosperity. The city has five private hospitals, one city hospital, and the hospital and medical school which are part of the University of Massachusetts. The courts and the banks contribute their share, and the city remains a center for retail trade.

Left
*Isaiah Thomas laid out a turnpike in a direct line to Boston. Route 9 follows that path. This 1945 aerial photograph by Paul Savage shows the straightness of the road. (WHM)*

Below
*Salisbury Pond at Institute Park in 1974. The pollution of the pond by industrial wastes has made the water murky and full of weeds. In the foreground interested neighbors scrutinize the situation. (WHM)*

*Here is the cast of the Foothills Theatre's production of* Viva Vaudeville. *Worcester's people have always enjoyed theater, both professional and amateur. (WHM)*

Worcester has private museums of art, medieval armor, science and history. It has libraries, both public and private, theatres and concert halls. Much of the city's social life centers around private clubs and organizations. Some are connected with churches, fraternal, or veterans organizations. Some, like the Shakespeare Club which has been going for more than a hundred years, have a serious purpose; in this case, the study of Shakespeare's plays. Many exist just for the amusement of their members.

These clubs remain largely invisible to the stranger visiting Worcester. It is only during great snowstorms that some hint of their numbers can be found in the announcements of cancelled programs on the radio.

Worcester's people tend to be modest about their city and newcomers are often slow to find her charms. But the charms are there. The hard work and imagination of past generations has made it a city where there is work for good hands, stimulation for good minds, a climate and care for good health, the comforts of religion, and the amusements of recreation. It is a strong, a vigorous, and a generous heart for the Commonwealth of Massachusetts.

Above
*Lincoln Square today. The railroad and trolley tracks are gone, but the traffic in the square still presents problems. The buildings of Worcester Vocational Technical High School, the successor to the Boy's Trade School, are on the right. The Worcester Boy's Club building is in front of them. The Auditorium, dedicated in 1933, is in the background. The traffic swirls around the flagpole of the memorial to the World War I soldiers, dedicated in 1933.*

Right
*The last of the mills built near Lincoln Square by the second Stephen Salisbury now houses a variety of shops and a restaurant.*

*The Crown Hill area of Worcester, a street of private homes rescued from oblivion under the guidance of the Heritage Preservation Society.*

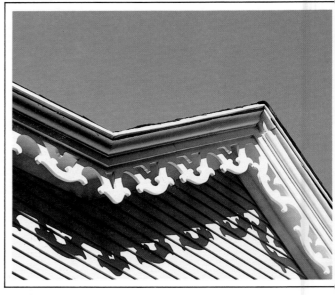

One of the colored-glass windows from a Buckley Lunch Wagon. Founded in 1899 by Thomas H. Buckley, the company decorated their lunch wagons with paintings, colored-glass windows, and bric-a-brac. The wagons were a feast for both the eye and the stomach.

*Stephen Earle designed this build-
ing for the Society of Friends in
1911. It replaced the earlier
wooden structure. Now it is the
home of the New England Reperto-
ry Theatre.*

*In 1978 the Worcester Society of Antiquity was renamed the Worcester Historical Museum. Concerned only with Worcester history, it maintains a library, the Salisbury Mansion, and of course, a museum. To the right is the Spanish War memorial made by Worcester sculptor Andrew O'Connor. Dedicated in 1917, the memorial stands in Armory Square.*

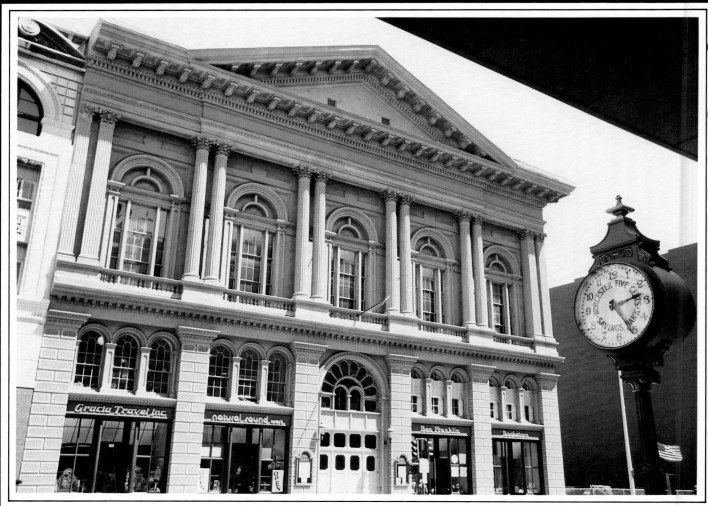

Above
*Mechanics Hall was completely refurbished in 1977, reopening on November 26. The clock in the foreground belongs to the Consumer's Savings Bank.*

Left
*The rear entrance to Mechanics Hall. One of the problems with the old building was that there was no elevator. The main concert hall is on the upper level. The problem was solved without disturbing the original structure by adding a new section to the back.*

Above
*This charming fountain of a boy with a dolphin stands outside the offices of the Freedom Federal Savings Bank offices on Pearl Street.*

Below
*East Park on Shrewsbury Street. Three deckers have not been built in Worcester since 1938, but they still continue to provide inexpensive, comfortable housing for many of Worcester's people. The Lion in the foreground is all that remains of the 1875 Union Station.*

Top
Lyman Gordon built this estate on Salisbury Street. He owned Wyman Gordon Company which made drop forgings. When the automobile industry began to grow, Gordon actively sought the business of making the forgings for automobile parts. The estate, which was later owned by Lucius Knowles of the Crompton and Knowles Loom Works, is now the convent connected with Notre Dame Academy.

Above
Assumption College began in 1904 with a school run by the Augustinian Fathers. The buildings of the school were badly damaged by the tornado of June 9, 1953 and it was then decided to move the college to a new campus on Salisbury Street. These buildings now house Quinsigamond Community College.

Above
*Sailboats at Regatta Point. This view, taken from the Shrewsbury side of the lake, shows the park where sailboats may be rented in the summer. In the background is the University of Massachusetts Medical School and Hospital. Behind that are the buildings of the Worcester State Hospital.*

Left
*Court Hill. On the left is the Unitarian Church, which was built in 1851 after a fire destroyed the earlier building. The facade of the courthouse next to it dates from 1898 with numerous additions in the rear.*

*The interior of the Galleria at Worcester Center.*

Above
*Fenwick Hall of The College of the Holy Cross replaces an earlier building that burned in 1852. The first permanent settlers lived on this hillside which had been the principle dwelling place of the Nipmuck Indians.*

Left
*The interior of the Worcester County Horticultural Society. The Society has regular horticultural displays, and conducts a series of lectures and classes.*

Top
A view of Worcester City Hall from
the tower of the Worcester County
National Bank. The Galleria of the
new Worcester Center is in the
background.

Above
Elm Park today. The recently
restored arched bridge is a favorite
setting for wedding photographs of
Worcester brides.

Top
The courtyard of the Worcester Art Museum. In the background is the modern wing of the building that houses the school.

Above
The Worcester Science Center, with its collections, displays, omnisphere, and zoo, is the successor to the old Natural History Society.

*This view of Worcester today shows the modern center of the city with its glass, steel, and concrete towers all centered near the old common.*

# Chapter Nine

# Partners in Progress

*Mechanics Hall was the expression of the pride of the manufacturers of Worcester in their own abilities and the beautiful city they were building. The architectural elements of the facade are of cast iron and were made in William Wheeler's foundry. The Central Exchange building is on the left and the Union Block is on the right. Courtesy of the Worcester Historical Museum.*

wo hundred years ago, few could have guessed that Worcester was destined to become an industrial giant, the home of a great educational complex, or even a major population center. Even though it had been named the shire town for the county in 1713, it still had fewer than 2,000 residents by 1780.

Several other nearby towns seemed to have better prospects than Worcester. Fitchburg, Southbridge, Oxford, Wesster, Rutland, and Charlton all had superior waterpower sites. The Brookfields boasted more desirable land. Westborough and Northborough had better potential access to the coast. Yet it was Worcester, with none of these natural assets, that developed the manufactories that produced goods and wealth in amounts sufficient to attract thousands of immigrants from all over Europe. It was Worcester that, by 1980, had become the second largest city in New England.

Nothing came easy to Worcester. It had to develop its early industries without the help of major waterfalls. Since it was not on a navigable waterway, it had to build, at great expense, a canal along the Blackstone River all the way to the sea. Since it had no natural access to Boston, it had to build a road, including a bridge across Lake Quinsigamond. In its search for energy sources other than wood, it could find only an inferior type of coal to mine.

In some ways, the rise of Worcester to its current metropolitan and industrial status is not easy to explain. But one of the clues to the puzzle surely must be the entrepreneurs and inventors that the community attracted from the earliest days of the nineteenth century. Beginning with Isaiah Thomas, printer of Worcester's first newspaper and builder of Worcester's first industry, a paper mill, a long list of enterprising businessmen and artisans came here to make their fortunes. They were metal workers, cabinet makers, architects, iron forgers, wire drawers, tinsmiths, inventors, and they called themselves "mechanics." They founded the Worcester County Mechanics Association in 1842, built up a technical library, and applied their ingenuity to advancing the Industrial Revolution. Mechanics Hall, built in 1857, is their monument.

Worcester today, still bustling, still prosperous, still inventive, carries on the legacy. It has come far in the last two centuries. It looks ahead with confidence and anticipation.

# BANCROFT AUTOMOBILE CLUB

Although the Worcester Automobile Club, ancestor of the Bancroft Automobile Club, Inc., was formally incorporated on November 28, 1905, its roots go back beyond that date. As early as 1900, when there were no more than twenty automobiles in Worcester, W.J.H. Nourse started an organization of car owners and enthusiasts. Nourse deserves to be remembered as the founding father of the Worcester Automobile Club, although James W. Bigelow was the first president of the original organization.

In late 1905, the club established its first headquarters in the Chase Building on Front Street. In that same year, the club held its first hill climb, up Dead Horse Hill on Stafford Street. The hill climb was an annual club event for years.

Membership in the club increased rapidly, reflecting the enormous and growing interest in the new "gas buggies." At the annual meeting in May 1906, president John P. Coghlin reported that the membership had jumped from 81 to 331 in one year.

During World War I, with all its demands on industry and society, the club lost a great deal of support, and by the end of the war, the club was moribund. However, in 1920, according to the records, fifteen men re-established the Worcester Automobile Club. Four years later, it was superseded by the Bancroft Automobile Club, an organization dedicated as much to practical problems of motoring as to the social and recreational aspects.

The Wachusett Automobile Club, a separate affiliate of the American Automobile Association, was founded in 1928 with membership in the northern part of Worcester County. It was dis-

*Below*
*It is apparent from this early 1920s photograph provided by the Worcester Historical Museum that the Franklin Square Garage was a popular rendezvous for the "gas buggy" set.*
*Right*
*As it looks to the future, the Bancroft Automobile Club remembers the past, represented by this 1913 Model T Ford Runabout.*

continued in 1934 and its membership merged with that of the Bancroft Automobile Club.

After 1930, the club had several locations before it moved into its new quarters at 290 Park Avenue.

Membership grew steadily as America developed its enthusiasm for the automobile. In 1948, the club enrolled its 3,000th member. In November 1980, its official seventy-fifth anniversary, the club boasted more than 36,000 members.

The Bancroft Automobile Club, through its affiliation with the American Automobile Association, offers its members a whole galaxy of services, including trip planning, travel guides, bail bond service, camping directories, hotel-motel reservations, certification of accommodations, emergency roadside assistance, and accident and warranty service, among many others.

As the club enters the last quarter of its first century, it looks forward to making automobile travel safer, more economical, more pleasant, and more useful to more people than ever before.

#  ENTRAL OIL COMPANY

Central Oil Company of Worcester, Inc., a retail and wholesale petroleum distributorship active in all facets of the petroleum and energy fields, was founded in 1934 by three brothers — Beton M. Kaneb, George D. Kaneb, and Kenneth A. Kaneb.

The venture began as a gas station and garage at 462 Grafton Street, known as the Square Deal Garage. Despite the effects of the Great Depression, the company bought a second gasoline station and bulk ter-

minal at 233 Southbridge Street in 1935. That acquisition started Central Oil in the business of wholesaling home heating fuel and range oil to the various fuel oil dealers in Worcester County.

The distribution of fuel oil products to fuel dealers opened a new chapter in the company's operation and led to new developments. The terminal operation was expanded to include five bulk plants; a home fuel oil division was inaugurated; and acquisitions and mergers expanded Central Oil's home fuel delivery system to include five fuel trucks servicing the heating needs of the community.

Later in 1935 the company in-

*Top*
*Modern tank trucks transport gasoline and fuel oil safely and efficiently.*
*Above*
*Central Oil Company's sophisticated tanks and distribution system, located on Putnam Lane, enable the firm to service many types of fuel throughout Worcester County.*

stituted an oil-burner service department and commenced to service home and industrial equipment throughout Worcester County. Central Oil's oil-burner service department has long been, and continues to be, a leader in this rapidly changing field.

The gasoline division grew with the fuel oil division to include twenty-five stations in the Worcester County region. Services included all automo-

tive repairs and inspection bays. Among the acquisitions of the company was the Mass 10 Truck Stop in Auburn, servicing the needs of over-the-road truckers.

The company, despite its steady growth, remains a family affair. A second generation of Kanebs has joined the enterprise, providing potential leadership for the years ahead. Technological innovations and changing energy needs have issued new challenges to all companies involved in energy and fuel. Central Oil has kept pace with the growing interest in alternative energy resources, including solar, wind, greenhouse, and wood-burning heating equipment.

The history of Central Oil Company, from its establishment in 1934 with a single gasoline service station to its present role as a dealer and distributor of a wide variety of energy sources and equipment, marks the growth of a significant Worcester business. Its strong position in 1981 signifies continued growth for many years to come.

# CHARLES MANOOG, INC.

One of Worcester's oldest and largest plumbing and heating supply houses began in 1927 when a young electrician and plumber from Watertown, Massachusetts, established a small cash-and-carry business at 53 Chandler Street. During the company's fiftieth anniversary in 1977, when its founder became chairman of the board, Charles Manoog was still energetically involved in all phases of what had become an enormous full-service plumbing and heating supply operation.

Manoog was born in 1903, the son of immigrants from the Middle East. He started his "Ma and Pa" plumbing business with a small capital investment and took care of the stock while his wife, Elizabeth, handled the cash register and the bookkeeping. The business was run on a strictly cash basis for sixteen years.

When Manoog made the crucial decision to expand to a full-service outlet, he soon discovered the need for more space. In 1946, the company moved to 9 Piedmont Street, where it has been located ever since. Old buildings on the site were renovated and enlarged to include a new office and showroom. Today, Charles Manoog, Inc., occupies more than 175,000 square feet of land and 60,000 square feet of warehouse and general office space at five locations in Worcester. Its warehouses stock plumbing and heating inventories as large as any in New England.

Through the years, a professional staff has provided service in all facets

*Above*
*Around 1930, Charles Manoog, Inc., sported this storefront on Chandler Street.*
*Below*
*Russell Manoog (seated) succeeded his father as president of the firm in 1977, and Charles Manoog became chairman of the board.*

of plumbing and heating. A pipe fabricating department serves general construction, mechanical trades, and industry with facilities to cut, thread, groove, weld, coat, and line hundreds of varieties, sizes, and grades of steel pipe.

In recent years, an international department has offered an assortment of products and services to customers abroad, supplying foreign markets with quality American products for overseas containerized shipments.

Charles Manoog, Inc., has pioneered in several directions, including the development of a computer code used by the American Supply Association. In the early 1950s, Manoog introduced an innovative salesmen's compensation program based on a percentage of gross profit. And he has constantly improved methods of handling the huge inventories of pipe and plumbing equipment in his extensive warehouses since that time.

In 1977, Charles Manoog stepped down from the president's post he had held for half a century to become chairman of the board. Although his son, Russell, is now president and treasurer, Charles Manoog continues his active involvement in the business with undiminished enthusiasm.

# CINCINNATI MILACRON-HEALD CORPORATION

Heald Machine began in Barre, Massachusetts, when Stephen Heald started making chair rods in his woodworking shop in 1826. Heald, later joined by his son, Leander, gradually expanded the family business to include lumber and grain milling; the manufacture of wooden wheels, sleighs and the like; and general repair work.

The addition of forge and foundry facilities in the mid-1800s led to the manufacture of stoves and improved farm implements such as corn-cob crushers, hay rakes, and hay tedders.

James N. Heald joined the company in 1884, following his graduation from Worcester Polytechnic Institute. He soon turned the firm in the direction of machine tool manufacturing and, in 1903, made the important decision to move the company to Worcester, where skilled machinists were readily available. There he concentrated on producing machine tools for world markets, with particular emphasis on meeting the needs of the infant automotive industry.

In the early years of the century, Heald Machine developed, in quick succession, a six-inch piston grinder, a planetary grinding machine for accurate grinding of engine block cylinder bores, and, in 1907, the Heald Model 70 internal grinder, which set new standards for accuracy and production of transmission gears.

The next fifty years saw Heald progressing from one engineering innovation to another. Under the management of James N. Heald's sons, Roger, Richard, and Robert, the firm became a world leader in machine tool manufacturing. Between the mid-1930s and the mid-1950s, Heald Size-Matic, Gage-Matic, Centri-Matic and Bore-Matic technologies were developed.

The firm became the Heald Machine Division of Cincinnati Milacron in 1955, making Cincinnati the largest machine tool manufacturing organization in the world, a position it retains today.

Heald continued its innovative machine tool technology and in 1960, the two-axis, numerically controlled Healdrill was introduced, heralding the modern machining center line of the 1980s. This new generation of

machines is equipped with automatic tool change, computer numerical control, self-diagnostic capability, and as many as five axes under control.

Heald's "Controlled Force" grinding principle, unveiled in 1963, was the first major breakthrough in grinding technology in thirty years. The space-saving IEF (electronic feed) internal grinding machines, introduced in 1978, carried the breakthrough still further, providing the same precision and productivity while occupying one-third less space.

Heald Machine continues to set standards for the industry as it has for over a century. The firm fully expects to be in the vanguard of invention and development for the next 100 years.

*Left*
*The firm's product line has changed significantly in the past 154 years. In the left foreground is a three-station cheese press built in the 1840s. A six-inch ring grinder produced in 1903 is pictured in the right foreground; and a vertical spindle computer numerically controlled machining center appears in the background.*

*Below*
*Heald's Greendale plant is bounded by West Boylston, New Bond, and Ararat streets. The original 1903 shop can be seen beneath the long cupola to the left of the smokestack.*

# COMMERCE BANK & TRUST COMPANY

In an era when new banks were a rarity, Commerce Bank & Trust first opened its doors. Worcester's youngest bank, it was incorporated in June 1955 and opened for business two months later. The first directors' meeting, with seven directors in attendance, was held on May 31, 1955.

The founder of Commerce Bank & Trust Company was Aaron Krock, a prominent Worcester civic leader and businessman. Mr. Krock's purpose was to serve the financial needs of small businesses and to provide financial services to the consumer public.

The new bank's original location was 240 Main Street in Worcester.

The original staff was comprised of seven people. Expansion first occurred in 1968 when Shrewsbury Bank and Trust, located on the heavily traveled Boston Turnpike, was merged into Commerce Bank & Trust Company.

The year 1972 witnessed a great deal of expansion. A branch office was opened in Webster, Massachusetts. Of even greater significance was the establishment of a new and larger main office at 386 Main Street, in the heart of downtown Worcester. The original headquarters building continues as a branch office with modern drive-up facilities and ample parking, plus four floors of administrative offices.

Commerce Bank & Trust today is a full-service bank with four offices and over 100 employees offering a wide variety of commercial and consumer services. Among these are free interest-bearing checking accounts; international credit cards; short-term and intermediate-term money market certificates; electronic computer bookkeeping systems and services; and computerized trust services.

Evidence of founder Aaron Krock's special interest in the small businessman can be found today in the bank's close relationship with the Small Business Administration. Commerce was the only bank in Worcester County and one of only three in the entire state to be selected for the new SBA Bank Certification Program designed to use the credit knowledge of the bank's loan officers to shorten the processing time on SBA loans. Also characteristic of the bank are innovative marketing techniques and a highly liberal approach toward developing special customer programs.

Barry Krock has been president of the bank since 1972, when his father, Aaron Krock, passed away. Since its inception in 1955, control of the bank has remained in the Krock family.

*Left*
*Aaron Krock, founder and first president of Commerce Bank & Trust Company, was a long-standing Worcester businessman and community leader.*
*Right*
*Barry Krock, son and successor of Aaron Krock, has been president of the bank since 1972.*

# DONAHUE INDUSTRIES, INC.

*Left*
*Irving James Donahue, Jr., is founder, president, and chief executive officer of Donahue Industries, Inc., and Donahue International, Inc.*
*Above*
*Donahue metal parts and assemblies for the grinding wheel industry are used around the world.*

Although the modern Donahue Industries, Inc., was launched in the mid 1950s, its roots go back to the turn of the century. The original company, founded in 1903, was a partnership of W.H. Stearns and G. Smith, specializing in the manufacture of drill presses. It was located at 133 Dewey Street, Worcester.

In 1928, the company name was changed to Stearns Pressed Metal Co., and production of small metal stampings was begun. In 1940, it was succeeded by the Carroll Pressed Metal Co., which manufactured small metal stampings and Carroll ski bindings. Charles A. Paul purchased the business in 1948 and continued the line of metal stampings.

The firm was purchased in 1957 by Irving James Donahue, Jr., and Roger C. Hager. After several years of steady growth and production, construction of a new building with 25,000 square feet of floor space in an industrial park in Shrewsbury was completed in 1969. The company name was changed to Donahue Industries, Inc., at that time.

Donahue, a graduate of Worcester Polytechnic Institute and Harvard Graduate School of Business, and a civic leader in both Worcester and Shrewsbury, is president and chief executive officer. He holds various patents in the specialized field that his company serves.

In 1980, Donahue Industries produced more than 300 different parts, assemblies, and components with various finishes for the grinding wheel industry. It uses steel, aluminum, fiber, and plastic with coatings of zinc, cadmium, zinc phosphate, and copper, depending on the specific needs of each customer.

The firm has developed many new products, including safety back bushings for portable cup wheels, throwaway metal screw-on adapters and reusable adapters for regular and high-speed depressed center wheels, metal-plastic adapters for depressed center wheels, track grinding wheel safety backs, disc wheel inserts, and various steel centers for cut-off wheels. In 1968, a new export corporation, Donahue International, Inc., was established. That enterprise has customers throughout the United States, Canada, and Europe.

Donahue Industries, Inc., the world's largest producer of metal components for the grinding wheel industry, has worked closely with the Grinding Wheel Institute in developing standards for designs and tolerances of components used in grinding wheels. It has also been closely involved in the development and implementation of safety standards for the industry.

# FALLON CLINIC/FALLON COMMUNITY HEALTH PLAN

*Top*
*The clinic's main office at 630 Plantation Street was opened in 1966. In 1973, 1977, and 1979, the facility was expanded to accommodate the growing number of patients and staff.*
*Above*
*The main lobby of the Fallon Clinic provides patients and visitors with an atmosphere of comfort and reassurance.*

Quality care and creative leadership have been the trademarks of the Fallon Clinic since Doctors John and Michael Fallon founded the medical group practice in 1929. Today, nearly every medical specialty is represented by the staff, which consists of 60 full-time physicians who work together as a group practice team. Extensive laboratory, radiology, and other ancillary services are available with a broad range of diagnostic, treatment, and prevention services provided by physicians and support staff.

From downtown Worcester, the practice was relocated in 1966 to new headquarters at 630 Plantation Street, where a modern ambulatory care center was constructed overlooking Lake Quinsigamond. In 1973, a second major expansion program culminated with the opening of the Meyers' Wing addition at Plantation Street.

A branch office of the clinic has been maintained in Westboro since 1977. Here members of the "Fallon Family" provide primary care services to the residents of Westboro and neighboring communities. Referral linkages and coverage arrangements have been developed between the central office and the branch office for the purpose of providing expanded access for Fallon patients. Additional expansion of the Westboro clinic and a new branch clinic in Auburn were completed in 1981.

The Fallon Clinic organization has been innovative in the area of health care delivery. In 1977, it established, in cooperation with Blue Cross of Massachusetts, a health maintenance organization (HMO) known as the Fallon Community Health Plan. The Plan is the first federally qualified HMO in central Massachusetts and is offered by more than 600 Worcester area employers as an alternative to their existing health insurance coverage. It is based on the concept of preventive medicine and the elimination of many out-of-pocket health care expenses. In 1980, the Plan became the nation's first site selected to offer HMO services to medicare recipients under a demonstration project. Already, the Plan has the largest community penetration of any HMO of its kind in New England.

The Fallon commitment to the health care needs of the community extends to programs of health education, health fairs, occupational health and medicine, smoking termination workshops, and community services. The recent golden anniversary of the Fallon Clinic brought recognition from the White House, with President Jimmy Carter conveying written congratulations and joining with Fallon "in looking forward to a future of continued excellence in providing health care."

# FREEDOM FEDERAL SAVINGS & LOAN ASSOCIATION

1877 — one-room office in downtown Worcester.

1980 — the largest savings and loan association in New England with eighteen full-service offices and five supermarket banking locations.

That, in short, is the story of Freedom Federal Savings and Loan Association, which began as the Worcester Cooperative Savings Fund and Loan Association on October 19, 1877. The next year, the association had assets of $33,000.

The founders — Harold H. Bigelow, Stephen C. Earle, Dorrance S. Goddard, John Jeppson, Iver Johnson, and Enoch H. Towne — led the institution to early success. Their achievements prompted another group of Worcester businessmen to organize two other associations, the first in 1882 and the second in 1887. The three operated out of the same office, and, by 1892, had combined assets of more than $1 million.

Two men figured prominently in the early growth of the three affiliated firms. Jeremiah J. Higgins, a building contractor, served the institutions for more than forty years; in the early 1900s, he was president of one of them. In 1937, when the three merged into the Worcester Cooperative Federal Savings and Loan Association, he became chairman of the board.

Raymond P. Harold joined the affiliated firms in 1927 as assistant treasurer. A year later, he was elected

*Above*
*The firm began in this one-room office in the Walker Building at Main and Mechanics streets October 19, 1877.*
*Left*
*Raymond P. Harold became chief executive officer in 1928, a post he held until his death in 1972.*
*Bottom*
*Joseph T. Benedict is president and chairman of Freedom Federal Savings.*

chief executive officer. Harold was also the first chairman of the Worcester Redevelopment Authority and the driving force behind the city's plans for urban renewal. Prior to his death in 1972, Harold was chairman and chief executive officer of First Federal Savings and Loan Association.

Freedom Federal, as it has been called since 1975, has posted its most substantial growth in recent years with Joseph T. Benedict, president and chairman, at the helm. Assets grew 113 percent between 1968 and 1978. This spectacular growth exceeded that of the institution's first ninety years. Assets at year-end in 1968 were $336 million. On December 31, 1979, they exceeded $733 million.

# GUARANTY BANK & TRUST COMPANY

Although the Skandia Bank & Trust Company was chartered in 1930, its origins trace back to 1915, when George Jeppson, Nils Bjork, and F. Julius Quist founded the Skandia Credit Union and opened for business in a small office at 18 Franklin Street. The purpose of the Skandia Credit Union was to provide second mortgages for Swedish immigrants who needed cash in times of emergency. Later, as capital accumulated, it went into home mortgages. George Jeppson, the first president, served for many years without pay.

Fifteen years later, the assets of the credit union had grown to more than $1 million and the state suggested that it be incorporated as a bank. Although the new bank was launched in the midst of the Great Depression, it never had a run and it was the first bank in Worcester to reopen after President Franklin D. Roosevelt's bank holiday.

The bank changed its name to Guaranty Bank & Trust Company in 1934 and enlarged its quarters in the Slater Arcade. Within six years, assets had increased to almost $7 million and the bank moved into even larger quarters, on the street-level floor of the Slater Building. By 1947, its assets exceeded $22 million.

Guaranty opened its first branch the following year, a drive-in at Central and Commercial streets. The Webster Square branch was opened in 1953 and the Gold Star Branch in 1957. By 1964, Guaranty had eleven offices in Worcester County. Within five years there were eighteen offices in fifteen communities. By 1980, the bank had offices in twenty-six locations.

In 1971, Guaranty built its new headquarters and office building at 370 Main Street, a historic spot. There had stood Stearns Tavern, where George Washington once spent the night. Later it was the site of the Levi Lincoln mansion. In more recent times, the Elm Street Theater stood there. The handsome, 12-story Guaranty building is a fitting part of a proud tradition.

In 1973, Guaranty Bank & Trust Company became a member of the Conifer Group, which has assets of more than half a billion dollars and constitutes one of the major commercial banking complexes in Massachusetts.

Presidents of Guaranty have been: George Jeppson, 1930-1941; Nils Bjork, 1941-1947; Roland Erickson, 1947-1964; and William D. Ireland, Jr., since 1964.

*Left*
*George N. Jeppson was the first president of the financial institution.*
*Below*
*The handsome, 12-story headquarters of Guaranty Bank & Trust distinguishes the corner of Main and Elm streets.*

# HOLBROOK DROP FORGE INC.

H.E. Holbrook Drop Forge Company was started in 1929 by Harrison E. Holbrook, Sr., with two hammers, one press, and five employees. The total payroll for the first week was $90. After a year in temporary quarters at Winona Street, the company moved to its current location at 40 Rockdale Street, where a new forge shop was built for a total price of $19,472. The company's main products in those early years were gun barrels, valves, textile parts of carbon, and stainless steel. Among its first customers were Crompton & Knowles, Harrington & Richardson, and American Steel & Wire.

The company survived the Great Depression and prospered during World War II by making gun barrels. In 1951, it was incorporated, with Harrison E. Holbrook, Sr., Harrison E. Holbrook, Jr., and Kenneth W. Holbrook as principals. Harrison Holbrook, Sr., died in 1958.

In 1965, the company built a new office and machine shop and increased the number of employees to thirty-five. On July 1, 1968, the company was purchased by Paul J. Kervick, owner of Providence Steel & Iron Inc., and Holbrook became an operating division. It was reincorporated as Holbrook Drop Forge Inc., in 1978, as an independent operating company of Kervick Enterprises Inc. In that same year, the company broke ground for a $4.5-million expansion, which included one of the first forge shops of its kind in the country built to the new and exacting environmen-

*Top*
*A forging crew took a break to pose for this photograph around 1937.*

*Above*
*In 1979, the facility at 40 Rockdale Street was renovated and expanded.*

tal standards. Capacity was increased by 60 percent.

Holbrook Drop Forge has steadily developed new product lines and improved old ones. It has customers across the United States as well as in Canada and Europe. It specializes in close-tolerance stainless steel, high-temperature alloy, superalloy, and titanium forgings used in the aerospace, petrochemical, missile, and medical markets.

One of the company's fastest growing lines is the forging of cobalt or titanium parts used as implants in

hip prosthesis and total elbow operations.

As compared to the original $90-payroll for the first week of production in 1929, the company's payroll has grown to over $40,000 a week. The annual payroll in 1980 exceeded $2.25 million to its more than 125 employees. Robert B. Kervick is president.

Kervick Enterprises Inc., the parent company, has sales in excess of $21 million a year. In addition to Holbrook Drop Forge, its member companies include F.A. Bassette Company, Springfield, Massachusetts; Providence Steel Inc., Providence, Rhode Island; Dave Russell Leasing Inc., Palmer, Massachusetts; and Kervick Realty Inc., Providence, Rhode Island.

# HOME FEDERAL SAVINGS AND LOAN ASSOCIATION

Since 1948, Home Federal Savings has played a proud role in Worcester's growth. And Home has grown by helping Worcester grow. The savings and loan was founded as the Home Cooperative Bank at 61 Pleasant Street and began innovative new policies almost from the day the doors opened. Traditional bankers' hours were a fading remnant of a bygone era. Banks were providing expanded services and longer business hours. Home was one of the first savings institutions to offer both to its customers.

After almost two decades of hard work and growth, a federal charter was granted in 1965 and the name was changed to Home Federal Savings and Loan Association of Worcester. Innovation followed innovation. Computer-compounded interest on savings started in 1966, giving customers the highest possible return on their money. Home was one of the first to offer savings certificates that paid the highest rate of interest permitted by law on passbook accounts. The more Home gave, the more it grew.

In 1968, the new main office opened at its current site on Main Street. The Worcester Center office was opened in 1971 and the drive-up office on Main Street in 1973.

Throughout its growth, Home never lost sight of tradition. The old Stearns Inn, a historic way station for the stage run between Boston and Albany, was purchased by Home Federal as a bicentennial project, carefully moved across town to the Park Avenue site near Webster Square, and completely restored. This preservation of a city landmark has resulted in one of the most unusual banking facilities in the country.

In July 1975, Home completed its merger with Montello Savings and Loan Association of Brockton. A new office was opened at West Yarmouth in 1976, serving thousands of Worcester people with homes on the Cape. In the same year, another branch opened on Gold Star Boulevard in Worcester and the main office expanded to four times its original size.

In 1981, Home's management team and directors forsee increased strength and a bright future. But the important services have not changed. Home is still a people's bank. The commitment to Worcester's tomorrow is stronger than ever before.

Patrick J. Gavin, Home's president and chief executive officer, has stated, "At Home, it's not important that we be the biggest ... only that we serve our customers to the best of our ability, and that we don't stop trying until everybody knows it."

*Left*
*Home Federal began in these modest quarters in 1948. By 1980, it had grown to be the second largest federally chartered savings and loan association in New England.*

*Right*
*In 1976, the association's main office quadrupled its original space.*

# HONEMATIC MACHINE CORPORATION

Honematic Machine Corporation was founded in 1956 by Allan Glazer, a graduate of Worcester Polytechnic Institute. The company began operations on one floor of a converted Farm Bureau warehouse on Thomas Street, Worcester, manufacturing and finishing cylinders and precision hollow components.

Mr. Glazer, who had experience in various aspects of metal machining and honing, became convinced that the honing process, generally used for light finishing operations in specialty applications, could also be used for the abrasive machining of metals. Honematic has successfully developed this concept.

The high degree of precision and quality control achieved by Honematic caught the attention of government and industry. The company produced shock tubes for testing space capsule reentry modules as early as 1957. Shortly afterward it produced the main rotor shafts for the first jet-powered helicopters, stainless steel fuel cells for nuclear reactors used on navy ships, expansion joints for the first commercial nuclear breeder reactor, periscope elevation cylinder assemblies for nuclear submarines, and many other applications.

The Honematic process, which began with relatively small cylinders and hollow components, was steadily utilized on larger units. The company now hones cylinders measuring up to twenty-four inches in diameter and twenty-five feet long.

*Top*
*In 1969, the family-owned company moved to its present location on Route 140, in Boylston, Massachusetts.*
*Above*
*Special equipment developed by Honematic Machine Corporation has given the firm a national reputation for its gun drilling, deep hole boring, trepanning, and honing capabilities.*

By 1967, the company was producing the first extendable, telescopic fueling probes for rescue helicopters. These were used for the in-flight fueling of the first nonstop helicopter flight across the Atlantic. In 1969, when the first men landed on the moon, their lunar lander was equipped with landing cylinders designed and manufactured by Honematic.

The firm has also designed and pro-duced sophisticated components for medical technology, stainless steel flow nozzles weighing up to three tons, titanium spars, oil drilling equipment, cannon barrels used for testing at the Aberdeen Ballistics Research Laboratory, and other specialized equipment for the nation's defense research and development labs.

In addition to the Honematic process, the company offers a full line of precision metal machining of the traditional type. It handles materials ranging from aluminum to zirconium.

The firm, still family-owned, employs about forty skilled craftsmen. In 1969 Honematic moved from downtown Worcester to a new plant at its present site on Route 140, in Boylston, Massachusetts.

# IDLE WILD FOODS

Idle Wild Foods, Inc., a holding company with one of the largest meat packing and processing operations in the United States as a subsidiary, had its beginnings near the turn of the century when Max Jacobson, newly arrived from Europe, started a cattle and kosher meat business in Worcester. Mr. Jacobson purchased cattle from farmers throughout Worcester County and processed and sold the meat at his store on Water Street.

The business steadily expanded over the years as five of Mr. Jacobson's six sons, Nathan, Robert, Eli, John, and Irving, joined him in the business. When the senior Mr. Jacobson died in 1931, Eli Jacobson became chairman of the board and served in that position until his passing in 1975. That year also marked the passing of Irving, a vice-president and a member of the company's board. Chicago Dressed Beef, a wholesale meat operation, was established in the 1930s when western dressed beef began to come into New England. It was the first independent wholesaler in New England to sell to the A & P food chain, which to this day remains a customer of the company. The L.B. Darling plant was acquired shortly thereafter. The Worcester Cold Storage & Warehouse complex was bought in 1944. In 1946, Central Packing of Kansas City was purchased from Campbell Soup Company. Idle Wild Farm in Pomfret, Connecticut, developer of the Rock Cornish Game Hen, was acquired in 1962 and has become nationally known for its high-quality prepared cooked and frozen food products.

*Mr. and Mrs. Max Jacobson and five of their eight children are seen in this photograph taken soon after their arrival in the United States.*

The company played a major role in the decentralization of the beef-packing industry. When the decade began, Swift, Armour, Wilson, Morell, and Cudahy, centered in Chicago, dominated the wholesale meat business. When the decade ended, independents such as Idle Wild's largest subsidiary, National Beef Packing Company, with its newly integrated slaughtering and processing plant in Liberal, Kansas, in the heart of the cattle country, were the rising stars of the industry. The Liberal plant, presently capable of processing over 2,300 head of cattle daily into uniform boxed beef, is one of the most modern in the world.

At about the same time, the firm started its trucking subsidiary, National Carriers, also located in Liberal, Kansas. National Carriers is an irregular common route carrier which transports a wide variety of commodities via its more than 500 refrigerated trailers.

In 1980 the company acquired Supreme Feeders, a 41,000-head-capacity custom feedlot located near its packing plant in Liberal, Kansas.

By 1980, Idle Wild Foods, Inc., was grossing over $600 million a year and was listed among the 500 largest corporations in the country by *Fortune* magazine. The present chairman of the board, John Jacobson, Sr., is the son of Max Jacobson, founder of the company. M. Howard Jacobson, the son of Eli Jacobson, is president and treasurer, and is the nephew of the chairman of the board and the grandson of the founder of the company. Other family members active in the company include N. Robert Jacobson and his son Kenneth, who is a vice-president of the company; John Jacobson, Jr., the son of the chairman, a company vice-president, and a member of the board of directors; and Arthur and David Jacobson, the sons of Nathan Jacobson who passed away in 1973 and was an officer of the company.

# JAMESBURY CORPORATION

In the valve industry, the ball valve was long regarded as a potentially ideal design, but production of high-performance ball valves eluded designers until 1954, when Howard G. Freeman, working from experiments in his home on Jamesbury Drive, founded the new company and began to fill modern industry's need for self-compensating valves and automatic controls while revolutionizing the valve industry.

The rapidly expanding company, under the leadership of the original entrepreneurs, Howard G. Freeman, Julian S. Freeman, and Saul I. Reck, moved to its present plant and headquarters at 640 Lincoln Street. The Lakeside plant in Shrewsbury was built in 1971 and expanded three years later. In 1977, a new research and engineering plant was opened at the Hillside site, and two years later, work was initiated on a new 86,000-square-foot building at the Lakeside location. In 1980, the firm employed 1,400 people and sales surpassed $100 million, with wholly owned subsidiaries in Canada, England, Japan, West Germany, and Singapore, and a joint venture in Mexico. A constantly expanding work force of competent, enthusiastic employees is considered the major ingredient to success.

In the late 1950s, Jamesbury worked closely with the U.S. Navy in developing ball-valve designs still used in nuclear submarines. Critical problems in the aerospace and other industries were and are solved by Jamesbury know-how and research. In 1968, the company introduced its unique Wafer-Sphere high-perfor-mance butterfly valve, which utilizes ball-valve technology and which is a product of utmost present and future value.

The company's ball valve, butterfly valve, and control products are used by industries involving chemicals and petrochemicals; pulp and paper; petroleum in all phases; food processing; synthetic fibers; steel and iron; pharmaceutical; nuclear and fossil fuel generation; marine, rail, and pipeline transportation; and air and water pollution controls.

Jamesbury, which manufactures valves ranging from an 8-ounce, 1/4-inch pipe-size ball valve to a 4-foot pipe-size butterfly valve weighing 2.5 tons, is one of the leading manufacturers of high-performance valves and controls in the world.

*Left*
*Howard G. Freeman (left) and Julian S. Freeman lend a hand at the groundbreaking ceremony for the new plant at 640 Lincoln Street.*
*Below*
*The main Jamesbury plant on Lincoln Street and the new engineering center (at lower right) constitute one of the largest capital investments in recent Worcester history.*

# JAMES J. MOYNIHAN & ASSOCIATES, INC.

James J. Moynihan & Associates, Inc., opened for business in 1968 at 40 Foster Street as a one-man operation. James Moynihan, the firm's founder and president, obtained a bachelor of arts degree in economics from Holy Cross, a master of business administration from Boston College, and is a graduate of the Pension and Profit Sharing Schools of Purdue University. He is also a licensed life insurance and pension advisor, a lifetime and qualifying member of the Million Dollar Round Table, and a qualifying member of the Top of the Table.

Within the life insurance industry, Jim Moynihan is past president of the Estate Planning Council of Worcester County, past president of the Worcester Chapter of Chartered Life Underwriters, and an active member of the Association for Advanced Life Underwriting.

Within the community, he is a corporator of the People's Savings Bank, vice-president of the Worcester Area Chamber of Commerce, community trustee of the United Way, member of the board of directors of the Mohegan Council of Boy Scouts, and trustee of the Worcester Historical Museum.

From the beginning, Jim's goal was to organize a financial consulting firm expert in the complex fields of estate planning, employee benefits, retirement plans, and executive compensation. Each client's needs were to be analyzed individually to assure the design of a program which would address all aspects of financial plan-

*This strikingly modern building at 55 Linden Street houses the offices of James J. Moynihan & Associates, Inc.*

ning.

The response has been gratifying. By 1975, the company had expanded to three employees and moved to a suite in the Mechanics Tower. Three years later, with eight employees, the firm moved into its new offices at 55 Linden Street. Although the firm continues to cover all facets of business insurance and employee benefit plans, Moynihan & Associates specializes in the design, installation, and administration of employee pension and profit sharing plans, which have become such an integral part of today's business world. Plan design and installation services, suggested drafts of plan and trust documents, employee announcement letters, and government form preparations are

but some of the services available to the client.

Annual actuarial valuations, maintenance of individual participant account records, preparation of personalized employee benefit reports, special computations for adding new employees and effecting retirements and terminations — all of these time-consuming administrative services are handled through a highly sophisticated, in-house computer system.

The company is steadily expanding, with clients throughout Massachusetts and in several other northeastern states, including New York, New Jersey, Connecticut, and Maine.

Still relatively young, James J. Moynihan & Associates, Inc., has already established an important niche for itself in Worcester and the Northeast and looks to the future with anticipation and confidence.

# HORNE & HASTINGS ASSOCIATES, INC.

The firm now known as Horne & Hastings Associates, Inc., was founded by Archie J. Horne in 1935. Mr. Horne, born in Scotland in 1903, came to the United States as a young boy and graduated from Worcester Polytechnic Institute. He began in the real estate business as an appraiser, soon developed a consulting business, and then later formed the brokerage division.

Mr. Horne (MAI, SREA), a member of the American Institute of Real Estate Appraisers and the Society of Real Estate Appraisers, has served as president of the Worcester Board of Realtors, director of the Massachusetts Association of Realtors, and president of the New England Chapter of the American Institute of Appraisers. He was named Realtor of the Year in 1967.

The company was originally located on Lovell Street, Worcester, and later moved to West Boylston Street. In 1978, new headquarters were built at 55 Linden Street to house Horne & Hastings Associates, Inc., and James J. Moynihan, Inc.

Mr. Horne formed a partnership with Calvin B. Hastings in 1963. Horne & Hastings Associates was incorporated in 1972. Mr. Hastings (RM, SRA), educated at Worcester Junior College and Clark University, is a member of the American Institute of Real Estate Appraisers and the Greater Worcester Board of Realtors. He was voted Realtor of the Year in 1976.

Horne & Hastings has four offices

serving central Worcester County, providing a wide range of services through its appraisal, consulting, brokerage, and development divisions. The firm has been involved in the financing and/or construction of developments in Worcester, Shrewsbury, Holden, and Boylston.

The company lists its properties by computer, thus making it possible for each office to search the records in a matter of seconds. Clients are given an instant picture of what is being offered on any particular day. As it has for many years, Horne & Hastings, Inc., with long experience in Worcester and Massachusetts, continues to offer a full range of services in all aspects of real estate.

*Top*
*In 1935, Archie J. Horne founded the firm now known as Horne & Hastings.*
*Left*
*Calvin B. Hastings joined the company as Horne's partner in 1963.*
*Below*
*This Greek-Revival house originally stood on what is now Linden Street, where the company's current headquarters (pictured on the opposite page) are located. In order to build the new facility, Calvin Hastings and James Moynihan donated the house to the Heritage Society. It was then moved to the historic Crown Hill area of Worcester.*

# L. HARDY COMPANY

In 1854, Levi Hardy decided to start a small company of his own to produce machine knives for the leather industry, and in 1980, the L. Hardy Company was still producing machine knives for the leather industry at the same location — 9-17 Mill Street, Worcester.

Hardy had learned the machine knife trade in partnership with Loring and Aury G. Coes. He continued that relationship until 1864, when he sold his share to the Coes brothers and concentrated on developing his own business. In 1880, Hardy retired, and Henry A. Hoyt assumed the firm's managerial reins. Under Hoyt's able hand, many improvements were made in Hardy knives. The company was incorporated in 1894 with a capitalization of $25,000.

Nahum Goddard, one of the company's employees before the turn of the century, married Hoyt's daughter; their son, Robert Goddard, would one day pioneer the rocket technology that would enable modern space exploration. Nahum displayed the family trait of inventiveness when he engineered an improved style of blade for cutting rabbit fur for hats.

In 1906, Charles H. Bliss, who had been treasurer, succeeded Hoyt as president, a position he held for twenty-two years. During his tenure, the company developed the composite material used in Hardy shock-absorbing knife bodies.

Bliss died in 1928. Three years later, his son-in-law, Thomas B. Moor, was elected president, treasurer, and chairman of the board. Wilber J. Birnie joined the company in 1938, became president in 1960, and retired in 1974. Robert Becker succeeded him as president in 1974.

For the first ninety-three years of its existence, L. Hardy Company was spared the misfortune of natural disasters. Then, in 1947, the firm was hit twice. A fire gutted the main manufacturing plant and office on April 28. A new steel and concrete structure was built to replace the old wooden plant. Production was just returning to normal when, on December 2, the rest of the original building went up in flames, leaving the company without production facilities for a second time.

In 1955, severe flooding in Webster Square left L. Hardy Company with a discouraging amount of mud and debris to clean up. Fortunately, the interruption was only temporary.

In 1980, the company was selling knives for leather, paper, textiles, and fur, as well as other related products, to both domestic and international markets. The firm had established an export department in 1950. Today, two-thirds of the company's output is sold abroad.

L. Hardy Company has grown steadily over the past generation. In 1960, shipments amounted to about $500,000. In 1970, they totaled about $1.4 million. By 1980, they had increased to $4 million. As the company approaches its 150th birthday in 1994, it looks back with pride and forward with optimism.

*Top*
*The L. Hardy Company's plant has occupied a site in the heart of Webster Square since 1854.*
*Left*
*Thomas B. Moor guided the firm through the depression years.*
*Right*
*Wilbur J. Birnie, president of the L. Hardy Company from 1960 to 1974, played a key role in establishing the firm's solid footing in the modern era.*

# L.C.H. FABRICATORS, INC.

In 1949, William Arnieri founded the William Manufacturing Company on Bartlett Street in Worcester. The new company, which primarily fabricated heating ducts, moved to 62 Washington Street in 1952.

The company faced severe financial difficulties in the early 1970s. In March 1973, letters were sent to customers announcing that liquidation was being considered. The company was on the verge of going out of business, but at the last moment, Leslie C. Haynes, Jr., who had been production manager, decided to buy the struggling firm. Encouraged by friends and associates and helped by a loan from the Guaranty Bank, Haynes signed the papers on May 1, 1973, that created L.C.H. Fabricators, Inc.

Starting with only two employees, Haynes switched production from conventional heating duct work to plant fabrication of all sorts of sheet-metal work done to customer specifications. The company quickly developed the capacity to work on light, medium, and heavy metal, including stainless steel, and by 1974 was successfully handling orders in all three varieties.

The company produces only one standard item of its own — stainless steel crosses that are fastened to gravestones and cemetery monuments. Almost all of its orders involve special custom work for clients ranging from Riley Stoker and Wyman-Gordon to smaller firms with particular needs for particular jobs. The company sells directly to customers nationwide and indirectly, through

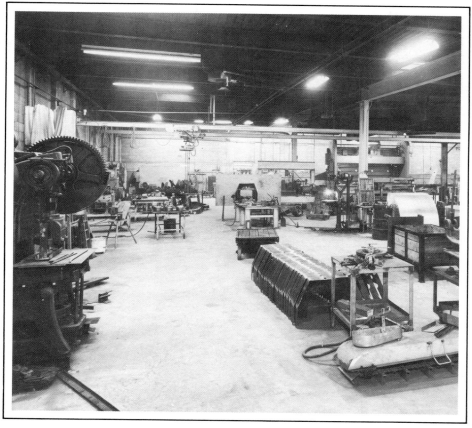

*Above*
*The company's modern plant contains a variety of machinery for the production of custom-fabricated sheet-metal orders.*
*Right*
*L.C.H. Fabricators is capable of manufacturing gear boxes like this one for industrial machinery.*

these customers, to companies in many parts of the world, including South America, South Africa, Taiwan, and the People's Republic of China.

The company's products range from internal panels for steam boilers to copper electrodes used in forging production to large gear boxes used on industrial machinery.

Leslie C. Haynes, Jr., is owner, president, and treasurer of the firm, which now employs about twenty. His wife, Irene, is vice-president.

Today, steadily increasing gross annual sales approach $800,000. L.C.H.

Fabricators, Inc., is actively exploring the possibility of expanding into various areas of production for the electronics industry.

# LODDING: A DIVISION OF THERMO ELECTRON CORPORATION

In 1929, with $1,000 of his own and another $1,000 borrowed from a relative, Frederick W. Lodding founded Lodding Engineering Corporation. Mr. Lodding had emigrated from Norway in 1908, at the age of eighteen. He was hired at the Fore River Shipbuilding Company in Quincy, then went to work for the Rice Barton Corporation in Worcester in 1915. When Mr. Lodding left Rice Barton to form his own company, he had attained the position of chief draftsman.

Lodding developed an improved method for securing doctor blades against the rolls of paper machines. In 1929, he applied for a patent on his holder and subsequently formed Lodding Engineering Corporation, even before his patent was accepted. The new company had a drill press, an engine lathe, a punch press, a primitive grinder, a long assembly bench, and not much else. Heavy machine work was subcontracted. It was ten years before the company moved to adequate first-floor quarters and acquired its first planer for the machining of doctor backs. But the business earned a national reputation almost from its inception, thanks to its association with the W.E. Greene Corporation, which also sold Stowe-Woodward paper-machine rolls.

The war years were difficult ones for the firm. When Frederick Lodding died in 1943, his son, Woodrow, was serving in the navy. The company

*Above*
*Frederick Lodding founded Lodding Engineering Corporation in 1929.*
*Below*
*Lodding products are manufactured in this modern plant in the Auburn Industrial Park.*

managed to survive largely due to the capable leadership of Marjorie Lodding, Woodrow's wife, who served as president for the next three years.

After the war, Lodding Engineering Corporation experienced substantial growth and renewed prosperity. By

1959, annual sales had increased fivefold to $2 million, and the company was able to move to its new quarters on Sword Street in Auburn. In 1969, Lodding was acquired by Thermo Electron Corporation of Waltham, and now operates as a division within Thermo Electron's Papermaking Equipment Group.

Lodding Engineering Corporation has had four presidents since Marjorie Lodding relinquished that position in 1946. They are: Woodrow C. Lodding; David J. Milliken; Howard W. Harding, Jr.; and, since 1978, David W. Lodding, the founder's grandson.

Today, the company employs about 200 people in the United States, most of them at the Auburn plant with its 65,000 square feet of manufacturing space and 15,000 square feet of office space. Lodding products are manufactured by subsidiaries in the United Kingdom, Canada, Mexico, and Brazil, as well as by licensees in France, Japan, and Sweden. But, as in 1929, its main efforts remain focused on the manufacture and service of specialty equipment for papermaking machines.

# LOWELL CORPORATION

Lowell Wrench Company was founded in 1869 by John E. Sinclair, head of the mathematics department at what is now Worcester Polytechnic Institute, and Milton P. Higgins, superintendent of the Washburn Shops there. The two had bought the patent rights to a new style ratchet. Their first wrenches were machined at the Washburn Shops.

Higgins later sold his interest in the company and went on to become one of the founders and the first president of Norton Company. But Sinclair continued as head of Lowell Wrench for the next thirty-seven years. In 1906, he selected John H. Dodge as president and general manager, posts that Dodge held for the next forty-one years.

Dodge guided the company through the boom years of World War I, when the demand for wrenches was great; through the uneven times of the 1920s; through the terrible depression of the 1930s; and the challenging years of World War II, when the demand for wrenches again required overtime and multishift production.

Upon the retirement of his father in 1947, John S. Dodge became president and general manager. He was ably assisted by Anna M. Greene, assistant general manager and vice-president. Together they embarked on a program of machine modernization, improvements in the bookkeeping system, and sales development. After only five years as president, Dodge died in 1952, and Mrs. Greene was appointed general manager. She succeeded in attracting many valuable new customers.

In 1959, H.S. Cummings, Jr., a direct descendant of John E. Sinclair, became general manager. He was named president in 1961. Cummings developed a new statement of corporate policy and a long-range plan for growth. Improved wage scales, fringe benefits, better working conditions, more efficient manufacturing

methods, product redesign and standardization, sales organization of representatives and distributors, and new products were some of the fruits of this plan.

In 1978, David S. Cummings, a fifth-generation descendant of the founder, joined the company as treasurer and director. He has expanded computer utilization and integrated financial systems throughout the company.

Today, Lowell's employees are seeking and generally finding the common objectives of earning enough money, gaining a sense of accomplishment, and enjoying their work. With well over a century of production and innovation behind it, this unique family business faces the future with pride and confidence.

*Left*
*John E. Sinclair, who teamed with Milton P. Higgins in 1869 to gain the patent rights to an innovative ratchet design, headed Lowell Wrench Company for thirty-seven years.*
*Below*
*In 1942, the firm won the coveted Army/Navy "E" Award for excellence.*

# MECHANICS BANK

Mechanics Bank was organized as a state bank on June 15, 1848, by Frederic William Paine, Henry Goulding, and William T. Merrifield. Francis H. Dewey was chosen clerk. At the first meeting, Charles Washburn, Francis H. Dewey, and William M. Bickford were selected to approach the Worcester County Institution for Savings, the Merchant & Farmers Mutual Fire Insurance Company, and the State Mutual Life Assurance Company to sell subscriptions to the stock of the new bank.

The bank first set up business in the rear of the Manufacturers & Mutual Fire Insurance Company. A few months later it moved to William Dickinson's building nearby. The bank was to stay in that same general location of North Main Street, near the Central Exchange Building, for the next 123 years.

For more than a century, the bank's history and fortunes have been closely linked to two Worcester families, the Washburns and the Deweys. Four generations of Washburns and three generations of Deweys have served as directors. In addition, Frederick B. Washburn, Rodney Washburn, Francis H. Dewey, Francis H. Dewey, Jr., and Francis H. Dewey III have all served as president. Francis H. Dewey III is presently a director.

In April 1861, following the attack on Fort Sumter and President Lincoln's call for 75,000 volunteers to defend the Union, the bank, along with the other banks of Worcester County, voted to contribute to an extraordinary loan of $300,000 to the state for military preparations.

*Above*
*The new headquarters of Mechanics Bank dominates Worcester Center.*
*Below*
*In 1929, the bank displayed art-deco elegance at its Central Exchange Building offices.*

The directors voted to convert the institution into a national bank on July 19, 1864, a change that was completed in March 1865. A capital of $350,000 was provided.

Over the years, through good times and bad, Mechanics Bank has grown steadily to become one of the major banks in Worcester County. In 1964, it merged with the former Industrial City Bank. In 1971, after almost 125 years in or near the Central Exchange Building, the bank moved to new quarters in the Worcester Center complex downtown.

Mechanics became an affiliate of Multibank Financial Corp., a statewide bank holding company, in 1972. The bank converted back to a state charter in 1977, dropping the designation "national" from its name. Presently, the bank operates nine offices, in Worcester and in the towns of Auburn, Holden, and Northboro.

# THE MEMORIAL HOSPITAL

Ichabod Washburn's bequest of $100,000 established a hospital as a living memorial to his two daughters, Eliza Ann Moen and Pamela Washburn. The hospital's mission, in his words, was to "afford care, comfort, and relief to the sick and suffering who require superior medical and surgical skill and science."

In 1869, the Washburn Free Dispensary opened in the converted Abijah Bigelow house at Front and Church streets. During 1876, it was moved to 11 Trumbull Street and, in 1886, to the Samuel Davis property on Belmont Street, where The Memorial Hospital was formally dedicated in 1888.

Lucia Jaquith became matron in 1892 and superintendent and director of the nursing school shortly thereafter. This remarkable woman, who in the early days often served as anesthetist, lab technician, and surgical assistant, headed the hospital until 1929. During her tenure, the Children's Building, the Newton and Morgan wards, Jaquith House, and the Higgins Building were constructed.

Until 1909, The Memorial Hospital treated only women and children. Men were first admitted as patients when the George L. Newton Building opened that year. During the period from 1894 to 1932, the only interns at the hospital were women.

Benefactors have given generously of their time and money to The Memorial Hospital. The Memorial Hospital Aid Society, founded in 1888 by a group of teenage girls led by Mabel Gage, underwrote innovative programs such as the hospital's dental clinic, the Worcester Visiting Nurse Association, and the social and occupational therapy departments.

With several additional wings constructed between 1946 and 1975, The Memorial Hospital now has 371 adult beds and 40 bassinets. It is regarded as one of the region's leading centers for health services, research, and education. It serves as a regional nursery for sick and premature infants, a treatment center for women with high-risk pregnancies, a comprehensive care center for patients with hemophilia and other blood disorders, and a regional center for patients requiring kidney dialysis treatment.

Throughout its history, The Memorial Hospital has reflected the changes and needs of a growing community. It continues to follow the directive written by Ichabod Washburn over a century ago — to provide the best possible services that medical science can offer.

*Below center*
*Lucia Jaquith, superintendent from 1892 to 1929, guided the hospital during its formative years.*
*Left*
*The Memorial Hospital moved to the Samuel Davis property on Belmont Street in 1886.*
*Right*
*The health care facility looked like this in 1906, three years before it admitted its first male patients.*

# MICRO NETWORKS CORPORATION

Micro Networks was founded in March 1969 by Robert Jay, who believed that there was a market opportunity in thin-film hybrid circuits, particularly for the military and aerospace industries. An engineering graduate of Notre Dame with an M.B.A. from Harvard, Jay had extensive experience in the semiconductor, transistor, and circuit fields with General Electric and Sprague Electric.

Financed by Tucker Anthony, R.L. Day, State Mutual Life Assurance Company, and Unitrode Corporation, Micro Networks started in June with a management team of three and a production crew of three. Settling into offices on the second floor of the old round house building at 5 Barbara Lane, the company spent its first months buying equipment and setting it up for production. The fledgling firm was manufacturing stable, thin-film nichrome resistor material by late 1969. Only a few months later, the company became the first in the industry to successfully use lasers to trim the tiny resistor patterns, which had line widths of as little as .001 inches.

Micro Networks soon expanded into new products, including a line of standard data converters in dual-in-line package. These tiny A/D circuits translate analog information into digital form which can be utilized by computers and microprocessors. The company's first volume order for digital-to-analog converters came in 1970 from Bendix Corporation. That same year, Micro Networks introduced the industry's first dual-in-line packaged hybrid D/A converter. Although originally skeptical, the military soon began to accept this new miniaturized approach, which offered high reliability and improved performance.

*Above*
*Robert Jay (1930-1980) founded Micro Networks in 1969.*
*Below*
*This product, manufactured by Micro Networks, is a thin-film hybrid 16-bit analog to digital converter.*

In 1973, the company introduced the industry's first hybrid A/D converter, further enhancing its reputation as a leader in the introduction and development of high-performance data conversion circuits. The company's 126 employees moved into their 14,000-square-foot plant at 324 Clark Street in 1974. Sales that year exceeded $1.5 million.

By early 1979, Micro Networks had increased its floor space to 53,000 square feet, its employees to 400, and sales to $14 million. The company currently serves more than 800 accounts in the United States and 300 overseas and has emerged as a key supplier to the military and aerospace industry of high-accuracy, broad-temperature-range data converters.

Micro Networks merged with Unitrode Corporation, one of the firm's original investors, in May 1979. With an aggressive plan for new product development, the company looks forward to continued rapid growth in providing advanced data-conversion products and interface circuits for microprocessor systems in military, industrial, and communications markets.

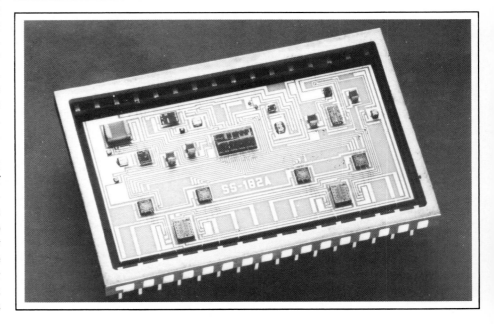

# NEW ENGLAND PLATING COMPANY, INC.

The New England Plating Company, Inc., was organized on February 15, 1933, when Dwight E. Priest, Leon E. Jorjorian, and Carl E. Soderberg acquired ownership of a business formerly operated solely by Jorjorian. It was originally located at 31 North Foster Street.

In 1938, after the corporation had purchased Jorjorian's stock, it moved into the Parker Manufacturing Plant at 149 Washington Street. Priest, who also owned a controlling interest in Parker, upgraded the plating facility to meet a Sears, Roebuck commitment that called for quality finishing.

That same year, Bruce E. Warner, a chemical engineer from Michigan, joined the company as general manager. He acquired 40 percent of the stock in April 1941. World War II interrupted Warner's service at New England Plating, and for three years he served as an anti-aircraft officer in the Pacific. His battalion saw extensive field service including the assault on Saipan. During his absence, the plant was managed by Robert C. Potter, later to become vice-president of operations, who successfully led the company from peacetime to defense production. Warner returned to the company after the war, and, in 1953, became sole stockholder as well as president, treasurer, and general manager.

The company moved to its current location at 31 Garden Street in 1953. Two years later, management made a crucial decision to replace the old system of hand-carrying dripping work from tank to tank with automatic plating conveyors. This program, completed in 1975, committed the company to much larger production runs and limited the finishes to those justified by volume operations.

During Hurricane Diane in 1955, the plant was flooded with water up to six feet deep in some places. The danger of flooding was not eliminated until the Mill Brook diversion project was completed in the 1960s.

Another crisis — this one financial — was precipitated when the state Water Quality Office forced the company to make major wastewater treatment expenditures. At one point, drained by these demands, operating capital was down to a mere $76. Fortunately, bank credit was available and the company survived. But the price it paid was several years of low growth. Then, in 1975, the company was able to launch a program of expansion. Management installed more automatic plating conveyors and converted to diesel equipment for trucking.

The key people in the New England Plating success story are Bruce Warner, civic leader, former director of the National Association of Metal Finishers, and officer and director of the Master Metal Finishers of New England; Robert C. Potter, retired vice-president of operations; Anne Merriam, vice-president of administration; and George W. Nilsson, vice-president of sales. As the company nears its half-century mark, the future looks bright indeed.

*Top*
*In 1953, the New England Plating Company moved to its current location at 31 Garden Street.*
*Bottom*
*This photograph shows the same building after the company spent thousands of dollars in modernizing and refurbishing efforts.*

# NORTON COMPANY

Norton Company, which evolved from a nineteenth-century Worcester pottery shop, is today a billion-dollar manufacturer of thousands of industrial products with people and markets throughout the world — and headquarters still in Worcester.

Norton's story began in 1858 when two young potters from Bennington, Vermont, set up shop in Worcester. Frank B. Norton gave the company its name.

During the 1870s, one of Norton's workers devised a formula for a reliable grinding wheel, the first ceramic-bonded wheel that could be precision made and mass produced. The grinding wheel business grew. But it remained a sideline to Frank Norton, whose interest was pottery. In 1885, he sold his grinding wheel business to seven Worcester men — John Jeppson, Milton P. Higgins, George I. Alden, Charles L. Allen, Horace A. Young, Fred H. Daniels, and Walter L. Messer. They went into business for themselves, keeping Norton's name on their own firm.

These men had the right idea at the right time. As the Industrial Revolution spurred the manufacture of more and more machinery, the new machines required more and more grinding wheels and other abrasives to shape and smooth parts and to keep cutting tools sharp.

Norton Company grew. Frequently adding new abrasive products to its business lines, the firm was soon serving markets throughout the world. In 1909, Norton Company began building plants overseas. Its German plant came first, followed by

*Norton Company's plant at Barbers Crossing in 1886 was just the beginning of what would become the company's sprawling modern complex near Indian Lake.*

plants in France and Canada ten years later, then in England, Italy, and Australia. By the middle of the twentieth century, Norton had become the world's largest manufacturer of abrasives, with products ranging from dental drills to sandpaper, massive pulp-crushing wheels to metal polishers.

But the company has also expanded far beyond the possibilities its founders saw in grinding wheels. During the 1970s, Norton undertook a planned program of diversification for

further growth. Through the acquisition of smaller companies and through discoveries of new uses for its traditional abrasive products, Norton added industrial ceramics, safety products, plastics, and chemical process products to its lines of industrial offerings.

In 1977 the company merged with Christensen, Inc., of Salt Lake City, Utah, which provides diamond drill bits and other equipment and services for the petroleum and mining industries.

Today, Norton Company has more than 120 manufacturing plants in 27 countries and is listed among the 500 largest corporations in the United States.

# PARKER MANUFACTURING COMPANY

Parker Wire Goods Company was organized and began production in the Pond Building on May 24, 1901. At the start and for many years after, the firm manufactured a complete line of bright wire goods such as cup hooks, gate hooks, oxen muzzles, and other items. In 1930, noting the trends in industry, Parker began producing small hand tools, and in 1943, the firm discontinued the manufacture of wire goods. That same year, the company banner was changed to Parker Manufacturing Company.

The firm's original location on Assonet Street was abandoned after a destructive fire in 1915. The company relocated to the Osgood-Bradley Building at 18 Grafton Street and, in 1923, moved again to its present location on Washington Street, where production facilities have been expanded several times.

Arthur H. Parker, the firm's first president, treasurer, and corporate clerk, resigned in 1922. Edward D. Priest, the actual founder and principal stockholder in the company, became chairman and chief executive that same year. He was elected president on May 14, 1927, and later resigned on February 4, 1931, because of poor health. He was succeeded by his son, Dwight E. Priest, who held the office of president until his death in December 1960. John Z. Buckley assumed the presidency until November 1966, when he was succeeded by Edward D. Priest, grandson of the founder.

In 1949, Parker Manufacturing Company purchased Ackermann-Steffan of Chicago, manufacturers of Trojan Saw Blades, and moved its manufacturing operations to Worcester. Another acquisition, in 1952, was Snell Manufacturing Company of Fiskdale. Recently, the acquisition of the King Fastener Company of Kingstown, Rhode Island, was completed. Parker ceased manufacture of its Parker line of products in late 1966 and since then has concentrated its efforts on the production of Trojan tools for hardware distributors and Craftsman tools for Sears, Roebuck and Co.

Parker Manufacturing is engaged in metal stamping and forming, and also welding, heat treating, grinding, and machining, in its production of hand tools and power tool accessories. In addition to its main plant and headquarters in Worcester, the company operates a modern 60,000-square-foot assembly, shipping, and warehousing plant in Northboro.

*Parker Manufacturing Company's headquarters and production plant on Washington Street lie just a few blocks from the office and shopping areas of downtown Worcester.*

# PAUL REVERE COMPANIES

1980 marked the fiftieth year of the founding of The Paul Revere Life Insurance Company — and the eighty-fifth anniversary of the formation of its parent. And, while the world has grown smaller over those years in terms of communications and accessibility, Paul Revere's world has grown larger in the service of satisfied customers across the North American continent and around the world.

If the Paul Revere organization got a head start toward recognized stature and success in the national insurance marketplace in 1930, it was because its pioneer parent in the disability insurance business had blazed a widely recognized and well-regarded trail ahead of it.

The Masonic Protective Associ-

*Above*
*Francis A. Harrington, three-time mayor of Worcester, founded the Masonic Protective Association and served as its first president.*
*Below*
*The old Knowles Building housed the association in its early years.*

ation was founded in Worcester in 1895 under the then-fraternal assessment company laws of the Commonwealth of Massachusetts. One of its founders and its first president was Francis A. Harrington, a respected community leader and a man who

was elected to three terms as mayor of Worcester.

Though the beginnings of the company in its early years were modest, its growth was nonetheless steady. And the combination of a sound product and an excellent distribution system through the fraternity gave it the kind of impetus that accelerated both expansion and profit. As a result, it was able to withstand the challenges of the catastrophic Spanish flu epidemic and a devastating Knowles Building headquarters fire in its early years.

The MPA's strength and stability also led to the founding of The Paul Revere Life Insurance Company on June 10, 1930, as a companion company to the original fraternal firm. Its broader, nonfraternal marketing horizons developed impressive growth. Moreover, in relatively rapid order, it outpaced its parent company significantly.

For nearly seventy-five years, the companies were guided largely by one family. Francis A. Harrington served as president from 1895 until his death in 1922. His son, Charles, was president from 1922 to 1945. Charles's nephew, Frank L. Harrington, led the firms from 1945 to 1966, and Frank L. Harrington, Jr., served as president from 1966 to 1969.

In 1967, the parent company was merged into the Paul Revere organization. Later that year Paul Revere became a part of the Avco Corporation, based in Greenwich, Connecticut. Shortly thereafter, George L. Hogeman became the first nonfamily president, serving until 1974 when he became president of Avco.

Today's Paul Revere Companies, headed by Aubrey K. Reid, Jr., operate across the United States and Canada — respected as national disability insurance leaders and as quality underwriters of life insurance, group insurance, and annuities.

# HALO CORPORATION

The Phalo Corporation was founded in 1943 by Herbert Raymond, Arvid Johnson, Levi Plante, and Oliver Plante. The name is an acronym derived from the *P* of Progressive Tool and Die, the parent company, and the first letters of the first names of the four men.

Phalo was organized to manufacture field wire, then in short supply, for the United States Army. The founders, all experts in machine design, developed their own equipment and set up shop at 1 Foster Street in Worcester. As World War II drew to a close, Phalo was well established in the wire and cable industry.

After the war, as the demand for television and consumer appliances grew dramatically, Phalo expanded its product lines to include cord sets, assemblies, molded plugs, and TV antenna wire. The company soon became one of the leading manufacturers of cord sets in the country.

By 1945, the Foster Street facility had been outgrown and the firm moved to larger quarters on Commercial Street. There it manufactured products for General Electric, Sylvania, Motorola, and other companies in growing volume.

In 1958, again pressed for space, the company built a new headquarters force has expanded to more than 500 employees. Sales exceeded $50 million in 1980.

Phalo products now range from audio and communications cable to highly specialized computer and telemetry cable. A sister plant in Westboro, Massachusetts, named the "Special Products Division," specializes in miniature planar and high-temperature constructions.

Comprising approximately 250,000 square feet, Phalo's Shrewsbury plant is considered one of the most modern

*Modern headquarters of Phalo Corporation are located in pleasant surroundings in Shrewsbury, Massachusetts.*

and plant in Shrewsbury, Massachusetts, where a steady line of new products was developed for the growing electronics, communications, telemetry, and aerospace industries. In 1963, Phalo was purchased by Transitron Electronic Corporation of Wakefield, Massachusetts.

Today, executive offices and administrative, sales, and manufacturing activities are located at the Shrewsbury facility. The local work electronic wire and cable facilities in the country. Approximately 30,000 square feet were added in 1980 to house the marketing, engineering, and sales staff. Production is more than 200 million conductor feet of wire each week.

Phalo management gives a great deal of credit to its workers — its engineers, technicians, production people, and sales staff — for keeping the company in the vanguard of the sophisticated and rapidly changing field of telecommunication and electronic wire and cable production.

# OLAR CORPORATION

Polar Corporation traces its roots back to 1882, when J. George Bieberbach, bottler of seltzer water, ginger ale, and mineral water, set up shop at 113 Summer Street. A few years later the company was reorganized as Bieberbach Brothers.

A second ancestor of Polar Corporation was the Arctic Polar Spring Water Corporation, which, on May 1, 1909, leased water rights to a spring of unusual purity located near the Leicester-Spencer county line. The company opened an office at 25 Mercantile Street in Worcester, and began to promote its product.

An early advertisement asserted that the water was "A cure for insomnia, catarrh, dispepsia, liver, summer complaint, general debility and nervous affections . . . All you can drink, 2c."

The Bieberbach Company was purchased in 1916 by Dennis M. Crowley, grandfather of the present owners. Two years later he acquired the Leicester Polar Spring Water Company and named the merged operation the Bieber Polar Ginger Ale Company, and later the Bieber Polar Company.

In those early days, the sparkling water of the Leicester-Spencer spring was in great demand and accounted for a large part of the business. The water was also used to make pale dry ginger ale, orange, root beer, and other soft drinks.

Dennis Crowley was assisted and eventually succeeded by his sons, who steadily expanded the business over the years. Presently, four of Mr. Crowley's grandsons, as well as

several great-grandchildren, are involved in the business.

By the late 1960s, it had become clear that, despite the addition of several pieces of adjacent property, the business had outgrown its old location at 113 Summer Street. In 1970 the company, which had changed its name two years earlier to Polar Corp., moved to a modern new plant on a six-acre site at Walcott Street. The plant has the capacity to bottle 20,000 cases of soft drinks per day.

Polar Corporation produces twenty flavors of drinks in cans, 32-ounce bottles, and two-liter plastic bottles; and deals in pre-mix, post-mix, ice-cube makers, and vending machines, as well.

In the days before World War I, the company's beverages were sold in a relatively small radius from the plant, limited to the distance a horse-drawn wagon could travel and return within a day. Today, trailer trucks deliver Polar beverages throughout New England and into the eastern part of New York State. Although still a Worcester owned and oriented company, it has acquired a regional reputation for the excellent quality of its soft drinks and customer service.

*Top*
*In the 1920s, this fleet of trucks delivered Polar beverages throughout Worcester County from the Summer Street warehouse.*
*Bottom*
*About 1902, Arctic Polar spring water was delivered and sold to downtown residents from this store on Mercantile Street.*

# REED ROLLED THREAD DIE COMPANY

*Above*
*The firm's plant in the Holden Industrial Park continues to push the state of the art in thread- and form-rolling technology.*
*Below*
*Precise measurement, symbolized by this early Reed micrometer, has been important to Reed's success in the thread-rolling and knurl business.*

On June 15, 1916, E. Howard Reed, a 1902 graduate of Worcester Polytechnic Institute, started Reed Small Tool Works on the third floor of the Baker Lead Company Building at the corner of Vine and Cherry streets. Reed's first product was a rolled thread micrometer, an innovation in that era. The demand created by World War I gave the fledgling company an impetus, but business slacked off when the war ended.

Reed, an inventive genius, then developed thread-rolling dies, using a lapping operation he had perfected. In 1925, needing more space, the company moved to 35 Hermon Street, and shortly thereafter to 237 Chandler Street. The Rolled Thread Die Company was incorporated independently in 1927, with M.C. Nelson, president; Howard Reed, treasurer; and Bradford Reed, a recent college graduate, clerk. Coates Clipper Manufacturing Company was acquired about the same time.

In 1930, the companies bought the knurl business and equipment of John and Russell Goodnow's Hardware Products Company. Howard Reed soon developed methods for lapping the teeth and holes and for grinding the sides, making it possible to produce the first completely finished knurl ever offered to the trade.

By the late 1930s, the companies were busy developing improved dies to roll Class-3 and Class-4 threads on semi-hard alloy steels, the first time the process had been accomplished

successfully. During World War II, Reed was virtually the only company capable of meeting the demand for dies of that type.

The war led to a tremendous increase in output by the companies. Dies, knurls, and micrometers were the main product lines. With the cooperation of Crompton and Knowles Loom Works, the company developed thread-rolling machines, which were soon in great demand from the military and from aircraft manufacturers.

After Howard Reed's death in 1943, his son, A. Bradford Reed, assumed the main responsibility for management, serving as president until his retirement in 1961.

The three companies were consoli-

dated into Reed Rolled Thread Die Company in 1947. Four years later, the firm built a new plant in Holden. Since 1951, Reed's plant in Holden has been expanded five times. In 1961, Reed Rolled Thread Die Company became a wholly owned subsidiary of Union Twist Drill Company; in 1968, Litton Industries acquired Union Twist Drill and Reed became a division of Litton Industries.

In 1970, Reed began a concentrated effort to export its products. The company received a Presidential "E" Award in 1975 for outstanding contributions to the United States' export expansion program. More than 20 percent of Reed's volume is exported.

Rossiter R. Holt became president of Reed Rolled Thread Die Company in 1961, upon the acquisition by Union Twist Drill. Holt changed Reed's position in the industry to become principally a die manufacturer with a limited line of thread-rolling machines. Edward A. Miller, Jr., was named president in 1978.

The automotive industry is the largest consuming industry serviced by Reed and Reed's customers. This market segment accounts for approximately 40 percent of Reed's sales. In addition, Reed's tools are used in the manufacture of aircraft fasteners and actuators.

In 1980 a 30,000-square-foot addition made it possible to increase production capacity by 45 percent. Today, Reed is the world leader in thread- and form-rolling technology, as it has been for forty years.

# SAINT VINCENT HOSPITAL

In 1893, Monsignor Thomas Griffin, pastor of Saint John's Church on Temple Street, purchased the Bartlett Farm on Vernon Street and invited the Sisters of Providence of Holyoke, Massachusetts, to operate a hospital that would care for the sick and injured without regard to color or creed. On September 8, 1893, a nucleus of five nuns opened a 12-bed hospital in the remodeled farmhouse, calling it the House of Providence.

During the first full year of operation, there were 101 admissions. The cost of a ward bed was one dollar a day, and private room accommodations were available for twenty dollars a week. The medical staff numbered seventeen — two consultants, four surgeons, six general practitioners, one orthopedist, two ophthalmologists, one pathologist, and one obstetrician.

To meet the increased demand for medical care, a new building was dedicated in 1895, and the facility was renamed Saint Vincent Hospital. The construction of a 150-bed brick building followed the hospital's incorporation in 1898. A 60-bed addition was built in 1918 and a residence for sisters and student nurses in 1922.

Responding to the need for nursing instruction, the hospital opened a school for lay nurses in 1900. There were fourteen students in training in 1908 and the number of sisters had increased to forty.

The "new" Saint Vincent Hospital was opened at the corner of Winthrop and Providence streets on the old George Crompton estate in 1954. Eleven years later, the Bishop Wright Pavilion was added, providing facilities for a 51-bed psychiatric unit,

a 45-bed maternity section, and a 52-bed surgical floor. At the same time, the building on Vernon Street was remodeled and became Providence House, a home for the elderly. St. Luke's Hall on Heywood Street opened in 1965, providing living accommodations for residents and interns. The Rose Building, containing laboratories and research facilities, was added in 1970.

The hospital is operated by a nonprofit corporation presided over by the Bishop of Worcester. Miss Helen Marie Smith has served as executive director since 1963.

Today, Saint Vincent Hospital is a 600-bed general hospital providing a wide range of acute patient care. Its modern and extensive teaching and research facilities, its sophisticated equipment, and its expertly trained staff combine to make Saint Vincent Hospital a superb regional medical center for all of central Massachusetts.

*Left*
*This 35-bed hospital building (adjacent to the 12-bed remodeled farmhouse) opened in 1895 but proved inadequate within five years.*
*Bottom left*
*In the 1920s, this six-bed ward provided the latest in health care.*
*Below*
*Today, the modern Saint Vincent Hospital dominates the heights of Worcester's Vernon Hill section.*

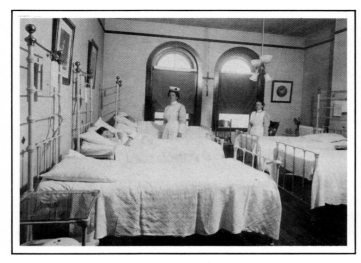

# STANDARD PAPER GOODS MANUFACTURING COMPANY

Standard Paper Goods Manufacturing Company evolved from Anglend Coin Wrappers, a business that was conceived one day in 1896 when Edgar H. Wilcomb was making a bank deposit. Ahead of him in line, a Salvation Army officer was depositing some wrapped coin. Mr. Wilcomb noticed that the wrappers were cut so that the end of the paper would follow the contour of the roll and fit snugly. He took the idea home and began to manufacture coin wrappers as a sideline, continuing to work nights at the *Worcester Telegram* as a compositor.

Gummed currency straps were added to the line about 1912, followed by sealed bill bands. During World War I, the business expanded rapidly, and in 1917 and 1918 a machine was developed to make coin tubes, the forerunner of Cartridge Cointainers, which are still widely used by banks.

Wilcomb retired in 1919 and sold the business to a newly formed corporation called Standard Paper Goods Manufacturing Company. Frank L. MacNeill was president; Welcome H. Hughes, vice-president; and Dewitt Clinton, treasurer. A month later, Stanley W. MacNeill joined the firm upon his discharge from the United States Navy.

The company, which has been located at Southbridge Street, Park Avenue, Eden Street, and, since 1964, Sherman Street, equipped its first machine shop in 1928 and proceeded to develop machines for the manufacture of Tubular Coin Wrappers. The first Cointainer machine was built in 1938; the Cointainer has continued to be one of the company's main lines.

Frank L. MacNeill continued as president until his death in 1945, when Stanley MacNeill became president and treasurer. He ran the operation as a one-man business until 1954, when he was joined by his son, Campbell. Clinton sold his interest in the company in 1930, and Hughes sold his in 1944.

In 1966, Stanley MacNeill was elected chairman of the board of directors, and Campbell MacNeill became the chief executive officer with the titles of president and treasurer. The elder MacNeill served as chairman of the board until his death in January 1973.

Frank J. Ricci was appointed vice-president/sales in 1975, and vice-president of the entire corporation in 1979.

Since its inception, the company has supplied related money-wrapping items produced by other firms to accommodate its customers. This service has been greatly expanded, and in 1979 the related products were responsible for 15 percent of total sales.

In 1919, Standard Paper Goods occupied 3,500 square feet of floor space. Today it occupies 30,000 square feet in a modern, single-story building. Sales have increased tenfold, the number of employees by 260 percent.

*Standard Paper Goods' production line turns out currency straps, bill bands, and tubular wrappers.*

# STARK, JOHNSON & STINSON, INC.

In 1919, the nucleus of one of Worcester County's largest and most prestigious independent insurance agencies began. During that year, James E. Stinson, along with William N. Stark, an independent agent, and Charles W. Johnson of the Factory Insurance Association, formed a partnership and opened an office in the Park Building at 507 Main Street, Worcester. The new firm, originally called William N. Stark & Company, became Stark, Johnson & Stinson in 1925, and relocated to expanded facilities in the new Chamber of Commerce Building at 32 Franklin Street. When Stark retired in 1928, Johnson and Stinson continued as a partnership until 1932, when due to rapid growth it became more prudent to incorporate, with the former becoming president, the latter treasurer.

Charles Johnson retired in 1936 and sold his share in the company to James E. Stinson. Richard F. Canton joined the agency as vice-president that same year and continued in that capacity until his retirement in 1958. Thomas B. Stinson, a former navy pilot, entered the firm in 1946 as assistant treasurer and became president upon the retirement of James E. Stinson in 1972. In 1959, W. Willard Travis joined the firm as vice-president and served in that position until his retirement in 1978.

Since its inception in 1919, the company has won recognition for its many creative techniques and promotional slogans designed to develop public awareness of the advantages of different types of insurance coverage. "The Little Messenger" and "Insurance to the Rescue" became household words in central Massachusetts because of the company's pioneering use of radio advertising as early as 1926 on station WTAG.

From 1945 to 1955, branch offices in Boston and Framingham were maintained to service the needs of various bus transportation companies, which became clients under an innovative program designed by the firm. The company formed the Insurance Credit Company to finance insurance premiums during that period. In 1972, Reidy, Coe & Company was acquired as part of Thomas B. Stinson's continued expansion program.

Stark, Johnson & Stinson was the first agency in Worcester to underwrite aviation insurance and to offer malpractice coverage to the medical profession. The agency was also a pioneer in explaining and promoting automobile insurance coverage following the passage of the Massachusetts Compulsory Automobile Insurance Laws in 1926.

Stark, Johnson & Stinson continues to offer quality insurance service and comprehensive counseling to a wide variety of commercial and industrial clients, which include banks, hospitals, and machinery manufacturers. The firm continues to operate out of expanded quarters at the Franklin Street location it has occupied for more than fifty-five years.

*Thomas B. Stinson joined the company in 1946 and has been president since 1972.*

# STATE MUTUAL LIFE ASSURANCE COMPANY OF AMERICA

State Mutual Life Assurance Company was founded in Worcester by the Honorable John Davis, former governor of Massachusetts and United States senator. The charter granted by the Commonwealth on March 16, 1844, established State Mutual as one of the first life insurance companies incorporated in the United States.

The firm's original office was located in the rear of the old Central Bank Building at 100 Main Street. In 1872, the company relocated to 240 Main Street and, in 1897, to 340 Main Street, where it stayed for sixty years. On November 30, 1957, the company moved into its new home office and company headquarters at 440 Lincoln Street.

The company issued its first policy on June 2, 1845, to Nelson Carpenter

*Above*
*The headquarters of State Mutual and The America Group is located on Lincoln Street.*
*Below*
*The impressive building at 340 Main Street served as the headquarters of State Mutual from 1897 to 1957.*

of Warren, Massachusetts. Carpenter paid an annual premium of $84.91 for his $3,000 policy. The provisions reflected the hazards of the times. Carpenter was forbidden "to travel to the Southern part of the country in the summer, could not participate in a duel, partake of any dangerous occupation, and never become so intemperate as to impair health."

As the nation grew, so did State Mutual. It soon expanded its coverage to residents throughout the United States and quickly became a leader of the young American insurance industry. State Mutual pioneered cash surrender values and paid its first cash surrender in 1848. Policyholders no longer had to forfeit their entire investments if they were unable to pay their premiums. That early State Mutual decision became law in Massachusetts in 1861. The firm later introduced such services as policy loans and deferred settlement options, as well as group and health insurance products.

State Mutual issued its first group

policy in 1945. Three years later, its total life insurance in force exceeded $1 billion. State Mutual of Worcester became State Mutual of America in 1957, and by the 1960s, the company was expanding beyond life and health insurance to more comprehensive concepts of total financial security. Through its affiliate companies, now collectively called The America Group, a comprehensive portfolio of financial services including variable annuities, property and liability insurance, and mutual funds was developed.

Shortly after the Surgeon General's report on "Smoking and Health" was published in 1964, State Mutual pioneered with insurance premium discounts to nonsmokers. This concept has been extended to State Mutual's individual disability income insurance and to other insurance products offered by affiliated companies of The America Group.

The fifth oldest life insurance company in the United States, State Mutual has continued to grow and change with the times. Under the leadership of W. Douglas Bell, chairman of the board and chief executive officer, the company entered the 1980s ranked among the nation's top twenty mutual life insurance companies with assets of well over $2 billion.

# THOMAS SMITH COMPANY

Thomas Smith, born in Rindge, New Hampshire, in 1819, and trained as a blacksmith, came to Worcester at the age of twenty to work for the Crompton-Knowles Loom Works. After gaining experience working on loom machinery, he started his own business in 1854, producing nuts and bolts. Smith's first shop was located on Commercial Street. He gradually expanded into farm machinery and the production of metal stampings, and soon became a major supplier to textile machinery manufacturers. To this day, Crompton-Knowles has remained one of the firm's customers.

After sharing the business with various partners, Smith bought sole control in 1875. He continued as president of the company until his death in 1896. Although he was forced into bankruptcy during one of the financial panics of the 1870s and had to settle with his creditors for twenty cents on the dollar, Smith some years later gave a banquet for his creditors. Under each plate was a check for the full amount owed to each, even though his legal obligations had already been fulfilled.

Thomas Smith was succeeded by his son-in-law, Frank W. Foy, who had started in the company as bookkeeper. He served as president from 1896 until his death in 1914, and was succeeded by his wife, Ella Smith Foy. She moved the company to its current location at 288 Grove Street and ran it until 1937, when she was succeeded by her son-in-law, William M. Mill. Mill, who had been manager since 1920, served as president from 1937 to 1964.

*Thomas Smith — blacksmith, handyman, self-taught engineer — founded Thomas Smith Company in 1854 and guided it until his death in 1896.*

Over the years, the company has expanded its sales and services beyond the textile industry, adapting to whatever changes the industrial revolution brought. It provides metal stampings for the electronic, computer, and high-technology industries, as well as for more traditional lines. A press designed and built by Thomas Smith, somewhat modified over the years, was used in daily production until 1978, when it was well over a century old.

Most of the firm's customers are located in New England, within 150 miles of the plant. A typical New England industry, Thomas Smith Company has remained small and flexible. In 1980, under the guidance of the present owner and president, Philip A. Peterson, the firm employs sixty-five people.

# WACHUSETT WIRE COMPANY, INC.

Wachusett Wire Company, Inc., was started on June 18, 1948, by George A. Jacobson. As foreman at Johnson Steel and Wire Company, he had been in the wire business since he was seventeen and had extensive experience in the field.

Beginning with three used Waterbury drawing machines, Jacobson energetically expanded operations. The first company headquarters, on McKeon Road, soon proved too small, so the business was moved to 35 Hermon Street within six months. Growth continued, and by 1953, Wachusett Wire was incorporated. In 1956, it moved to its current location at 641 Cambridge Street.

Wachusett Wire has grown from a tiny business into a sophisticated corporation, which sells both nationally and internationally. It has 216 wire-drawing machines, plus furnaces, die-making machines, and respooling facilities. It is essentially a fine wire redraw mill with wire sizes ranging from .032 to .004 annealed wire, and from .020 to .003 drawn wire. Wire is supplied both hard-drawn and annealed, and all wire is put on different-sized spools.

The company also makes fishing wire of stainless steel and monel wire, in 20-pound to 75-pound test, for deep-sea fishing. Fine wire is produced in stainless steel, inconel, monel, and aluminum. Bobbin-bound wire of multiple ends is put up on braider spools for the weaving industry. Wire for the manufacture of cables, sponges, jewelry, and knitted and woven products are among the company's lines.

On September 1, 1978, Wachusett Wire's majority stock was purchased by Jacobson, his two sons-in-law, and their families. Sandra Jacobson Heeps serves as clerk and director and her husband Richard A. Heeps, who has been with the firm since 1958, is president and director in charge of production. Karen Jacobson Wyman is vice-president and director, and her husband, Kenneth P. Wyman, is treasurer and director in charge of the nonproduction aspects of the business.

The founder and driving force behind the company, George A. Jacobson, has served as chairman of

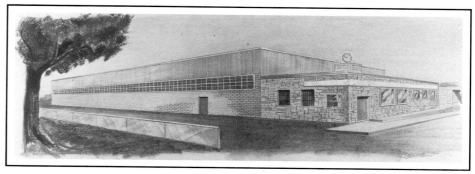

*Above*
*This Cambridge Street site became home for Wachusett Wire in 1956.*
*Left*
*Founder George A. Jacobson poses with Wachusett Wire Company's first wire-drawing machine.*
*Right*
*The company had a modest beginning in this small building on McKeon Road.*

the board since 1948. Katherine Jacobson retired in 1976 after twenty-six years as the company's bookkeeper. The business she and her husband started together now employs twenty-five people and looks forward to many productive years in Worcester.

# THE WHITE & BAGLEY COMPANY

The White & Bagley Company began in 1888 at the dawn of the automobile era, three years after Karl Benz of Germany invented the first workable internal-combustion engine. That device helped to propel the development of the machine age, with its demand for thousands of specialized products, including all types of lubricants.

The company was founded by Herbert P. Bagley, then only twenty-one years old, and his brother-in-law, Frederick W. White. With a combined capital of $300, they commenced business in a small barn on Woodland Street. In 1894, White resigned and Bagley bought the site on Foster Street, where the company is still located today. Bagley once stated that his aim was to "specialize and pioneer" in oils and lubricants, and that goal has never changed.

Bagley himself was an indefatigable experimenter, constantly mixing batches of oils and lubricants tailored for specific industrial demands. In 1905, the company began to market "Oilzum," one of the first brand-name motor oils. The new product took the risk and guesswork out of car lubrication. Oilzum is still marketed and enjoys the same excellent reputation today that it has since it was first introduced.

In 1907, White & Bagley, in cooperation with Norton Company, developed the first lubricant for wet-grinding. Designed as a coolant as well as a lubricant, the new compound was used to grind the rolls for

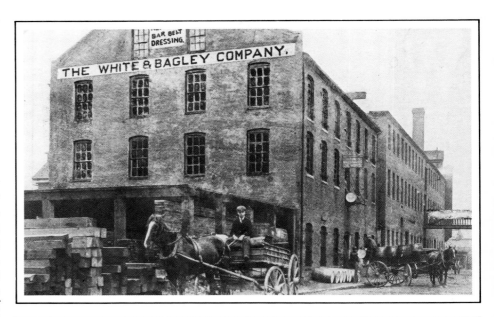

*Top*
*Although the original building is still recognizable and still serves as headquarters for White & Bagley, the structure has been supplemented by many additions.*
*Bottom*
*A modern blending and packaging plant was recently built.*

the locks of the Panama Canal, then undergoing construction. During World War I, the lubricant was utilized to grind military projectiles, and it was later used to grind parts of Lindbergh's *Spirit of St. Louis.*

The depression of the 1930s dealt White & Bagley a severe blow when the major gasoline companies told their service stations to sell only house brands of motor oil. That edict eliminated 90 percent of the firm's outlets for Oilzum. But the company survived without laying off a single worker. When their were no orders to

fill, employees were given brooms and paintbrushes to clean and renovate the plant.

Herbert Bagley died in 1952 and the presidency was assumed by his son, Edwin G. Bagley. He, in turn, has been succeeded by his son, H. Prescott Bagley II. Edwin G. Bagley continues to serve as treasurer. In 1980, he marked his fifty-seventh year of company service.

Although the company headquarters have been located in the same building since 1894, the establishment has been expanded until it covers a city block. Further expansion took place in 1969 with the purchase in Detroit of a plant and equipment with capabilities similar to the Worcester operation. A branch factory in Los Angeles helps to serve the western demand for White & Bagley products.

# WIRE AND METAL SEPARATIONS, INC.

At the dawn of this century, in 1900, Bernard Cotton started a junk and scrap business in Worcester. Cotton, an immigrant from Lithuania, traveled countless miles through Worcester County with his horse and wagon, collecting metal, rags, paper, and anything else that could be salvaged and resold.

That original enterprise was called Bennie Cotton, Inc., and it continued to be known as such for many years. Its first location was on Harding Street. In 1920, the company moved to Southbridge Street, not far from the current location of Wire and Metal Separations, Inc., its corporate descendant. It moved to its current location on Southbridge Street in 1932.

In the ensuing years, Cotton was joined in the business by his sons, Louis, Bennie, and Maurice. They expanded operations by buying trucks, a baling press for junked automobile bodies, derricks, electrical magnets, and the other heavy equipment that a modern salvage system requires.

Bernard Cotton died in 1942. Wallace and David Cotton, Bernard's grandsons, joined the business about that time. They established the first copper recycling operation in Massachusetts, an achievement that grew in importance as metals became scarcer and more expensive. The operation processes insulated copper wire through a completely mechanized system, and recovers the copper without causing pollution, an important consideration. Lawrence Cotton has represented the fourth generation of

the family-owned business since he joined the firm in the 1970s.

Wire and Metal Separations, Inc., keeping pace with technological developments, has entered the field of exotic alloys and has installed sophisticated equipment to identify and analyze space-age metals and alloys. A sensitive computer can identify all of the components of a load of scrap at the touch of a button.

The company continues to expand with the burgeoning recycling industry, contributing both to the nation's economic self-sufficiency and to Worcester's prosperity. David Cotton is president of the firm and Wallace Cotton is vice-president and treasurer.

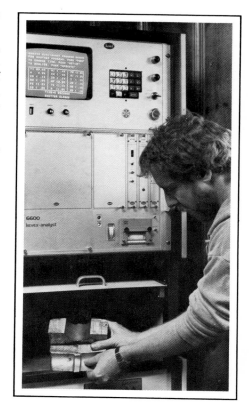

*Right*
*This computer-analyzer separates alloys and space-age metals from base metals. It can identify up to eighteen elements in five seconds.*
*Below*
*Scrap steel is prepared in the yard by means of shears, torch cutters, and cranes.*

# WORCESTER AREA CHAMBER OF COMMERCE

On December 15, 1873, a group of prominent businessmen met at the Bay State House to establish the Worcester Business Exchange. The following year it was renamed the Worcester Board of Trade, and in 1913 it merged with the Merchants Association to form the Chamber of Commerce. The goal from the start was to represent and promote business in the Worcester area.

In its early years, the organization busied itself combating such problems as high fuel prices and the lack of local emergency medical treatment. During the first World War, it housed the War Savings Campaign, the County Food Administration, and the Worcester Fuel Committee, which processed 10,000 emergency fuel orders and obtained 100,000 cords of wood to back up tight coal supplies.

After the war, the Chamber organized bureaus for industrial development, foreign trade, merchandising problems, traffic control, and several other areas. It helped promote the construction of the Lake Quinsigamond Bridge, pressed for a decrease in telephone fees, and helped bring to Worcester the Bancroft Hotel, one of the then-largest hotels in the Northeast.

The Chamber moved in 1926 to a new building at 32 Franklin Street, where it remained for many years. It now is located across the Common in Mechanics Tower.

The organization has steadily expanded its services, not only to business and industry, but to the community as a whole. The Chamber's Economic Development Department staffs the Worcester Business Development Corporation, which created the Higgins, Goddard, Gold Star, Holden, and Worcester Airport industrial parks. The Chamber has helped make available $40 million in business financing in recent years. Its Convention and Visitors Bureau works to bring major conventions to the area, and its Central Massachusetts Tourist Council actively promotes the various attractions of the region. The Chamber is working with the city of Worcester on administering an Urban Development Action Grant to rebuild and revitalize North Main Street with the addition of a new hotel.

In 1980, the Chamber outlined its future goals for the community. They include the creation of more jobs, the conservation and increase of resources, and the bettering of Worcester as a place to live and work.

Although the Chamber's priorities have evolved with the passage of time, its fundamental goal remains unchanged — to strive for a better Worcester tomorrow, today.

*Left*
*The elegantly redesigned Common and the new $130-million Worcester Center, with its office buildings and galleria housing 100 stores, are symbols of the Worcester of the 1980s.*

*Right*
*Higgins Industrial Park is one of several that the Chamber has helped to develop through the Worcester Business Development Corporation.*

# WORCESTER COUNTY NATIONAL BANK

Although the 1800 Census counted 2,411 people in Worcester, a respectable number for an inland town in that era, the community had no bank. Trade and commerce were carried on largely by barter, with little money changing hands. Daniel Waldo, later first president of the Worcester Bank, accepted eggs and hay in exchange for nails and windows at his hardware store. It was a cumbersome system.

On a cold December evening in 1803, "an association of gentlemen," including Daniel Waldo and Isaiah Thomas, met at Barker's Tavern to plan the incorporation of a "country bank." On March 8, 1804, after 1,500 shares had been sold at $100 each, the bank was chartered by the Massachusetts Legislature with a capitalization of $150,000. That day, and for sixty years after, the chief function of the Worcester Bank was to loan and issue money in the form of bank notes. Securing money on deposit was a much later idea.

In 1864, the Worcester Bank became the Worcester National Bank, "an association for banking purposes under the laws of the United States." In April 1917, the name was changed again to the Worcester Bank and Trust Company; in 1935, to the Worcester County Trust Company; and in 1959, to the Worcester County National Bank.

Since its establishment, the bank's history has been intertwined with the history of Worcester. As the product of thirty-six mergers and consolidations over the years, its story is a large

part of the city's banking chronicle.

Firmly rooted in the past, Worcester County National continues to grow and contribute to the economy of Massachusetts. Its new headquarters, at 446 Main Street, opened in 1974 and stands as a striking vote of confidence in the future of downtown Worcester.

By 1980, Worcester County National had assets of $692 million.

With thirty-two banking centers located in Worcester County, it is the lead bank of Worcester Bancorp, Inc., a $900-million asset, multibank holding company with other subsidiaries in Amherst, Greenfield, Marlboro, and Orleans. Through the holding company's form of organization, the scope of the original bank, which started with $150,000 in capital, now provides full-service banking to five Massachusetts counties and is backed by a capital base in excess of $46 million.

*Top*
*The first president of the Worcester Bank was Daniel Waldo, Sr. (1724-1808).*
*Left*
*John D. Hunt is the current president of the bank.*
*Right*
*Worcester County National Bank's new headquarters rise dramatically over downtown Worcester.*

# WORCESTER CONSORTIUM FOR HIGHER EDUCATION

Founded in 1968, the Worcester Consortium for Higher Education is a cooperative association of ten area colleges which have full membership, and ten institutions with associate memberships. Higher education is a major Worcester industry, employing 4,800 people full time, 800 part time, and generating an estimated $157 million a year in college, student, and visitor expenditures.

## Anna Maria College

Anna Maria College opened in 1946 in temporary quarters in a section of St. Ann Academy in Marlboro. In 1953, it moved onto its new campus in Paxton, where eight new buildings were built over the next sixteen years. In April 1980, the Sisters of St. Ann, which had governed the college since its founding, dissolved all legal ties with Anna Maria and appointed a 24-member board of trustees to run the college.

Anna Maria is a coeducational institution committed to the principle of quality liberal arts education in the Christian tradition. It offers liberal arts and career-oriented undergraduate courses, as well as graduate programs.

## Assumption College

In 1904, Assumption College was founded by the Augustinians of the Assumption to prepare Franco-American men for further studies leading to the priesthood.

The college began conferring bachelor degrees in 1917. For the next thirty-five years, it offered a unique bilingual education, with admission limited to men fluent in French. Since 1952, all courses except foreign languages have been taught in English.

Women were first admitted in 1969, and now constitute half of the 1,400 undergraduate students. Today, this Catholic liberal arts college offers graduate degrees in fourteen areas, and operates a growing Center for Continuing and Professional Education.

## Becker Junior College

With campuses in Leicester and Worcester, Becker Junior College enrolls students from nearly every eastern state, as well as from several foreign countries.

Becker opened in 1887, became coeducational in 1969, and merged with Leicester Junior College in 1974. Since this consolidation began, new academic programs in physical-therapist assisting, horticulture, veterinary assisting, and travel services were added to the curriculum. Enrollments have increased every year for the past five years at Becker, where students are attracted by the unique academic program, small classes, and a reputation for teaching excellence.

## Central New England College

Located in the heart of Worcester, Central New England College began in 1888 as the educational division of the YMCA. Consisting of Worcester Junior College and the Central New England College of Technology, the college offers associate degrees in such fields as applied technology, management, aviation, computer science, humanities, pre-law, and engineering. Bachelor degrees are offered in engineering technology, industrial distribution and management, and management and technology.

This coeducational institution provides for reductions in tuition based on students' grade point averages, and requires all students to study economics before graduation.

# Clark University

In 1887, Jonas G. Clark founded Clark University, the second graduate school in the United States. Female graduate students were admitted in 1900, male undergraduates in 1902, and female undergraduates in 1942. G. Stanley Hall, the university's first president, established Clark's worldwide reputation in psychology. Wallace W. Atwood, the second president, did the same in geography.

A liberal arts college and university, Clark offers thirty-one undergraduate programs, eighteen masters programs, and ten doctoral programs. It has an enrollment of about 1,900 undergraduates and 400 graduate students, with a student body drawn from around the world. Clark is a founding member of the Association of American Universities.

# Holy Cross

The College of the Holy Cross was founded in 1843 by the Most Reverend Benedict J. Fenwick, the second Bishop of Boston. It is the oldest Catholic college in New England, offering a liberal arts education in the Jesuit tradition to 2,500 undergraduate men and women from thirty-six states and six foreign countries. The bachelor of arts curriculum includes fifteen majors, plus academic internships available through independent study projects with the Office of Special Studies.

In 1972, the college admitted women, who now compose about 45 percent of the student population. The recently renovated Dinand Library has 365,000 volumes and 2,270 periodicals available to students at all Worcester Consortium schools.

# Quinsigamond College

Founded in 1963, Quinsigamond, the second largest institution in the Worcester Consortium, enrolls 2,000 day and 3,500 evening students each semester. In addition to offering high-quality traditional liberal arts programs at low tuition, the college continuously assesses its mission to assure its responsiveness to community needs in furthering the quality of life in the greater Worcester community. Its developmental education program, through outreach centers, strives to meet the needs of the minority and educationally disadvantaged population. The college's Center for Lifelong Learning, with four extension centers, offers a wide variety of courses as well as student support and counseling services.

# University of Massachusetts Medical Center

The University of Massachusetts Medical School, created by an act of the legislature in 1962, opened with its first class of sixteen students in September 1970 in temporary quarters. The new medical school building opened three years later, and the ajoining teaching hospital received its first patients in January 1976.

Today, the University of Massachusetts Medical Center includes the Medical School, the University Teaching Hospital, and programs for educational and service programs in health care throughout the state. In addition to the degree in medicine, the Medical School offers a Ph.D. in medical sciences and provides clinical training to approximately 500 allied health students each year.

# Worcester Polytechnic Institute

Worcester Polytechnic Institute, founded in 1865, is the nation's third oldest engineering college. WPI's competency-based academic program, implemented in 1971, represents a significant departure from the traditional engineering curriculum.

The goal of the WPI Plan is to integrate the broadening influence of the humanities into a technological curriculum to educate men and women sensitive to the social implications of their professional work. Part of their educational experience involves solving real-world problems in the surrounding community. WPI also conducts an extensive continuing education program to serve the graduate study needs of working professionals throughout central New England.

# Worcester State College

The college began as a normal school in 1874 to train teachers. In 1932, it became Worcester State Teachers College, awarding bachelor degrees in education.

In 1960, it became a multipurpose institution offering a wide variety of liberal arts and professional career programs. Today, it is the largest four-year institution of higher learning in the city, serving 3,000 full-time day students and 6,000 part-time evening students. Worcester State offers undergraduate, graduate, and continuing education, as well as community service. These four general divisions are housed on a 62-acre campus located in the residential section of Chandler Street.

# ORCESTER HAHNEMANN HOSPITAL

On June 26, 1896, the Commonwealth of Massachusetts granted a charter to the Worcester Hahnemann Hospital "for the purpose of the care and treatment of the sick, suffering and injured upon the principles of Homeopathy." Homeopathy is a system of medical care developed by German physician Samuel Christian Frederick Hahnemann (1775-1843) advocating the treatment of disease with simple drugs capable of producing symptoms of an illness, or removing similar symptoms produced by other causes.

Homeopaths were not admitted to practice in every hospital, but at Hahnemann all qualified physicians, including homeopaths, were welcomed. As homeopathy declined in popularity, physicians practicing more generally accepted systems of care succeeded the homeopaths.

The hospital was first located on Providence Street, on land deeded to Dr. John K. Warren by Mrs. Elizabeth Colburn. Dr. Warren, who had opened his Warren Surgical Hospital in 1893 at 78 Pleasant Street, became the first president of Worcester Hahnemann. The hospital Auxiliary, consisting of twenty-one women headed by Mrs. Warren, was founded in 1897.

In 1908, David Hale Fanning presented the J.R. Roche estate at 281 Lincoln Street to the hospital. The cornerstone for the new facility was laid in December, and the building with 35 beds began serving patients on November 1, 1909. The south wing

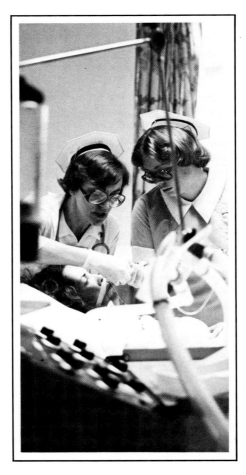

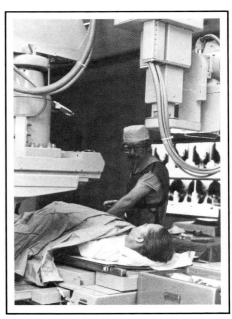

*Above*
*The very active Radiology Department at Worcester Hahnemann Hospital provides services and general radiology, fluoroscopy, nuclear medicine, and ultrasound.*
*Left*
*A patient receives special nursing attention in the intensive care unit.*

was built in 1923, after a $350,000 fund drive, bringing the number of beds to 100.

In the 1930s, the hospital increased its beds to 150. During U.S. involvement in World War II, Hahnemann's strong nursing school, established in 1906, educated record numbers of nurses, many of whom served in the U.S. Cadet Nurse Corps.

When a devastating tornado struck Worcester on June 9, 1953, the Hahnemann medical and nursing staffs, in limited emergency facilities, treated more than 250 victims.

A $2-million fund drive in 1969 provided for a decade of spectacular growth. In 1972, the McEvoy Building was opened to accommodate, with modernized existing buildings, services in family-centered maternity and pediatrics, medical-surgical, in-

tensive and coronary care, and expanded ambulatory and emergency services.

The following year the hospital helped organize the Great Brook Valley Health Center, and in 1975 opened the Hahnemann Family Health Center to provide comprehensive ambulatory health services for entire families, as well as to train resident physicians in family practice medicine. The hospital assumed responsibility in 1980 for the Hahnemann Rehabilitation Center at 535 Lincoln Street, the most comprehensive not-for-profit rehabilitation unit in central Massachusetts.

By 1980, Worcester Hahnemann Hospital had a medical staff of more than 290 physicians practicing 38 medical and surgical specialties. More than 11,000 patients were being admitted yearly, in addition to 75,000 ambulatory and emergency visits.

# WORCESTER HISTORICAL MUSEUM

In January 1875, Daniel Seagrave, Richard O'Flynn, John G. Smith, and Franklin P. Rice received a letter from Samuel E. Staples that said, in part, "It has been proposed to form a Society for the purpose of increasing an interest in Archaeological science, and to rescue from oblivion such historical matter as would otherwise be lost . . ." This letter was the seed of what was first called the Worcester Society of Antiquity, later the Worcester Historical Society, and, since 1978, the Worcester Historical Museum.

It was not the first Worcester organization devoted to preserving the past. The American Antiquarian Society had been started by Isaiah Thomas in 1812. The AAS was an exclusive group, however, dedicated primarily to cataloging and preserving newspapers and printed matter. The Worcester Society of Antiquity was interested in local history and artifacts.

The society grew slowly at first. It had 37 members when it was legally incorporated in 1877, but by 1885 it numbered 160 members, boasted a library of 18,000 titles, and had assembled 3,000 pages of unpublished local history. It was rapidly outgrowing its two rented rooms on Foster Street.

In 1889, Stephen Salisbury III, benefactor of so many of Worcester's institutions, donated land at Wheaton Square and $25,000 for a building. It was dedicated on November 24, 1891, and reportedly cost nearly $50,000. The building remained largely unchanged until 1963, when a three-story addition with an elevator was built.

Since the beginning, through boom and depression, through war and peace, the museum has steadily amassed a vast quantity of books,

*Left*
*Among the items in the collections of the museum is this 1843 patent printer manufactured by the firm of Ethan Allen and Charles Thurber.*
*Right*
*The Worcester Historical Museum's building was dedicated in 1891.*

pamphlets, handbills, costumes, furniture, shoes, paintings, tools, musical instruments, and artifacts of every description. Indeed, by 1973, the years of haphazard accumulation had clogged the building with so much uncataloged material that the museum was closed for a year while staff and volunteers sorted each artifact to determine what should remain. That was the start of a systematized effort to augment and catalog the museum's collection. The library, with more than 50,000 volumes, was given larger quarters and was gradually organized into a first-class research facility.

William D. Wallace, a professional museum administrator, became director in 1976. Since then, the museum has mounted periodic and elaborate exhibits, hosted lectures on historical topics, made important acquisitions, attracted a steady flow of dedicated volunteers, and secured new funding.

In 1980, the trustees signed an agreement with the Salisbury Mansion Associates assigning the museum the responsibility of developing the Salisbury Mansion into a museum furnished in the style of the 1830 to 1850 period. It was a mark of the esteem felt by the community for the revitalized Worcester Historical Museum.

# WORCESTER TELEGRAM & GAZETTE, INC.

Worcester's newspaper history began with a rattle of drums when Isaiah Thomas, youthful patriot, printer, and gadfly, sneaked his handpress out of Boston under the noses of the British redcoats in April 1775. On May 3, the first Worcester edition of the *Massachusetts Spy* appeared, complete with a heart-wringing account of the Battle of Lexington.

Although today's Worcester newspapers cannot claim direct lineage from the *Spy,* which folded in 1904, they have deep roots in Worcester's journalistic history. The *Evening Gazette,* launched as the *Worcester Evening Gazette* on January 1, 1866, is the senior survivor of an era of numerous Worcester newspapers. It was a continuation of the *Evening Transcript,* founded as a morning paper in 1851 and bought from Caleb Wall by Charles A. Chase and Dr. S.B. Bartholomew, a Woonsocket dentist, in 1865.

They were an odd couple — Chase, a conservative and member of one of Worcester's leading families, and Bartholomew, something of a radical populist. In 1869, he gave up and resumed his dental practice in Woonsocket. After a period of reorganization, Chase brought in Charles H. Doe from the *Boston Daily Advertiser.* Doe edited the *Gazette* for the next twenty-seven years until he retired in 1896 and was succeeded by David B. Howland of Springfield.

The *Gazette* was sold to two young men from New Haven, John Day

Jackson and George F. Booth, in 1899. Jackson, later publisher and owner of the *New Haven Register,* never was active in Worcester. But Booth was to wield power in Worcester journalism for the next fifty-five years, with only a brief hiatus from 1920 to 1925.

The *Telegram* sprang from the mind and energy of one man, Austin P. Cristy, who at thirty-three left his post as assistant clerk of the Central District Court, borrowed $300, and started the *Worcester Sunday Telegram* on November 30, 1884. His *Worcester Daily Telegram* appeared May 19, 1886.

His publications fit the Hearst-Pulitzer mold of "yellow journalism." Cristy covered crime, sports, political corruption, and personal scandal in a splashy way, reveling in gory details. He made sensational charges against public figures and carried on lively feuds with those who disagreed with him.

Although many deplored A.P. Cristy and his doings, he was extremely successful. Circulation for both the daily and the Sunday papers mounted spectacularly. By the turn of the century, he was threatening to crowd out both the *Gazette* and the *Spy.* The *Gazette* was saved by the efforts and imagination of George F. Booth, but the *Spy* — venerable and respected — succumbed in 1904, after a disastrous fire and years of declining circulation. For the next fifteen years, the *Telegram,* the *Gazette,* and the *Worcester Evening Post* fought a running battle for circulation.

Theodore T. Ellis, former foreman of the *Telegram* pressroom, became the next personality to enter the field. An inventive genius who had made a fortune with a new type of fiber press blanket, Ellis startled Worcester when he bought the *Telegram* from Cristy for a reported $1 million on November 18, 1919. Roland F. Andrews was his editor. Ellis shocked the community again a year later, on

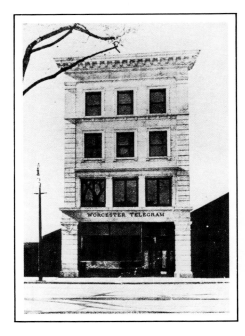

*Above*
The Telegram *emanated from this austere structure in 1910.*
*Below*
*Austin P. Cristy practiced a Hearst-like form of "yellow journalism" at the* Worcester Telegram *in the late 1800s.*

December 31, 1920, when he purchased the *Gazette.* Five years later, on September 23, 1925, he purchased Worcester's only active radio station, WCTS, from the C.T.

Sherer department store, renaming it WTAG.

Then, on December 5, 1925, he surprised the city again by selling the whole package to the Worcester Telegram Publishing Company, whose principals were George F. Booth and Harry G. Stoddard. Stoddard, president of Wyman-Gordon and one of Worcester's most active civic leaders, had known Booth for years. He became president of the new company, and Booth became editor and publisher, holding both posts until his death in 1955. During his second newspaper career, Booth became one of the best-known newspaper figures in New England and beyond.

In 1938, after a losing circulation battle, the *Worcester Evening Post* was sold to the Worcester Telegram Publishing Company. In 1968, the *Marlboro Enterprise* and the *Hudson Daily Sun* were also acquired by the company. Since 1938, Worcester has had one morning paper, one evening paper, and one Sunday paper, all published by the same, locally owned company. Since 1775, all Worcester newspapers have been locally owned.

After Booth's death at the age of

*Left*
*George F. Booth bought the* Worcester Gazette *with John D. Jackson in 1899, sold it in 1920, and reacquired it with Harry G. Stoddard in 1925.*
*Right*
*Today the* Worcester Telegram *and the* Gazette *are produced in this modern facility on Franklin Street.*

eighty-five, Forrest W. Seymour was appointed editor; Howard M. Booth, publisher; and Richard C. Steele, general manager. Steele became associate publisher in 1957, publisher in 1961, and, after Howard Booth's retirement in 1963, president and publisher. Robert W. Stoddard succeeded his father as chairman of the board. Robert C. Achorn became editor in 1970, on the retirement of Seymour.

As is the case with all newspapers, the Worcester newspapers have undergone more technological changes in the past twenty years than they had in the eighty years preceding. Steele's main task was to guide the company from the age of linotypes, hot lead, and iron chases to the era of computers, photographic negatives, plastic plates, and pasteups. This required significant changes in the

workload, including the elimination of some whole job categories, notably stereotypers. These complex changes posed challenges to established composing room procedures and union rules and were not easily effected.

The concept of journalism also continues to evolve. Achorn, a careful student of the newspaper business, has put increased emphasis on local news coverage, interpretive background reporting, news analysis, and informed editorial comment. But he also has noted the obstacles that are put in the way of comprehensive reporting by some judges, court officials, and public office holders, not to mention libel laws. For all the technical progress in hardware and software, the news business is still a human enterprise, limited by human fallibilities but inspired by the human determination to help and to inform.

As the Worcester newspapers head down the final lap of the twentieth century and look toward the twenty-first, they have reason for confidence. With a *Telegram* circulation of more than 55,000, a *Gazette* circulation of more than 85,000 and a *Sunday Telegram* circulation of more than 110,000, the papers blanket the central part of the state and also sell well in northeastern Connecticut.

For all the print that has flowed in the past century or more, the Worcester newspapers still see their task as primarily one of community service. As Steele said a few years ago: "It is the responsibility of newspapers to do for the public what it doesn't have the time or faculties to do for itself — gather information, select that which is important, and present it to the reader."

That echoes the editorial that ran in the very first *Gazette* ever published: "We will furnish our readers with the news of the day, local and general, fully, promptly, and impartially." The techniques change; the goals remain the same.

# WYMAN-GORDON COMPANY

Almost a century has passed since 1883, when two young graduates of Worcester Polytechnic Institute, Win Wyman and Lyman Gordon, started a forging business on Bradley Street in Worcester. Their first advertisement, in January 1884, announced: "Iron and Steel Drop Forgings. Parts of machines of all kinds, firearms, machine tools, carriage, agricultural, hardware, etc." It was an ambitious start. For the first few years, however, the main business of the new company was forging parts for looms manufactured by Crompton & Knowles.

In 1887, Wyman and Gordon hired a promising 18-year-old, George Fuller, as bookkeeper. Fuller soon became a driving force in the development of the company and in the forging business in general. He became general manager in 1912, president in 1916, and chairman in 1931.

One of Fuller's proudest boasts was that he hired Harry G. Stoddard as vice-president and general sales manager in 1911. Stoddard worked closely with Fuller in guiding the company through the critical years of both world wars and into the postwar period. He served as president of the company from 1931 to 1955 and as chairman of the board from 1955 to 1967. He was succeeded by his son, Robert W. Stoddard, president from 1955 to 1967, chairman from 1967 to 1972, and honorary chairman since 1972.

With the dawn of the motoring age, Wyman-Gordon Company commenced the production of technically advanced forgings for transportation applications. The skills developed over the decades in forging crankshafts and other components have served the firm well in building its reputation as the industry leader.

The maiden flight of the Wright Brothers opened up a new field that the company was quick to enter. Wyman-Gordon forged its first aircraft part in 1916. During World War I, when aircraft suddenly became important as military weapons, Wyman-Gordon was among the first to meet the new stringent requirements for forgings fashioned to hitherto unknown tolerances and specifications. Wyman-Gordon forgings were in Lindbergh's airplane engine in 1927, when the *Spirit of St. Louis* made its epochal flight from New York to Paris. From those days to the present, Wyman-Gordon has never relinquished its leadership in forgings for aerospace applications.

World War II brought new demands. The need for larger and more complex aircraft parts made from lighter alloys and forged on large presses emerged. Once again, Wyman-Gordon responded to the challenge. Late in the war, the government asked the company to build and operate a plant in North Grafton containing presses larger than any others in the world. Experimental production began in 1946. By 1955, one 35,000-ton press and one 50,000-ton press were put into operation. The 50,000-ton press is still the largest of its kind in the free world.

Development and research in the increasingly sophisticated field of forgings has continued and now includes areas such as powder metal technology and microstructural control.

In 1974, Wyman-Gordon made the far-reaching decision to build an entirely new crankshaft forging plant at Danville, Illinois. This plant, utilizing a 16,000-ton screw press and other sophisticated equipment and techniques, will represent a capital investment of almost $50 million when current plans to double its capacity are completed.

*Below*
*The "knuckle gang," shown here around the turn of the century, forged parts called knuckles used in coupling systems on railway cars.*
*Right*
*Wyman-Gordon's plant at North Grafton contains a press rated at 50,000 tons.*

Wyman-Gordon has three plants in its eastern division, at Worcester, Millbury, and Grafton; two in its midwestern division, at Harvey and Danville, Illinois; four subsidiaries in other parts of the United States and in Brazil; and three affiliated companies, in Bombay, Mexico City, and Sao Paulo. Among the non-forging operations is Rome Industries, Inc., which designs and manufactures heavy-duty equipment attachments used for land development, agriculture, construction, and forestry. The company has approximately 5,000 employees and 2,000 stockholders. It is listed among the 500 largest industrial companies in the United States by *Fortune* magazine.

The company's forging sales represent more than 10 percent of total sales made by the entire forging industry. Wyman-Gordon parts are found in many types of industrial and military machinery, from submarines to power generators. At its Millbury plant, the firm conducts the most sophisticated research and development program in the forging industry.

In early 1980, John R. Bullock, group vice-president in charge of forging, was elected president and chief operating officer. Joseph R. Carter is chairman and chief executive officer; he was elected president in 1967 and chief executive officer in 1972.

# WRIGHT LINE INC.

In January 1934, Wright and Company was organized on the strength of one man's idea and ingenuity. E. Stanley Wright, then with Riley Stoker Corporation, had been reading about a new record-processing method marketed by IBM. The system involved punching holes into odd-sized cards and putting the cards through machines that read the holes, did calculations, and printed out tabulated results. Wright also knew that no company, including IBM, was manufacturing an index or guide for the cards.

Working in his Shrewsbury home basement with only one employee, his wife, Alice, Wright started experimenting with cardboard, celluloid, a paper cutter, and an electric iron. His first catalog and price list included fifteen vertical guides and eight horizontal guides. Gradually the business expanded. During World War II, when steel was scarce, a woodworking plant headed by a brother, Henry, made files and indexes out of wood. Some of them were still in use almost fifty years later. The plant reverted to metal production as soon as the war ended.

The firm soon outgrew its first office, in the State Mutual Building on Main Street, and the company moved to 100 Exchange Street, with manufacturing operations on Commercial Street. In 1954, a new plant was opened on Gold Star Boulevard and the entire firm relocated there two years later.

Wright, founder and spearhead of the company, died in September 1959, shortly after the company's twenty-fifth anniversary. In September 1960, the board of directors, under the chairmanship of R. Perry Collins,

*Above*
*E. Stanley Wright guided the firm through its first quarter-century.*
*Below*
*The Wright Line plant was one of the earliest to be built on Gold Star Boulevard in 1954.*

voted to merge with Barry Controls, Inc., of Watertown, Massachusetts, to form the Barry Wright Corporation.

The next twenty years produced rapid growth and a steady development of new products. The Gold Star File was put on the market in 1960, the Disk Pack data storage system and the Tape-Seal® computer tape filing system in 1965, the Databank™ safe line for the protection of magnetic media records shortly thereafter, the Optimedia® Filing cabinet line in 1972, and the Docu-Mate® filing system in 1975.

During this period, the company expanded its warehouse space at Gold Star Boulevard and, in 1967, acquired the ElectroMechanics Corporation in High Point, North Carolina, a manufacturer of card punches. Direct sales operations were established in West Germany in the 1970s.

E. William Housh became president of the company in 1971. Under his leadership Wright Line has expanded its product line and the markets it serves.

From E. Stanley Wright's basement in 1934, Wright Line has grown into an international enterprise, employing 1,000 people, half of them in Worcester, and serving 150,000 customers with more than 1,000 different products. The firm operates from the five locations in the Worcester area, with space totaling approximately 370,000 square feet.

# Index

## Suggestions For Further Reading

The first *History of Worcester* was written by William Lincoln in 1836 and was reprinted in 1862 by Charles Hersey. In 1919, Charles Nutt's *History of Worcester and Its People* was published. These books have long been out of print and are not generally available for purchase. The Worcester Society of Antiquity, the predecessor of the Worcester Historical Museum, had an active program of publishing Worcester's records for many years. Their bulletins contain much useful information. All of these works, plus many more, are available in the library of the Worcester Historical Museum. They also have a large collection of manuscripts, prints, and photographs all relating to the history of Worcester.

The Worcester Free Public Library has a large collection of Worcester material. Their extensive clipping file is very useful.

The American Antiquarian Society has a large collection of material relating to Worcester, especially the early period.

## Acknowledgments

I would like to express my appreciation to the staff of the Worcester Historical Museum, who have put all their resources at my disposal while writing this book, and especially to the Assistant Librarian, Dorothy Gleason, to whom this book is dedicated.

To all those who have been left out because of the limitations of space I present my apologies. They are not forgotten. Their hard work and generosity have made Worcester the attractive and prosperous city it is today. If you would know them better look for their memorials all about you. Look for their histories in the library of the Worcester Historical Museum.

Margaret A. Erskine

THIS BOOK WAS SET IN CAMBRIDGE AND PALATINO TYPES,
PRINTED ON 80LB. ENAMEL AND BOUND BY WALSWORTH PUBLISHING COMPANY.
COVER & TEXT DESIGNED BY ALEXANDER D'ANCA
LAYOUT BY RANDY HIPKE, DAURI PALLAS, MELINDA WADE, AND LISA SHERER

# Designed to Win

Roger Marshall

# Designed to Win

W · W · NORTON & COMPANY
New York · London

Library of Congress Cataloging in Publication Data

Marshall, Roger.
  Designed to win.

  Bibliography: p.
  Includes index.
  1. Yacht–building.   2. Sailboats.   3. Yacht
racing.   I. Title.
VM331.M37      623.82′2      79–24406
ISBN 0–393–03229–9

1 2 3 4 5 6 7 8 9 0

# Contents

# Foreword

As anyone who has sailed for any length of time knows, deck layouts have changed dramatically over the years. It has been interesting to observe this transition. Not too long ago, a competitor felt extremely fortunate to have perhaps one small ratchet winch on either side of the boat to help trim the biggest headsail and minimize the need to luff in order to get the sheets in. On a modern racing boat, in contrast, virtually every line has its own winch—except when, in the interest of efficiency, various lockoff devices are used to allow one winch to serve several lines efficiently.

Not only has the amount of equipment of a racing deck changed over the years, but the sophistication and capabilities of gear have altered too, in no small way. Take winch technology, for example. In general, winch sizes and power have gradually increased, first with the introduction of two-speed winches, later with three-speed, and also with pedestal-drive and modular linked winch systems that interconnect either on deck or below.

But although certain deck gear has undergone great strides in development, some of the basic problems of racing deck layout have not changed much at all. There still is, and always has been, the most profound relationship between what is feasible on deck and what is desirable below deck. Midship crew cockpits, for example, make handling on deck safer and more efficient, but they inevitably take a pretty big chunk out of what could be the largest area for accommodation. Trade-offs such as these can only be settled by establishing, for a particular owner, the relative importance of efficiency on deck versus comfort below.

In this book, Roger Marshall reviews some of the general trends that have taken place in ocean racing deck layout, much of the latest equipment available, and a number of critical and continuing problems that designers face in attempting to plan a deck for maximum efficiency. A unique combination of technical training, drafting and drawing ability, accompanied by a love of sailing and an opportunity to compete in top-level racing, provide the author with the necessary background to compile and present information which is of great use to all involved with the sport of sailing. Owners as well as crewmen, designers as well as builders, can all learn much from the study of this text and its illustrations.

Useful guidance is provided not only for laying out the deck of an ocean racer, but also for handling a sailboat under a wide variety of conditions. Even the most complex manoeuvres become relatively clear by virtue of the excellent interplay of text and drawings. The drawings reflect the virtue of careful planning. What's more, they allow the numerous possible design combinations to be carefully analyzed, so that basic decisions can be made in an orderly manner.

Congratulations to Roger Marshall for so clearly summarizing a great many of the choices that should be considered in the design stage.

Roderick Stephens Jr.

8

# Acknowledgements

Books–particularly first books–come into being for many different reasons. The initial impetus for this book is largely due to an old sailing friend, now editor, Jeremy Howard-Williams. It was he who, over more than a few beers in various Cowes watering holes, persuaded me to tackle the subject of ocean racing deck layouts. And it was he who had the patience to keep pushing me to the finish.

I have been very fortunate in writing this book that so many people–other designers, manufacturers' agents, and sailing friends–have been kind enough to share their knowledge of deck gear and deck layout with me. In particular, grateful thanks are due to Olin and Rod Stephens who have so generously allowed me to use the office files and drawings. My thanks, too, go to other members of the Sparkman & Stephens design staff, without whose help, both directly and indirectly, this book would have been so much the poorer. Of these, Chris Wick deserves special mention for his careful reading of the manuscript and his many helpful suggestions, as does Bruce McPherson for his good eye in reviewing drawings.

I also greatly appreciate the assistance given to me by the staff members of various manufacturers. Both Ian Nichols of Barient Winches and Steve Prime of North Sails were kind enough to read the manuscript and offer their excellent advice. And Dick Rath of Lewmar, Ian Godfrey of Hood Sails, Tim Stearn of Stearn Sailing Systems, and Ben Bradley of H. R. Spencer all supplied very valuable information in their areas of expertise.

Various designers have been extremely generous in allowing me to use some of their deck plans. They are Raymond Wall of Camper & Nicholson, Scott Kaufman, Gary Mull, Rob Mazza of C & C Design Group, Ron Holland, and German Frers.

A debt of gratitude must also go to Vera Miller and Gerry Barille who did so much of the typing in their spare time. And last, but certainly not least, thanks to my wife Mary without whose editorial skills, encouragement, and patience this book would never have made it to the publisher.

There are many others, of course, too numerous to mention, who have helped me to formulate my ideas on deck layouts and the best way to handle sails on an ocean racer. Usually, such a sharing of ideas has come while on watch during the small hours of the morning. To all of them, I give my thanks.

Roger Marshall

INTRODUCTION
# The Evolution of Racing Decks

The modern offshore racer has a long and fascinating history of development. The direction of its evolution, of course, has been greatly influenced by the various rating rules in effect over the years. Other factors, too, have influenced the pace of evolution. During most of the last century, improvements in racing yachts were introduced quite slowly. Not until the last few decades have innovations in all areas of yacht design accelerated to their present rate, where new ideas are seen at almost every major regatta.

One of the most important areas of change has been in deck gear and deck layout. Consider, for example, the deck plan of the racing yacht *Ghost*, designed in 1890, almost ninety years ago, and compare it with the deck of a modern ocean racer, *Sunbird V*. (See Figures Intro-2 and Intro-3.) The two boats are fairly close in size, *Ghost* being 46 feet 1 inch on the waterline and 60 feet overall, and *Sunbird V* 39 feet 6 inches LWL and 54 feet LOA. But there the similarity ends. *Ghost* has a displacement of 68,000 pounds, *Sunbird V* of 36,000. While *Sunbird* has a total of fifteen winches, *Ghost* with its larger sail area does not have one, unless the windlass is counted as a winch. *Ghost* also has no instruments, no sail tracks, no spinnaker gear, and no lifelines, in stark contrast to *Sunbird*.

This is not to denigrate *Ghost*, which was a product of her time and sailed as competitively as any of today's ocean racers. The intention here is simply to point out the vast strides that have been made in racing deck layout over the last hundred years. And what is even more impressive is the fact that many of these developments have been extremely recent. If you look at a boat like Fife's beautiful *Evenlode* designed in 1937 and a top British yacht until after World War II, you realize how little change in deck layouts had occurred since *Ghost*'s era. (See Figure Intro-1.) Although *Evenlode*, unlike *Ghost*, did have lifelines, two winches, and spinnaker gear, the simplicity of her deck was still a far cry from the complex and technologically advanced layouts of many of the very latest ocean racers.

With racing decks having reached their present level of sophistication, and with new innovations being introduced every year, deck design is no longer a job for the amateur. This does not mean, however, that the average owner or sailor should leave all decisions about deck layouts to the experts. Even if he cannot design a deck completely on his own, he should at least be familiar with the elements that go into making an efficient, modern deck so as to be able to discuss the various options knowledgeably with a designer. Only then can an owner be sure that the deck of his boat will be designed or modified with his particular needs in mind. And this, quite naturally, will increase both his enjoyment of sailing and his performance on the race course.

*Figure Intro-1.* Chris Ratsey's *Evenlode*, the lovely Fife-built 50-foot double ender, racing in the Solent in 1948. There are only two halyard winches and two sheet winches, the latter mounted on deck outside the cockpit coaming. The runners are operated via a system of pulleys, and sweated up by hand (levers were considered by the owner to be too dangerous). It would appear that the spinnaker pole is being topped up at the mast. No danger of broaching here. (*Photo Beken*)

## A Note on Reading a Drawing

Because deck and interior plans show three-dimensional objects on only two planes, they are often difficult to visualize. But a few simple techniques can help. Most important, always refer to the layout and the profile plans simultaneously to get a sense of both horizontal dimensions and depth. Imagine a winch, for example.

Viewed from above, as in a layout plan, the diameter of the winch is clearly apparent (drawing a), but one has virtually no idea of its depth. Only when the winch is viewed in profile (drawing b), is its height indicated. Now by mentally putting these two views together, one can imagine the winch as it would usually appear on a boat (drawing c).

Many other items on a boat, of course, are more difficult to visualize than a winch. But using this same technique, you can usually get a general idea of how much space an object will take up—both its length and width, and its height. From here it is only a short step to imagining that object as it actually would appear if you were standing on deck or in the interior below.

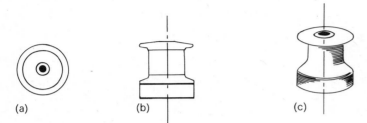

(a)    (b)    (c)

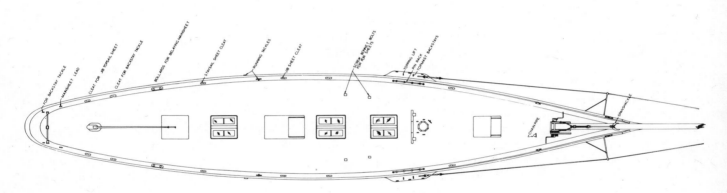

*Figure Intro-2.* Deck plan of the 20 rater *Ghost* designed by C. P. Clayton in 1890.

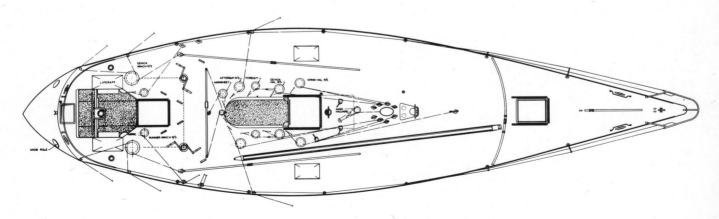

*Figure Intro-3.* Deck plan of Mr Tatsumitsu Yamasaki's *Sunbird V* designed by the author in 1974 when he was with Sparkman & Stephens.

12

# PART I

# The Background to Deck Design

Before a deck can be designed with any assurance that it will work efficiently, a person must be familiar with the techniques and equipment that will be used on the race course. The first part of this book is intended to help the average owner and sailor, or the novice designer, acquire this essential knowledge. As we will see, it is only by carefully evaluating each sailing operation and each piece of deck gear on board a modern ocean racer that improvements in deck layout are eventually made.

The chapters that follow review the basics of three factors that critically affect deck layout: sails and sail-handling techniques, deck gear, its proper use and maintenance, and the various racing rules. Where appropriate, these chapters also discuss the best of the most recent ideas that have emerged in these three key areas. When one has a thorough knowledge of this fundamental background to deck design, he can then begin the actual process of laying out an efficient, modern deck.

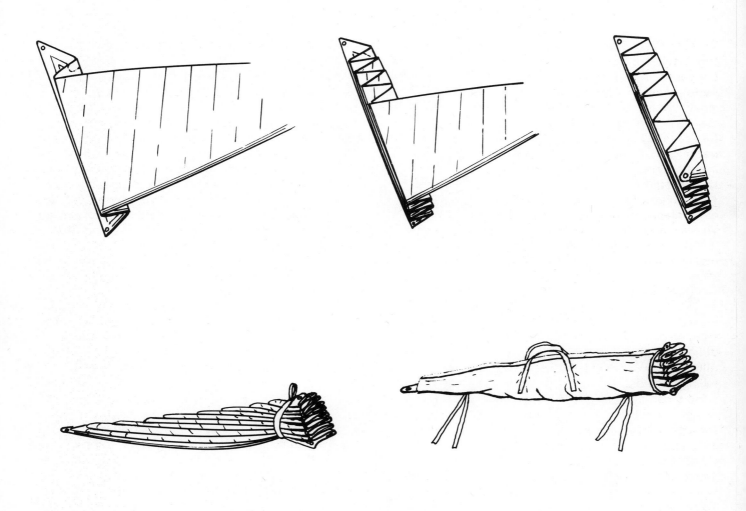

*Figure 1-1.*   Flaking the luff of a genoa. If there is no lacing line, a sail tie around the luff will hold it in place while the sail is stowed in the sausage.

# CHAPTER ONE
# Sails and Handling Techniques

All over the world racing is becoming keener. This is the inevitable result of steady advances in design concepts, in sail and gear technology, and in crew performance. Each new development in itself may be small. Designers introduce new hull features that reduce a boat's rating by one tenth of one foot. Sailmakers use computers to create sails that are fractionally faster than previous ones. And crews practise long hours to better the speed of an operation by a matter of mere seconds. The cumulative effect of these relatively minor improvements is an ever-increasing sophistication of boats and equipment, and an ever-increasing professionalism of offshore crews.

Yet even with the best in hull and sail design, equipment technology, and crew experience, a boat will never win races if its deck is laid out inefficiently. A hatch located where you want to put the tack of the staysail, a wheel positioned so that the helmsman cannot easily see the luff of the genoa, a winch that is sited so close to a stanchion that turning the handle is difficult—all these flaws and many others can make the difference between staying at the head of the fleet or falling behind.

How can one achieve maximum efficiency in a deck design? Answers to this question will be offered throughout this book, but here we begin by considering sails and sail handling techniques. Sails, after all, are what power a boat, so it stands to reason that a deck which is carefully planned to meet sail handling needs will have a definite edge over many of its competitors. To accomplish this aim, however, the person designing the deck must have a thorough knowledge of sailing techniques and their sequencing during a race. This chapter reviews this basic information. Hopefully, it will give even the most inexperienced crewman a good understanding of why a deck is generally laid out as it is.

## Techniques for Genoa Handling

Genoas are changed often during a race, and every change takes time. It pays to organize a drill carefully for this operation and then design the deck to suit it. Thoughtful planning can save seconds, and when racing, seconds often make the difference between first place and an also-ran. The following pages describe some of the drills that I have used for changing, as well as for hoisting and tacking genoas. They are, of course, not the only ways that genoas can be handled. The regular crewmen on a boat should decide which drills work best for them and design the deck accordingly.

### Hoisting a Single Genoa

When not in use, a genoa is usually folded and stored inside a sausage, a sail cover closed with a velcro strip or zipper. In addition to making the sail compact, folding helps preserve a more uniform surface, which can increase boat speed. Inside the sausage, the luff of the sail is carefully flaked and tied off either with a sail tie or with a lacing line passed through the grommets, as shown in Figure 1-1. The head and tack are clearly marked. The luff is then stowed in the forward end of the sausage, and the sail is usually folded in thirds so that the clew is at the aft end. Generally, the clew is allowed to poke through a hole so that sheets can be fastened to it without opening the sausage.

The single-sail genoa hoist is a simple operation. A crewman carries the sausage to the bow and ties it down to the toerail or to a handy cleat. After opening the forward end to expose the luff and removing the sail tie or lacing, he feeds the head into the guide and then into the luff groove, or, if the sail has hanks, he hanks it on. Next, he attaches the tack. With a double

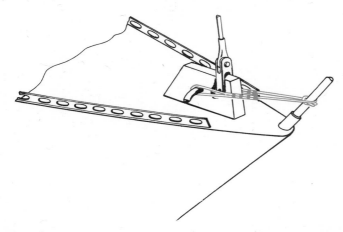

*Figure 1-2.* Shock cord or bungee is hooked over the tack of the sail to hold it in place while hoisting.

luff groove device, snarl-ups are prevented by using the halyard, luff groove, and tack fitting on the same side. Also, if the tack fitting is simply a horn, shock cord, used as in Figure 1-2, keeps the sail from sliding off.

If the genoa is not to be set immediately, it can be secured with a sail tie, as illustrated in Figure 1-3. Then, when ready to hoist it, make a quick mental check of all the necessary preparations. Is the genoa fairlead on the correct track and in the correct hole? Are the halyards clear and not wrapped around the spreaders? Are the sheets led outside the shrouds? Do you have a handle ready? Is someone ready at the mast to help you? Is someone at the genoa sheet winch to trim the sail when it is up? If everything looks right, hoist.

**Tacking a Genoa**

Tacking should be done with a minimum of effort. Be aware of things that might slow the operation. For example, remember to: (1) keep crew weight outboard as long as possible; (2) reduce windage; (3) send the lightest person forward to help the sheet around the mast; (4) warn the crew that the boat is about to be tacked; (5) complete preparations as quickly as possible and avoid wasted motions.

As for the specific steps involved in a tack, here is the sequence I have found best.

1. One man, not the tactician, continues to watch and trim the genoa. Someone else makes sure the tail of this sheet is cleared of snarls.

2. Another man pulls tight the weather sheet, which should have been placed on the winch immediately after the previous tack. He should begin with two turns on the drum, and then add more as needed when the sheet load increases.

3. With non-linked winches, the man who will be operating the new leeward winch keeps a double-grip handle ready. With linked winches, the man on what is now the leeward winch inserts a handle after throwing off the sheet. And with pedestal-driven winches, two men go to the pedestal, and what is now the weather winch is connected. Finally, the man who is going to tail the new sheet moves into position.

4. On the order 'Helm's a lee', the crewman who has been trimming the genoa eases the sheet a little and watches for the break—the moment when the sail starts to luff. On a big boat, it is often useful to call this moment. As soon as the break is apparent, the old sheet is cast off and the new tailer starts hauling in. A man at the mast can help the bowlines around the shrouds and, in lighter winds, pull the clew gently aft. Once the sail is coming aft on the new tack, the winch operators start winding. If they begin to wind any sooner, they only tire themselves before the genoa is completely home. Both the man who is tailing and the men winding must watch the sail so that they do not overtrim it and stall the boat. Their visibility, therefore, is a crucial point to consider when positioning winches.

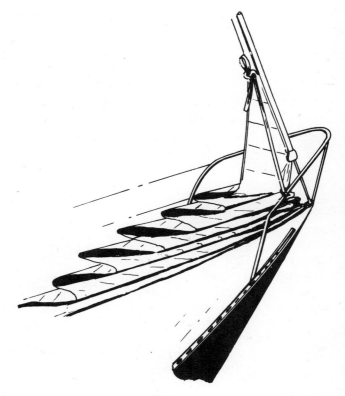

*Figure 1-3.* A sail tie fastened to the halyard with a slip knot will hold the sail until ready to hoist. Note that the sail must be tied down if it is to be left on deck for a long period of time.

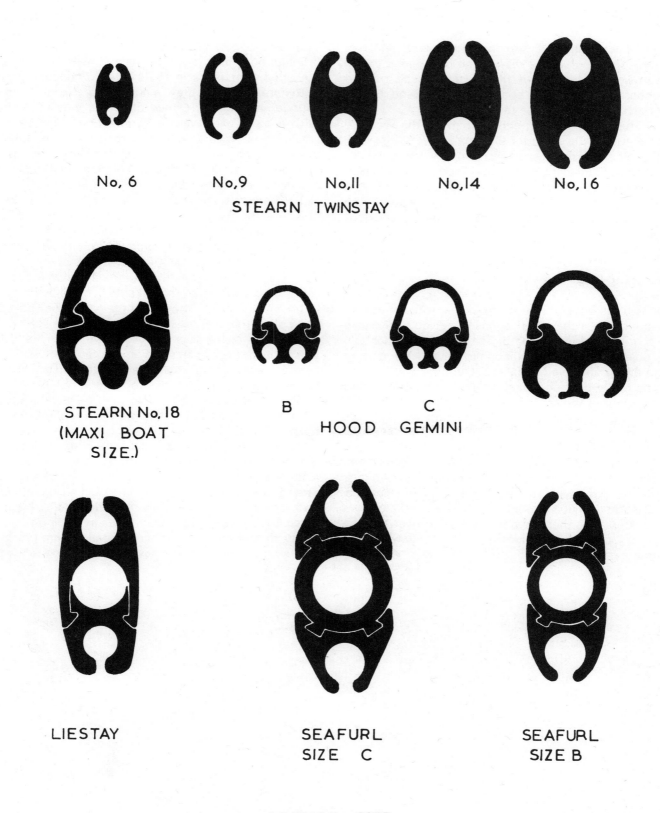

No, 6     No,9     No,11     No,14     No,16

STEARN TWINSTAY

STEARN No,18
(MAXI BOAT
SIZE.)

B       C

HOOD GEMINI

LIESTAY       SEAFURL       SEAFURL
SIZE C         SIZE B

ACTUAL SIZE

*Figure 1-4.*   Some current luff groove devices.

5. Now that the sail is in on the new tack, one man is left to trim while the rest of the crew goes to the weather rail. The sooner their weight is distributed outboard, the sooner the boat settles down and regains any speed lost during the tack.

6. The man nearest to the winch on the weather side prepares the sheet for the next tack.

For top performance, job assignments cannot be left to chance. Each man should have a specific task which he continues to perform on every tack, in every race. Only in this way can the entire crew acquire the proficiency needed to make their boat a consistent winner.

## Changing Genoas

'All you do is pull the blank-blank rope' was the introduction to changing genoas I received many years ago. Unfortunately, it isn't quite that simple when you are changing from a number one to a number two using a double luff groove headstay system.

The method of changing genoas varies depending upon whether the sail is equipped with hanks or made for a luff groove device. Nowadays, most racing boats use some form of luff groove. Cross sections of several designs currently on the market are shown in Figure 1-4. The earliest type was the Hood C-stay, a one piece extrusion made to measure. Later, single-groove systems were made in light alloy or plastic sections, designed to be fitted to an existing stay. It was only a small step from there to putting two grooves side by side or opposite one another. This, to date, is the ultimate refinement in luff groove devices.

### Changing Genoas with Hanks

It need not take long to change genoas that are equipped with hanks. In 1971, *Quailo III* had headsails with hanks, and the crew managed to change genoas in under 40 seconds. *Quailo*, of course, was a big boat with a crew of eleven; a bareheaded change on a smaller boat with a smaller crew often takes longer and causes more ground to be lost. Nevertheless, a well-organized drill can cut the time required to a minimum. Here is the drill we used on *Quailo*.

1. One man takes the new sail forward and hanks it on below the lowest hank of the old sail. If this bottom hank is very low, it may be unfastened to make room.

2. The weather sheet is removed from the old sail to make it easier to remove the leeward sheet.

3. The crewmen take the positions shown in Figure 1-5. Because this arrangement puts five people forward of the mast, the men should not ready themselves until just before the change.

4. A man at the mast eases off the halyard a little, while the first bowman removes the tack.

5. The halyard and sheet are thrown off. The second bowman presents the hanks to the first bowman, who removes them. The other two men on the foredeck gather the old sail and stuff it into the forehatch. A man at the cockpit removes the sheet from the old sail and ties it onto the clew of the new sail. He also moves the genoa fairlead along the track to its new position.

6. The first bowman finishes unhooking the hanks. The second bowman takes the halyard off the old sail and clips it onto the new sail. Then the order to hoist is given. Bowman number two assists in hauling the sail up the mast. Bowman number one makes sure that the hanks run freely while the new sheet is being taken to

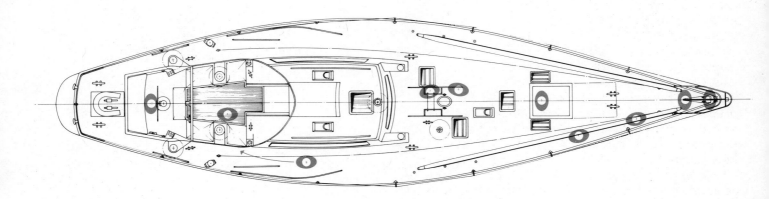

*Figure 1-5.* Positions of the crew on *Quailo III* during a genoa change. 1 *No 1 Bowman.* 2 *No 2 Bowman.* 3 and 4 *Sail gatherers.* 5 *Navigator, who pulls sail down the hatch.* 6 and 7 *Mastmen, one to tail and one to wind winch.* 8 *Man who changes bowlines and then winds the sheet winch.* 9 *Sheet tailer.* 10 *Helmsman.*

the primary winch and the spare or weather sheet is re-led around the weather side.

*Quailo* had large hanks which made unhooking easier and quicker. Another innovation that speeds the handling of hanks is the use of a U-shaped device, around which the hanks are slipped. Then, when the first sail is dropped, the U is slid over the forestay above the old sail, and the open hanks slide off as the second sail is raised.

*Changing Genoas with a Luff Groove System*
Refinements in genoa hanks have been largely over-shadowed by the vast strides taken in luff groove technology. One device, which still requires a bare-headed change, is the single luff groove. The new sail is taken forward and the luff tape is led into a feeder at the bow. Next, the crewmen simply follow steps 2, 3, and 4 for the genoa change with hanks, except that in this case the number two bowman grabs the tack of the old sail, and, when the halyard and sheet are thrown off, he runs along the weather side pulling the old sail down. The halyard is then clipped onto the new sail, which is fed into the groove and hoisted. This method

WELD    ¼" OR 6mm. BAR

*Figure 1-6.* A typical short sheet hook for boats over Two Ton size.

is faster than unclipping hanks, and on *Morning Cloud* it enabled us to change headsails in 20 to 30 seconds. But as with hanks, we lost speed and ground by being bareheaded for that amount of time.

In an attempt to compensate for this loss, some people set a staysail inside the genoa during a bareheaded change. But the technique has several limitations. For one thing, it adds to the activity on the foredeck, and for another, speed is still lost because a staysail is much smaller than a genoa. Consequently, this procedure is generally not worth the effort if a crew can perform a snappy genoa change.

Twin-foil headstays were developed to avoid the inevitable loss of speed during a bareheaded change. With this system, one simply carries the new sail forward, hooks the tack onto the free tack fitting, and feeds the head of the sail into the spare groove. Using the halyard on the same side as the tack fitting, the

new sail is then hoisted and sheeted, and the old sail is lowered at leisure. It is illegal, however, to fly the two sails any longer than necessary.

The advantages of this system can be enhanced if a few tips are remembered. First, lead the halyard (which should exit from the mast about 8 feet above the deck) through a padeye block to a winch where a crewman can tail it using one wrap around the drum. Second, use a special short sheet to allow the sheets on the old sail to be removed and attached to the new sail. (Figure 1-6 shows a typical short sheet hook.) And third, try to make the sail change with the new sail on the inboard side, a technique that can save a great deal of time.

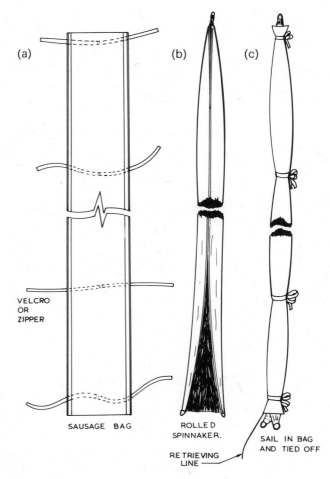

(a)    (b)    (c)

VELCRO OR ZIPPER

SAUSAGE BAG

ROLLED SPINNAKER.

RETRIEVING LINE

SAIL IN BAG AND TIED OFF

*Figure 1-7.* A spinnaker sausage. In drawing (b) the spinnaker is rolled up tightly with the luff tapes together. Then the sausage shown in (a) is wrapped around it. The velcro edges of the sausage are pressed together or the zipper closed, and the tube is tied off at intervals, as seen in drawing (c). Before hoisting, the ties are undone and the sausage retaining line is attached to a handy cleat. When the sail is fully hoisted, pulling on the sheet snaps the velcro or zipper open and the sausage falls to the deck.

19

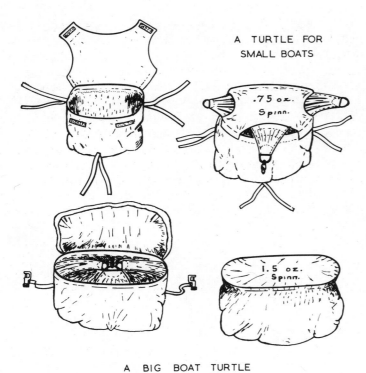

A TURTLE FOR
SMALL BOATS

.75 oz.
Spinn.

A BIG BOAT TURTLE

*Figure 1-8.* Different types of spinnaker turtles.

## Techniques for Spinnaker Handling

When you think that spinnakers can be carried when the apparent wind is only 55 degrees off the bow, you realize why a chute is such an important part of a sail wardrobe. A sloppy set can waste precious minutes during a race. Consequently, a crew should carefully work out its drills for spinnaker handling and design the deck to suit them.

### Hoisting a Spinnaker

Hoisting a spinnaker really amounts to no more than hauling on a halyard. But preparation for the hoist is more complex than for genoas, with greater penalties for failure to remember essential details.

On most boats, spinnakers are usually stowed in turtles, circular bags which are closed at one end with velcro or with an elastic strip around a wire frame. (See Figure 1-8.) The spinnaker inside is carefully flaked or, in the case of heavier sails such as the heavy runner and the starcut, it is stopped, as illustrated in Figure 1-9. When a spinnaker has been properly flaked or stopped, its three corners will be apparent at the top of the pile.

A stopped spinnaker is both easier and safer to hoist in heavy air than a flaked one because it can be raised to the masthead and the halyard cleated off before sheeting. An unstopped spinnaker, on the other hand, could fill in heavy air and pull an uncleated halyard through a man's hands, or it could flog and throw off the sheet. One way to guard against serious accidents with a spinnaker halyard when the sail is not stopped is to use a halyard jammer. Then, if the sail fills half way up, the jammer will stop the halyard, and the crew can winch the sail the rest of the way.

What are the proper techniques for hoisting a spinnaker? On most boats a crewman first carries the sail to the foredeck and ties the turtle down on the leeward side. (Sailmakers love people who forget to tie turtles down, although owners do not share this

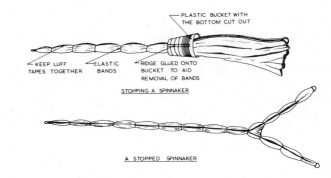

*Figure 1-9.* Stopping a spinnaker.

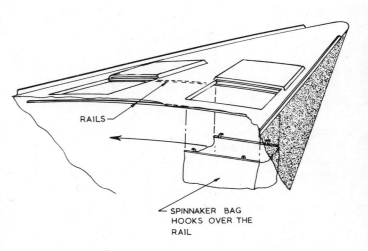

RAILS

SPINNAKER BAG
HOOKS OVER THE
RAIL

*Figure 1-10.* Details of a spinnaker bag designed for hoisting out of a hatch. On a gybe set, there must be some form of stop to hold the bag to windward. Also, make sure that the hatch corners are rounded and any potential snags removed.

20

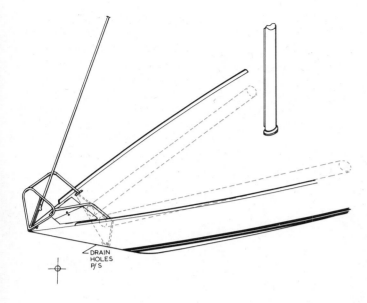

*Figure 1-11.* Spinnaker launching and retrieval tubes. A patch in the middle of the spinnaker has a take-down line attached to it which runs through the tube.

fondness.) Sometimes, however, a boat is designed so that the spinnakers can be hoisted right out of the forehatch. Usually, this requires one hatch to port and another to starboard, and the hatches must be of adequate size. Also, there must be some device for holding the sail under the hatch, as illustrated in Figure 1-10.

The steps to follow in setting up for the hoist vary, depending for one thing on the size of the boat. More and more smaller boats are being designed with under-deck spinnaker tubes and a pulpit that is specially shaped to help the sail go up cleanly. A typical example is shown in Figure 1-11. The pole on these boats is often permanently attached to the mast. The spinnaker can be stowed in the tube before the start of the race, provided the crew knows which one they are likely to be using. When the sail is properly in position, only its three corners are visible in the bow well. The hoist simply amounts to hooking on the sheet, guy, and halyard, raising the pole, and hauling when ready.

On larger boats, the spinnaker pole is either permanently attached to the mast or in an easily accessible position so that setting up can be handled by one man. It is important at the design stage to consider the placement of the pole and how it affects other aspects of the deck layout. A pole attached to the mast and carried in a trough on the centreline, for instance, renders a centreline hatch useless. Moreover, some pole arrangements restrict one's options for future alterations. A pole in a centreline trough, to use the

same example, makes changing to 160 per cent J poles virtually impossible. (See Figure 1-12.)

The actual hoist on a larger boat requires careful attention to details. After the spinnaker sheet, guy, and halyard have been clipped onto their respective corners of the sail, the crewman at the mast who will do the hauling should check off mentally: does the man tailing the halyard have at least one turn around a winch in case the sail fills half way up? Are the foreguy and topping lift secure, either cleated or being held by a man? Are the sheets and guys led cleanly, not wrapped in the pulpit? Is the jockey pole in, if required? If you are reaching, is the fairlead led correctly? (It should be further forward for a starcut.) Are there any tangles or halyard wraps aloft? If all is correct, hoist. Before the sail is fully up, the guy should be hauled aft and the sail sheeted to prevent wrapping. But do not sheet too soon, or else you may find a crewman disappearing up the mast as the chute fills!

When the sail is up and drawing, crew weight in the right place helps increase boat speed, so winch positions must be carefully considered. On a run, crew weight is usually best aft, while on a reach, it is best on the high side. A designer must consider these different requirements, as well as a number of other factors, when making his final decision about where to site spinnaker winches. Typically he settles on the best of several compromise positions.

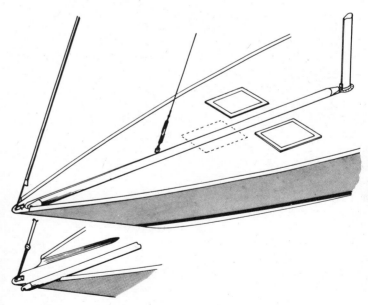

*Figure 1-12.* A spinnaker pole permanently attached to the mast rests in a deck trough. Note that twin hatches are required and that the midstay must be slightly to one side of the trough. Drawing below shows an alternative arrangement.

21

## Gybing a Spinnaker

There are three principal methods of gybing a spinnaker: the twin-pole gybe, the dip-pole gybe, and end-for-ending the pole. Each requires different techniques and gear.

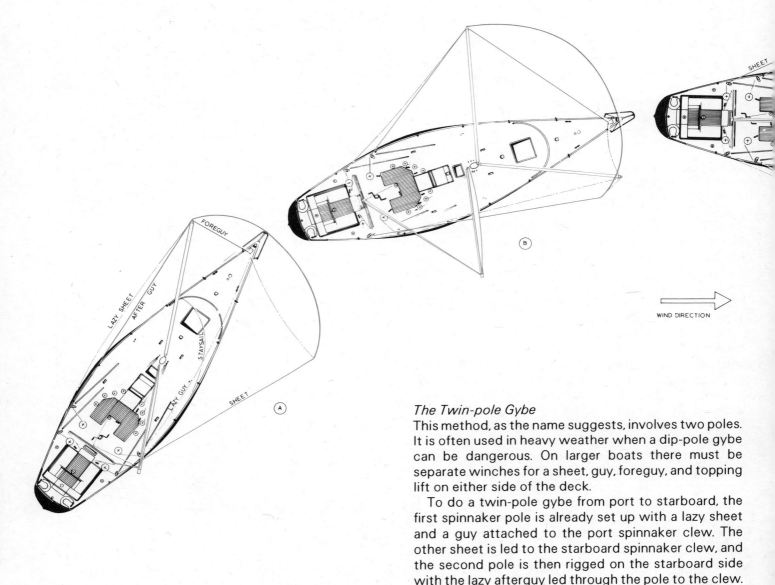

WIND DIRECTION

*The Twin-pole Gybe*

This method, as the name suggests, involves two poles. It is often used in heavy weather when a dip-pole gybe can be dangerous. On larger boats there must be separate winches for a sheet, guy, foreguy, and topping lift on either side of the deck.

To do a twin-pole gybe from port to starboard, the first spinnaker pole is already set up with a lazy sheet and a guy attached to the port spinnaker clew. The other sheet is led to the starboard spinnaker clew, and the second pole is then rigged on the starboard side with the lazy afterguy led through the pole to the clew. (See Figure 1-13.) On the gybe, pole two is hoisted and cranked aft to take the weight off the sheet. The mainsail is handed across, and the port guy is triggered and allowed to float free of pole one. The new working sheet, which was the former lazy sheet, is trimmed as required.

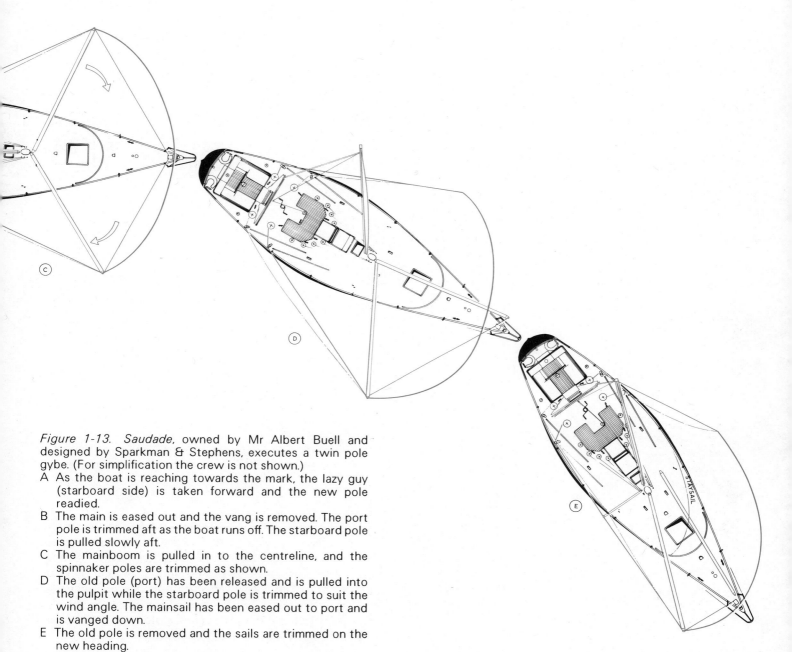

*Figure 1-13. Saudade*, owned by Mr Albert Buell and designed by Sparkman & Stephens, executes a twin pole gybe. (For simplification the crew is not shown.)

A As the boat is reaching towards the mark, the lazy guy (starboard side) is taken forward and the new pole readied.

B The main is eased out and the vang is removed. The port pole is trimmed aft as the boat runs off. The starboard pole is pulled slowly aft.

C The mainboom is pulled in to the centreline, and the spinnaker poles are trimmed as shown.

D The old pole (port) has been released and is pulled into the pulpit while the starboard pole is trimmed to suit the wind angle. The mainsail has been eased out to port and is vanged down.

E The old pole is removed and the sails are trimmed on the new heading.

*Figure 1.14.   America Jane III*, owned by Mr George Tooby and designed by Scott Kaufman, shows a dip-pole gybe technique.

A  The boat approaches the mark with sails trimmed to suit the wind.

B  The mainsail is held on the centreline while the spinnaker pole is released from the port guy and swung forward through the foretriangle. Note that the lazy guy (starboard side) has been taken to the pulpit.

C  The starboard guy is clipped into the pole and has been wound aft. The pole is raised and both sails trimmed to suit the wind angle.

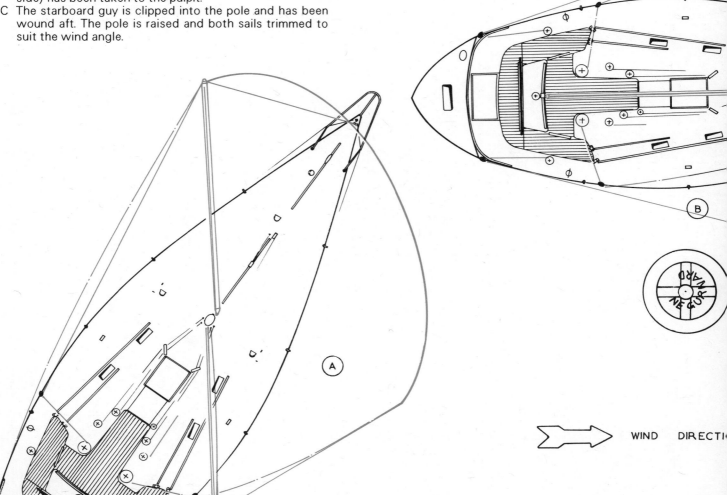

WIND   DIRECTI

### The Dip-pole Gybe

This technique gets its name from the fact that a single pole is dipped under the forestay during the gybe. Sheets and guys are attached to the clews of the spinnaker, with the weather guy going through the end of the pole. On the leeward side, the sheet controls the chute, and the lazy guy is led forward to the pulpit. On the order to gybe, the pole is first raised on the inboard end so that the outer end can be passed through the foretriangle. (The height to which the inboard end is raised is usually marked on the mast.) The pole is then squared aft as the boat runs more away from the wind, and the guy is tripped and allowed to float clear. Next,

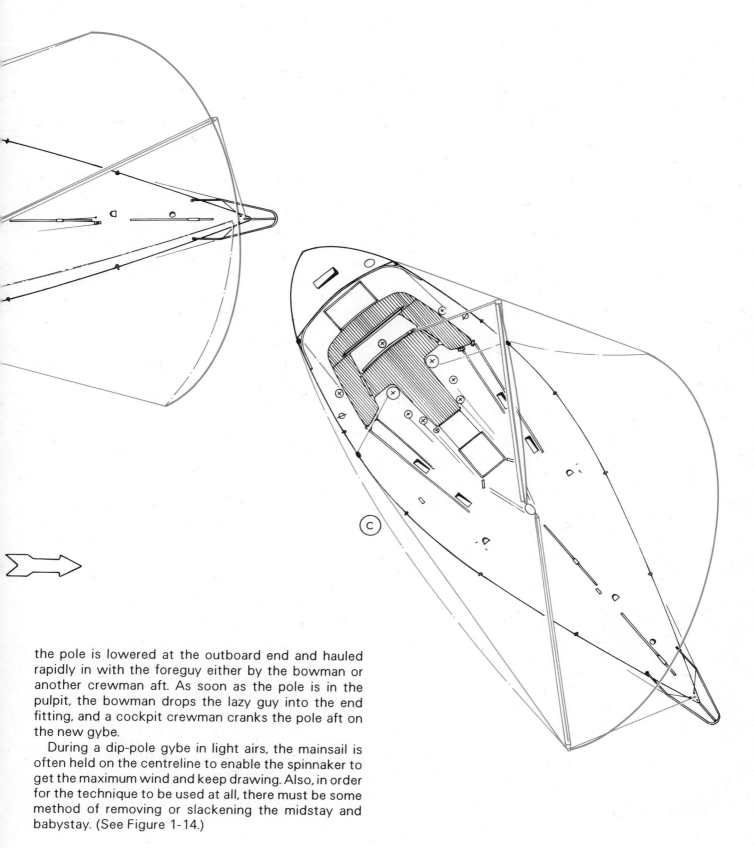

the pole is lowered at the outboard end and hauled rapidly in with the foreguy either by the bowman or another crewman aft. As soon as the pole is in the pulpit, the bowman drops the lazy guy into the end fitting, and a cockpit crewman cranks the pole aft on the new gybe.

During a dip-pole gybe in light airs, the mainsail is often held on the centreline to enable the spinnaker to get the maximum wind and keep drawing. Also, in order for the technique to be used at all, there must be some method of removing or slackening the midstay and babystay. (See Figure 1-14.)

*Figure 1-15.* An end-for-end gybe on a C & C Half Tonner. A The sails are trimmed to suit the wind angle as the boat approaches the mark. B The boat is steered dead down wind with the main boom on the centreline. The outboard end of the pole is unclipped, then the inboard end, and the pole is handed across the fore-deck. C The pole is re-attached to the sail and the mast. The mainsail is eased out and both sails are trimmed to suit the wind angle.

B

A

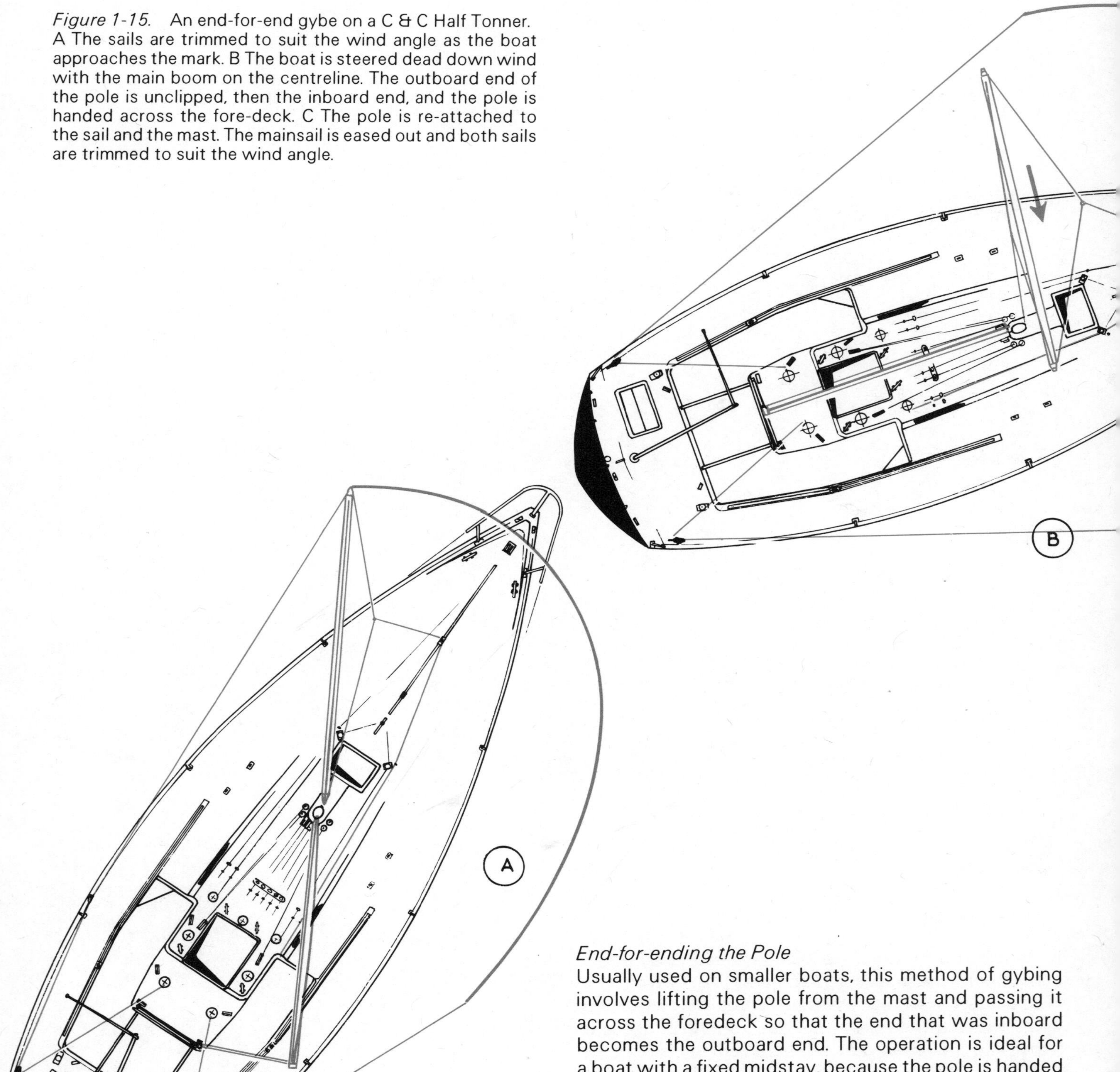

### End-for-ending the Pole

Usually used on smaller boats, this method of gybing involves lifting the pole from the mast and passing it across the foredeck so that the end that was inboard becomes the outboard end. The operation is ideal for a boat with a fixed midstay, because the pole is handed between it and the mast. (But note that the topping lift must be attached to the mast at a point below the midstay or else the pole must be passed forward of the midstay. In heavy weather, though, a crew may want to set the deck up for a twin-pole or dip-pole gybe as well, in case end-for-ending appears too dangerous.

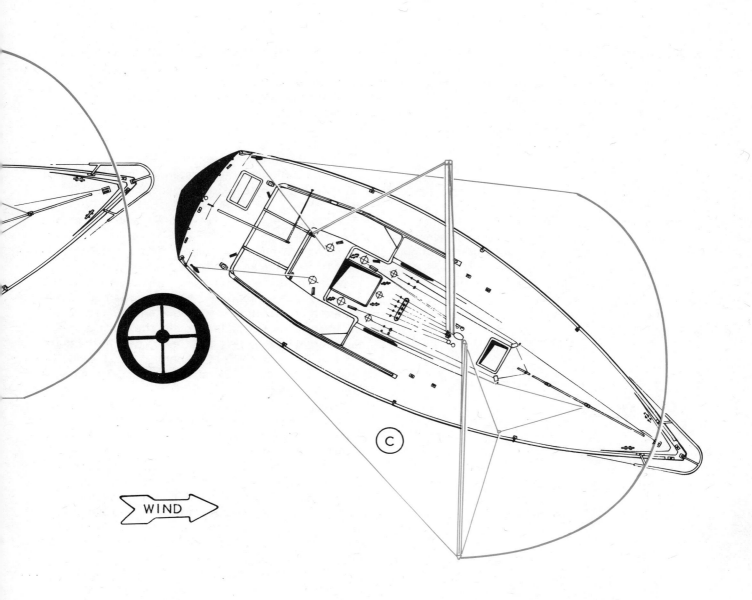

WIND

Ⓒ

When end-for-ending a spinnaker pole, only a single sheet/guy is attached to each clew of the sail. On the order to gybe, the guy is triggered and freed from the outboard end of the pole. The inboard end is then removed from the mast. With the weight taken by the topping lift, the pole is passed through the foretriangle. For efficiency, this step requires a bridle on the pole. The former inboard end is then attached to the former sheet. At this stage the mainsail can be handed across, or, in lighter airs, it can be held on the centreline. Next, the pole is hooked back onto the mast, and the sails are trimmed on the new gybe, as shown in Figure 1-15.

## Changing Spinnakers

Just as there are several ways to change genoas, so there are several ways to change spinnakers. Most top-class racing boats use the peel change, but smaller boats with only one halyard must change bareheaded.

*The Peel Change*
A peel change cannot be done without certain gear: two spinnaker halyards, an extra sheet, and a peeling strop, shown in Figure 1-16. The actual method of doing a peel change varies depending upon whether the new sail is to be set inside or outside the old one. The following steps describe how to perform an inside set. The boat in this example is a one tonner on port gybe flying a 1.5 ounce spinnaker. The crew decides to change to a starcut because the wind is heading and rising steadily.

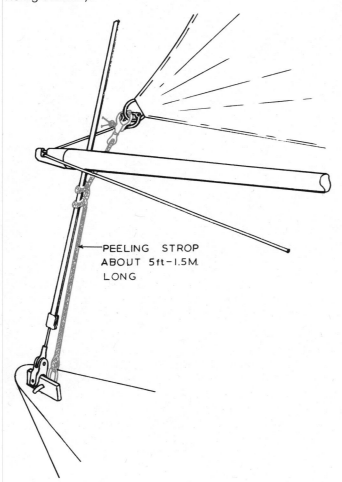

PEELING STROP
ABOUT 5ft – 1.5M.
LONG

*Figure 1-16.* Peeling: after the old spinnaker has been taken down, the guy is attached to the new one, and the peeling strop can be removed.

1. The men trimming the chute concentrate on obtaining maximum boat speed and ignore the change preparations.
2. The starcut is taken forward and tied down.
3. A spinnaker changing strop or pennant is made fast on the headstay and hooked onto the clew of the starcut, see Figure 1-16.
4. A new sheet is rigged to the desired position, run forward, and clipped onto the starcut clew. (Remember that different size sails do not necessarily lead to the same fairlead.)
5. The spare halyard is cleared and led to the leeward rail.
6. The crewmen take their positions: one man in the pulpit to clear the sail on the hoist; one at the mast to lower the pole, if required, raise the new halyard, and lower the old one; another man aft to gather the old sail; another operating the foreguy and the afterguy; a man at the forward rail first to clip the halyard on and make sure it runs cleanly and then to help at the mast; and a person on the old spinnaker sheet who will eventually take the new one. The helmsman completes the seven-man crew.
7. Just before the hoist, the foredeck boss should mentally check: is the sheet clear? Is the new tack clipped on? Are the halyards clear? Is everyone in position and ready?
8. On the word go, the new sail is hoisted inside the present one. The halyard is made fast. There are now two spinnakers flying–the old 1.5 ounce sail which is set on the leeward starboard halyard and the starcut on the port halyard. The new sail must go aloft in such a way that its halyard does not foul the halyard of the original sail. This is illustrated in Figure 1-17.
9. Next, the pole is lowered and brought forward to the man in the pulpit who unhooks the 1.5 ounce spinnaker. This sail then peels back, ready to be taken down. The bowman hooks the guy into the tack of the starcut. (Remember to give him enough slack in the guy.) Once the guy is clipped on, the weight can be taken off the peeling strop by pulling the guy aft. The peeling strop can then be unhooked from the starcut and the pole can be winched aft as required.
10. While these steps are being taken on the bow, the old spinnaker is gathered in and cleared off the deck. The old sheet and halyard are re-run, if necessary, and finally, the old sail is repacked.

These are the techniques for an inside set. The method of doing an outside set is similar, except that the new sheet and halyard must be led outside the sail that is presently flying. Then, when the change is made, the old sail must be sheeted in very hard to pull it inside the new one. If this point is neglected, the old spinnaker will wrap around the luff of the new one and cause it to collapse.

*The Bareheaded Change*

The preparation for a bareheaded change is largely the same as steps 1 to 7 for a peel change. The only difference is that instead of using a changing strop, the new sail is simply led forward around the headstay.

Once everything is ready, the order is given and the old spinnaker is released at the bow and taken in either on the foredeck or aft. The same halyard is then carried forward outside the lee shrouds and clipped onto the head of the new spinnaker. At the same time, the old guy is also clipped onto the new sail, which can then be hoisted and sheeted home. This method of changing a spinnaker is simpler than the peel change, but the loss in speed while the boat is bareheaded is a real handicap in top flight competition.

## Taking a Spinnaker Down

The methods of taking a spinnaker down vary, depending upon the location of the hatch through which the sail is taken below. The three major methods are the aft, the middeck, and the foredeck takedowns. Most good crews use all of them at one time or another, but every owner should decide which method will be used most frequently and design the deck to facilitate it.

*Takedown Aft*

This is a common method of taking down a spinnaker. The sail is simply unhooked from the guy and the lazy sheet at the end of the pole and allowed to blow aft into the lee of the mainsail, where it is gathered in as the halyard is eased. Usually, the spinnaker is then stuffed down the aft hatch for flaking later. The big disadvantages of the takedown aft are that it concentrates weight on the leeward quarter, and the flapping sail obscures the genoa/jib for a crucial few minutes during the transition from running or reaching to beating. The sail also blocks the slot for a short time and can foul winches or other afterdeck gear.

*Middeck Takedown*

Another common location for taking down a spinnaker is on the middeck just abaft the mast. A few seconds before lowering the sail, the lazy guy is wrapped around a handy cleat. Then, when the spinnaker is released from the pole, the weight is on the guy and the sail can

be easily hauled in and stuffed down a midship hatch for flaking later. One of the advantages of this method is that the sail is close to the boat when it is let fly, but as during the aft takedown, it sometimes fouls winches or other middeck gear.

*Foredeck Takedown*

Quite often it is easier to take a spinnaker down on the foredeck than to take it down aft. For a foredeck takedown, a short sheet (often the lazy foreguy) is led through the genoa tack fitting and up to the tack of the spinnaker, where it is made fast. When the tack is let go, the weight is on the short sheet, which pulls the luff of the spinnaker into the lee of the genoa. The spinnaker can then be gathered in under the headsail and stuffed down the forehatch. The most significant disadvantages of this technique are that two or three men must be positioned on the foredeck to gather in the sail, and

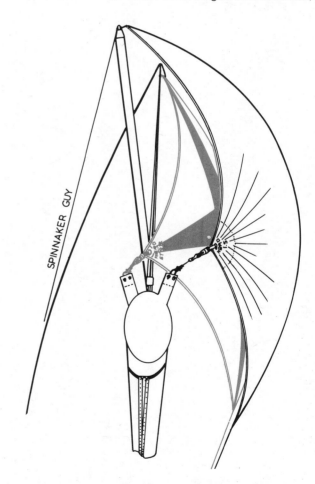

*Figure 1-17.* From this view looking down on the masthead you can see that the halyards will not cross when the 1.5 ounce spinnaker peels away ready to be taken down.

29

that the air flow on the leeward side of the genoa is disturbed. On the positive side, this method allows a crew to make a quick tack while the spinnaker is still being gathered, provided the outboard end of the pole has been dropped and the topping lift unhooked.

Note that for a foredeck takedown, as for an aft or middeck takedown as well, the tack of the spinnaker need not be unhooked from the guy. Sometimes it is easier simply to let the guy run out through the end fitting of the pole. But if this is the technique used, always be sure that the lazy sheet is not made fast.

An aid to spinnaker takedowns recently appearing on larger boats is the pull-down patch (or belly button) located in the middle of the sail. The retrieving line attached to the patch can be led under the genoa and taken down the forehatch. Without unclipping the guy at the pole, the halyard can be released and the sail pulled down below. The guy and sheet can then be allowed to run free as the spinnaker vanishes through the forehatch. This technique, of course, is not new, since it has long been used on dinghies. Another development seen more and more often on small offshore boats, which has also been borrowed from dinghy racing, is the use of spinnaker launching and retrieval tubes. In the future, even large offshore racers may be fitted with such devices, especially if restrictions are placed on the number of spinnakers carried.

## Techniques for Mainsail Control

In terms of how a crew must handle it, a mainsail is decidedly different from a genoa or spinnaker. While genoa and spinnaker handling often requires heavy work, mainsail handling is more a matter of proper control.

By itself, the mainsail is not a particularly efficient sail, due to the effect of the mast in front of it. But when used in conjunction with a genoa, the efficiency of both sails is increased beyond their separate potentials. To get the maximum boat speed possible from this mainsail/genoa combination, the sails must be adjusted to suit varying wind conditions. This is accomplished by using a series of control mechanisms, most of which are on the mainsail because it is difficult to control the cloth of the genoa. Here we discuss the basic techniques for using a kicking strap and vang, a mainsheet, an outhaul, a cunningham, a flattening reef, and a variety of reefing devices. Of course, mast bend, too, is used to control the mainsail, but because it does not influence deck layout we will not consider it here.

*Figure 1-18.* A three-part rope kicker aboard *Desperado,* *(author)* and a hydraulic vang aboard *Scandalous. (author)*

The deck of the Swan 65 *King's Legend* when sailing under spinnaker. Note how the mainsheet and spinnaker sheet cross near the starboard grinder drum. Also, sheet tail bags would come in handy. On the coachroof is an inboard 6 degree staysail sheet track, with halyard winches just forward of it. *(Alastair Black)*

## The Kicking Strap and Vang

The word vang is often applied to anything that holds down the boom, whether it is a multi-part rope tackle, an adjustable steel bar or wire, or a hydraulic ram. (See Figure 1-18.) Kicking strap, on the other hand, is an English term which refers only to a rope tackle attached to the boom.

Regardless of their various constructions, however, kickers and vangs serve similar functions. One is controlling the roach of the main. The most effective part of a mainsail is approximately the after third, so a large roach extending this area increases the sail's efficiency. But unfortunately, a sail with a large roach is often difficult to handle. This problem is partially solved by a kicking strap or vang, which pulls downward on the boom and helps control the amount of twist in the mainsail, thus affecting the angle at which the wind leaves the leech. (See Figure 1-19.)

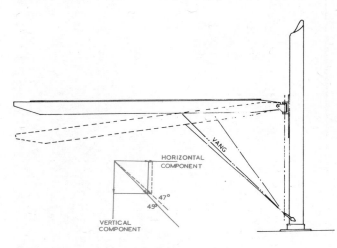

*Figure 1-19.* About 45 degrees is the maximum angle for a kicker or vang. If the angle is greater than this, increasing the load on the vang tends to increase the load on the gooseneck, leading to compression failure of the gooseneck.

## The Mainsheet

Due to the influence of the IOR, mainsails have become much smaller in recent years. This reduction in size has occurred primarily along the boom, since the minimum luff length is defined by the rule. The result has been higher aspect ratio mainsails which require greater leech tension than sails in the past. On larger boats, this need has been met with hydraulic vangs. But on most smaller boats, where the high cost and extra weight of hydraulics often prohibit a hydraulic vang, the mainsheet must help tension the leech, especially when sailing to windward in heavier winds. Older boats with long booms pose slightly different problems. Because their booms usually bend, both vang and sheet tension is needed to hold the leech tight.

In addition to its function of tensioning the leech of the mainsail, the mainsheet also serves to position the boom on the horizontal plane. When the boom moves beyond the range of the main traveler, a preventer (usually a single-part line taken to a spare winch) is used in conjunction with the mainsheet to hold the boom in the desired position. Figure 1-20 shows several arrangements that take into account the various purposes the mainsheet serves.

## The Outhaul

This is basically a device for controlling the depth of the camber in the lower part of the mainsail. A main that can be made fuller in lighter air and progressively flatter as the wind increases is often advantageous. This is accomplished by adjusting the outhaul. Various types of outhauls are shown in Figure 1-21.

## The Cunningham

In fresh breezes, the maximum camber in the mainsail tends to move aft. Tensioning the luff of the sail pulls the camber forward again, but the main halyard can only tension the sail within the limits of the black bands. Once these limits have been reached, the cunningham is used to exert even greater tension on the luff. The principle by which the cunningham operates is best shown visually, as in Figure 1-22.

## The Flattening Reef

When the mainsail has been made as flat as possible using the outhaul and the cunningham, a further advantage may be gained by taking in the flattening reef, which is fitted on most boats. To gain a little more sail area under the IOR, a mainsail is often designed for a downward-sloping boom, and the flattening reef usually removes this extra cloth while also flattening the sail.

The technique for taking in the flattening reef is similar to that for slab reefing, discussed later. Boats with roller reefing, too, can have flattening reefs similar to the slab reefing type, and they often have a zipper in the foot to tidy up the loose sail cloth and allow it to be rolled easily. The mainsail on a boat without a flattening

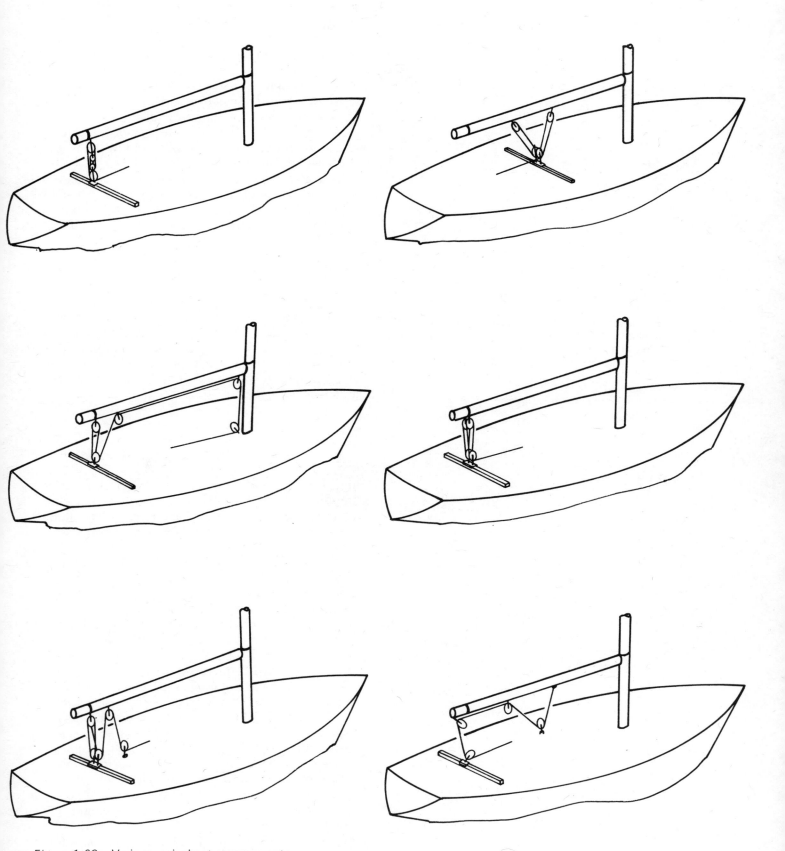

*Figure 1-20.* Various mainsheet arrangements.

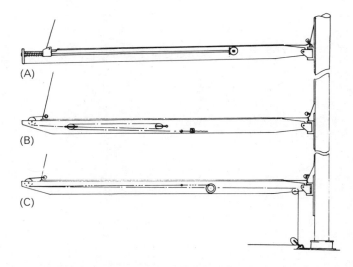

*Figure 1-21.* Various types of outhauls. A: screw arrangement inside the boom—it may be driven by a winch handle from either end. B: A 3- or 5-part purchase inside the boom. C: A single-part line taken to a winch either on the boom or on deck—there is usually some form of jammer in the system.

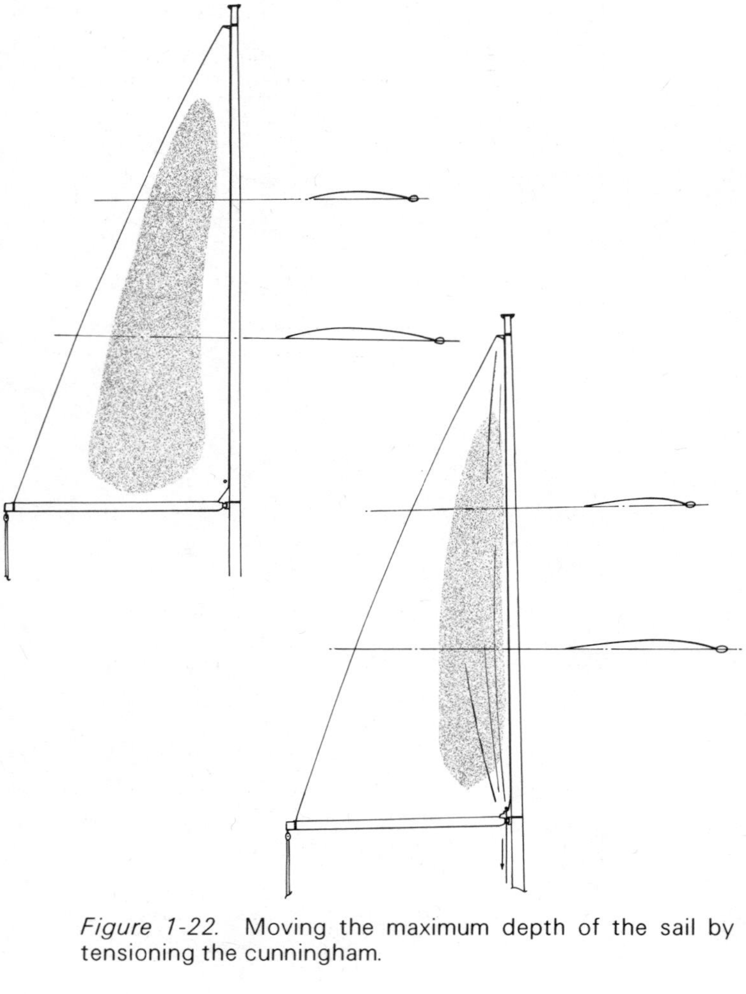

*Figure 1-22.* Moving the maximum depth of the sail by tensioning the cunningham.

reef is usually a little smaller than maximum along the foot so that outhauling the foot achieves the desired flatness. Again, a zipper is sometimes used to stow the loose sail; it is also used to create a new foot line when the cunningham on a boat with roller reefing is pulled down as far as possible. Current trends, however, are not to fit a zipper for this purpose, but rather to allow the sail to roll in as it will.

In general, when adjusting both the flattening reef and the cunningham, remember that they should be taken in by small increments in order to achieve the desired sail flatness without easing the main halyard.

## Reefing Devices

When the wind picks up to such an extent that carrying a full main is no longer possible, the sail must be made smaller by reefing. Reefing systems must be considered even before the boat is designed. Basically, there are two major systems currently manufactured: slab reefing and roller reefing. Each requires a different boom and deck arrangement.

### Slab Reefing

Often called jiffy reefing because it can be done in a jiffy, a slab reefing system uses a boom laid out as in Figure 1-23. A few points are not apparent in this drawing. First, there must be a cringle in the leech of the sail at every reef point. Second, there should be a pennant for each reef which is long enough to be passed up through the leech cringle and down again to the boom, while still leaving sufficient length at the bitter (or inboard) end to wrap twice around a winch at the mast. Third, each pennant should have a whipped eye termination, shown in Figure 1-24, to enable it to be pulled through the cringle with a light nylon messenger. This makes it unnecessary to climb on the outboard end of the boom, which in heavy weather is both difficult and dangerous. And fourth, because the reefing lines are used infrequently, it is a good idea to sew the upper messengers lightly to the leech of the sail so that they will not flap in the breeze and tangle or snag on things. A similar solution is to press the messengers on velcro patches.

The actual method of reefing varies from boat to boat, but a system that works well is as follows.

1. Take up the slack on the topping lift or adjust the hydraulic vang to stop the boom from drooping.

2. If there is a stainless steel track on the side of the boom, set the slide about 2 to 5 inches further aft than the cringle in the sail.

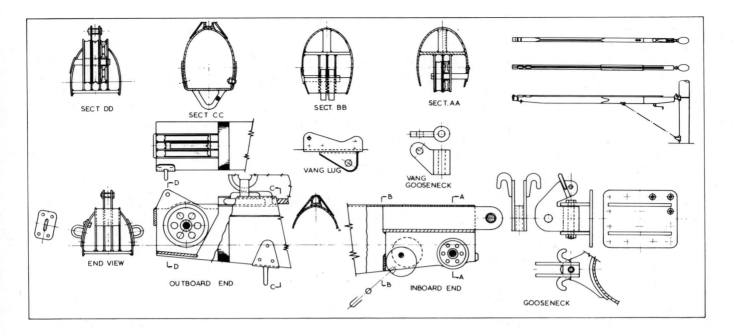

Figure 1-23. A jiffy reefing boom layout. *(Courtesy of Sparkman & Stephens Inc.)*

3. Open the lockoff cam for the first reef and draw enough of the reef pennant through to go up to the reefing eye in the leech of the sail and down again.

4. Pass the pennant through the cringle and dead end it in the adjustable slide. If no slide is fitted, pass the pennant around the boom and tie it off.

5. Take the bitter end of the pennant to a winch. All this can be done while the sail is trimmed and drawing.

6. Slacken the vang and remove the cunningham; it will only get in the way.

7. Now comes the actual reefing. First, ease the mainsheet. (Some people think it is not necessary to slacken the sheet, but since this makes the operation easier and therefore quicker, the loss in boat speed is more than compensated for.)

8. Next, have one crewman ease the main halyard to a predetermined mark or until the cringle at the luff of the sail can be passed over the hook at the inboard end of the boom.

9. While this is being done, have another man wind down the reefing pennant at the leech until the reef is taken in.

10. When the reef is fully in, wind up the main halyard again and lock off the pennant at the inboard end of the boom. Then sheet the newly reefed sail home.

11. The same procedure can be followed for the next reef, using another pennant and taking it to the same winch, as shown in Figure 1-25.

If a main is going to be reefed for a long period of time, the sail should be carefully rolled and a few light lashings put on it using the reefing eyes, including an extra lashing on the clew. To lash the mainsail on a reach or when the wind is abaft the beam, the crewmen should work from the outboard end toward the mast. To lash the sail when the boat is close hauled, they

Figure 1-24. A whipped eye terminal.

should work from the middle of the boom toward the ends.

The technique for shaking out the reef is quite simple. Remove all the lashings, tighten the topping lift, and ease the mainsheet, the main halyard, and the boom vang or kicking strap. Remove the sail from the hook at the mast end of the boom and undo the lockoff. Take up on the main halyard, making sure that the luff of the sail feeds into the luff groove properly. Finally, take up on the mainsheet to trim the sail.

Like any system, slab reefing offers both advantages and disadvantages. Its primary positive feature is the ease with which sail shape can be maintained, no matter how many reefs are put in. On the negative side, however, the amount of area taken out of the sail with each reef is always quite large. Slab reefing does not allow for small adjustments in mainsail size.

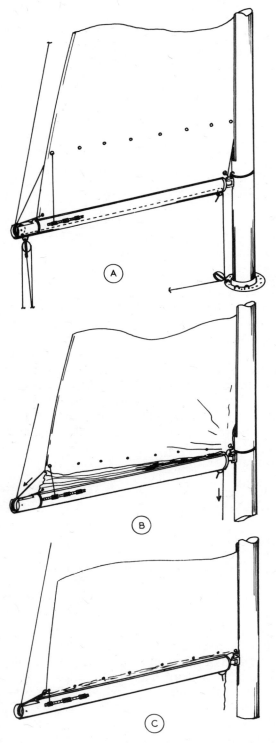

*Figure 1-25.* How to take in a jiffy reef. First lower the cringle at the luff and then pull the leech down. (a) Ready to reef. (b) Halyard has been eased and reefing cringle is on gooseneck hook: halyard is tensioned while clewline is wound down. (c) The sail reefed: it could now be tied in if desired.

## Roller Reefing

Roller reefing systems have lost popularity in recent years, mostly because of the difficulties they create for maintaining good sail shape. While the reef points of a slab reefing system can have slight upward curves to make the sail flatter as it is reefed, a roller reefing system can only allow the sail to be wound around the boom. Often the reefed sail is padded with towels or sail bags in an effort to improve sail shape. But this method is not very effective unless the padding is carefully fitted as the reefs are put in, and who could accomplish this in 25 knots of wind!

Roller reefing, however, does have one big advantage over slab reefing: any amount of sail can be taken in. This means that you can adjust the size of the main to the maximum area possible for any given wind strength, thus gaining extra power during a race. In addition, a more minor advantage of a roller reefing system is the ease with which the mainsail can be stowed on the boom when the boat is docked or anchored. With a slab reefing system, on the other hand, the mainsail must be carefully flaked down and tied.

A typical roller reefing system is illustrated in Figure 1-26. The boom is rolled by means of teeth at the end of it, which in turn are driven by a hand-operated worm gear. No locking device is needed for such a system, since it is impossible for the worm gear to rotate backwards.

A through-the-mast system is one of the later developments in roller reefing. An extension of the gooseneck fitting passes through the mast and terminates at the forward face in a winch handle socket. This arrangement, of course, does require a ratchet lock to prevent the boom from possibly unrolling. Figure 1-27 shows a typical through-the-mast roller reefing design.

To reef the main with roller reefing, the following method works well.

1. Remove the vang. (Usually it is fitted either to a keyhole in the boom or to a stainless steel eye which can be pushed up inside the boom.)

2. Insert the handle in the roller reefing socket on the boom or on the forward face of the mast.

3. Tighten the topping lift to help the sail stay at the outboard end of the boom, and so avoid having to pull it out at the leech.

4. Let go of the mainsheet.

5. Ease the main halyard and wind the reef in on the boom. Try to finish with the boom either straight up or completely upside down, the two strongest positions especially if the boom is an eliptical one.

6. When the reefs are in, wind up the main halyard, ease the topping lift, take up on the mainsheet, and

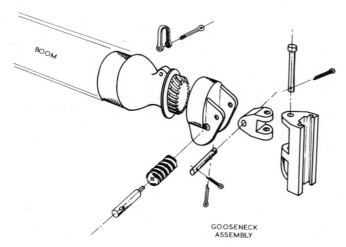

BOOM

GOOSENECK
ASSEMBLY

*Figure 1-26.* An exploded view of a roller reefing boom.

remove the handle.

To shake out a reef, simply perform these same steps in the reverse order.

## Techniques for Handling Other Sails

### Staysails

There are various types of staysails, each serving a different function. The windward staysail, the close reaching staysail, the tallboy and the spinnaker staysail are the most well known.

The windward staysail and the close reaching staysail are both used in conjunction with a high-clewed reacher of the same sail area as the genoa. This two headsail rig not only gives an efficient double slot effect, but the staysail also provides extra sail area. The windward staysail, however, is usually slightly smaller than the CRS. Both the windward staysail and the close reaching staysail require extra track on the foredeck centreline, extending from about 20 per cent of J to 40 per cent J aft of the bow, plus additional track for the sheet fairlead. (Chapter 4 discusses these requirements in more detail.) Talk with your sailmaker, though, before installing this track. On the race course, the disadvantages of the windward and close reaching staysails are the difficulties of sheeting and trimming them, and the restrictions they impose on the helmsman's view of the luff. Also, with the ability of a modern boat to carry a spinnaker when the wind is well forward, these staysails are used less frequently.

A tallboy or banana staysail, which is used under a spinnaker when the boat is running downwind, is positioned so as to clear the stalled air from behind the mainsail. It requires a circular track on the foredeck, about 30 to 40 per cent of J forward of the mast, to enable the sail luff to be kept close to the spinnaker pole. This particular staysail would probably be sheeted to the rail on the lee side. The spinnaker staysail is used under a spinnaker when the boat is reaching. It may be tacked either on the track for the windward and close reaching staysails or on the track for the tallboy. The sheet is led to the rail, or alternatively to one of the other tracks aft of the mast. Consequently, no extra gear is required for this sail.

The halyard and winch requirements for staysails vary, depending upon the size of the boat. Larger boats should have a separate halyard than can serve for all the staysails, plus an extra halyard winch. On smaller boats, however, rather than include another winch, the staysail halyard can be led to a spinnaker or genoa winch when either sail is not in use. As for sheeting, staysail lines can be led to any unoccupied winch, so no special hardware need be added for this purpose.

### High-clewed Reachers

A high-clewed reacher is simply a sail with the same overall area as a genoa, except that the clew is positioned much higher. It is used in conjunction with a CRS when the boat is close reaching. With the wind at 40 degrees or more, this sail combination offers a definite speed advantage, but when the wind goes aft of 55 to 60 degrees, a spinnaker should be used instead. The tack and head of a reacher are positioned like those of a genoa, although the clew is usually sheeted through a block on the quarter where it is then taken to a genoa sheet winch. Thus, no special fittings, other than the block, are needed.

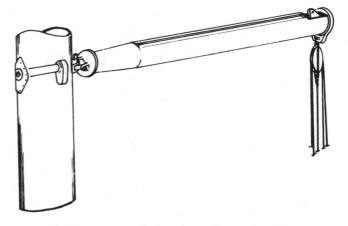

*Figure 1-27.* A through-the-mast roller reefing boom.

## Bigboys or Bloopers

Used on the opposite side of the boat to the spinnaker, a bigboy or blooper is hoisted outside the spinnaker sheet, usually on the spare spinnaker halyard. Bigboys or bloopers must almost always be taken down when the spinnaker is changed or gybed. Methods have been developed for gybing a bigboy or blooper, but they tend to cross the halyards.

## Combined Sail Handling Techniques

Having discussed each sail handling technique separately, it is time to turn to several sequences in which two or three operations are combined. For the purposes of deck design, the main reason for reviewing these sequences is to see which pieces of equipment are used and at what stages. Of course, gear requirements vary for boats of different size, so we will look at a particular boat for each operation—first a gybe set and then a take down and tack.

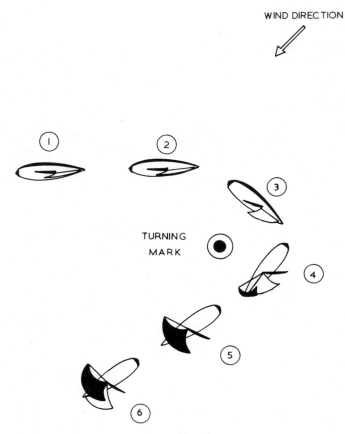

WIND DIRECTION

TURNING MARK

Figure 1-28.   A gybe set mark rounding.

## A Gybe Set

Some combined operations require more steps than others. A gybe set, which involves gybing the headsails as the boat rounds a mark and then setting a spinnaker, is one of the most difficult. Consider the boat in Figure 1-28, a typical Admiral's Cup design. At position 1 it is close hauled on port tack.

At position 2 the sails are being eased a little as the boat edges toward the mark. The tactician is keeping an eye out for any starboard tack boats and also watching the setting up procedures on deck. At the mast, the pole is hooked on and the inboard end raised to the required height, while in the cockpit, the sheets and guys are slacked off and led to winches. The spinnaker is taken forward and tied down on the weather side. The sheets, afterguys, and halyards are clipped onto the sail and the slack taken up. The foreguy is then slackened off a few feet and cleated, the exact amount of slack depending upon the wind strength and the resulting height to which the spinnaker pole will be raised. At this stage, the pole topping lift, which should be under the genoa sheet, is hooked on but held back at the mast.

At position 3 the genoa and mainsail are eased out fully on the port gybe, and the spinnaker hoist is started on the weather side. The genoa and main are gybed and trimmed.

At position 4 the outboard end of the pole is raised and started aft. The spinnaker should now be almost completely up and the sheet should be pulled aft to get the sail open just a little more quickly. The foreguy can be set up and cleated off. Note, too, that there is often no need for the crew to raise the pole because the spinnaker will pull the pole up until it is stopped by the foreguy. But if using this technique, be sure to keep the inboard end of the pole low, or else it will not lift. And be careful not to allow the spinnaker to collapse before the topping lift is made up.

At position 5 the spinnaker is up and drawing, the pole is being hauled aft, and the spinnaker sheet is being eased. The genoa is now being lowered, and when it is down, a bigboy or blooper is set on a spare halyard.

Position 6 shows that while the foredeck crew is doing this, one of the afterguard is easing the main outhaul, cunningham, and kicker, and putting a preventer on the boom. At this stage, with the bigboy or blooper set, the kite drawing, and the mainsail fully out, some crews like to set a tallboy or slot staysail slightly to weather just in front of the mainsail.

From a design point of view, of course, it is not the sail handling techniques themselves that are important, but rather the relationship between handling techniques and the positioning of equipment on deck. One of the most critical factors is the location of the various winches involved. Table 1-30 summarizes the winches required for the gybe set just described.

## Winch Requirements

| Position | Gybe set (Admiral's Cup boat) | Take down and tack (Half Tonner) |
|---|---|---|
| 1 | genoa halyard winch<br>genoa sheet winch<br>main halyard winch<br>main sheet winch<br>Cunningham winch in heavier winds | main halyard winch<br>main sheet winch<br>spinnaker halyard winch<br>spinnaker sheet winch<br>spinnaker guy winch |
| 2 | same as for 1 | same as for 1 |
| 3 | same as for 1, plus:<br>spinnaker halyard winch<br>spinnaker sheet winch<br>spinnaker guy winch | same as for 1 |
| 4 | same as for 3, plus:<br>topping lift winch<br>down haul winch | same as for 1 |
| 5 | main halyard winch<br>main sheet winch<br>spinnaker halyard winch<br>spinnaker sheet winch<br>spinnaker guy winch<br>topping lift winch<br>down haul winch | same as for 1 |
| 6 | same as for 5, plus:<br>genoa sheet winch for bigboy or blooper sheet<br>spinnaker halyard winch for bigboy or blooper halyard | same as for 1, plus:<br>genoa halyard winch<br>genoa sheet winch |
| 7 | | genoa halyard winch<br>genoa sheet winch<br>main halyard winch<br>main sheet winch<br>cunningham winch in heavier winds |

Table 1–30

## A Takedown and Tack

Suppose a Half Tonner is sailing on the course shown in Figure 1-29. There is a strong tidal stream to one side of the buoy. Two possible courses exist. One is to do what boat A is doing and come from position 1 to position 4 about 100 yards short of the mark, gybe the spinnaker, and round the mark on starboard, taking the spinnaker down at the mark and tacking as soon as possible. The second alternative is what boat B is doing–namely, to stay in the tidal stream as long as possible, then sharply head up for the buoy, taking the spinnaker down at position 8, gybing the genoa and main to round the mark, and tacking immediately. Obviously, these are tactical decisions and the question of which is better does not concern us here. But because the first operation is the more complex one, let us review the steps it calls for.

At position 2 the boat leaves the tidal stream, heading high enough to allow the crew sufficient time to clean up the deck after the gybe in preparation for the spinnaker take down. At position 3 the bigboy and any staysails are removed and stuffed down the forehatch. At 4 the spinnaker and main are gybed and

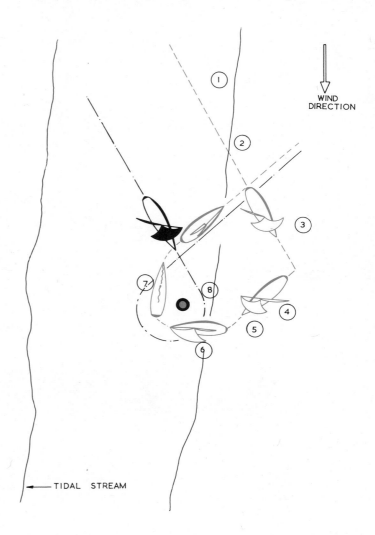

WIND DIRECTION

TIDAL STREAM

*Figure 1-29.* A take-down and tack sequence.

the boat heads up slightly, sailing for the mark at maximum reaching speed. At 6 the pole is put on the forestay and the genoa is hoisted. The boat is now sailing at top speed. The spinnaker is tripped, and as soon as it leaves the guy, the pole is lowered, and the topping lift is unhooked and led back to the mast. If the genoa sheet has been led over the pole, the boat should now be free to tack (at position 7), even if the spinnaker has not been fully gathered. For this operation, an aft spinnaker takedown is usual because it prevents the sail from tangling with the lazy genoa sheet.

Again, the winches used in this sequence are listed in Table 1-30. By working up lists of this sort, one can determine such things as which winches are used simultaneously and therefore can be placed close together, or which winches are used infrequently and therefore suggest fitting lockoffs which can free the winch for some other job. All this is important information that a person should have clearly in mind before beginning the process of laying out a racing deck.

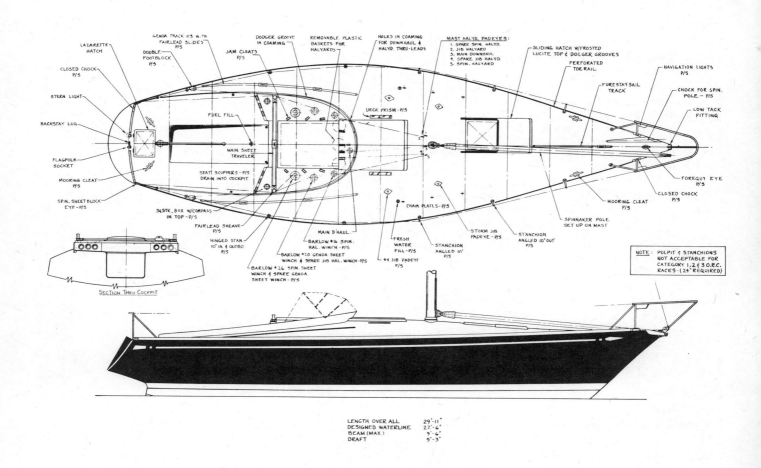

Sparkman & Stephens plan no. 2098, a stock Half Ton cupper.

CHAPTER TWO
# Winches

Sailors have used winches for hundreds of years. The earliest winch was a capstan, used to haul the anchor. Compared with contemporary winches, it was grossly inefficient. On large eighteenth-century warships, dozens of men had to struggle to turn the capstan—a far cry from the ease with which a single crewman pulls in loads up to 10,000 pounds using a modern sailing winch.

Although the principle of the winch has been known for a long time, winches were not used to control sails until the early part of this century. Before then, sails were handled with running rigging which consisted of numerous blocks and multi-part tackles. Such a system was unwieldy at best. But once the sheet winch was introduced, winch technology advanced steadily. Today, a large ocean racer might be equipped with a three-speed, modular linked winch system so sophisticated that it requires a technical expert to repair and maintain it. No wonder, then, that many boat owners have only a limited knowledge of modern winches. This chapter attempts to broaden that knowledge. First it discusses the types of winches that are available, their construction and special features, as well as the factors affecting their power and speed. Next, it covers the proper way to operate a winch, and finally how to select the best winch for each job on a given boat.

## Types of Winches and Their Uses

Without some knowledge of the winches that are currently available and how they operate, one cannot even begin the job of choosing the most efficient set of winches for a particular boat. Various kinds of winches are on the market today, ranging from the simple snubbing winch to the highly complex linked winch systems. We will first describe the different types of standard sheet winches, and then turn to special-purpose and special-feature winches.

### Sheet Winches

*Snubbing Winches*
Without a winch a man can pull only about 150 pounds, or perhaps a little more if he gives a good, hard jerk. And if this load is on a sheet and the man must hold it for any length of time, he will soon tire and eventually allow the sheet to slacken. The snubbing winch is a small, handleless winch intended to overcome this problem of fatigue: it allows the crewman to haul in whatever load he is capable of pulling and then to hold it without quickly tiring.

Because of the limited loads for which it is intended, the snubbing winch is usually found on small keelboats, such as Solings or Tempests. Its design is quite simple. A drum is fitted around a central spindle, and pawls on the spindle allow the drum to revolve in one direction only. The spindle is also equipped with bearings which help reduce friction.

*Single-speed Winches*
When the load on a sheet becomes too great for a person to comfortably handle using a snubbing winch, it is necessary to use a larger winch instead. The next step up is the single-speed winch, which is really just a larger version of a snubbing winch with a square hole in the top for a handle. With a few exceptions, almost all single-speed winches are direct drive, meaning that the drum revolves at the same speed as the handle.

The single-speed, direct-drive winch is similar in construction to the snubbing winch in that both have a central spindle with pawls and bearings, over which is fitted a drum. The difference between the two, of course, is that the single-speed winch is operated by a handle. Most are top-action winches—that is, the handle is inserted in the top. But there are also some bottom-action models which have a flat handle that is inserted in a slot at the base of the winch; the drum is then

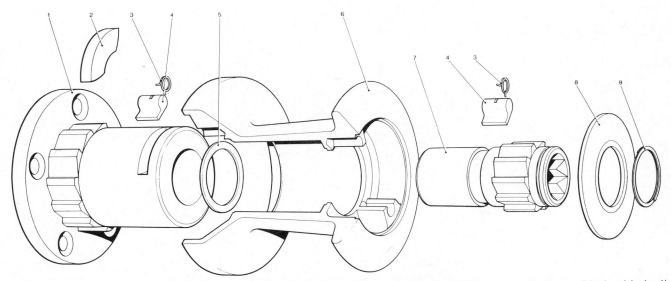

*Figure 2-1.* An exploded view of a Lewmar single-speed winch, numbers 6 and 7. *(Courtesy of Lewmar Marine Limited)*
1 Centre Stem, 2 Key, 3 Pawl Spring, 4 Pawl, 5 Washer, 6 Drum (Bronze or Alloy), 7 Spindle, 8 Top Cap, 9 Circlip

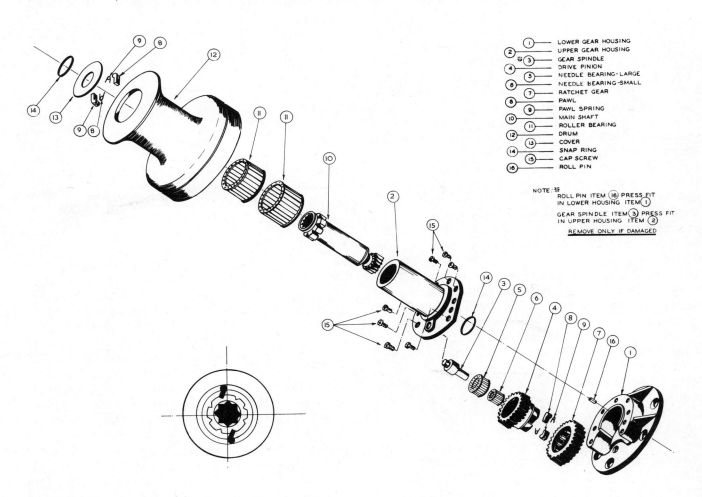

1    LOWER GEAR HOUSING
2    UPPER GEAR HOUSING
※3   GEAR SPINDLE
4    DRIVE PINION
5    NEEDLE BEARING-LARGE
6    NEEDLE BEARING-SMALL
7    RATCHET GEAR
8    PAWL
9    PAWL SPRING
10   MAIN SHAFT
11   ROLLER BEARING
12   DRUM
13   COVER
14   SNAP RING
15   CAP SCREW
16   ROLL PIN

NOTE:※
ROLL PIN ITEM 16 PRESS FIT
IN LOWER HOUSING ITEM 1

GEAR SPINDLE ITEM 3 PRESS FIT
IN UPPER HOUSING ITEM 2
REMOVE ONLY IF DAMAGED

*Figure 2-2.* An exploded view of a Barient two-speed winch, number 26. *(Courtesy of Barient Company)*

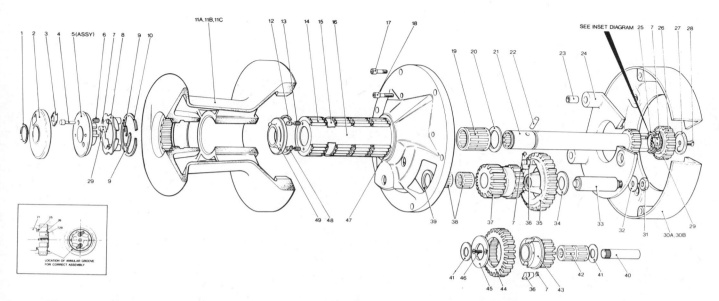

*Figure 2-3.* An exploded view of a Lewmar three-speed winch, number 65. *(Courtesy of Lewmar Marine Limited)*
1 Circlip, Spirolox, 2 Top Cap Cover, 3 Push Button, 4 Plunger, 5 Top Cap Assembly, 6 Spring, 7 Pawl Spring, 8 Closing Ring, 9 Spring, 10 Circlip, 11A Drum, Bronze, 11B Drum, Alloy, 12 Plunger, 13 Spring, 14 Cage Assembly, 15 Spacer, 16 Centre Stem, 17 Socket Head Cap Screw $\frac{3}{8}$" 16 UNC × $\frac{3}{4}$" long, 18 Socket Head Cap Screw $\frac{5}{16}$" 18 UNC × 1$\frac{1}{2}$" long, 19 Cage Assembly, 20 Washer, 21 Spindle, 22 Drive Pin, 23 Hollow Dowel, 24 Bridge Piece, 25 Spacer, 26 Ratchet Gear, 27 Spindle End Cap, 28 Countersunk Screw $\frac{1}{4}$" UNC × $\frac{1}{2}$" long, 29 Pawl, 30A Base, Bronze, 30B Base, Alloy, 31 Locknut, $\frac{1}{2}$" BSF, 32 Washer, 33 Spindle, 34 Washer, 35 Pawl Gear, 36 Pawl, 37 Output Gear, 38 Cage Assembly, 39 Washer, 40 Spindle, 41 Washer, 42 Cage Assembly, 43 Pawl Gear, 44 Ratchet Gear, 45 Retaining Plate, 46 Countersunk Screw 2 BA × $\frac{3}{8}$" long, 47 Washer, 48 Collet, 49 Clutch Plate

wound by a ratcheting motion. Figure 2-1 shows a Lewmar single-speed winch.

Although often assumed to be an insignificant part of the winch system, the lowly winch handle plays a far more important role than most people suspect. Careful design of a handle is essential. Some measurements, of course, have become standardized. Most handles are 10 inches long, which reflects a compromise between increased power and the average man's reach. (This is the handle length used to calculate power ratios.) Also, the $\frac{11}{16}$ inch stud is now accepted as the international norm. Other aspects of handle design, however, are left to the judgment of the winch manufacturer. Some key considerations are the size and shape of the hand grip (a good grip should fit the hand well) and the total handle weight (a heavier handle has a higher energy potential which makes it easier to wind at the furthest point in the turning circle, but too much weight is cumbersome).

*Multiple-speed Winches*
The next step up in winches, beyond the single-speed type, is some kind of geared winch. These are designed so that winding the handle in one direction gives you a high-speed drive, while reversing the handle direction causes the drum to revolve at a lower speed for the same number of handle turns. Multiple-speed winches are essential on larger boats. The high-speed drive is used during a tack to get most of the genoa sheet in rapidly, while the lower, second speed allows the last few inches to be pulled in. And for trimming under load, which requires a good deal of power on larger boats, genoa winches often have a third speed. This slowest drive is brought into play either by pressing a button on the winch or by depressing the handle and winding in the reverse direction from second speed.

Multiple-speed winches are much more complex in construction than single-speed. A typical two-speed winch has a gear wheel which is driven by a central shaft. This gear wheel, in turn, drives another gear which ultimately winds the winch drum. Reversing the direction in which the handle is turned brings other gear wheels into play between the shaft and the drum, and these gears lower the speed at which the drum revolves. Spring loaded pawls stop the drum movement from reversing when the handle is wound in the opposite direction. In order to reduce friction as much as possible, there are needle roller bearings between the shaft and the drum, and the gears operate on low-

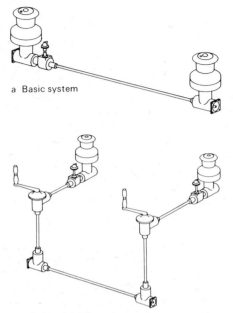

a Basic system

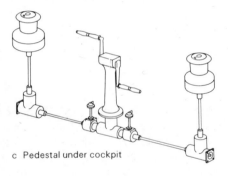

b Double molehill arrangement

c Pedestal under cockpit

*Figure 2-4.* Some of the linked winch variations. *(Courtesy of Lewmar Marine Limited)*

*Figure 2-5.* A Barient integral pedestal grinder, MK XII. *(Courtesy of Barient Company)*

friction bearings. On larger winches, pawls that work off an idler gear also reduce friction and allow the drum to freewheel easily as the slack in the sheet is taken in.

Most three-speed winches are similar in construction to the typical two-speed winch except that they have a by-pass mechanism which allows the winch to be driven directly. Barient, however, has developed a line of three-speed winches that are fully geared in every speed.

Figure 2-2 shows an exploded view of a two-speed Barient sheet winch, and Figure 2-3 shows a three-speed Lewmar sheet winch. The two-speed type is generally used for primary sheets on smaller and medium-sized boats, and also for halyards; the three-speed models are used for primary sheets on larger boats.

## Linked Winches

Most boats do not require sheet winches more powerful than the largest multiple-speed, top action winch. But a sizable minority of offshore racers are now being equipped with linked winches which can be operated by a pedestal, and also by a winch handle for trimming. Designed for larger boats with greater sail area and consequently more sheet load, the linked winch system is a good alternative to the development of, say, a four-speed winch, or perhaps a three-speed with a longer and more cumbersome handle.

The earliest linked winch systems were composed of two winches joined together by extending the shaft of each out through the bottom of the winch and bolting a bevel gear onto the extension. The bevel gear drove another gear, which gave a 90 degree turn. By mounting the second gears on either end of a drive shaft, it was possible for one winch to be used to drive another. This design was first introduced by Lewmar on the 1971 *Morning Cloud*. From here it was an easy step to incorporate a pedestal, a molehill, or additional winches. Figure 2-4 shows some of the possibilities.

Linked winches have several obvious advantages. They allow any number of men to be used to drive a winch, depending upon the type of linkage. Of course, a large number of bodies is rarely needed to power a single winch, but another big plus for the linked system is that the winchman can now operate the winch from the weather rail if required. The system also allows a designer to use a molehill or a cross-linked pedestal so as to position the winder where he is clear of both the winch and the tailer. There is, however, one drawback that must be considered when linking winches: every right angle turn introduces friction and lowers the efficiency of the system by about 5 to 8 per cent.

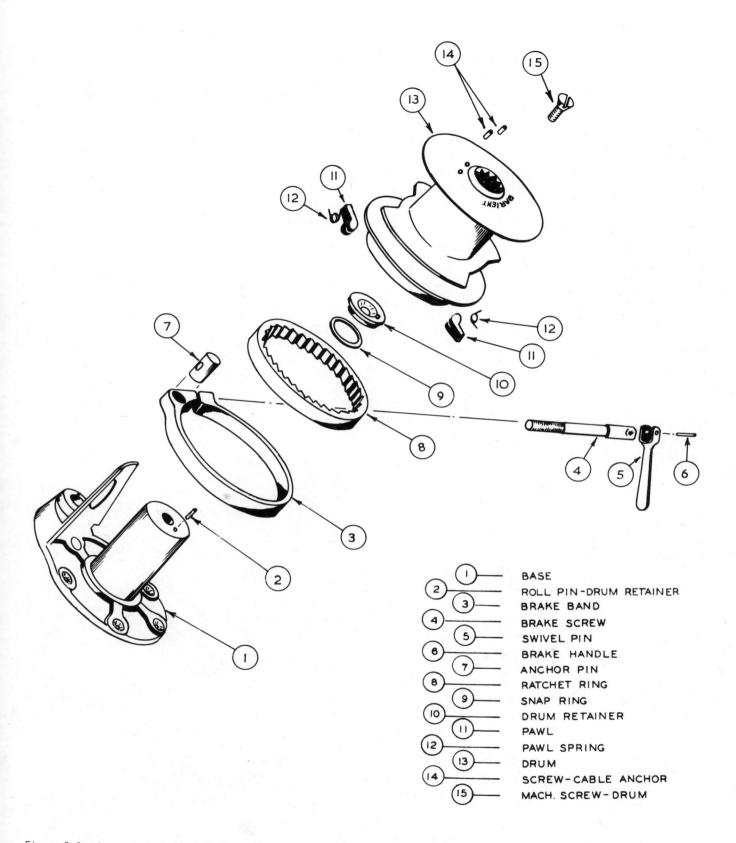

| | |
|---|---|
| 1 | BASE |
| 2 | ROLL PIN-DRUM RETAINER |
| 3 | BRAKE BAND |
| 4 | BRAKE SCREW |
| 5 | SWIVEL PIN |
| 6 | BRAKE HANDLE |
| 7 | ANCHOR PIN |
| 8 | RATCHET RING |
| 9 | SNAP RING |
| 10 | DRUM RETAINER |
| 11 | PAWL |
| 12 | PAWL SPRING |
| 13 | DRUM |
| 14 | SCREW-CABLE ANCHOR |
| 15 | MACH. SCREW-DRUM |

*Figure 2-6.* An exploded view of a Barient two-speed reel winch, number 3. *(Courtesy of Barient Company)*

### Integral Pedestal Winches

Large boats, with extremely high genoa sheet loads, often have a pedestal winch with an integral, large diameter drum. These winches, more commonly referred to as 'coffee grinders,' are operated by turning the pedestal handles which revolve a shaft or chain. The drum is connected to this shaft or chain by various gears and linkages. To change the speed at which the drum revolves, one must reverse the direction in which the handles are turned. Three-speed grinders have a push button or control knob on the top of the drum which engages the third speed when the handles are turned in the opposite direction from second speed. Figure 2-5 shows a Barient integral pedestal grinder. The difference between this and a linked winch system, of course, is that with the coffee grinder the drum and pedestal are integral parts of a single structure.

### Special-purpose Winches

For some jobs, the standard sheet winch may not be ideal, and a special-purpose winch is preferable. When lowering a sail, for example, a halyard reel winch may be preferred because it stores the halyard on a reel rather than having it coiled on deck. Similarly, when lowering a centreboard, a special purpose centreboard winch has the advantage of doing the job smoothly, with no damage to the board or stops.

### Halyard Reel Winches

When a boat has wire halyards it is sometimes more convenient to store the wire on a reel winch than to wrap it between winch and cleat. A reel winch is slightly different in construction from a standard winch. Like a standard winch, the drum is turned by gears and pawls prevent the drum from revolving in the wrong direction. But the pawls on a reel winch operate on the inside of a brake drum, and only when the brake is screwed down tightly does that drum stop revolving. Thus to lower the sail, one simply slacks off the toggle-operated brake lever and allows the drum to slip. For safety reasons, a crewman should never insert a handle in the winch when the brake is about to be released. Also, halyard reel winches should never be oiled because oil can permeate the brake drum with disastrous results. Figure 2-6 shows an exploded view of a Barient two-speed reel winch. Except for the larger reel winches, like this one, most are single-speed.

The last few turns on a typical reel winch are taken up on a step located on the inboard end of the drum. Crewmen should be careful to pass the wire over the guard correctly and onto this step. This prevents the wire leaving the winch from crushing the turns underneath, and it also reduces leverage on the winch base by keeping the halyard close to the mast.

In spite of its advantages, the halyard reel winch also has several drawbacks. There is always a possibility that the winch may slip, and it is difficult to make fine adjustments to the halyards. For these reasons, an ordinary sheet winch with a horn is preferable on a pure racing boat. Reel winches are usually found on boats that both cruise and race, although even here they should be used only for the main halyards.

### Centreboard Winches

All boats with a centreboard must have some method of raising and lowering the board. On small to medium-sized boats, a special winch is typically used for this purpose. A centreboard winch differs from a sheet winch in that the drum is turned by a worm drive which permits the load to be held in any position. The board can thus be raised or lowered simply by changing the direction in which the handle is rotated. Figure 2-7 shows a typical centreboard winch.

*Figure 2-7.* A centreboard winch. *(Courtesy of Merriman-Holbrook, Inc.)*

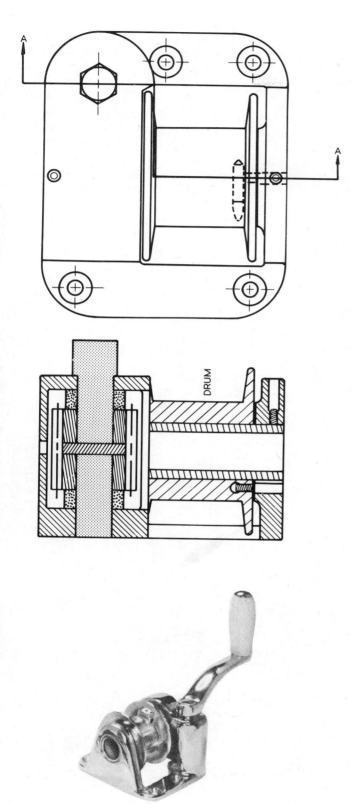

*Figure 2-7b.* A Merriman-Holbrook worm gear drive winch for centreboards on smaller boats.

## Special-feature Winches

In addition to winches designed for special purposes, winches with special features are also available. The most common of these are probably self-tailing winches, winches with backwind, and electric-drive winches.

### Self-tailing Winches

A self-tailing winch is similar to an ordinary sheet winch except that it has a special mechanism to remove the line from the drum as the winch is wound. The only other possible difference between a self-tailing and a standard winch is that the self-tailer is fully geared in all speeds while the ordinary model may or may not be. In recent years, all the major manufacturers have developed some form of self-tailing device, although specific designs vary. Figure 2-8 shows an exploded view of a Lewmar self-tailing winch. Any self-tailing winch, of course, can also be used like an ordinary winch simply by removing the sheet from the self-tailing mechanism.

Experience has shown that the self-tailing winch is most suitable for the spinnaker afterguy and foreguy, and for the pole topping lift (all of which should be positioned within reach of one crewman), as well as for the mainsheet, the runners, and on larger boats the inboard end of the spinnaker pole lift. Where a boom vang or handy billy is used, a self-tailing winch can also be helpful.

To install a self-tailing winch, the rope shedder should be placed at about 15 degrees to a line from the operator through the centreline of the winch. This is shown in Figure 2-9. When using the winch, the operator should put at least three turns on the drum before putting the sheet into the self-tailer. If only one turn is put on the drum, the line will slip, and if the line snaps out of the self-tailing device while under load, the operator's hand can be pulled into the winch. Figure 2-10 illustrates the correct method of putting a sheet on a self-tailing winch.

### Winches with Backwind

With today's high aspect ratio rigs, sheet loads are very large, and the simple job of easing a sheet off a drum can be hazardous business. Lewmar had this in mind when it designed a grinder with backwind. The sheet can be eased under load by reversing the direction of the drum. This allows the sheet to be eased out without the usual sharp jerks which disturb the airflow over the sail. Also, a riding turn can be easily wound out,

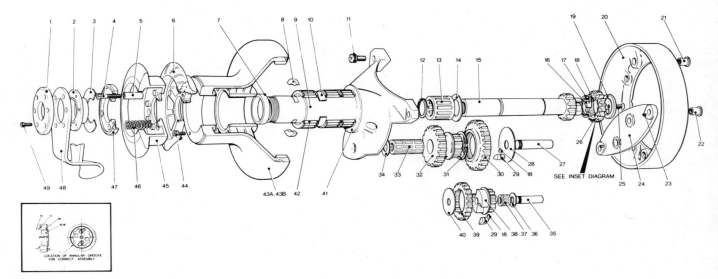

*Figure 2-8.* An exploded view of a Lewmar self-tailing winch. *(Courtesy of Lewmar Marine Limited)*
1 Top Plate, 2 Nut, 3 Thrust Washer, 4 Socket Head Cap Screw $\frac{1}{4}$" × 20 UNC × $1\frac{3}{4}$" long, 5 Spacer, 6 Lower Crown Plate, 7 Collar, 8 Key, 9 Centre Stem, 10 Spacer, 11 Socket Head Cap Screw $\frac{3}{8}$" × 16 UNC × $\frac{3}{4}$" long, 12 Circlip, Spirolox, 13 Cage Assembly, 14 Washer, 15 Spindle, 16 Pawl, 17 Spacer, 18 Pawl Spring, 19 Spindle End Cap, 20 Base, 21 Dowel, 22 Dowel, 23 Spirol Pin, 24 Bridge Piece, 25 Countersunk Screw $\frac{1}{4}$" × 20 UNC × $\frac{1}{2}$" long, 26 Ratchet Gear, 27 Shaft, 28 Washer, 29 Pawl, 30 Pawl Gear, 31 Circlip, 32 Ratchet Gear, 33 Cage Assembly, 34 Washer, 35 Shaft, 36 Washer, 37 Cage Assembly, 38 Pawl Gear, 39 Ratchet Gear, 40 Washer, 41 Washer, Drum, 42 Cage Assembly, 43A Drum, Stainless Steel, 43B Drum Alloy, 44 Socket Head Cap Screw $\frac{1}{4}$" × 20 UNC × $\frac{3}{4}$" long, 45 Upper Crown Plate, 46 Spring, 47 Retaining Plate, 48 Stripper Plate, 49 Socket Head Cap Screw $\frac{1}{4}$" × 20 UNC × $\frac{1}{2}$" long.

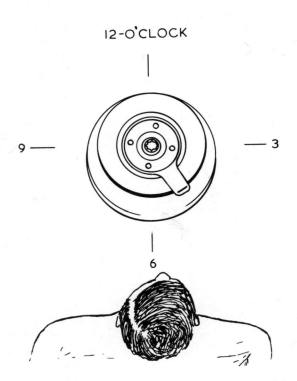

*Figure 2-9.* How to position the line lifter on a self-tailing winch. When the tailer stands facing the winch in the normal operating position, the line lifter should be positioned at 5 o'clock. *(Courtesy of Barient Company)*

*Figure 2-10.* The correct method of putting a sheet on a self-tailing winch. Note the number of turns on the drum. *(Courtesy of Lewmar Marine Limited)*

48

especially when wire sheets are used. Reversible drums are operated either by a worm gear mounted on the drum or by a gear train inside the winch.

*Electric Winches*

Electric winches are not generally used on racing boats, but some of the larger cruiser/racers have one or two for shorthanded cruising. The power consumption of an electric winch is high, extremely so, and as the load increases, so does the power required. For a 12 volt winch, the circuit breakers should be set at about 90 ampères. Of course, electric winches can be ordered with motors to suit most common voltages. The higher the voltage, the less amperes required under load.

With many electric winches, the drum can freewheel when the electric drive is not in use. The winch can also be operated with a handle. When the handle is inserted, it depresses a plunger in the winch which makes it safe for manual use. When the motor is in use, it is operated by a foot switch located near the winch. Ideally, of course, an electric winch should also be self-tailing, so the operator is completely free of work and need only press the button.

## Winch Maintenance

Closely related to the topic of winch construction is that of winch maintenance. When a designer is aware of the problems that may arise in maintaining different types of winches, he is more likely to appreciate the need for easy access to winch mechanisms—especially from underneath where linkages and angle drives are located. Of course, any information on winch maintenance included here must necessarily be very general due to the differences in models produced by different manufacturers. Almost all winch makers have booklets on maintenance, and if you intend to do your own servicing you should obtain the relevant ones. Nevertheless, the basic maintenance principles that follow are a good starting point.

To gain access to the interior workings, the drum of a winch must usually be removed. On smaller sized Barlow winches, the drum is secured with a machine screw set inside the winch handle socket. The smaller size Barient winches use a circlip or snap ring over a washer to hold the drum in place. Larger winches by these manufacturers have a specially designed, keyed nut which screws into the top of the spindle until it is flush with the drum. Lewmar winches, regardless of their size, are designed similar to the smaller Barient

winches—with a snap ring fitted over a washer, which in turn holds the drum.

Once the drum has been removed, the gears and roller races are exposed. Always be sure to note how the various parts fit together so that they can be replaced correctly. Most single-speed winches simply have a central spindle which has pawls set into it and is surrounded by a roller race with various spacers and washers. Two- and three-speed winches are more complex in that they have several gear trains and sets of pawls.

With the winch stripped down, inspect for broken pawl springs, bent pawls, gears, and spindle, roller races that do not move freely, and any shards of metal embedded in the winch grease which could be a sign of future trouble. On reel winches, inspect the brake drum for cracks. The component parts, except the brake parts on a reel winch, should then be immersed in paraffin or kerosene to remove all grease. Afterwards, the parts should be carefully dried.

Now is the time to decide whether you want to oil your winches weekly or simply clean and grease them twice a year. The maintenance schedule you chose affects the procedures you should follow. If you plan a weekly routine, the parts should be oiled lightly and then reassembled. If, on the other hand, you opt for a much less frequent schedule, the parts should be greased rather than oiled before reassembly. But avoid putting grease on the springs and pawls; it can react with salt water to form a sticky gum which can render the winch useless.

The next step is to bolt the winch back in place, greasing each bolt to facilitate its later removal. When securing winches back to the deck or base plate, beware of putting dissimilar metals together because this can cause corrosion in a marine environment. Use a bedding compound to seal the through-bolts and prevent any leaks. And if you use one of the more gooey compounds, be sure not to get any into the winch or the winch drainage holes.

If the sails are the engine of a boat, the winches might be considered the throttle. Without winches, the sails cannot be regulated at all. It pays, therefore, to always keep winches in top working order.

## Winch Size and Selection

Which winch? This is one of the biggest questions facing the inexperienced owner who wants to design his own deck. Fortunately, he has all the expertise of the winch manufacturer's staff to help him answer it. But many owners feel they should also acquire some technical knowledge of their own. What is the relationship between winch power and speed? What do the manufacturer's winch numbers mean? And how does one make an estimate of the winch size needed for a particular job? These are some of the topics we will consider in the following section.

## The Trade-off Between Speed and Power

The basic purpose of a winch, of course, is to reduce the load on a sheet to a manageable load on a handle. Theoretically, a winch could be produced that would allow an average crewman to haul in an incredibly large sheet load with no difficulty at all. The only trouble would be the equally incredible snail's pace at which the winch drum would revolve. The job of getting the genoa home could take hours! This is because there is a trade-off between winch power and speed. For every gain you make on one side of that trade-off, you must give up something on the other. To understand how this inverse relationship works, it helps to review the concepts of gear ratio and power ratio.

*Gear and Power Ratios*
The gear ratio of a winch is the number of times you must turn the handle in order to rotate the drum once.

## Half Ton Cup Boat Sail Data (a)

| Sails | | Wind mph | Weight oz. | L.P. | Luff | Area | Remarks |
|---|---|---|---|---|---|---|---|
| Main sail | 1 | all | 6.5 | see | plan | | Reefs: 1=flat'n'g, 2=4' 0", 3=5'0" ± |
| Trysail | R | — | 6.5 | 9.5' | 14.75' | 70 | Reef: 3' 6"=42f; rope tack pen. |
| No. 4 (storm jib) | R | 40–50 | 7.5 | 7.0' | 21.0' | 74 | 1 ft tack pen., 17.75 ft head pennant |
| (Reefed no. 3) | | 30–40 | 6.5 | 12.0' | 29.0' | 174 | Same sail as below |
| No. 3 Genoa | 2 | 22–30 | 6.5 | 15.0' | 34.0' | 255 | 5.75' head pennant |
| No. 2 Genoa | 3 | 16–22 | 6.5 | 17.0 | 36.5' | 310 | 3.25' head pennant |
| No. 1 Genoa | 4 | 4–16 | 4.5 | 18.6' | 39.75' | 365 | Design for slack rig in light wind |
| Lt No. 1 Genoa | 6 | 0– | 3.0 | 18.6' | 39.75' | 365 | Choose betw'n Lt No. 1 or 110% st'ys'l. |
| Reacher | 5 | 3–22 | 3.0 | 18.6' | 39.75' | 365 | Doubles as drifter |
| 110% staysail | 6A | — | 3.0 | 13.6' | 35.0' | 238 | Reefs: 1: 6' 8". Fly on spin. Hal'd |
| Blooper | 7 | — | 0.75N | 18.6' | 39.75' | 375 | |
| Starcut spinnaker | 8 | — | 1.5D or N | | | | Storm dimensions, narrow shoulder |
| Heavy spinnaker | 9 | — | 0.75N | rule | max | 859 | Tri radial, foot only 92% smw |
| Light spinnaker | 10 | — | 0.5N | rule | max | 859 | Tri radial, foot only 92% smw |

## Sheet Loads for a Half Ton Cup Boat (b)

| Sail | Wind range (knots) | Area (sq ft) | % Area | Wind Speed (knots) | | | | | | | | | | | | |
|---|---|---|---|---|---|---|---|---|---|---|---|---|---|---|---|---|
| | | | | 5 | 10 | 15 | 18 | 20 | 25 | 30 | 35 | 40 | 45 | 50 | 55 | 60 |
| Storm jib | 40–50 | 74 | 20 | | | | | | | | | 510.3 | 645.8 | 797 | | |
| Reefed No. 3 | 30–40 | 174 | 48 | | | | | | | 674.9 | 918.7 | 1200 | | | | |
| No. 3 Genoa | 22–30 | 255 | 70 | | | | | 439.6 | 687 | 9892 | | | | | | |
| No. 2 Genoa | 16–22 | 310 | 85 | | | 300.6 | 432 | 534.4 | 835 | | | | | | | |
| No. 1 Genoa | 4–16 | 365 | 100 | 39.3 | 157.3 | 354 | | | | | | | | | | |
| Lt No. 1 Genoa | 0.8 | 365 | 100 | 39.3 | | | | | | | | | | | | |
| Reacher | 3–22 | 365 | 100 | 39.3 | 157.3 | 354 | 629.3 | | | | | | | | | |

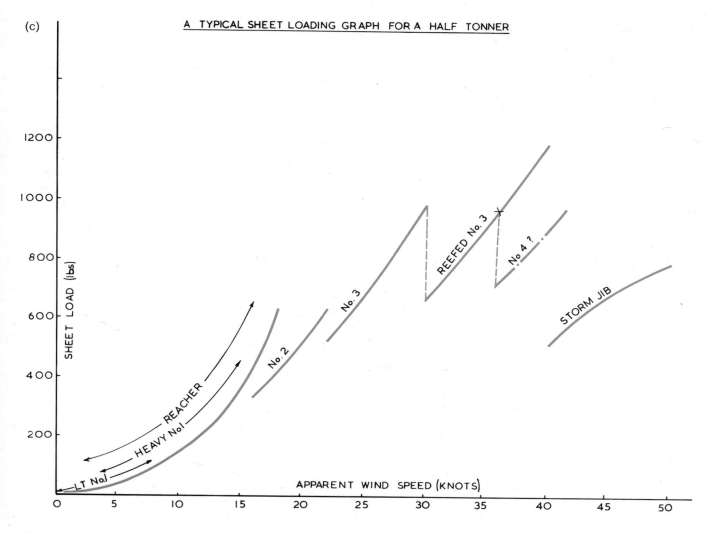

(c)

A TYPICAL SHEET LOADING GRAPH FOR A HALF TONNER

*Figure 2-11.* (a) The sail inventory for a typical Half Tonner. (b) The sheet loads for the sails shown in drawing (a). (c) The same sheet loads graphically illustrated. Note that the reefed No. 3 carries the highest load. It may be better to reef the No. 3 again at X to lower the strain on the winches.

The formula is:

$$\text{Gear ratio} = \frac{\text{Number of handle revolutions}}{\text{Number of drum revolutions}}$$

A single-speed direct-action winch, for example, has a gear ratio of 1 to 1 (1/1=1), meaning that the drum revolves once for every turn of the handle. If a winch has three speeds, the first may have a gear ratio of 1 to 1. In second speed, however, you may have to turn the handle 5 times for every one drum revolution; the gear ratio is 5 to 1 (5/1=5). And in third speed, it may take 12 turns of the handle for a single revolution of the drum, thus giving a gear ratio of 12 to 1 (12/1=12).

Power ratio is the winch manufacturer's term for mechanical advantage. It depends on three factors: the gear ratio, the length of the winch handle, and the

diameter of the drum. The relationship between these variables is shown in the following equation:

Power ratio =

$$\frac{\text{Gear ratio} \times \text{diameter of circle described by handle}}{\text{Diameter of drum}}$$

Thus, if the three-speed winch just described has a drum diameter of 4.5 inches and the handle is 10 inches long, the power ratio in first speed is:

$$\frac{1 \times (2 \times 10)}{4.5} = 4.44 \quad \text{(or 4.44 to 1)}$$

In second speed the power ratio is:

$$\frac{5 \times (2 \times 10)}{4.5} = 22.22 \quad \text{(or 22.22 to 1)}$$

51

## The Admiral's Cup Boat Sail Data

| Sail | WT | Luff | LP | Area | Remarks |
|---|---|---|---|---|---|
| Main | 8.0 | 50.0 | 13.2 | 330 | 3 reefs; flatting reef shelf w/o zipper |
| Storm trys'l | 8.5 | 20.0 | 12.5 | 125 | |
| Storm jib | 8.5 | 36.5 | 8.5 | 155 | |
| Storm stays'l | 8.5 | 21.0 | 7.0 | 7.4 | |
| No. 4 Jib 80% | 8.5 | 47.0 | 15.4 | 363 | With reef to reduce area to 260 ft |
| No. 3 solent jib | 2.50 | 55.0 | 18.8 | 517 | |
| No. 2 genoa 125% | 8.5 | 56.0 | 23.12 | 647 | Reef with blast R |
| No. 1 heavy genoa | 7.2 | 57.0 | 26.7 | 761 | |
| No. 1 light genoa | 5.0 | 57.0 | 26.7 | 761 | |
| Drifter reacher | 2.2 | 57.0 | 26.7 | 761 | |
| Wind seeker 140% | .75 | 56.0 | 24.9 | 701 | Wire luff |
| Reacher 150% | 4.5 | 57.0 | 26.7 | 761 | Trims to stern |
| Dual stays'l 110% | 3.2 | 53.3 | 19.6 | 522 | Reefs to genoa stays'l |
| Blooper 150% | .75 | 57.0 | 26.7 | 761 | Radial tack; head |
| Storm spin | 1.5 | 51.5 | 24.0 | | |
| Spinnaker | 1.5 | 55.4 | 32.0 | | Reacher |
| Spinnaker | 1.5 | 55.4 | 32.0 | mid-girths | |
| Spinnaker | .75 | 55.4 | 32.0 | | |
| Spinnaker | .50 | 55.4 | 32.0 | | Floater |

(a)

## Sheet Loads for an Admiral's Cup Boat

| Sail | Wind range (knots) | Area sq ft | % area | Wind speed knots | | | | | | | | | | | | |
|---|---|---|---|---|---|---|---|---|---|---|---|---|---|---|---|---|
| | | | | 7 | 10 | 15 | 18 | 20 | 25 | 30 | 35 | 40 | 45 | 50 | 55 | 60 |
| Storm trysail | 60+ | 131 | 14.5 | | | | | | | | | | | | | 1708 |
| Storm jib | 50–60 | 108 | 12 | | | | | | | | | | | | 1408 | 1675 |
| Fore staysail | 35–40 | 240 | 27 }54 | | | | | | | | 1267 | 1655 | 2094 | 2586 | | |
| No. 3 jib topsail | 35–45 | 240 | 27 | | | | | | | | 1267 | 1655 | 2094 | 2586 | | |
| No. 4 Genoa | 32–40 | 495 | 55 | | | | | | | | 2613 | 3414 | | | | |
| No. 3 Genoa | 25–35 | 656 | 73 | | | | | | 1767 | 2545 | 3463 | | | | | |
| No. 2 Genoa | 15–25 | 790 | 88 | | | 776 | 1103 | 1362 | 2128 | | | | | | | |
| Hvy No. 1 Genoa | 10–18 | 887 | 98 | | 388 | 873 | 1257 | 1552 | | | | | | | | |
| Lt No. 1 Genoa | 2–7 | 900 | 100 | 190 | 388 | | | | | | | | | | | |
| Drifter | 0–3 | 900 | 100 | Hand held | | | | | | | | | | | | |

(b)

52

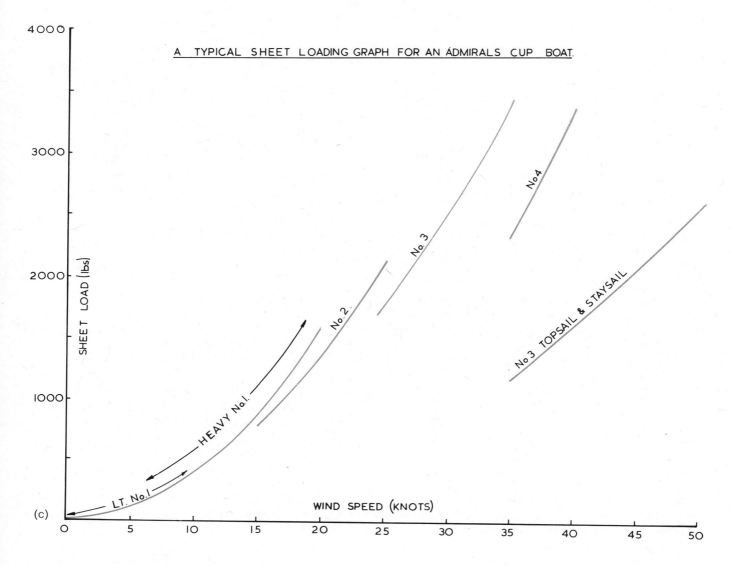

*Figure 2-12.* (a) The sail inventory for an Admiral's Cup boat. (b) The sheet loads calculated. (c) The sheet loads graphed.

And in third speed the power ratio is:

$$\frac{12 \times (2 \times 10)}{4.5} = 53.33 \quad \text{(or 53.33 to 1)}$$

### Achieving an Optimum Balance

Obviously, gear and power ratios are very closely linked. The higher the gear ratio (and the lower the speed), the higher the power ratio (and the greater the sheet load that can be pulled in for a given amount of effort). This means that with a low gear ratio–say, 1 to 1–the sheet can be brought in very quickly, but the power that the winch operator must exert is very high. In our earlier example, one pound on the handle of the winch would only pull in a 4.44 pound load on the sheet. So if a man can exert 50 pounds on a winch handle, the maximum sheet load he can pull in is 50 × 4.44 or 222 pounds. If the sheet load exceeds this, the winch operator must switch to second speed which gives a higher power ratio. His 50 pounds of force would now be enough to pull in a sheet load of 1111 pounds, or five times what he could handle previously. But he will also have to increase his turns of the winch handle five fold. And at third speed, the operator would have to wind the handle twelve times to revolve the drum once, although the sheet load he could haul in would be 2666.5 pounds! Manufacturers have carefully developed their winches to achieve the optimum balance between speed on the one hand and power on the other.

## What the Winch Numbers Mean

Some manufacturers use power ratios to govern their winch numbering systems. A Lewmar 40, for example, has a power ratio of 40 to 1 in second gear, and 1 to 1 in first gear.

But this relationship between power ratio and winch number is far from universal. Barient and Barlow number their winches according to the working load divided by 100. Thus a Barient 22 would normally be used for loads of about 2200 pounds.

Both these numbers are, of course, useful. The Barient/Barlow numbering system gives an instant guide to the working load of the winch. The Lewmar system, on the other hand, gives an easy way of calculating the size load a crewman can actually handle using a given winch. For example, if the average person can exert 45 pounds of pressure on the handle of a winch, then the load on the drum he is capable of turning is the power ratio multiplied by 45. Thus, with a Lewmar 40 (power ratio of 40) an average crewman could handle 40 × 45 = 1800 pounds of pressure on the drum.

## Estimating Your Winch Requirements

When a designer selects a winch for a certain purpose, he does so on the basis of several factors: his calculation of the sheet load, the manufacturer's recommendations, and his past experience using winches under varied sailing conditions. Here we will look at one method of calculating sheet load to find the required winch size.

Note, however, that the other factors just mentioned also contribute to the final decision of which winch to choose.

The manufacturer's recommendations, especially, should never be disregarded. All the major winch makers have compiled tables matching sail area or displacement to winch size. These guidelines are used because sheet load is directly proportional to sail area and wind strength, and sail area is directly related to displacement. Beware of winch tables that relate winch size to boat length, because the sail areas or displacements of boats of equal length can vary tremendously. Although the following pages describe one way to calculate winch requirements without consulting manufacturers' tables, don't make the mistake of completely ignoring the winch maker's advice. He is far more likely to know the extent of load a particular winch can handle than are you, the beginning deck designer.

### Selecting Sheet Winches

Theoretically, the load in lbs on a genoa sheet can be calculated approximately by the formula:

sail area (sq ft) × wind velocity $^2$(knots) × 0.00431

This formula has been experimentally verified with a dynamometer on wire sheets. Figures 2-11 and 2-12 show typical sheeting load curves for a Half Tonner and a boat of Admiral's Cup size. Note, however, that boats with higher righting moments may impose slightly higher loadings than are indicated here. As can be seen from the graph, the smaller headsails have the higher loadings.

To select a genoa winch, take the sheet load calculated under the heaviest wind conditions and multiply by a safety factor (2.0 for small boats, decreasing to 1.2 for larger ones). The result can then be compared to the manufacturer's 'recommended working loads' for particular winches. Table 2-13 is a table of most of the winches currently produced, with their working loads if available.

The same method used to select a genoa sheet winch can also be used to select a staysail sheet winch. For spinnaker sheet winches, experience suggests that you should probably select a model one or two sizes smaller than the genoa sheet winch. The exact size, of course, depends on the boat's stability and whether it can carry a starcut because the starcut imposes the greatest spinnaker sheet load.

The load in lbs on a main sheet of a medium displacement boat can be calculated using still another formula:

$$\frac{E \times P^2 \times 0.0043\,V^2}{\text{Leech length}}$$

Where E is the foot length, P is the hoist (both in feet) and V the wind speed in knots.

This calculation should be made for wind strengths up to and including the maximum reefed position. Figure 2-14 plots the results for the same Admiral's Cup boat used to illustrate how genoa sheet loads are calculated. Note that this formula, like the one for genoa sheets, does not take into account any shock loads imposed on the winch. Consequently, a safety factor of 1.5 or more must be used. Thus, if the mainsheet in our example has a three-part tackle, the calculated load on the winch should be $\frac{3000}{3}$ × 1.5 = 1500 pounds.

Having calculated the loads that will be exerted on various sheets and the different winch sizes that can handle them, the next factor to consider is the ability of one's crew. As is clear from Figure 2-15, a pro can operate a winch much more efficiently than a novice, and a husky 200-pounder can exert far more brute

# Single Speed Winches

| Manufacturer | Model No. | Drum dia mm | Drum dia inches | Base dia mm | Base dia inches | Height mm | Height inches | Gear ratio | Power ratio | Material | Weight Kg | Weight lbs |
|---|---|---|---|---|---|---|---|---|---|---|---|---|
| Aldo | 10 | 65.6 | $2\frac{5}{8}$ | 102 | 4 | | | 1/1 | 7.6/1 | AL | 1.6 | $3\frac{1}{2}$ |
| | | | | | | | | | | BR | 2.3 | 5 |
| Barbarossa | C1 | 52 | 2 | 76 | 3 | 66 | $2\frac{5}{8}$ | 1/1 | 8/1 | AL | 0.21 | $\frac{1}{2}$ |
| Barient | 9 | 56 | $2\frac{3}{16}$ | 90 | $3\frac{9}{16}$ | 90 | $3\frac{9}{16}$ | 1/1 | 9.3/1 | AL | 1.02 | $2\frac{1}{4}$ |
| Enkes | AR6 | 45 | $1\frac{3}{4}$ | 80 | $3\frac{1}{8}$ | 72 | $2\frac{5}{8}$ | 1/1 | 8.8/1 | AL | | |
| Gibb | 1 | 51 | 2 | 77 | 3 | 84 | $3\frac{5}{16}$ | 1/1 | 8.5/1 | AL | 0.8 | $1\frac{3}{4}$ |
| Goiot | 50 | 65 | $2\frac{1}{2}$ | 138 | $5\frac{5}{8}$ | 126 | 5 | 2/1 | 8/1 | AL | 1.3 | 3 |
| Merriman-Holbrook | 8 | 45 | $1\frac{3}{4}$ | 80 | $3\frac{1}{8}$ | 63 | $2\frac{1}{2}$ | 1/1 | 11/1 | AL | 1.1 | $2\frac{5}{16}$ |
| | | | | | | | | | | SS | 1.81 | 4 |
| Lewmar | 6 | 59 | $2\frac{5}{16}$ | 94 | $3\frac{11}{16}$ | 83 | $3\frac{1}{4}$ | 1/1 | 8.6/1 | AL | 0.5 | $1\frac{1}{8}$ |
| | | | | | | | | | | CH | 1.1 | $2\frac{5}{16}$ |
| Aldo | 16 | 73 | $2\frac{7}{8}$ | 138 | $5\frac{7}{16}$ | | | 1/1 | 6.9/1 | AL | 3.2 | 7 |
| | | | | | | | | | | BR | 5.4 | 12 |
| Barbarossa | C5 | 70 | $2\frac{3}{4}$ | 115 | $4\frac{1}{2}$ | 90 | $3\frac{1}{2}$ | 1/1 | | AL | 1 | $2\frac{3}{16}$ |
| | C6 | | | | | | | | | | | |
| Barient | 10 | 67 | $2\frac{5}{8}$ | 102 | 4 | 94 | $3\frac{11}{16}$ | 1/1 | 7.6/1 | AL | 1.53 | $3\frac{3}{8}$ |
| | | | | | | | | | | BR | 2.16 | $4\frac{3}{4}$ |
| | | | | | | | | | | CH | 2.27 | 5 |
| | | | | | | | | | | SS | 2.31 | $5\frac{1}{16}$ |
| Barlow | 16 | 67 | $2\frac{5}{8}$ | 102 | 4 | 100 | $3\frac{5}{16}$ | 1/1 | 6.1/1 | AL | 1.36 | 3 |
| | | | | | | | | | | BR | 2.95 | $6\frac{1}{2}$ |
| Enkes | 8 | 60 | $2\frac{3}{8}$ | 98 | $3\frac{7}{8}$ | 92 | $5\frac{5}{8}$ | 1/1 | 8.46/1 | SS | | |
| Gibb | 2 | 63 | $2\frac{1}{2}$ | 95 | $3\frac{3}{4}$ | 78 | $3\frac{1}{8}$ | 1/1 | 8.5/1 | AL | 0.9 | 2 |
| Goiot | 52 | 65 | $2\frac{1}{2}$ | 120 | $4\frac{3}{4}$ | 90 | $3\frac{1}{2}$ | 1/1 | 8/1 | AL | 1.3 | 3 |
| Merriman-Holbrook | 10 | 57 | $2\frac{1}{4}$ | 102 | 4 | 83 | $3\frac{1}{4}$ | 1/1 | 8/1 | AL | 1.39 | $3\frac{1}{16}$ |
| | | | | | | | | | | SS | 2.5 | $5\frac{1}{2}$ |
| Lewmar | 7 | 65 | $2\frac{9}{16}$ | 108 | $4\frac{1}{4}$ | 102 | 4 | 1/1 | 7.9/1 | AL | 0.8 | $1\frac{3}{4}$ |
| | | | | | | | | | | CH | 2 | $4\frac{3}{8}$ |
| | 8 | | | | | | | | | AL | 1.5 | $3\frac{5}{16}$ |
| | | | | | | | | | | CH | 2.4 | $3\frac{1}{4}$ |
| Barbarossa | C8, C9 | 70 | $2\frac{3}{4}$ | 125 | $4\frac{7}{8}$ | 105 | $4\frac{1}{8}$ | 1/1 | 7.15/1 | AL | 1.5 | $3\frac{1}{3}$ |
| Barient | 16 | 73 | $2\frac{7}{8}$ | 138 | $5\frac{7}{16}$ | 132 | $5\frac{3}{16}$ | 1/1 | 6.9/1 | AL | 3.63 | 8 |
| | | | | | | | | | | SS | 5.44 | 12 |
| Barlow | 20 | 73 | $2\frac{7}{8}$ | 117 | $4\frac{5}{8}$ | 119 | $4\frac{11}{16}$ | 1/1 | 6.96/1 | AL | 1.82 | 4 |
| | | | | | | | | | | BR | 4.2 | $9\frac{1}{4}$ |
| Enkes | 12 | 70 | $2\frac{3}{4}$ | 102 | 4 | 97 | $3\frac{13}{16}$ | 1/1 | 7.25/1 | S.S | | |
| Gibb | 3 | 67 | $2\frac{5}{8}$ | 111 | $4\frac{3}{8}$ | 102 | 4 | 1/1 | 8/1 | AL | 2.4 | 5 |
| | 5/1 | | | | | | | | | | | |
| Goiot | 53 | 70 | $2\frac{3}{4}$ | 140 | $5\frac{1}{2}$ | 110 | $4\frac{1}{4}$ | 2/1 | 7/1 | AL | | |
| Merriman-Holbrook | 16 | 76 | $2\frac{7}{8}$ | 114 | $4\frac{1}{2}$ | 108 | $4\frac{1}{4}$ | 1/1 | 6/1 | AL | 2.44 | $5\frac{3}{8}$ |
| | | | | | | | | | | SS | 3.88 | $8\frac{1}{2}$ |
| Lewmar | 10 | 76 | $2\frac{7}{8}$ | 123 | $4\frac{13}{16}$ | 120 | $4\frac{3}{4}$ | 1/1 | 6.7/1 | AL | 2.2 | $4\frac{7}{8}$ |
| | | | | | | | | | | CH | 3.4 | 7.5 |

*Material abbreviations*
AL–Anodized aluminium alloy
BR–Bronze or chromium plated bronze
CH–Chromium
SS–Stainless steel

*Table 2–13*

# Two Speed Winches

| Manufacturer | Model No. | Drum dia mm | in | Base dia mm | in | Height mm | in | Gear ratio 1st | 2nd | Power ratio 1st | 2nd | Material | Weight Kg | lbs |
|---|---|---|---|---|---|---|---|---|---|---|---|---|---|---|
| Barlow | 18 | 70 | 2¾ | 102 | 4 | 111 | 4⅜ | 1/1 | 2.33/1 | 5.8/1 *(7.27)* | 13.6/1 | AL | 2.2 | 5.9 |
|  |  |  |  |  |  |  |  |  |  |  |  | BR | 4.1 | 9 |
| Enkes | 18 | 70 | 2¾ | 120 | 4¾ | 110 | 4⅜ | 1/1 | 2/1 | 7.25/1 | 14.5/1 | SS |  |  |
| Gibb | 16 | 67 | 2⅝ | 121 | 4¾ | 105 | 4 3/16 | 1/1 | 2/1 | 8/1 | 16/1 | AL | 1.4 | 3⅜ |
|  | 5/2 |  |  |  |  |  |  |  |  |  |  | AL | 1.4 | 3⅜ |
|  |  |  |  |  |  |  |  |  |  |  |  | CH-BR | 3.4 | 7½ |
| Lewmar | 16 | 64 | 2½ | 114 | 4½ | 108 | 4¼ | 1/1 | 2/1 | 8/1 | 16/1 | AL | 2.3 | 5 |
|  |  |  |  |  |  |  |  |  |  |  |  | BR | 3.2 | 7 |
| Barbarossa | B-25 | 76 | 3 | 130 | 5⅛ | 115 | 4½ | 1/1 | 3.5/1 | 7/1 | 23/1 | BR | 5 | 11 |
|  | B-25LL | 80 | 3⅛ | 134 | 5¼ | 115 | 4½ | 1/1 | 3.5/1 | 7/1 | 22/1 | AL | 3.9 | 8 9/16 |
| Barient | 21 | 68 | 2 11/16 | 140 | 5½ | 138 | 5 7/16 | 1/1 | 4/1 | 7.5/1 | 29.5/1 | AL | 3.8 | 8⅜ |
|  |  |  |  |  |  |  |  |  |  |  |  | CH | 4.76 | 10½ |
|  |  |  |  |  |  |  |  |  |  |  |  | SS | 4.88 | 10¾ |
| Enkes | 20 | 72 | 2 13/16 | 126 | 5 | 124 | 4⅞ | 1/1 | 4/1 | 7.1/1 | 288/1 | SS |  |  |
| Gibb | 28 | 76 | 3 | 140 | 5½ | 124 | 4⅞ | 1/1 | 4/1 | 7/1 | 28/1 | AL | 2.25 | 5 |
| Goïot | 61 | 85 | 3¼ | 188 | 7½ | 185 | 6½ | 1/1 | 4.1/1 | 5.85/1 | 24.4/1 | AL | 6.3 | 14 |
|  | 62 | 105 | 4 | 220 | 8⅝ | 205 | 8 | 1/1 | 5/1 | 5.7/1 | 28.6/1 | AL | 8 | 18 |
| Merriman-Holbrook | 20 | 76 | 3 | 114 | 4½ | 108 | 4¼ | 1/1 |  | 7/1 | 24/1 | AL | 2.78 | 6⅛ |
|  |  |  |  |  |  |  |  |  |  |  |  | SS | 4.31 | 9½ |
| Lewmar | 30 | 72 | 2.84 | 141 | 5.55 | 135 | 5.3 | 1/1 | 4.3/1 | 7/1 | 30/1 | AL | 16.5 | 7½ |
|  |  |  |  |  |  |  |  |  |  |  |  | BR | 20.8 | 9 7/16 |
| Aldo | 22 | 83 | 3¼ | 146 | 5¾ |  |  | 1/1 | 7/1 | 6.4/1 | 35/1 | AL | 5 | 11 |
|  |  |  |  |  |  |  |  |  |  |  |  | BR | 7.3 | 16 |
| Barbarossa | B-40LL | 85 | 3¼ | 152 | 6 | 140 | 5½ | 1/1 | 6/1 | 28.2/1 | 35.5/1 | AL | 5 | 11 |
| Barient | 22 | 85 | 3¼ | 146 | 5¾ | 152 | 6 | 1/1 | 5.2/1 | 6.4/1 | 33.4/1 | AL | 4.76 | 10½ |
|  |  |  |  |  |  |  |  |  |  |  |  | BR | 7.26 | 16 |
| Barlow | 24 | 83 | 3¼ | 146 | 5¾ | 140 | 5½ | 1/1 | 5.2/1 | 6.15/1 | 32/1 | AL | 3.4 | 7½ |
|  |  |  |  |  |  |  |  |  |  |  |  | BR | 6.7 | 14¾ |
|  |  |  |  |  |  |  |  |  |  |  |  | SS | 6.35 | 14 |
| Enkes | 22 | 76 | 3 | 148 | 5⅞ | 146 | 5¾ | 1/1 | 6/1 | 7/1 | 40/1 | SS |  |  |
| Gibb | Super 6 | 76 | 3 | 165 | 6½ | 148 | 5⅞ | 1/1 | 5.7/1 | 7/1 | 40/1 | SS | 6 | 13 |
| Merriman-Holbrook | 22 | 81 | 3⅛ | 152 | 6 | 140 | 5½ | 1/1 |  | 7/1 | 30/1 | AL | 4.62 | 10 3/16 |
|  |  |  |  |  |  |  |  |  |  |  |  | SS | 6.92 | 15¼ |
| Lewmar | 40 | 76 | 3 | 140 | 5½ | 140 | 5½ | 1/1 | 6/1 | 7/1 | 40/1 | AL | 3.9 | 8 9/16 |
|  |  |  |  |  |  |  |  |  |  |  |  | BR | 6.2 | 13⅝ |
| Aldo | 28 | 101.6 | 4 | 197 | 7¾ |  |  | 2.5/1 | 7.4/1 | 12.8/1 | 37/1 | AL | 9.6 | 21 |
|  |  |  |  |  |  |  |  |  |  |  |  | BR | 13.6 | 30 |
| Barbarossa | B-40 | 76 | 3 | 150 | 5⅞ | 140 | 5½ | 1/1 | 6/1 |  | 39.5/1 | CH-BR | 6 | 13 |
| Barient | 26 | 95 | 3¾ | 178 | 7 | 118 | 7 | 1/1 | 6.9/1 | 5.3/1 | 37/1 | AL | 6.35 | 14 |
|  |  |  |  |  |  |  |  |  |  |  |  | SS | 9.98 | 22 |
| Enkes | 26 | 90 | 3 9/16 | 175 | 6⅞ | 172 | 6¾ | 1/1 | 7.63/1 | 5.64/1 | 42.3/1 | SS |  |  |
| Goïot | 63 | 120 | 4¾ | 260 | 10¼ | 207 | 8¼ | 1/1 | 8/1 | 5/1 | 40/1 | AL | 12 | 27 |
| Merriman-Holbrook | 28 | 102 | 4 | 203 | 8 | 187 | 7⅜ |  |  | 12/1 | 37/1 | AL | 10.44 | 23 |
|  |  |  |  |  |  |  |  |  |  |  |  | SS | 14.97 | 33 |
|  |  |  |  |  |  |  |  |  |  |  |  | BR | 9.5 | 21 |
| Lewmar | 43 | 89 | 3.5 | 170 | 6.69 | 168 | 6.63 | 1/1 | 75/1 | 5.7/1 | 43/1 | AL | 5.8 | 12¾ |
|  |  |  |  |  |  |  |  |  |  |  |  | CH | 9.5 | 21 |

# Two Speed Winches—*continued*

| Manufacturer | Model No. | Drum dia mm | Drum dia in | Base dia mm | Base dia in | Height mm | Height in | Gear ratio 1st | Gear ratio 2nd | Power ratio 1st | Power ratio 2nd | Material | Weight Kg | Weight lbs |
|---|---|---|---|---|---|---|---|---|---|---|---|---|---|---|
| Aldo | 32 | 121 | 4¾ | 240 | 9½ | | | 2.5/1 | 11/1 | 12/1 | 37/1 | AL | 13.6 | 30 |
| | | | | | | | | | | | | BR | 22.6 | 50 |
| Barbarossa | B45 | 112 | 4⅜ | 153 | 6 | 140 | 5½ | 1/1 | 6/1 | | 35.5/1 | AL | 3.75 | 8¼ |
| | A60LL | 120 | 4¾ | 210 | 8¼ | 180 | 7⅛ | 4/1 | 10.5/1 | | 44.5/1 | AL Light-weight | 13 | 28⅝ |
| Barient | 28 | 102 | 4 | 204 | 8 | 198 | 7¹³⁄₁₆ | 2.5/1 | 7.4/1 | 12.8/1 | 37.7/1 | AL | 5.9 | 13 |
| | | | | | | | | | | | | AL Light-weight | 9.5 | 21 |
| | | | | | | | | | | | | SS | 8.2 | 18 |
| | | | | | | | | | | | | SS with AL Base | 12.5 | 27½ |
| | | | | | | | | | | | | SS | 13.6 | 30 |
| Barient | 30 | 121 | 4¾ | 241 | 9½ | 225 | 8⅞ | 2.4/1 | 9/1 | 10/1 | 37.8/1 | ⎰AL | 13.6 | 30 |
| | 32 | 121 | 4¾ | 241 | 9½ | 225 | 8⅞ | 2.4/1 | 11/1 | 10.2/1 | 47/1 | ⎱SS with AL base / SS | 20 / 21.8 | 44 / 48 |
| Aldo | 35 | 146 | 5¾ | 257 | 10⅛ | | | 6.4/1 | 16/1 | 22/1 | 54/1 | AL | 19.5 | 43 |
| | | | | | | | | | | | | BR | 28 | 62 |
| Barbarossa | B50 | 90 | 3⅝ | 178 | 7 | 170 | 6⅝ | 1/1 | 9/1 | | 50/1 | CH-BR | 11 | 24¼ |
| | B50LL | 95 | 3¾ | 180 | 7¹⁄₁₆ | 170 | 6⅝ | 1/1 | 9/1 | | 47.5/1 | AL | 8.3 | 18.4 |
| | B55 | 95 | 3¾ | 180 | 7¹⁄₁₆ | 170 | 6⅝ | 1/1 | 9/1 | | 47.5/1 | AL | 5.4 | 12 |
| | A60 | 100 | 3¹⁵⁄₁₆ | 205 | 8 | 180 | 7¹⁄₁₆ | 4/1 | 10.5/1 | | 52.5/1 | CH-BR | 15 | 33 |
| Barient | 34 ⎫ | | | | | | | 5.6/1 | 13.3/1 | 20/1 | 47/1 | ⎧ AL | 1.8.1 | 40 |
| | 35 ⎬ | 146 | 5¾ | 257 | 10⅛ | 276 | 10⅞ | 6.4/1 | 15.5/1 | 22.4/1 | 54.5/1 | ⎨ SS with AL base | 26.3 | 58 |
| | 36 ⎭ | | | | | | | 6.4/1 | 19.4/1 | 22.4/1 | 69/1 | ⎩ SS | 27.2 | 60 |
| Gibb | 9 | 95 | 3¾ | 203 | 8 | 162 | 6⅜ | 1/1 | 9/1 | | 50.4/1 | CH-BR | 9.25 | 20½ |
| | 10 | 114 | 4½ | 210 | 8¼ | 203 | 8 | 3.4/1 | 10.5/1 | | 50/1 | CH-BR | 12.5 | 28 |
| | 12 | 133 | 5¼ | 248 | 9¾ | 229 | 9 | 5/1 | 15/1 | | 60/1 | CH-BR | 20 | 45 |
| Goïot | 63 | 120 | 4¾ | 220 | 10¼ | 207 | 8¼ | 1/1 | 8/1 | 5.5/1 | 44/1 | AL | 12 | 27 |

## Three Speed Winches

| Manufacturer | Model No. | Drum dia mm | Drum dia in | Base dia mm | Base dia in | Height mm | Height in | Gear 1st | Gear 2nd | Gear 3rd | Power 1st | Power 2nd | Power 3rd | Mat | Weight Kg | Weight lbs |
|---|---|---|---|---|---|---|---|---|---|---|---|---|---|---|---|---|
| Lewmar | 44 | 90 | $3\frac{17}{32}$ | 180 | 7 | 181 | $7\frac{1}{8}$ | 1/1 | 3.7/1 | 7.6/1 | 5.7/1 | 20.9/1 | 4.4/1 | BR | 10.7 | 23.5 |
| Barient | 28 | 102 | 4 | 209 | $8\frac{3}{16}$ | 241 | $9\frac{15}{32}$ | 1.75/1 | 4/1 | 8/1 | 8.75/1 | 20/1 | 40/1 | AL | 7.3 | 16 |
|  |  |  |  |  |  |  |  |  |  |  |  |  |  | SS | 16.3 | 36 |
| Barlow | 28 | 102 | 4 | 203 | 8 | 200 | $7\frac{7}{8}$ | 1/1 | 2.5/1 | 7.1/1 | 5/1 | 12.5/1 | 35.5/1 | AL | 13.6 | 30 |
|  |  |  |  |  |  |  |  |  |  |  |  |  |  | SS | 14 | 31 |
|  |  |  |  |  |  |  |  |  |  |  |  |  |  | AL | 9.1 | 20 |
|  |  |  |  |  |  |  |  |  |  |  |  |  |  | BR | 15 | 33 |
| Enkes | 28 | 104 | $4\frac{1}{8}$ | 210 | $8\frac{1}{4}$ | 213 | $8\frac{3}{8}$ | 1/1 | 3.15/1 | 10.4/1 | 4.88/1 | 15.4/1 | 30.9/1 | SS | NA | NA |
| Lewmar | 48 | 103 | $4\frac{1}{64}$ | 210 | $8\frac{1}{4}$ | 205 | $8\frac{1}{64}$ | 1/1 | 3.4/1 | 9.5/1 | 5.1/1 | 17/1 | 48/1 | BR | 13.4 | 29.5 |
| Barlow | 30 | 121 | $4\frac{3}{4}$ | 246 | $9\frac{11}{16}$ | 233 | $9\frac{3}{16}$ | 1/1 | 2.4/1 | 8.9/1 | 4.2/1 | 10.1/1 | 37.3/1 | AL | 8.4 | 18.5 |
|  |  |  |  |  |  |  |  |  |  |  |  |  |  | AL | 11.8 | 26 |
|  |  |  |  |  |  |  |  |  |  |  |  |  |  | BR | 19.7 | 43.5 |
|  |  |  |  |  |  |  |  |  |  |  |  |  |  | SS | 18.2 | 40 |
| Barbarossa | 80 | 145 | $5\frac{11}{16}$ | 225 | $8\frac{27}{32}$ | 195 | $7\frac{11}{16}$ | 2.5/1 | 6.25/1 | 15.6/1 | 8.5/1 | 21/1 | 54/1 | AL | 14 | 30.8 |
| Barient | 32 | 119 | $4\frac{11}{16}$ | 241 | $9\frac{1}{2}$ | 270 | $10\frac{5}{8}$ | 1.75/1 | 5.2/1 | 11.6/1 | 7.5/1 | 22.2/1 | 49.5/1 | AL | 15.9 | 35 |
|  |  |  |  |  |  |  |  |  |  |  |  |  |  | SS | 20.4 | 45 |
| Barlow | 32 | 121 | $4\frac{3}{4}$ | 246 | $9\frac{11}{16}$ | 233 | $9\frac{3}{16}$ | 1/1 | 2.4/1 | 10.4/1 | 4.2/1 | 10/1 | 44/1 | AL | 11.8 | 26 |
|  |  |  |  |  |  |  |  |  |  |  |  |  |  | BR | 19.7 | 43.5 |
|  |  |  |  |  |  |  |  |  |  |  |  |  |  | SS | 18.2 | 40 |
| Enkes | 32 | 114 | $4\frac{1}{2}$ | 240 | $9\frac{7}{16}$ | 235 | $9\frac{1}{4}$ | 1/1 | 4.7/1 | 13.5/1 | 4.46/1 | 21/1 | 59.6/1 | SS | NA | NA |
| Lewmar | 55 | 115 | $4\frac{1}{2}$ | 238 | $9\frac{3}{8}$ | 240 | $9\frac{7}{16}$ | 1/1 | 4.75/1 | 12.3/1 | 4.5/1 | 21/1 | 55/1 | AL | 10.9 | 24.0 |
| Barlow | 34 | 146 | $5\frac{3}{4}$ | 260 | $10\frac{1}{4}$ | 275 | $10\frac{13}{16}$ | 1/1 | 6.4/1 | 15.5/1 | 3.5/1 | 22.2/1 | 54/1 | BR | 18.4 | 40.5 |
|  |  |  |  |  |  |  |  |  |  |  |  |  |  | AL | 14.5 | 32.0 |
|  |  |  |  |  |  |  |  |  |  |  |  |  |  | BR | 27.2 | 60,0 |
|  |  |  |  |  |  |  |  |  |  |  |  |  |  | SS | 26.3 | 58 |
| Barbarossa | 90 | 160 | $6\frac{5}{16}$ | 250 | $9\frac{27}{32}$ | 220 | $8\frac{21}{32}$ | 2.5/1 | 7.2/1 | 21/1 | 7.8/1 | 22/1 | 65/1 | AL | 23 | 50.7 |
| Barient | 35 | 146 | $5\frac{3}{4}$ | 257 | $10\frac{1}{8}$ | 287 | $11\frac{5}{16}$ | 2/1 | 6.4/1 | 19.4/1 | 7/1 | 22.5/1 | 68.2/1 | AL | 21.4 | 47 |
|  |  |  |  |  |  |  |  |  |  |  |  |  |  | SS | 27.9 | 61.5 |
| Barlow | 36 | 146 | $5\frac{3}{4}$ | 260 | $10\frac{1}{4}$ | 275 | $10\frac{13}{16}$ | 1/1 | 6.4/1 | 19.4/1 | 3.5/1 | 22.2/1 | 67.5/1 | AL | 14.5 | 32 |
|  |  |  |  |  |  |  |  |  |  |  |  |  |  | BR | 27.5 | 60 |
|  |  |  |  |  |  |  |  |  |  |  |  |  |  | SS | 26.3 | 58 |
| Enkes | 36 | 142 | $5\frac{19}{32}$ | 280 | $11\frac{1}{64}$ | 282 | $11\frac{3}{32}$ | 1/1 | 5.78/1 | 19.8/1 | 3.57/1 | 20.6/1 | 70.7/1 | SS | NA | NA |
| Lewmar | 65 | 140 | $5\frac{1}{2}$ | 280 | $11\frac{1}{64}$ | 280 | $11\frac{13}{32}$ | 1/1 | 6.9/1 | 17.8/1 | 3.7/1 | 25/1 | 65/1 | AL | 19 | 43 |
| Barlow | 38 | 190 | $7\frac{1}{2}$ | 260 | $10\frac{1}{4}$ | 275 | $10\frac{13}{16}$ | 1/1 | 6.4/1 | 15.5/1 | 2.7/1 | 17/1 | 41.3/1 | BR | 32.3 | 71 |
|  |  |  |  |  |  |  |  |  |  |  |  |  |  | AL | 16.9 | 38 |
|  |  |  |  |  |  |  |  |  |  |  |  |  |  | BR | 32.5 | 71.5 |
|  |  |  |  |  |  |  |  |  |  |  |  |  |  | SS | 31.3 | 69 |
| Barient | 735 | 180 | 7 | 257 | $10\frac{1}{8}$ | 287 | $11\frac{5}{16}$ | 2/1 | 6.4/1 | 19.4/1 | 5.7/1 | 18.3/1 | 55.5/1 | SS/AL | 27.7 | 61 |
| Barlow | 40 | 190 | $7\frac{1}{2}$ | 260 | $10\frac{1}{4}$ | 275 | $10\frac{13}{16}$ | 1/1 | 6.4/1 | 19.4/1 | 2.7/1 | 17/1 | 51.7/1 | AL | 16.9 | 38 |
|  |  |  |  |  |  |  |  |  |  |  |  |  |  | BR | 32.5 | $71\frac{1}{2}$ |
|  |  |  |  |  |  |  |  |  |  |  |  |  |  | SS | 31.3 | 69 |

## Self Tailing Winches

When self tailing jaws are put on top of a three speed winch which has a direct drive first gear the direct drive pawls have to be removed. This means that a three speed self tailing winch must be fully geared in all three speeds.

Almost all self tailing winches have the same gear ratios as the non self tailing winches of the same number. The major areas of difference is in the weight of the winch where the self tailing jaws add a little extra.

Rather than duplicate the data given in the earlier lists I am simply listing the self tailing winches made by each manufacturer.

| Manufacturer | Single speed | Two speed | Three speed |
|---|---|---|---|
| Barbarossa | — | — | 82, 92 |
| Barient | 20 | 23, 27, 28, 30, 32, 34, 35, 734, 735, 736 | 28, 32, 35, 735 |
| Barlow | 23, 24 | 27, 28, 30, 32, 34, 36 | — |
| Lewmar | 16, 30 | 42, 44, 48, 55, 65 | 65/3 |

# Reel Winches

**Single Speed**

| Manufacturer | Model No. | Drum dia mm | Drum dia in | Base dia mm | Base dia in | Height mm | Height in | Gear ratio | Power ratio | Drum capacity m. 4 mm | 5 mm | 6 mm | Mat | Weight Kg | lbs |
|---|---|---|---|---|---|---|---|---|---|---|---|---|---|---|---|
| Barbarossa | H28 | 72 | $2\frac{27}{32}$ | 188 | $7\frac{13}{32}$ | 142 | $5\frac{19}{32}$ | 1/1 | 7.5/1 | 24 | 20 | 18 | AL | 4.27 | 9.4 |
| | H25 | 52 | $2\frac{1}{8}$ | 145 | $5\frac{23}{32}$ | 130 | $5\frac{1}{8}$ | 1/1 | 9.5/1 | 22 | 16 | — | AL | 2.23 | 4.9 |
| Barient | 3 | 60 | $2\frac{3}{8}$ | 144 | $5\frac{11}{16}$ | 124 | $4\frac{7}{8}$ | 1/1 | 8.4/1 | 43 | 27 | 14 | SS | 5.0 | 11 |
| | 3A | NA | NA | 167 | $6\frac{9}{16}$ | 138 | $5\frac{7}{16}$ | 1/1 | 8.4/1 | 43 | 27 | 15 | AL | 4.1 | 9 |
| Barlow | 2H | 57 | $2\frac{1}{4}$ | 141 | $5\frac{9}{16}$ | 119 | $4\frac{11}{16}$ | 1/1 | 8.8/1 | 20 | 14 | — | BR | 3.86 | $8\frac{1}{2}$ |
| | 4H | 57 | $2\frac{1}{4}$ | 159 | $6\frac{1}{4}$ | 140 | $5\frac{1}{2}$ | 1/1 | 8.8/1 | 16 | 12 | — | BR | 5.78 | $12\frac{3}{4}$ |
| | 5H | 67 | $2\frac{5}{8}$ | 178 | 7 | 165 | $6\frac{1}{2}$ | 1/1 | 7.6/1 | 23 | 14 | — | BR | 7.94 | $17\frac{1}{2}$ |
| Gibb | 869 | 44 | $1\frac{3}{4}$ | 108 | $4\frac{1}{4}$ | NA | NA | 1/1 | 11.4/1 | 14 | 9 | — | BR | 1.93 | $4\frac{1}{4}$ |
| | 870 | 57 | $2\frac{1}{4}$ | 140 | $5\frac{1}{2}$ | 93 | $3\frac{5}{8}$ | 1/1 | 4.6/1 | — | 24 | 17 | BR | 4.31 | $9\frac{1}{2}$ |
| Gibb | 3 | 70 | $2\frac{3}{4}$ | 14.6 × 164 | $5\frac{3}{4} \times 6\frac{5}{8}$ | 140 | $5\frac{1}{2}$ | 1/1 | 7.5/1 | — | 27 | 16 | AL | 5 | $11\frac{1}{4}$ |
| Lewmar | 1 | 89 | $3\frac{1}{2}$ | 140 | $5\frac{1}{2}$ | 98 | $3\frac{7}{8}$ | 1/1 | 4.6/1 | 40 | 26 | 14 | BR | 4.88 | $10\frac{3}{4}$ |
| | 2 | 82 | $3\frac{1}{4}$ | 198 × 203 | 7.8 × 8 | 133 | $5\frac{1}{4}$ | 1/1 | 6.2/1 | 40 | 25 | 15 | BR | 7.9 | $17\frac{1}{2}$ |
| Merriman-Holbrook | 1 | | | | | | | | | | | | | | |
| | 2 | | | | | | | | | | | | | | |

**Two Speed**

| Manufacturer | Model No. | Drum dia mm | Drum dia in | Base dia mm | Base dia in | Height mm | Height in | Gear ratio 1st | 2nd | Power ratio 1st | 2nd | Drum capacity m 5 mm | 6 mm | 8 mm | Mat | Weight Kg | lbs |
|---|---|---|---|---|---|---|---|---|---|---|---|---|---|---|---|---|---|
| Barbarossa | H40 | 90 | $3\frac{1}{2}$ | 150 | $5\frac{7}{8}$ | 100 | $3\frac{7}{8}$ | 1/1 | 6/1 | 5.7/1 | 33/1 | — | — | — | BR | 5.39 | 11.9 |
| Barient | 1 | 64 | 2.5 | 219 | $8\frac{5}{8}$ | 181 | $7\frac{1}{8}$ | 1/1 | 4/1 | 8/1 | 32/1 | $^{76}/_{51}$* | $^{58}/_{39}$* | $^{43}/_{29}$* | BR | 18.15 | 40 |
| | 2 | 63 | 2.47 | 430 | $6\frac{15}{16}$ | 145 | $5\frac{11}{16}$ | 1/1 | 3.4/1 | 8.1/1 | 27.4/1 | 29 | 15 | — | BR | 9.9 | 22 |
| | 2A | 63 | 2.47 | 430 | $6\frac{15}{16}$ | 173 | $6\frac{13}{16}$ | 1/1 | 3.4/1 | 8.1/1 | 27.4/1 | 45 | 25 | — | BR | 11.34 | 25 |
| Barlow | 6 | 70 | $2\frac{3}{4}$ | 189 | $7\frac{7}{16}$ | 173 | $6\frac{13}{16}$ | 1/1 | 5.25/1 | 7.3/1 | 38.2/1 | — | 27 | 19 | BR | 10.9 | 24 |
| | 8 | 102 | 4 | 264 | $10\frac{3}{8}$ | 256 | $10\frac{1}{16}$ | 1/1 | 8.34/1 | 5.1/1 | 41.6/1 | 30 m × 11 mm–40 m × 9.5 mm | | | BR | 2.9 | 64 |
| | 10 | 102 | 4 | 264 | $10\frac{3}{8}$ | 298 | $11\frac{3}{4}$ | 1/1 | 8.34/1 | 5.1/1 | 41.6/1 | 38 m × 11 mm–50 m × 9.5 mm | | | BR | 31.3 | 69 |
| Lewmar | 3 | 155 | $6\frac{1}{8}$ | 235 × 241 | $9\frac{1}{4} \times 9\frac{1}{2}$ | 178 | 7 | 1/1 | 5.2/1 | 3.3/1 | 17.5/1 | 81 | 56 | 37 | BR | 15.4 | 34 |

* Large capacity drum/small capacity drum

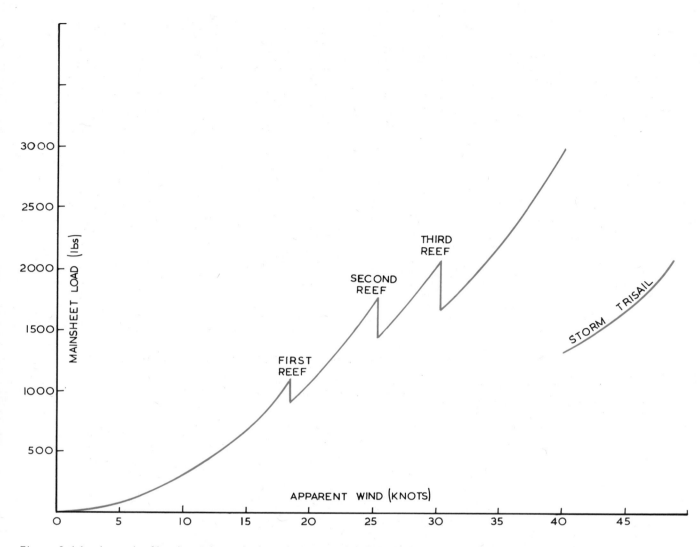

*Figure 2-14.* A graph of loads on the mainsheet for a typical Admiral's Cup design. Note that a reduction in area reduces the load only slightly, but because it takes sail from aloft and flattens the mainsail, heel angle is considerably reduced.

strength than can the owner's wife or children. So if there is a good possibility that less able or less experienced crew members will be aboard for several races, an owner may want to consider increasing the sheet winches by one size, or perhaps, if the option is available, selecting three-speed instead of two-speed models. There is, however, one potential problem in making such adjustments. You may go so far toward accommodating the needs of the weakest members of your crew that the experts on board overpower the equipment and end up tacking the headsail faster than the boat tacks. To avoid this problem, it is sometimes better to install a linked winch system, which allows more than one person to operate a winch when your crew is less experienced than usual.

*Selecting Halyard Winches*
There is no simple formula for selecting a halyard winch. The best method is to use the manufacturer's tables. The halyards for which different sized winches can be used are listed in Table 2-13.

One halyard winch with special sizing considerations is the reel winch, where the halyard wire is wound on a self-contained drum. Selection of the correct size, of course, depends on both the diameter of the wire and the storage capacity of the drum.

*Selecting Wires and Ropes*
Selecting the proper sized halyards and sheets is equally important as selecting the proper sized winches.

61

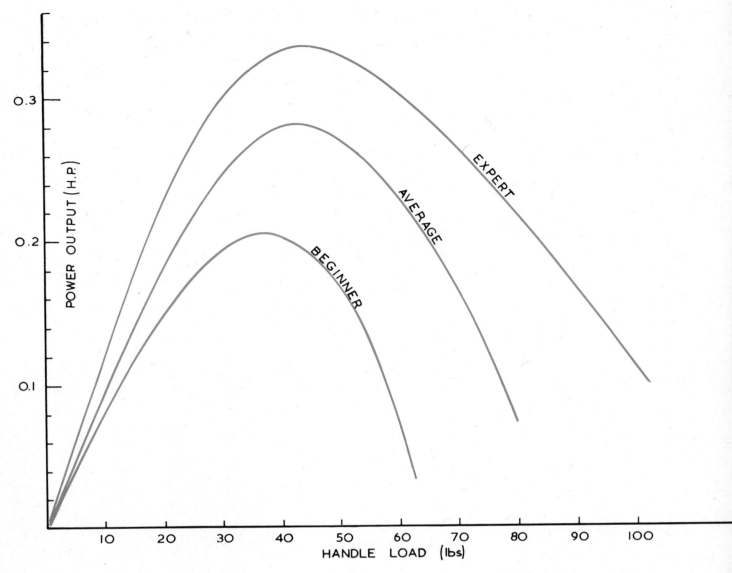

*Figure 2-15.* A graph plotting power output against handle load. *(Courtesy of Lewmar Marine Limited)*

A halyard that is too small, for example, will stretch excessively and be inefficient. Table 2-16 gives the appropriate halyard sizes for genoas and mainsails. Rope tail sizes are found by doubling the wire halyard size and using one size smaller. To select genoa sheets, find the load as described earlier and multiply by a safety factor of 1.25 to 1.5 to allow for the fact that the sheet will lose some strength at the knot. The required rope size can then be found from the manufacturer's tables. When choosing sheets to suit a particular winch, however, remember that winch makers design their drums with certain diameter ropes in mind. Using too large a rope relative to the size of the drum may cause the rope to slip because too few turns can be put on.

On the other hand, using too small a rope relative to drum size may cause kinking and riding turns because too many turns round the drum are required.

### Fitting Out an Admiral's Cup Boat

Having discussed how to size winches according to sail area, let's take a particular boat–say, the Admiral's Cup boat used earlier as an example–and specify the winches. Figure 2-12c shows that the maximum genoa load is 3463 pounds, and multiplying this times a safety factor of 1.2 gives us 4155 pounds. Based on this figure, we could select stainless steel Barient 35's or

# Halyard sizes for genoas and mainsails

| Approx boat size | Headstay 1×19 Dia | Breaking strength Galv | ss 302 | ss 316 | Genoa halyard 7×19 Dia | Breaking strength Galv | ss 302 | Main halyard 7×19 Dia | Breaking strength Galv | ss 302 |
|---|---|---|---|---|---|---|---|---|---|---|
| | 3/32″ / 2 mm | 1,200 | 1,200 / 840 | | | | | | | |
| 14–16 ft DWL micro ton | 1/8″ / 3 mm | 2,100 | 2,100 / 1,900 | 1,827 | 3/32″ | 1,000 | 920 | 3/32″ | 1,000 | 920 |
| 16–18 ft DWL mini ton | 5/32″ / 4 mm | 3,300 | 3,300 / 3,360 | 2,871 | 7/64″ | | | | | |
| 18–20 ft DWL ¼ ton | 3/16″ / 5 mm | 4,700 | 4,700 / 5,250 | 4,089 | 1/8″ | 2,000 | 1,760 | 3/32″ | 1,000 | 920 |
| | 7/32″ / 6 mm | 6,300 | 6,300 / 7,300 | 5,481 / 6,500 | 5/32″ | 2,800 | 2,400 | 1/8″ | 2,000 | 1,760 |
| 20–23 ft DWL ½ ton | 1/4″ / 7 mm | 8,200 | 8,200 / 9,950 | 7,134 | 5/32″ | 2,800 | 2,400 | 1/8″ | 2,000 | 1,760 |
| 23–26 ft DWL ¾ ton | 9/32″ / 8 mm | 10,300 | 10,300 / 13,000 | 8,961 / 12,000 | 3/16″ | 4,200 | 3,700 | 5/32″ | 2,800 | 2,400 |
| 26–30 ft DWL 1 ton | 5/16″ / 9 mm | 12,500 | 12,500 / 16,500 | 10,875 / 14,500 | 7/32″ | 5,600 | 5,000 | 3/16″ | 4,200 | 3,700 |
| 31–36 ft DWL 2 ton | 3/8″ / 10 mm / 11 mm | 17,500 | 17,500 / 20,500 | 15,225 / 17,600 / 23,000 | 1/4″ | 7,000 | 6,400 | 7/32″ | 5,600 | 5,000 |
| 37–43 ft DWL | 7/16″ / 12 mm | 23,400 | 23,400 / 29,400 | 20,360 / 25,300 | 9/32″ | 8,000 | 7,800 | 1/4″ | 7,000 | 6,400 |
| 44–51 ft DWL | 1/2″ / 14 mm | 30,300 | 29,700 / 38,500 | 25,840 / 33,370 | 5/16″ | 9,800 | 9,000 | 9/32″ | 8,000 | 7,800 |
| 52–59 ft DWL | 9/16″ / 16 mm | | 37,000 | 32,190 / 42,000 | 5/16″ | 9,800 | 9,000 | 9/32″ | 8,000 | 7,800 |
| 60–70 ft DWL | 5/8″ / 19 mm | | 46,800 | 40,710 | 3/8″ | 14,400 | 12,000 | 5/16″ | 9,800 | 9,000 |
| | 3/4″ | | 59,700 | 50,745 | 7/16″ | 17,600 | 16,300 | 3/8″ | 14,400 | 12,000 |

Note: if rope tails are used, they should be twice the thickness of the wire for halyards up to 1/4″ diameter. For halyards of 9/32″ diameter wire and larger, the rope tail should be one size smaller than twice the diameter of the wire.

*Table 2-16.* Halyard sizes for genoas and mainsails.

stainless steel Lewmar 65's for the primary winches. For the secondary or spinnaker winches, we could use Barient stainless steel 32's or Lewmar stainless steel 55's; either choice should be self-tailing. The load on the main sheet is 1500 pounds, suggesting a self-tailing Barient 21 or a self-tailing Lewmar 27. And if the main must be wound in quickly, a winch one or two sizes larger might be preferable. As for the halyard winches, the main halyard, with a theoretical load of 2900 pounds, requires a Barient 28 or a Lewmar 48. This same size could also be used for the genoa halyard and spinnaker halyard winches. All that remains is the sizing of the smaller winches. These decisions are usually based on the manufacturer's recommendations, coupled with experience. Winches for the runner, the foreguys, and the spinnaker pole could be self-tailing Barient 23's or Lewmar 40's. Often, a smaller model, such as a Lewmar 16 or a Barient 18, is used on the main boom as a jiffy reefing/foot outhaul winch with lockoffs.

Once the winches are selected, it is an easy matter to choose the proper diameter genoa and main sheets. For this Admiral's Cup boat, the genoa sheets would be 16-strand 5/8 inch diameter rope, and the main sheet would be 16-braid 3/8 inch diameter rope. Knowing this, the various blocks and other fittings can also be sized.

Halyard sizes should be selected with a safety factor of between 1.3 and 1.5 in mind. This allows room for rope tails and shackles to be spliced on. Again, for our Admiral's Cup design, the main halyard should be a

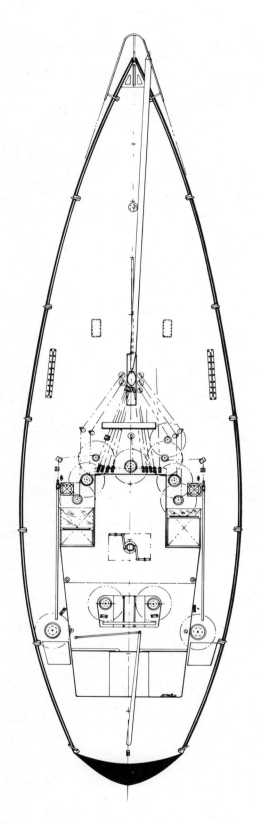

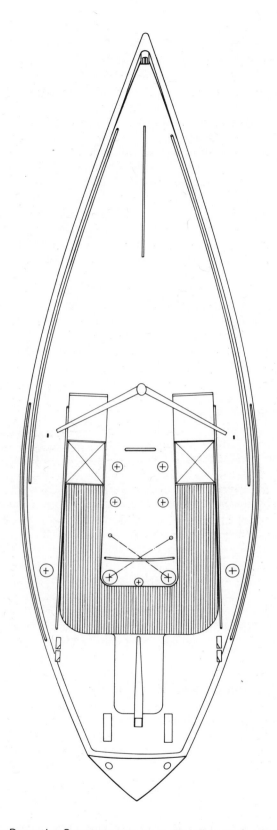

*Marauder*, the Canada's Cup design by C & C. The photo shows how the plan looks in real life.

*Golden Dazy*, the Canada's Cup design by Ron Holland that raced against *Marauder*.

$\frac{7}{32}$ inch 1 × 19 galvanized wire with a $\frac{1}{2}$ inch diameter rope tail. It should be long enough to reach the mainsail headboard when hoisted and still have at least six or eight turns of wire on the winch. Note that when the sail has three reefs in, there will be rope on the winch. The jib halyards should be $\frac{1}{4}$ inch diameter 1 × 19 wire with a $\frac{1}{2}$ inch diameter rope tail spliced on. They should be long enough to give about four or five turns of wire on the drum, with the splice between the winch and the cleat. A shorter luff headsail should have a wire pennant to allow the halyard wire to remain on the winch.

Staysail and spinnaker pole topping lifts are generally one size smaller than the genoa halyards. The best spinnaker halyards are all-rope, because they can stretch and absorb the shock loads when the sail collapses. (Some of the pre-stretched ropes on the market are ideal for this purpose.) Wire halyards were used on *Quailo* in 1971 and the crew tore the head out of the starcut three times during the early part of the season. For the Fastnet, the owner decided to try rope halyards. The rope broke the first night out but was easily replaced. If wire halyards had been used, the sail would probably have been lost, and that would have meant forfeiting second place.

## The Basics of Winch Positioning

Where do the winches go? Almost always in a position where they have to be moved later! This is because the drawings of a deck layout are only in two dimensions, making it difficult to tell on paper how well a particular arrangement will work. The only truly effective way to site winches, therefore, is to go to the boatyard when the boat is being fitted out and physically move winches and run leads until everything has a place where it will not foul anything else. But before this stage, the following points offer some basic advice on positioning sheet and halyard winches.

### Positioning Sheet Winches

Because a winch is circular, sheets can approach it from any side, but they cannot approach from just any vertical angle. A sheet should never be led to a winch at an angle less than 90 degrees; otherwise, you will end up with riding turns. For best results, a sheet should approach a winch at a vertical angle of 95 to 105 degrees.

For a genoa sheet, foot blocks are often used to maintain the correct angle in relation to the winch and

to ensure a fair lead with no possibility of overrides. Unfortunately, foot blocks introduce friction into the system, so many people do not like them. They do, however, have the definite advantage of keeping the lead to the winch constant regardless of the sail that's in use. If foot blocks are installed, it is essential to avoid placing the block too close to the winch because this is likely to cause foul-ups when the sheet is thrown off. Twenty to 30 inches between winch and block is best, and certainly no closer than 18 inches. Another point to remember when using foot blocks is the need for deck reinforcement where the blocks are located. If there is a 3000 pound load on the genoa sheet, the force is almost doubled at the turning block.

Sometimes, with careful positioning, one winch can be made to do the job of two. An example is locating a single genoa sheet winch in the middle of a cockpit bridge deck. Because one genoa sheet has to be thrown off before the other can be overhauled, this is a perfectly feasible system on a small boat. But remember that if a single winch does two jobs, both leads must be fair. There is no reason, though, why a second line must be led half way around the boat with numerous blocks to achieve this fairness. On larger boats, careful design will enable the genoa sheet pedestal winch to be aligned with the genoa or spinnaker halyard winches, thus making it possible for the pedestal winch to be used to hoist the genoa quickly and easily. The genoa halyard can then be locked off and the load taken on the halyard winch for fine tuning.

Winches should always be sited where the operator has room to work. At the very least, the winder must be able to make a smooth, full circle with the winch handle, thus maintaining his momentum. If he must stop and ratchet the winch because a stanchion or another winch is in the way, he loses efficiency and speed. Similarly, a winch tailer should be located well away from the winder, so that the tailer does not hinder the winder's movements.

Winch height is also critical, for speed and power are easily lost if the handle is too high or too low. The ideal height is discussed in Chapter 6. To gain the maximum leverage, winches should be sited near or around cockpits, and for inshore racers, they can also be located around a hatch which can be fitted with a platform for the operator to stand on.

Even a winch arrangement that looks fine at the dock can turn out to be useless when the boat is well heeled. For this reason, it is advisable to draw sections through the cockpit to ensure that the operator will be able to winch no matter what the heel angle and no matter what the accompanying sheet load. One

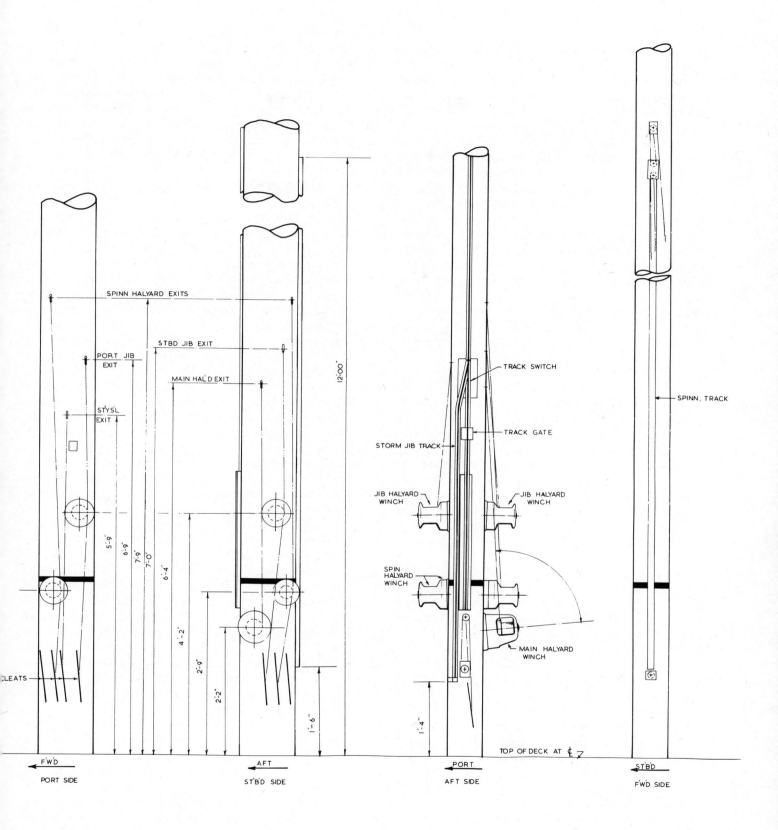

*Figure 2-17.* A typical winch and cleat arrangement plan. *(Courtesy of Sparkman & Stephens, Inc.)*

problem to watch out for are winches that are angled outboard to get a fair lead from the foot block. This is bad practice because when the boat is heeled over, the winch ends up almost horizontal and it is extremely difficult for the operator to maintain his balance while winding.

In addition to such questions as ideal angle, spacing, and height, designers must also determine the most efficient place to locate winches on a given deck. Where the sail trimmer is going to sit is a prime consideration in locating primary winches. Some racing pundits argue that on all but the very largest boats cross-linked winches should be used to keep crew weight high on the weather side while still being able to trim the genoa. Unfortunately, from this position it is impossible to see if the spreader has poked a hole in the sail unless the hole extends to the luff! When locating primary winches, therefore, it is desirable for the sail trimmer to sit to leeward where he can watch the sail and make allowances for differences in wind strength.

The best fore and aft placement of primary winches is also subject to some debate. Traditionally, they have been placed on the cockpit coamings, but increasingly they are being moved forward to the sides of a crewpit situated just aft of the mast. This arrangement is facilitated on boats of two ton size or larger by placing the drums outboard and putting a linked pedestal in the crewpit. Again, Chapter 6 explains the details. If this arrangement is used, care must be taken that the boom and boom vang do not interfere with the pedestal or tailing operations.

### Positioning Halyard Winches

With the type of middeck work area just discussed, halyard winches can be situated at the forward end of the crewpit, or if necessary on a reinforced hatch top. The advantages of this arrangement are that it allows crewmen to operate the winches at a height that gives them the best possible leverage, and it also tends to reduce windage as compared with the alternative positioning of halyard winches on the mast.

Although the modern trend in racing boats is to locate halyard winches on the deck, some owners who like to use their boats for cruising as well prefer to have certain winches mounted on the mast. If this is the case, careful planning is required to achieve an arrangement where each halyard leads to a winch and then to a cleat without fouling another halyard or winch. A winch and cleat arrangement, such as the one shown in Figure 2-17, is drawn for this purpose. Notice

how the winches have been carefully positioned to allow a full turn of the handle even when the mainsheet is fully extended and the boom is on the shrouds. Also note that no winches are protruding forward of the mast to foul genoa sheets when tacking. Each winch has been positioned to allow the best possible access and ease of winding without crossing halyards or lines.

### Winding and Tailing a Winch

How do you wind a winch efficiently? Although this question may not relate directly to the problem of deck layout, it does relate indirectly in that knowing how to wind a winch properly will help you answer such questions as how much work space is needed surrounding a winch. A firm understanding of sailing techniques, therefore, makes for a better design.

Actually, the correct method of winding a winch is quite simple. As you start to wind, try to get the winch drum moving as quickly as possible. A fast turning drum not only pulls the sheet in more rapidly, it also builds up momentum and this makes your job that much easier. Winding at this stage requires arm movement—a lot of it. So do not position rails or stanchions too close to the primary winches. As the load on the winch increases, add the power of your shoulder and back muscles. Eventually, you should be exerting your full force: arms locked, chin over the winch, with your entire body from the hips up powering each turn. As soon as you can feel the winch start to slow down and you really must work to turn the handle, change to a lower gear to get the sail in the rest of the way.

Meanwhile, the tailer, having initially put no more than two or three turns on the drum, should be using an elbowing motion to pull the tail off the winch. By using this particular motion, the tailer can get a great deal of sheet in before the sail fills and winding becomes difficult for the winch operator. As soon as the sail starts to fill, the tailer should get more turns on the winch and keep pressure on the sheet. At this stage he needs room to lean backward, as well as adequate space in which to swing his elbows.

In the future, much of the hard work of winding a winch may be eliminated by the use of foot-driven pedal winches, or by the development of hydraulic winches. The twelve metre *Sverige* used pedal winches in the 1977 America's Cup try-outs. After a tacking duel her winch winders were still relatively fresh compared with those on some of the other twelves, where winders had to be changed numerous times. The main problem with introducing foot-driven winches is where to put them: below deck and thus eliminate a cockpit, or in a large cockpit on deck?

The second alternative to conventional winches—hydraulic winches—opens up far more possibilities than even the foot-driven model. With hydraulic winches a crewman can wind the handle at any time to store up power in the system and then when the winch is needed the valve is simply released and the drum turns automatically. The obvious advantage is that one man alone can operate a battery of winches, thus cutting down on necessary crew size. The major drawback to hydraulic winches at the present time is the problem of power loss in a low-pressure system versus the problem of maintaining a high-pressure system on a yacht. Whether and how these difficulties are eventually overcome remains to be seen. But in any case, racing sailors can be assured that future advances in winch technology will make the modern winch even easier to operate.

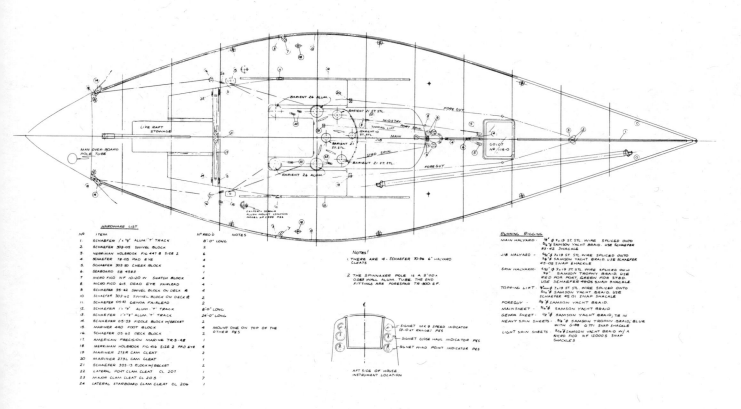

*Hot Flash*, a Half Tonner by Gary Mull.

The working area on the Two Tonner *Iorana*. Note the pedestal-driven winches, the runner winches aft of them, the instrument positions, and the locking backstay adjuster and hydraulic vang. *(Courtesy of Lewmar Marine)*

# CHAPTER THREE
# Masts and Rigging

The sails are the engine of a boat. Much of the gear and equipment on deck has one single purpose: to help harness the power of the wind via the sails. Because the sails of a boat are so all-important, it is not surprising that a book on deck layout should include a chapter on masts and rigging. The design of a deck, after all, can only be fully understood in relation to the sail plan.

First we will discuss the mast, both its positioning on the boat and its optimum design and construction features. Then we will take a look at the rig, examining the functions of the various stays and shrouds and reviewing the pros and cons of different rig configurations. And finally, we will turn to one of the more recent developments in ocean racing technology–hydraulics. In particular we will consider how hydraulics can be used, what systems are available, how they are installed, and how they are operated and maintained.

## The Mast

What makes for an ideal mast? The answer involves several considerations. Some have to do with the

## Weight & Centre of Gravity Summary

| Group | Weight | VCG | Moment | LCG | Moment | Notes |
|---|---|---|---|---|---|---|
| A. Hull Structure | 5,592 | 2.89 | 16,160.9 | 0.543 | 3,036.5 | |
| B. Superstructure | 42 | 3.87 | 162.54 | 0.62 | 26.04 | |
| C. Joiner Work | 1,250 | 2.59 | 3,238.75 | 0.563 | 703.75 | |
| D. Hull Fitting & Equipment | 1,468 | 3.10 | 4,553.74 | 0.627 | 920.44 | |
| E. Spars, Rig and Gear | 1,400 | 9.40 | 13,160.0 | 0.42 | 558.00 | |
| F. Machinery & Associated Piping | 812 | 2.28 | 1,853.79 | 0.64 | 522.12 | |
| G. Hull & Ship Systems | 215 | 2.80 | 602.0 | 0.725 | 155.88 | |
| H. Electrical | 400 | 2.70 | 1,080.0 | 0.690 | 276.00 | |
| I. Outfit | 506 | 3.07 | 1,555.44 | 0.638 | 322.83 | |
| J. Soakage & Bilge Water (5% of A, B, C) | 344 | 1.82 | 626.0 | 0.52 | 178.88 | |
| K. Paint (3% of A, B, C) | 207 | 2.59 | 536.13 | 0.54 | 111.78 | |
| Total (No margin or ballast) | 12,236 | 3.557 | 43,529.36 | 0.559 | 6,842.16 | |
| Margin (5%) | 604 | 3.557 | | 0.559 | | |
| Total (No ballast) | 12,840 | 3.557 | 45,678.1 | 0.559 | 7,179.92 | |
| Inside Ballast | | | | | | |
| Outside Ballast | 10,000 | 1.13 | 11,300 | 0.504 | 5,040.00 | |
| Light Ship | 22,840 | 2.495 | 56,978.1 | 0.535 | 12,219.92 | |

*Table 3-1*  A typical table of weights, showing desired location of keel weight.

positioning of the mast relative to the keel, while others have to do with design and construction features of the mast itself. Here we will cover both topics.

## Mast Positioning

When specifying the location of a mast, a designer must start with a good weight study. This means calculating the weight, vertical centre of gravity (VCG), and longitudinal centre of gravity (LCG) of everything on the boat—a long and tedious job. Once the LCG of the hull is known, the designer can then determine the position of the ballast weight to make the boat float level in sailing condition. (Note that in IOR measurement condition it may be preferable for the boat to be slightly bow down if the crew are to be positioned aft.) The next step is to design a keel and establish its position on the hull. Table 3-1 shows a typical weights table with the keel location established.

From here, it is a simple matter to find the centre of lateral resistance (CLR) of the boat. To do so, make a cut-out of the underwater portion of the hull to the rudderstock. (Ignore the rudder since it is movable.) Figure 3-2 shows how. Then locate the point where the cut-out can be balanced on the tip of a pin; this is the CLR. On the actual boat, the CLR is the point at which a line attached to the hull could tow the boat sideways without swinging it fore or aft.

Once the centre of lateral resistance is established, the centre of effort (CE) of the sail plan must also be found. This is done by finding the centre of each sail and then applying moments to calculate their combined centre. Figure 3-3 illustrates the process.

By projecting the CE and CLR to the waterline, the distance from the bow to each point can be measured and expressed as a percentage of the waterline length. The difference between the two is known as the lead. For a sloop, the lead should be on the order of 17 per cent plus or minus, depending on the BWL/LWL ratio. Figure 3-4 is a typical graph plotting the lead against BWL/LWL. If the lead is much greater than 18 per cent, the boat will suffer from lee helm; if, on the other hand, the lead is much smaller than 17 per cent, weather helm will result. By altering the position of the mast fore and aft, or the fore and aft position of the keel, the designer can correct these problems and balance the helm.

## Mast Design and Construction

### The Mast Section
To reduce windage, the mast should be as clean and as narrow as possible. This means a small mast section. My personal preference is for a thick-walled, small section spar. The mast should also have interior tangs, which are both easily accessible from the outside (not requiring 40 foot arms to reach!) and replaceable at sea.

### The Masthead and Halyards
Internal halyards are now fitted on modern racing boats, again, to reduce windage. Even so, they exert a considerable influence on the arrangement of halyard winches, making their layout an important consideration in deck design.

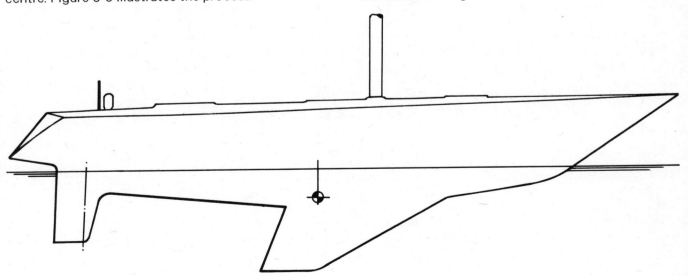

*Figure 3-2.* Locating the position of the centre of lateral resistance (CLR).

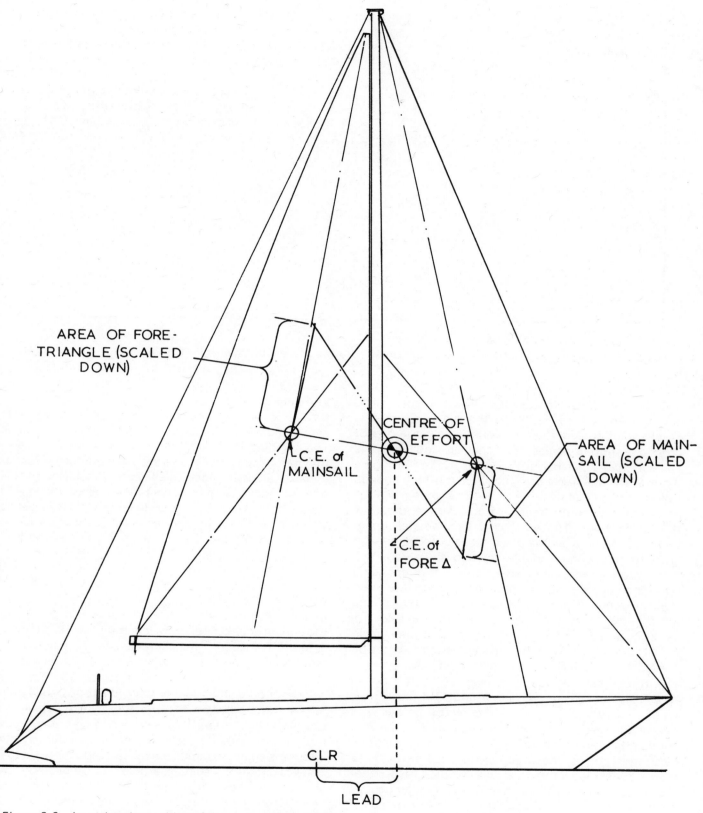

*Figure 3-3.* Locating the position of the centre of effort (CE).

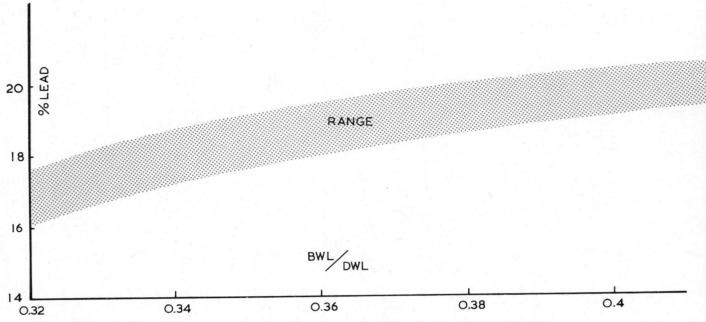

*Figure 3-4.* A typical graph plotting lead (as a percentage of waterline length) against BWL/DWL.

Figure 3-5 gives a good idea of how a mast is laid out, showing where the halyards enter and exit. It is essential, of course, that the various halyards do not cross one another, or else a slack halyard could become jammed in another halyard exit box. Notice in Figure 3-5 that the spinnaker pole topping lift is high enough to form an angle of no more than 45 degrees when the pole is at the top of the mast track. Notice, too, how the staysail halyard enters the mast immediately under the midstay, thus allowing the staysail to be hanked onto the stay when a double-head rig is required.

Halyard systems vary from boat to boat depending upon the purpose for which a particular boat is used. Long-distance racing boats usually carry two genoa halyards, two spinnaker halyards, and one main halyard, as well as a topping lift. Some carry a spare main halyard below deck, with a messenger already inside the mast. Figure 3-6 shows such a masthead.

With hydraulic vangs, or screw-type solid vangs, a topping lift is no longer essential; and if the messenger for the spare main halyard is removed together with one of the genoa halyards, a designer can achieve a substantial weight reduction at the masthead, plus one less turning block and winch at the base of the mast. Figure 3-7 shows a three-halyard masthead. Note that the two outside halyards can be used for either genoas or spinnakers, while the centreline halyard is used exclusively for fore and aft sails.

*The Spreaders*
Moving down the mast, the inboard spreader ends should be as 'clean' as possible to reduce windage. They should also be easily accessible in case a temporary repair job is required. The outboard spreader ends should be padded to alleviate sail chafe, but this does not mean huge lumps of tennis balls, packing, and tape. A small wadding taped securely in place is just as effective and creates far less windage. It is easier to cut away, too, when inspections or repairs are made.

*The Spinnaker Pole Track*
Below the spreaders are the spinnaker pole track and the uphaul cheek block. The pole track can be either an external T-shaped fitting, screwed to the mast, or an internal, integral part of the mast extrusion, as shown in Figure 3-8. On boats rating up to 35 feet, the spinnaker pole lift should probably be rope and should run from the bell over the cheek block to a cleat. On boats above this size, chain and wire drives are usually best. These can be either external or internal, but internal is again preferable because it reduces windage. The bottom of the spinnaker pole track typically ends about 18 inches above the deck, unless the pole is permanently fixed to the mast, in which case it should be carried down to deck level.

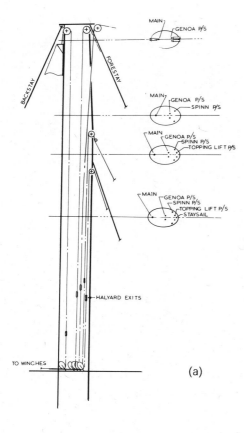

(a)

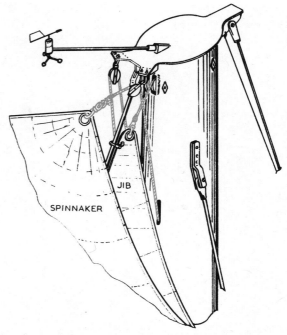

*Figure 3-6.* An ocean racer's masthead showing two genoa halyards and two spinnaker halyards.

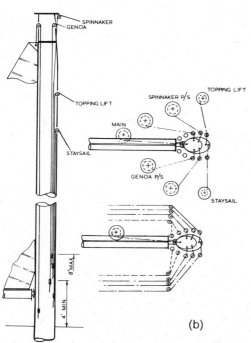

(b)

*Figure 3-5.* (a) A mast arrangement plan showing how halyards enter and leave the mast without crossing over. (b) How the deck might be laid out at the base of the mast.

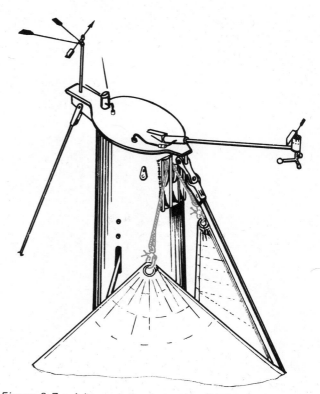

*Figure 3-7.* A low windage masthead using three halyards. Only the two outside halyards are used for spinnakers, while any of them may be used for the genoa. Also note the interior tang.

*Figure 3-8.* A spinnaker pole track set into the mast to reduce windage. Note the mast collar which allows variable attachment points for the halyard tails.

*Figure 3-9.* The chainplates on *Scaramouche* have been designed to pivot on a single.pin. Thus, when the genoa is sheeted in tightly on the lee side, the shrouds move inboard, allowing a smaller sheeting angle and improved pointing ability. *(author)*

*The Halyard Exit Boxes and the Mast Base*

The headsail halyards should exit on either side of the spinnaker pole track, starting about 8 to 9 feet above the deck. This height makes hauling up the sail easier. Headsail halyards should go to turning blocks at the base of the spar and then to a winch. At the base of the mast there should also be spare padeyes and blocks to lead the cunningham, vang, reefing lines, or any other lines to a winch. A bale at the front of the spar serves as a place to secure halyards in a regular order so that they may be found easily at night.

All these blocks and gear should be sited far enough away from the mast base to allow a good mast collar to be bolted or welded to the deck. The collar must be sufficiently wide to allow hard rubber wedges to be inserted fore and aft of the mast.

*The Spinnaker and Jockey Poles*

In addition to design aspects of the mast itself, places must be planned on deck for the spinnaker poles, and at times for the jockey pole, although it is often stowed below deck. The length of the spinnaker poles should be equal to the length of J, unless the designer intends penalty poles. The traditional stowage position is on either side of the deck at the bow. This location might be improved upon, however, by having one pole permanently attached to the mast and resting in a trough on the foredeck, while the second pole is constructed in two pieces and can be stowed below deck ready to assemble as needed. The length of the jockey pole, or reaching strut, should be at least one and a half times the distance from the mast to the vertical shrouds. It can be stowed in an easily accessible place below deck.

## The Rigging

If a boat had no rigging, the mast would have to be extraordinarily thick-walled and heavy, with an extremely large section. Obviously, from an aerodynamic standpoint, this would be undesirable. So various wires are used to support the mast, which enables much lighter construction and a far smaller section.

Supporting the mast on a boat, however, is not easy. Unlike the supports for a radio mast on land, the stays for the mast on a boat can only be spread over a limited area—the surface of the deck. Designers, of course, use the available space as best as possible. The forestay and backstay, for instance, often go from the masthead to the extreme stem and stern. Amidships, however, a special problem arises. Here the mast must be supported in an athwartship direction, even though a sailing boat is relatively narrow. To solve the problem, spreaders are used to increase the angle between the diagonals and the mast. Ideally, from a support point of view, the spreaders should be as long as possible, but excessive length may mean that the spreaders would poke through the genoa when it was sheeted in tightly on the leeward side. Therefore, the lower spreader is made about the same length as the distance between the mast and the vertical chainplate. Figure 3-9 shows a way of pulling this chainplate inboard when it is on the lee side for closer sail sheeting.

Needless to say, there are many different methods of supporting a mast. These vary especially with the size of the boat and the purposes for which the boat is intended to be used. Figure 3-10 shows a simple rig plan. All the stays are labelled, but depending upon the company you keep, you might be accustomed to calling certain ones by different names. This is why it is helpful to use the notations shown in parentheses alongside the names given in the drawing. Everyone can agree upon what a D1 shroud is, thus eliminating the confusion of calling it either a lower, or a lower diagonal, or a diagonal.

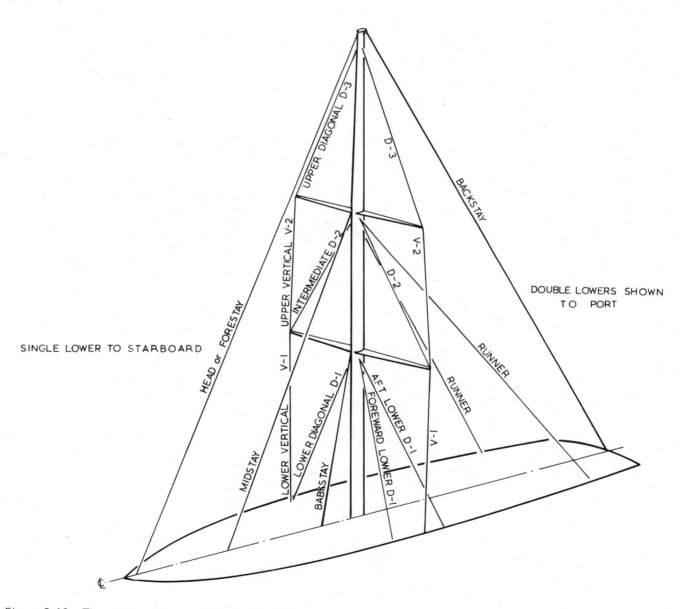

*Figure 3-10.* The names of the standing rigging.

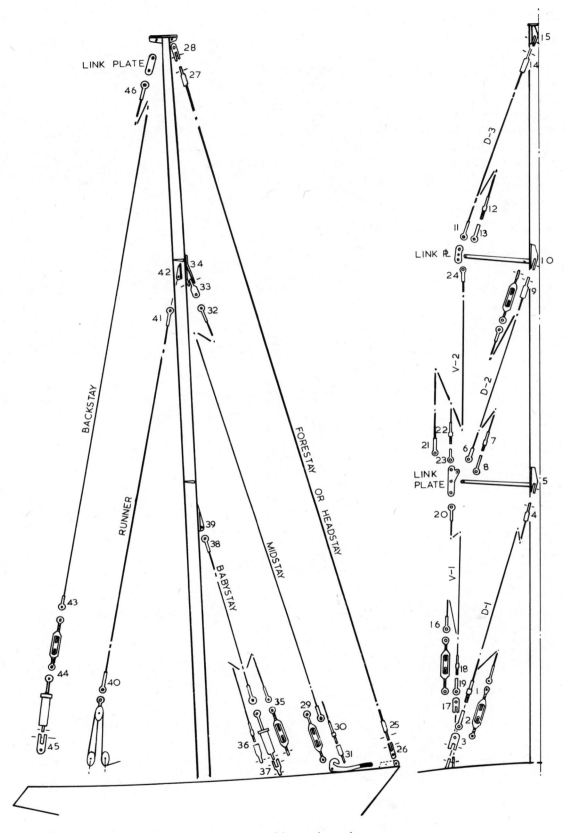

LINK PLATE

BACKSTAY

RUNNER

BABYSTAY

MIDSTAY

FORESTAY OR HEADSTAY

LINK PLATE

LINK PLATE

D-3

D-2

D-1

V-2

V-1

*Figure 3-11.* A rigging assembly plan showing all turn-buckles and toggles.

# Rigging Assembly Summary

| Boat—<br>Owner— | | Rigging Assembly Summary<br>RJM 23-7-75 | | Design—<br>Date— | |
|---|---|---|---|---|---|

| Shroud | | | | Size | Drawing No. | Checked |
|---|---|---|---|---|---|---|
| D-1<br>1 × 19 | Lower end | (1) | Threaded sleeve | | | |
| | | (2) | Eye terminal | | | |
| | | (3) | Double jaw toggle | | | |
| | Upper end | (4) | Eye terminal | | | |
| | | (5) | Tang | | | |
| D-2<br>bar | Lower end | (6) | Jaw terminal | | | |
| | Upper end | (9) | Eye terminal | | | |
| | | (10) | Tang | | | |
| D-2<br>1 × 19 | Lower end | (7) | Threaded sleeve | | | |
| | | (8) | Jaw terminal | | | |
| | Upper end | (9) | Eye terminal | | | |
| | | (10) | Tang | | | |
| D-3<br>AR | Lower end | (11) | Jaw terminal | | | |
| | Upper end | (14) | Eye terminal | | | |
| | | (15) | Tang | | | |
| D-3<br>1 × 19 | Lower end | (12) | Threaded sleeve | | | |
| | | (13) | Jaw terminal | | | |
| | Upper end | (14) | Eye terminal | | | |
| | | (15) | Tang | | | |
| V-1<br>bar | Lower end | (16) | Eye terminal | | | |
| | | (17) | Double jaw toggle | | | |
| | Upper end | (20) | Jaw terminal | | | |
| V-1<br>1 × 19 | Lower end | (18) | Threaded sleeve | | | |
| | | (19) | Eye terminal | | | |
| | | (17) | Double jaw toggle | | | |
| | Upper end | (20) | Jaw terminal | | | |
| V-2<br>bar | Lower end | (21) | Eye terminal | | | |
| | Upper end | (24) | Jaw terminal | | | |
| V-2<br>1 × 19 | Lower end | (22) | Threaded sleeve | | | |
| | | (23) | Jaw terminal | | | |
| | Upper end | (24) | Jaw terminal | | | |
| Headstay<br>bar/1 × 19 | Lower end | (25) | Eye terminal | | | |
| | | (26) | Double jaw toggle | | | |
| | Upper end | (27) | Eye terminal | | | |
| | | (28) | Double jaw toggle | | | |
| Forestay<br>1 × 19 | Lower end | (29) | Eye terminal-turnbuckle | | | |
| | | (30) | /Threaded sleeve | | | |
| | | (31) | Toggle | | | |
| | | (—) | Quick release gear | | | |
| | Upper end | (32) | Eye terminal | | | |
| | | (33) | Double jaw toggle | | | |
| | | (34) | Tang | | | |
| Midstay<br>1 × 19 | Lower end | (35) | Eye terminal-turnbuckle | | | |
| | | (36) | /Threaded sleeve | | | |
| | | (37) | Toggle | | | |
| | | (—) | Quick release gear | | | |
| | Upper end | (38) | Jaw/Eye terminal | | | |
| | | (39) | Tang | | | |
| Runner<br>1 × 19 | Lower end | (40) | Jaw/Eye terminal | | | |
| | Upper end | (41) | Eye terminal | | | |
| | | (42) | Tang | | | |
| Backstay<br>bar/1 × 19 | Lower end | (43) | Eye/Jaw terminal | | | |
| | | (44) | Turnbuckle/Backstay pump | | | |
| | | (45) | Toggle | | | |
| | Upper end | (46) | Eye/Jaw terminal | | | |

*Table 3-11b*

## The Functions of Stays and Shrouds

The basic rigging plan for a typical boat is familiar to all sailors. But in addition to their general function of supporting the mast, what exactly does each stay or shroud do? Why is it necessary to have so many wires going aloft? Let us review the purpose of each component of the rigging, beginning with the longitudinal stays.

### The Headstay
The headstay supports the luff of the genoa either by hanks or a luff groove device. It also serves to hold the masthead in a longitudinal direction. Ideally, the headstay should be either a rod bar with a luff groove fitted over it, or a solid luff groove device like the Stearn twinstay.

### The Backstay
The backstay counters the forces imposed by the headstay in holding the masthead in a longitudinal direction. By adjusting the headstay/backstay lengths, therefore, one can vary the rake of the mast. On a boat designed for ton cup racing, the backstay is best made of rod; but for long-distance racing, $1 \times 19$ wire is better because of its greater shock-absorbing capacity. (Wire will stretch about twice as much as rod for similar diameters.)

### The Midstay
The midstay positions the upper third of the mast when sailing. It is used to exert some forward bend in the spar, thus flattening the mainsail. It is also used in conjunction with the runners to prevent the upper third of the mast from flexing and changing the shape of the sails.

### The Runners
Runners prevent the mast from bending too far forward due to the midstay load. By highly tensioning the runners, a straight mast or some reverse bend can be obtained, which increases the fullness of the upper half of the mainsail for extra drive in light winds. Alternatively, if the mainsail is already full, tension the runners and midstay lightly to steady the upper portion of the mast.

Runners are usually $1 \times 19$ wire with a single or three-part tackle which can be taken to a winch on a large boat or to a cleat on a small one.

### The Babystay
A babystay, which eliminates the need for forward lowers, can be used to control mast bend. It has the advantage of not having to be removed for each tack, although it must be removed for a dip-pole gybe. Babystays are best made of $1 \times 19$ wire, which can be taken back to the mast on a gybe. If hydraulics are used, the babystay may be a rod bar.

The headstay, backstay, midstay, runners, and babystay are the most common longitudinal components of the rigging. Laterally, the parts of the rig vary in number, depending upon the arrangement. The basic styles are the single or double spreader, with single or double lowers. Recently, however, triple spreader rigs have also been experimented with.

### Double Lowers
A rig with double lowers (D1's) is the simplest type to set up. The lowers should be $1 \times 19$ wire and set fairly tight. They are usually positioned between 5 and 10 degrees out from the athwartship centreline of the mast. A babystay is not required with this rig, as it is with single lowers.

### Single Lowers
Single lowers (D1's) are set just aft of the vertical shrouds and thus do not exert much force against the forward pull of the babystay. They are best used with a flexible mast which can be bent to get the best performance from the sails. This kind of mast is usually found on a pure racing boat. Like double lowers, single lowers should ideally be $1 \times 19$ wire.

### Vertical Lower Shrouds
Vertical shrouds (V1's) carry the load from the upper shrouds and intermediate diagonals down to the chainplates. They are best made of round or lenticular rod.

### Intermediate Diagonals
Intermediate diagonals (D2's) which are found on boats with double spreader rigs, brace the middle section of the mast and keep the spar in column. They are usually lenticular or round rod.

### Upper Diagonals
Upper diagonals (D3's) do the same job as the intermediate diagonals for the top part of the mast. Again, they are either lenticular or round rod.

80

*Upper Vertical Shrouds*

The upper shrouds (V2's) carry the load of the upper diagonals down to the intersection of the intermediate diagonals and the vertical shrouds, where they are joined to the vertical shrouds. Occasionally, the upper shrouds are carried all the way to the deck, but this tends to increase windage more than is necessary. They are usually lenticular or round rod.

## Toggles and Turnbuckles

All the stays and shrouds just discussed must be adjusted to keep the mast in optimum tune, and some of these adjustments are made using turnbuckles. Also, because of the unavoidable movement of the rigging caused by the motion of the sea, toggles are required at the rigging attachment points so that there will not be any 'hard spots' where fatigue might occur.

While toggles are used on all components of the standing rigging, on racing boats turnbuckles or bottlescrews are used mainly on the shrouds, which

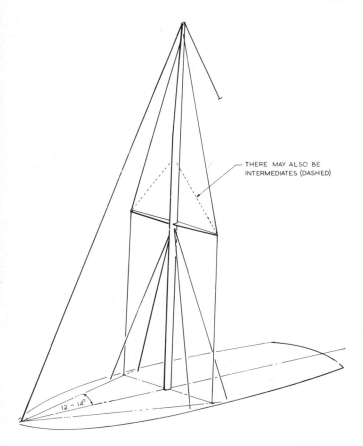

THERE MAY ALSO BE
INTERMEDIATES (DASHED)

12 - 14°

*Figure 3-12.* A double-lower, single-spreader rig.

are set up and adjusted at the dock and not readjusted during the race. This means that the D1's, the D2's, and the V1's are typically fitted with turnbuckles. A turnbuckle, which is attached directly to the end of the shroud, is pinned to the toggle, which in turn is fastened to the chainplate. Special turnbuckles have been developed for rod rigging, an example of which can be seen in Figure 3-9. The exact design varies, of course, from manufacturer to manufacturer. Also, when an owner does not want to invest in hydraulics, turn-buckles are often used to adjust some of the stays. A rigger should always be given a list of all the turnbuckles and toggles to be fitted on the boat, or a rigging assembly drawing like the one shown in Figure 3-11.

## The Pros and Cons of Different Rigs

Which rig is best? As with any other equipment, it always depends on the boat. Here we will simply review some of the various rig configurations, their advantages and disadvantages.

The simplest rig is the double-lower, single-spreader type shown in Figure 3-12. It is usually found on stock boats. The great benefit of this rig is that once it is set up, it does not need much adjustment other than pumping up the backstay. The major drawback is that a single spreader means there is more unsupported length of spar than with a double spreader; hence, higher mast inertias are required. This translates into a thicker and heavier mast, which adversely affects performance.

To obtain a thinner spar section, one usually goes to a double-spreader rig, which may have either single or double lowers. A double-spreader rig is usually pre-ferred over a single-spreader one for most racing boats, even though it is more difficult to tune because of the greater number of components. As mentioned earlier, triple-spreader rigs, and even 4- and 5-spreader rigs, have also been seen at recent regattas. In the 1977 Admiral's Cup, for example, *Moonshine* used an exper-imental triple-spreader rig with an extremely thin spar. (See Figure 3-13.) This arrangement, however, was even more difficult to tune than a double-spreader design, and I would imagine it was also easier to bring down! However, the ITC reacted to such rigs promptly, by placing a limit on rigging attachments to the mast below 25% of I.

With either a single-spreader or a multiple-spreader rig, hydraulics can be used to bend the mast. Also, any of these configurations can be used on a masthead or non-masthead design. Figure 3-14 shows some of the possibilities.

*Figure 3-13. Moonshine's* triple spreader rig. *(author)*

A rig that is not as flexible as those outlined above is the Bergstrom-Ridder, with its distinctive swept-back spreaders. (See Figure 3-15.) The Bergstrom-Ridder rig does, however, have other advantages. For one thing, the spreader sweepback helps increase tacking speed. This can prove especially useful for match racing, such as the Canada's Cup. B & R rigs should be set up with some mast bend, and a hydraulic headstay adjuster should be used to straighten the spar as required.

There are, of course, other rigs with swept-back spreaders. The non-masthead rig in Figure 3-16 is able to eliminate runners because the D2 shrouds are swept back and prevent the mast from moving forward at the headstay attachment point, while the D1's prevent the middle of the mast from moving aft. This means that tension must be kept on the backstay to bow the mast forward, or else the bend might reverse.

So far we have discussed only the rigs of sloops. But any of the previous rig configurations can also be applied to the mizzen mast of a yawl or ketch. With a two-masted boat, it is preferable to stay both masts separately. Then, if one mast is lost, the other can still get you home.

## Hydraulics

As sailing boats become more sophisticated, so too does the equipment they use. Ten years ago, the only method of tensioning a backstay was by means of either a turnbuckle with handles or blocks and tackles. Today, however, with modern advances in sailing technology, almost all boats have some form of hydraulic tensioner, at least on the backstay. The latest racing boats, of course, have much more.

There are many reasons why hydraulics are being used so frequently nowadays. One is the precision of control they allow. With hydraulics, the load on a stay can be viewed on a pressure gauge and adjusted with a high degree of accuracy. Another reason for the switch to hydraulics is efficiency. Hydraulics allow high loads to be moved short distances without first having to release the load. Also, adjustments can be made from a centrally-located control panel, saving crew time and movement. And because hydraulic leads usually go under the deck, complicated systems of deck hardware are eliminated and clutter is reduced. For these basic reasons, then, hydraulics provide the perfect answer where the load is high and the stroke short.

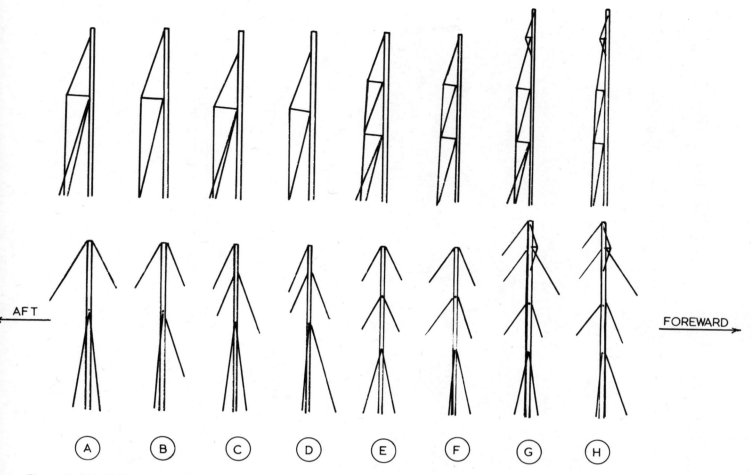

*Figure 3-14.* Various rig configurations.
A: single spreader, double lowers rig. B: single spreader, single lower and babystay rig. C: single spreader, double lowers with runners and removable midstay. D: single spreader, single lower and babystay with runners and removable midstay. E: double spreader, double lowers with runners and removable midstay. F: double spreader, single lower and babystay with runners and midstay. G: non-masthead rig with double spreaders, double lowers, double runners, jumper shrouds and midstay. H: as G but with single lowers and babystay.

## The Uses of Hydraulics

Hydraulics are currently used for many different purposes. Adjusting the backstay, the headstay, the babystay, and the boom vang are among the most common uses. But there are many others as well. The mast partners, the boom outhaul, the spreaders, the cunningham, the flattening reef adjuster, the genoa car tracks under load, above deck mast support struts and the mast step are some additional areas where hydraulics may be employed. Here we will discuss some of the more typical functions of hydraulics in greater detail.

*Backstay Adjuster*
The original hydraulic ram was always used on the backstay, generally for controlling headstay tension. With today's hydraulic systems, backstay tension is adjusted almost as often as sheet and halyard tension to control headstay sag and alter the amount and position of draft in the genoa. In heavy air, tensioning the backstay moves the masthead aft and tightens the headstay, which flattens the genoa and pulls the draft forward. In light going, on the other hand, easing the backstay moves the draft aft, thus increasing the fullness of the genoa and the drive that can be obtained from it.

*Figure 3-15.* A Bergstrom-Ridder rig on Mr Breene Kerr's *Winds of War. (author)*

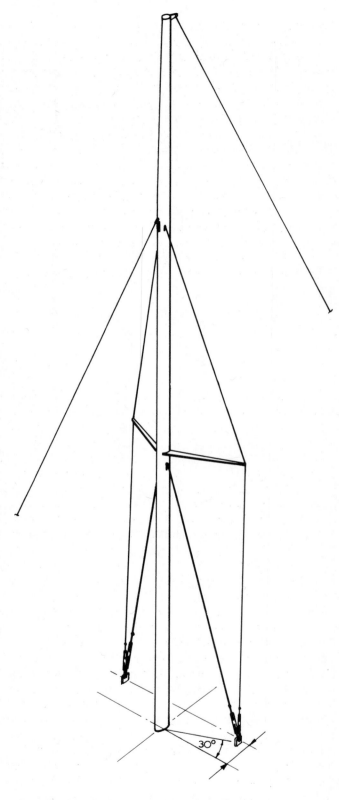

*Figure 3-16.* A non-masthead rig with swept back spreaders, which eliminate the need for runners and a midstay.

84

## Headstay or Forestay Adjuster

When a hydraulic backstay adjuster is used in conjunction with a headstay adjuster, the fore and aft rake of the mast can be varied. On a One Tonner, for example, up to 18 inches of fore and aft movement is possible using the Stearn hydraulics and mast system. The latest systems use a mast raking device that allows the operator to pump directly from one cylinder to another. Thus, the backstay/headstay tension can remain constant while the rake is adjusted. The ability to adjust mast rake is essential in order to obtain maximum hull speed under any given conditions. The general rule is to rake the mast aft in light air and forward in a good breeze so as to keep between 3 and 5 degrees of weather helm. Note that raking the mast necessitates moving the jib lead and adjusting the halyard tension.

Fore and aft movement of the mast really comes into its own on a reach. The mast can be cranked all the way forward which almost completely eliminates extreme weather helm (when the rudder acts as a brake). Needless to say, this greatly increases potential boat speed.

The ORC no longer allows hydraulic headstay adjusters on IOR boats. The only exception is a boat with clearly swept-back spreaders, where a headstay adjuster is essential. This exception is intended to allow boats with Bergstrom-Ridder rigs to continue to race under the IOR. All other boats must have a fixed headstay, although they are allowed an adjustable backstay.

## Babystay Adjuster

Mast bend can be controlled by using a hydraulic backstay adjuster together with a babystay adjuster. This, in turn, helps adjust the mainsail. More mast bend frees the leech of the mainsail and reduces the fullness of the sail, while less tension tightens the leech and makes the sail fuller, thus increasing drive in light air.

## Hydraulic Boom Vang

The hydraulic vang has almost totally replaced the mainsheet as an instrument for tightening the mainsail leech. Of the various types of hydraulic adjusters available, the best for a vang is the single-acting kind which is spring-loaded or uses compressed air. Either device ensures that the boom will lift when the vang is released. On a compressed air model, the pressure can be varied to control the lifting action of the boom, but a bicycle pump is needed to pump up the vang if it goes 'soft'.

Whatever type of adjuster you select, make sure that the designer is aware at an early stage that you intend to use a hydraulic vang because it necessitates reinforcing the boom in the area of the vang attachment point, and may also require changes in the deck layout.

## Hydraulic Mast Partners

A hydraulic ram at the mast partners can help bend the mast when used in conjunction with other mast controls. There are restrictions, however. It is illegal under the IOR to have hydraulic mast partners with a pump attached. This kind of system is used mainly on twelve metre boats. On IOR boats, the mast at the partners may only move up to 10 per cent of its fore and aft diameter, so hydraulic mast partners may not be necessary. For those who want them, though, systems are available. Stearn Sailing Systems has a form of mast partner that is a simple two-way cylinder in which the fluid may flow from one side to the other. A valve, when closed, essentially locks the mast in the desired position.

## Hydraulic Boom Outhaul

Hydraulics can also be used to tension the foot of the mainsail. The twelve metres *Courageous* and *Enterprise* had hydraulic boom outhauls, as well as hydraulic rams at the mast partners.

When hydraulic boom outhauls are used, the black band is put on the adjuster rather than on the outboard end of the boom.

## Types of Rams

The simplest and easiest kind of ram to use is the single-acting type, shown in Figure 3-17a. Although it is most commonly fitted as a backstay adjuster, it has also found favour lately for use on the headstay and midstay—or wherever one-way power adjustment is needed. Stearn Sailing Systems has developed a locking adjuster, seen in Figure 3-17b, which can be used for the same purposes as the single-acting ram. Its mechanical locking mechanism reduces wear on the system, and the device can still be adjusted mechanically if the hydraulics fail. Obviously, it is wise for offshore boats to install this type of ram since hydraulic failure at sea can be quite hazardous. Figure 3-18 shows a section through a Stearn locking adjuster.

For boom vangs, adjusters should preferably be able to both support the boom and lower it when the sail is full. A simple single-acting ram can be used for the boom vang, although it requires a compression rod to take the weight of the boom. And because it does not have an up stroke, the single-acting ram can only lower

85

*Figure 3-17.* (a) A non-locking, single-acting adjuster. (b) A locking adjuster. Note the screw thread and jaws that can be used to wind the ram down if pressure is lost from the system. *(Courtesy of Stearn Sailing Systems)*

the boom, not raise it as well. A double-acting ram, with its separate up and down strokes, has the advantage of being able both to lower and raise the boom. This system does not require a second valve or pump, but it has the drawback of possibly being damaged if the up stroke is not released before trimming the mainsheet. The best type of ram for boom vangs is probably a single-acting, spring-loaded model, or one that has a compressed air chamber. When this vang is tensioned, the spring is loaded or the air in the chamber compresses. Once the tension is removed, the ram returns to its original position supporting the boom.

This kind of adjuster has the advantage of eliminating the need for a topping lift, which can chafe the leech of the mainsail.

**Installing a Hydraulic System**

Having reviewed the uses of hydraulics on modern racing boats, and discussed some of the types of rams available, how should the total system be set up? How many pumps are needed? Where should the control panels go? And how is the entire system connected? This is the stage in the use of hydraulics where good design planning enters the picture.

*How Many Pumps?*
Suppose an owner wants to install a fairly complete system of hydraulics on his boat. How many pumps does he need and where should they be positioned? He could, perhaps, install a separate pump at each ram. Although such a solution is very simple from an installation point of view, it is also extremely expensive. Moreover, when the system is in use, the crewmen have to go to each hydraulic separately to make an adjustment or just to read the pressure. This could be dangerously slow if a ram has to be let off quickly, and it also requires more crew movement than is desirable. What is more, sheets can easily catch on pump handles, fouling a tack and possibly damaging the equipment.

Another solution, of course, is to site the rams as required and then locate the pumps in more easily accessible positions, connecting the two with hose. Obviously, this is preferable to the first system in terms of speed and ease of operation, but it still has some disadvantages—namely, the extra weight and cost of separate pumps plus the weight and cost of the hoses.

A much better system employs a single pump and a number of valves on a central control panel. The valves control the flow of hydraulic fluid to each ram, and each ram has its own pressure dial on the central control panel. The panel shows the load on the system even when the valves are closed. A reservoir from which fluid can be drawn is also indicated on the central panel, and all rams can be fully extended at any time. The pioneer manufacturers of this type of system are Stearn Sailing Systems in the United States and David Carne in England.

*Siting the Control Panel*
Where should the control panel be sited? There is no hard and fast rule. Several key factors, however, should

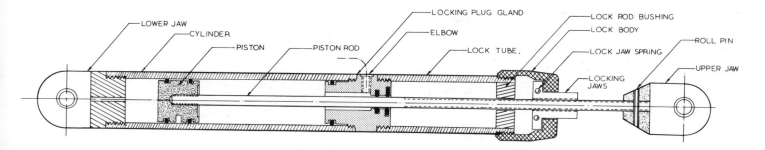

Figure 3-18.   A section through a locking adjuster. *(Courtesy of Stearn Sailing Systems)*

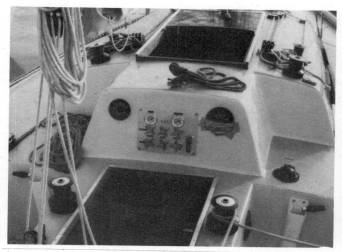

*Figure 3-19.*   (a) The hydraulic panel on Mr Bruce Mc-Pherson's Half Tonner *Maltese Cat.*

*Figure 3-19.*   (c) As *Marionette's* rig is adjusted, the wire ring on the cylinder moves, allowing the operator to duplicate any setting with ease.

*Figure 3-19.*   (b) A David Carne hydraulic panel aboard *Marionette.* The three gauges monitor backstay/forestay, babystay and kicker pressure, and the open/shut control valve can be seen in the middle of them. The switch at the top right allows the masthead to be moved forward or aft without removing the load from the system.

always be considered.

1. Visibility. The panel should be sited where the dials can be easily seen, and more importantly, where the ram being adjusted can be seen. Figure 3-19 shows an ideal location.

2. Ease of operation. The panel should be within easy reach of the operator to avoid excessive crew movement.

3. Interference with other equipment. The panel should be located where it does not snag lines or sheets. It should also be placed well clear of compasses, because the hoses leading from the panel are steel sheathed.

4. Maintenance. For easy maintenance, the panel should be accessible from inside the boat. Of course, the pump, too, must be easily accessible for priming, and the fluid reservoir (which must be higher than the pump) requires easy access for topping up.

*Connecting the Hoses*

With the rams, pump, and panel installed, the next step is to connect the hoses. The procedure varies from system to system, so consult the manufacturer's manual before attempting assembly. In general, however, the following instructions are helpful.

1. Tape the ends of all the hoses and lead them through the boat to the required positions. Do not kink the hose or lead it around a radius smaller than 8 inches. Allow extra length—in the order of 5 per cent—for contraction under pressure.

2. Cut the hose to length and assemble the end fittings according to the manufacturer's instructions. Make sure that the hose is cleaned of all metal filings and dirt before assembly. Dirt in the valves can ruin the entire system.

3. Connect the hoses to the rams and to the panel. Again, keep everything clean. When all the adjusters are connected, the system is ready to be filled. Like automobile brakes, all the air must be removed before the mechanisms will work properly.

4. The fluid to be used varies among manufacturers. At this time, a Stearn system uses Stearn hydraulic fluid or 10 W HP oil. A David Carne system uses Shell Tellus 27, or its equivalent. Almost all manufacturers warn against the use of brake fluid or automatic transmission fluid, because it may ruin the rubber seals.

5. To prime each cylinder, loosen the hose connection at the cylinder end and allow the air to escape. Pull the cylinder out to its fully extended position and pump until fluid flows from the loosened fitting. As soon as fluid flows, tighten the connection and repeat the procedure for the other adjusters. Remember to top up

the fluid reservoir after working on each cylinder. After all the cylinders have been bled, fill the reservoir to within one inch of the top.

## Operating and Maintaining Hydraulics

Now comes the moment of truth. You are ready to operate the system. Open a valve and pump up. Watch what happens to the rig. If anything looks unusual, release the pressure and find the cause of the problem before applying pressure again. Once the gauge reaches the desired figure, the valve can be closed. As far as how much pressure can be applied is concerned, a general rule of thumb is not to let the load on a given wire exceed one-third of its breaking strength.

What should you do when trouble arises with hydraulics? Different problems, of course, require different solutions, but here are some basic things to look for.

If there is any pressure loss in the system, the first thing to do is to make sure that all the valves are closed. This prevents the remaining pressure from draining away, leaving the rig slack. If pressure is being lost through a particular cylinder, check the appropriate valve carefully to see if it is fully closed. Then check the hose fittings. Any leak will be indicated by seeping fluid. Check the cylinder seals as well. A cylinder with a faulty seal will show fluid where the piston rod emerges. Also remember to check for leaks at the pump end of the system; or perhaps the pump itself may be leaking, which calls for new pump seals. If there is still no visible sign of a leak, the pump valve may be obstructed by dirt. A temporary solution is to undo the valve as far as possible and pump, hoping that the fluid will remove the obstruction. If it does not, the pump should be stripped down as soon as possible and cleaned.

Suppose the cylinders cannot be pumped up. If this is the case, there may be air in the system. (Remember how a car's brake system feels spongy when air is in the hose.) The solution is to bleed the system again. But before doing so, make sure to check if the fluid reservoir is full, or you may simply be pumping more air into the hose.

If the pump won't work, check first for materials caught in the valves, and then to see if any springs or other components are damaged. Unless you happen to have a hydraulics engineer among your crew, replacement is the best solution for damaged parts. Consequently, you should always carry a kit of spares, supplied by the manufacturer, on board.

Like everything else on a boat, attending to hydraulics only when they break down is not enough. The system also requires routine maintenance to stay in tip-top condition. Again, here are a few general guidelines.

- After every race, wipe the cylinders and rods clean.
- Every month, check the oil level, check for any signs of leakage, and check the tightness of the fittings.
- Annually, flush out the entire system to remove dirt and refill it with fresh oil. Check the hoses and fittings for signs of wear.
- Every two years, return all cylinders and pumps to the manufacturer for new seals and a complete professional inspection.

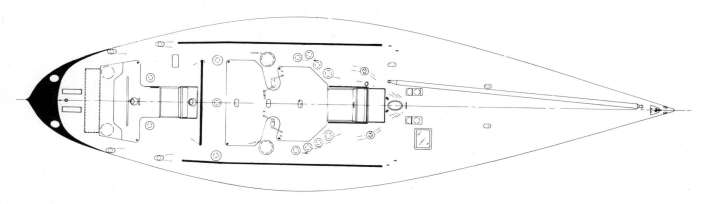

*Scandalous*, designed by Sparkman & Stephens for Mr William T. Pascoe.

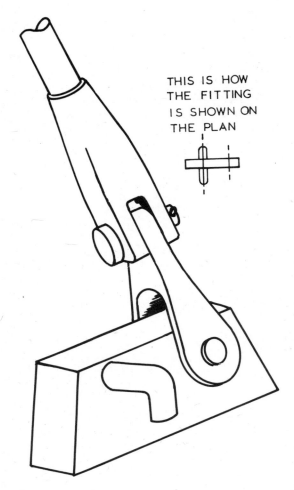

THIS IS HOW
THE FITTING
IS SHOWN ON
THE PLAN

*Figure 4-1.* An inverted horn tack fitting. Note that all tack hooks should be a minimum of 2½ inches aft of the headstay.

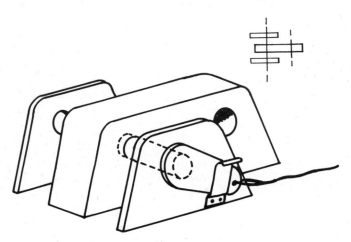

*Figure 4-2.* A tack fitting that holds the sail captive between two plates.

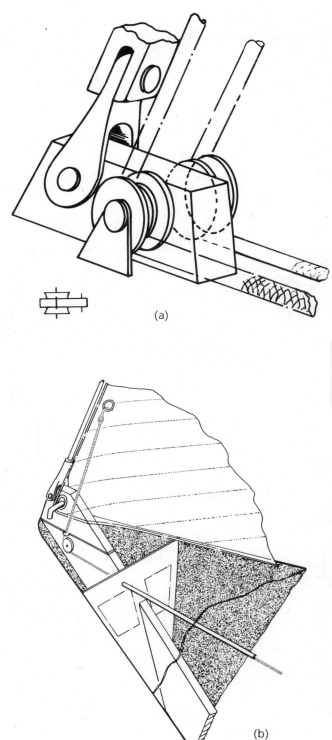

(a)

(b)

*Figure 4-3.* (a) A combination tack hook and foreguy. Often one side can be used as a tack hook and the other as a cunningham, or either one can be used as a foreguy. (b) An underdeck foreguy can also be used as a cunningham if it is positioned near the tack fitting.

90

CHAPTER FOUR
# Other Deck Gear

In Chapters 2 and 3 we discussed winches and hydraulics in great detail, the kinds manufactured, how to select them, and how they should be maintained. But however important good winches and hydraulics may be to optimum sailing performance, they are far from being the only equipment on a modern racing boat. Every boat has a large assortment of other deck gear–cleats for sitting on, fairleads for stubbing toes on, and a host of blocks and tracks, all of which help lead various lines to the winches and enable the power of the sails to be harnessed. In this chapter, we will review a wide variety of other deck gear. In particular, we will focus on the different types of equipment available, which kinds are generally best for different types of boats, and how each piece of gear can be integrated effectively into a good, workable deck arrangement.

## Rigging-related Deck Gear

### The Tack Fitting

Let us consider the tack fitting first. The simplest design is the inverted horn, shown in Figure 4-1. Careful consideration should be given to the strength of the horizontal member, which should be able to support at least 1½ times the calculated sheet load in bending and shear. Because the inverted horn is such a simple shape, one of its problems is that the tack can slip off when the sail is being hoisted. (Figure 1-2 in Chapter 1 shows a way of retaining the tack.)

A slightly more complex and also more widely used type of tack fitting is one that holds the sail captive between two metal plates while a pin is inserted through the plates and the sail tack cringle. (See Figure 4-2.) The major disadvantage of such a fitting is the ease with which the tack pins can be lost, although this can usually be avoided by tying the pin to a nearby fitting with a short line.

The combination tack hook and foreguy is a much more sophisticated fitting, often seen on level rating class boats. Figure 4-3 shows two variations. In drawing (a), one line is used as the running tack and the other as a cunningham or a foreguy. Both are led back to the cockpit with underdeck lines. The system in drawing (b) uses separate genoa tack hooks. The foreguy can be led around a sheave below the tack hook and used as a cunningham if required.

### The Foreguy

As already mentioned, the foreguy can be either combined with the tack fitting or entirely separate from it. The foreguy can also be fitted above deck or below. When led above deck, a swivel block attached to a through-bolted padeye is often the simplest and cheapest arrangement. When led below deck, be sure that the box containing the sheave is easily accessible for repair and maintenance. Figure 4-4 shows a typical underdeck foreguy exit box.

Before fitting the foreguy, consider your method of gybing. For a dip-pole or end-for-end gybe, the foreguy must be positioned so as to be used on either gybe. If, on the other hand, you intend to use a twin-pole gybe, there should be two foreguy padeyes which can be further forward than if a bridle is to be used in an end-for-end gybe.

### Chainplates and Rigging Attachment Points

The tack fitting is a multipurpose unit which, in addition to holding the tack of the genoa and possibly serving as a mounting for the foreguy sheaves, can also incorporate the headstay chainplate. If it does, care must be taken at the design stage to ensure that the

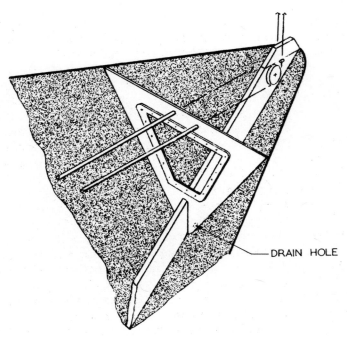

Figure 4-4.    A typical underdeck foreguy box.

battens), and whether the helmsman has enough room (a miscalculation here could break heads!).

The point where the midstay contacts the deck does not require a chainplate as such, but it does require an easily adjusted or removed attachment point with reinforcement going through to the hull or backbone. Figure 4-6 shows some of the variations for midstay attachment points. One system we used on *Morning Cloud*, employs a hydraulic ram below deck attached to the midstay by a length of wire and a drop-nose pin. A different system, using a six-part block and tackle, takes the midstay to a winch. And yet a third, and probably the most common arrangement, uses a highfield lever which tensions the stay when pushed down. The big disadvantage of this last system is the difficulty of adjusting it. First the stay must be let go, then the turnbuckle wound up or down, and finally the stay has to be reconnected. The lever is often set in a well in the foredeck, and a better finger crusher I have yet to meet!

toggles and pins holding the headstay to the chainplate can swivel freely and do not interfere with the operation of the tack fitting.

Care must also be taken when determining how the chainplates are to be fitted. Strong construction is of course essential since the chainplates attach the shrouds to the hull and hold up the mast. These decisions are best left to a competent naval architect.

The positioning of the chainplates on the deck is also critical, and this, too, should be left to an architect. On a boat with single or double lower shrouds, a designer usually locates each vertical shroud chainplate at the point where the athwartship centreline of the mast crosses a line 12 to 14 degrees from the centreline of the tack fitting. The aft lower chainplate is then positioned slightly inboard and aft of this line, and the forward lower is aligned slightly outboard of it, as in the port side of the boat shown in Figure 4-5. When a single lower and babystay are desired, the aft lower is positioned a few inches aft of the vertical shroud, illustrated on the starboard side of Figure 4-5. If a different rig is to be used, for instance a Bergstrom-Ridder rig, the shroud chainplate positions should again be determined by a competent naval architect.

As for the positioning of the backstay chainplate, it is always set on the centreline, with the fore and aft location decided upon by the designer when he draws up the sail plan. In making this decision, he will consider such things as whether the sail leech touches the backstay when tacking (an oversight here could break

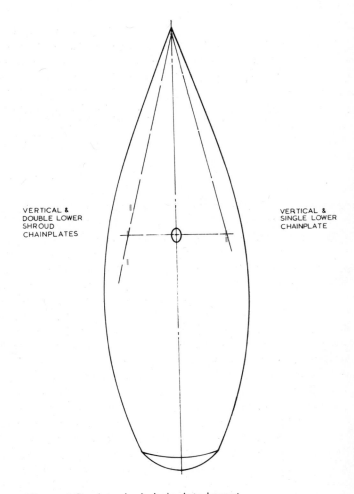

Figure 4-5.    A typical chainplate layout.

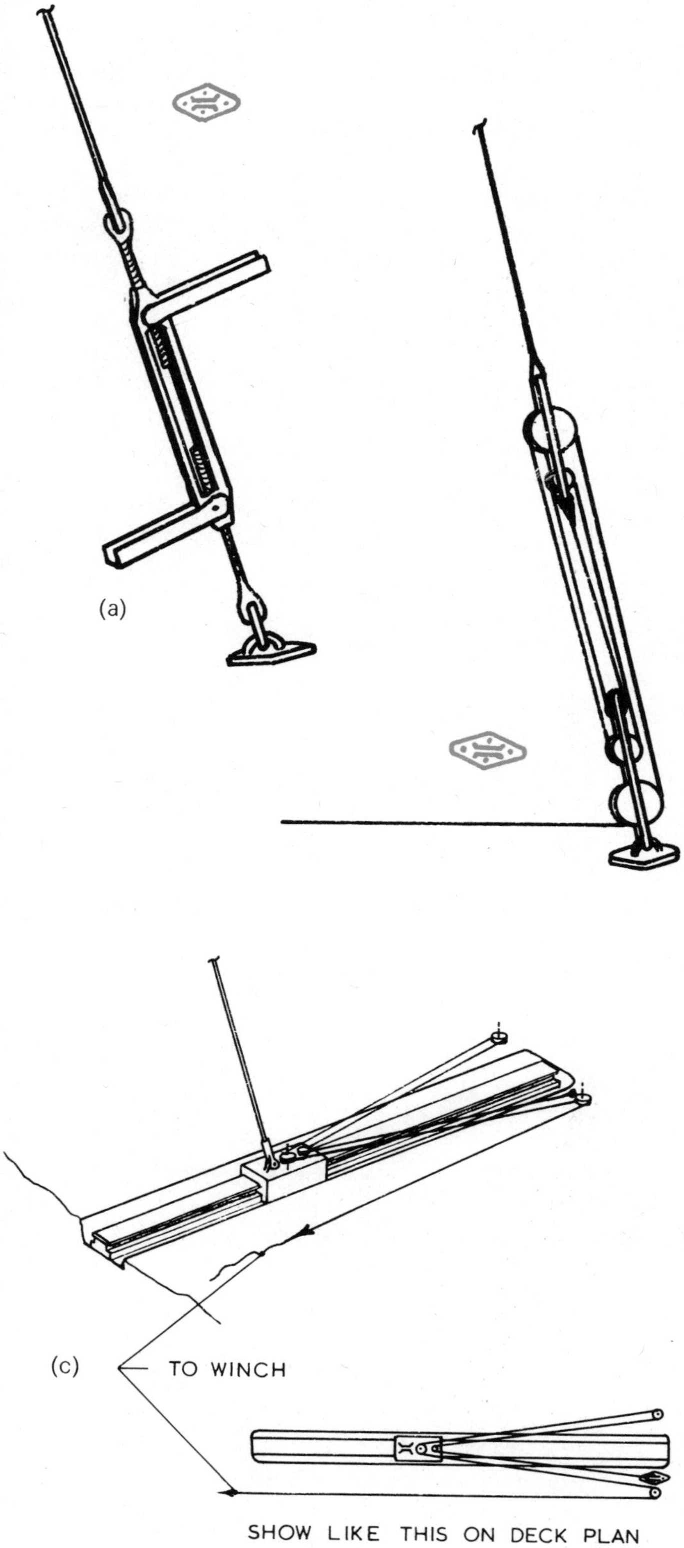

(a)

(c) ← TO WINCH

SHOW LIKE THIS ON DECK PLAN

*Figure 4-6.* (a) A turnbuckle adjuster for the babystay or midstay. (b) A five-part tackle adjuster for smaller boats. (c) A babystay adjuster using a track on the deck.

The babystay, which is set inside the midstay, is usually left connected except during a dip-pole gybe. This stay can be attached to the deck by any of the systems mentioned above, or it can have a short length of centreline track with a four-part tackle taken to a winch, as shown in Figure 4-6c. Again, there must be a tie rod or bulkhead to take the load to the hull.

Runners are also taken to a winch on larger boats, but a three-part, rather than a four-part tackle is generally used. If runners come far forward, they should be positioned inside the genoa sheet so they can be left set up to leeward without crossing and chafing the genoa leech. Padeyes or the toerail are often used as attachment points for the runners. For these, as well as for all other rig attachment points, the upwardly-exerted force should be transmitted to the hull of the boat or, if possible, to the keel by some form of bracing or reinforcement.

## Tracks

### Headsail Tracks

The fore and aft positions of the headsail sheet tracks are found by taking the working sail plan of a boat and drawing in the sheet leads. The points at which the sheets contact the deck determine where the track must be. On the sail plan shown in Figure 4-7, the sheet leads have been drawn in for all headsails. (To get the approximate sheet lead, simply bisect the angle at the clew.) The track would probably be positioned as indicated with a separate padeye for the No. 5 genoa. The reaching genoas would be sheeted to the toerail and would not require track.

At the design stage it is worth considering whether, some time in the future, the boat is likely to need 160 per cent overlap rather than 150. For example, if the boat does not go well under ten knots of wind, 160 per cent genoas might improve the light air performance for a small increase in rating. If this is a possibility, a 160 per cent genoa sheet should be drawn in, together with the drifter sheet. The tracks should then be taken even a little further aft than the points where the sheets meet the deck in order to allow for minor sheeting adjustments.

Athwartships positioning of the headsail tracks varies from designer to designer and from smaller to larger boats. One arrangement is shown on the port side of the boat in Figure 4-8a. The aft end of the track intersects a line drawn at 7 degrees from the tack fitting. When there is only one track, as shown here, it is usually placed parallel to the centreline so that the

93

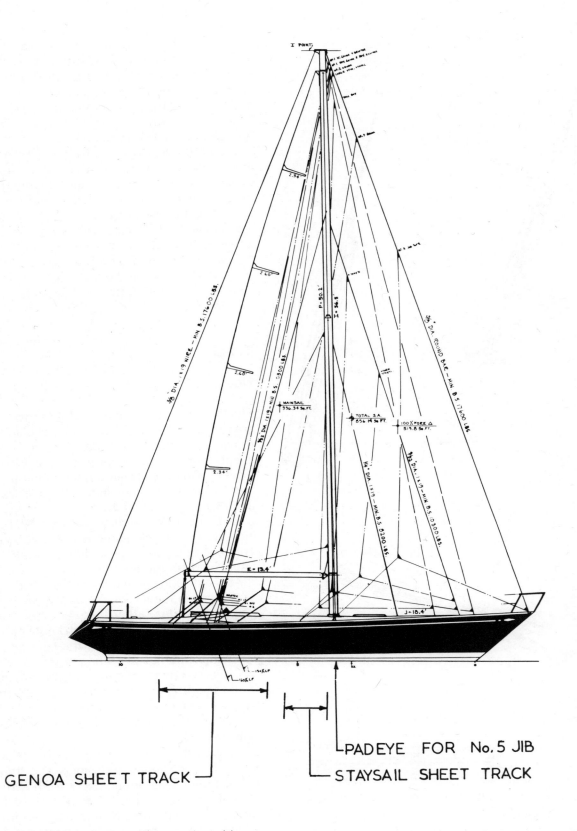

GENOA SHEET TRACK

PADEYE FOR No. 5 JIB
STAYSAIL SHEET TRACK

*Figure 4-7.* A sail plan showing the sheet track positions.

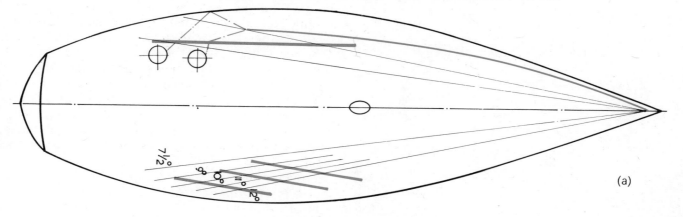

A SINGLE TRACK WHICH CAN BE BARBER HAULED TO THE RAIL

3 TRACKS GIVE A VARIETY OF POSITIONS

(a)

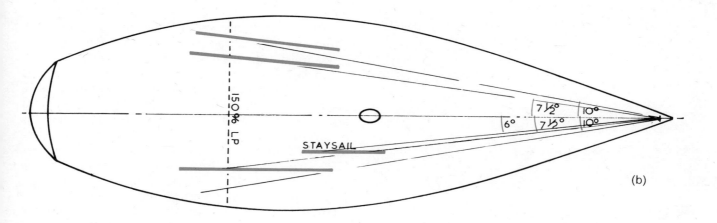

AN ATHWARTSHIP TRACK ARRANGEMENT.

(b)

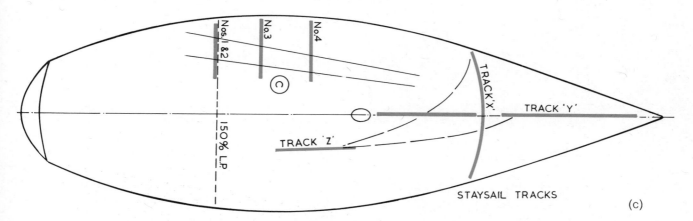

(c)

*Figure 4-8.* (a) and (b) Various genoa sheet track positions. (c) Athwartships genoa track and various staysail track positions.

*Figure 4-9.* (a) The Half Tonner *North Star*'s genoa track arrangement. *(author)* (b) Athwartship genoa tracks aboard the Half Tonner *Krakemut*. Note the mechanical vang and mast collar for the spinnaker pole. *(author)*

smaller headsails for higher wind strengths are sheeted on the 10 degree line, thus allowing the slot to open slightly. With this arrangement, the genoa sheet could also be barberhauled to the toerail. Figure 4-8 illustrates other variations as well. The starboard side of the boat in drawing (a) shows a three-track arrangement with a large number of sheeting points. On boat (b), the port side has a twin-track system, where the sheet could be barberhauled between both tracks if necessary. And finally, in drawing (c), the port side has a possible athwartship genoa track system suitable for smaller boats.

Provided one's sailmaker can be trusted to do a good job, it is often preferable on smaller boats to have athwartship tracks with some form of downhauler to give the slight vertical adjustment sometimes required. Figure 4-9a shows such an arrangement as used on *North Star* during the 1976 Half Ton world championship. This system is certainly easy to trim athwartships, but the sails must be very carefully cut to suit the track. Often, one piece of track is required for each sail, which tends to limit the total range of the system.

Staysails are usually sheeted on a 6 or 7 degree line when under double headsail rig, but when under a spinnaker the luff of the staysail should be kept at right angles to the pole and as close to it as possible. This necessitates another track for the tack of the staysail, usually at about 40 per cent of J forward of the mast, as illustrated by line x in drawing (c) of Figure 4-8. The exact distance varies depending upon the sailmaker, so check with yours before setting the track. Another alternative is to have a fore and aft track on the centreline for the tack of the staysail. This is illustrated by line y in Figure 4-8 (c). And finally, line z in the same drawing is a simple staysail sheeting track on the 6 degree line.

## The Toerail

Although the alloy toerail is a comparatively recent development in offshore racing, it is undoubtedly here to stay. The large number of holes enables a snatch block to be clipped on almost anywhere, thus allowing the best possible lead. On fibreglass boats, a properly selected and fitted toerail adds considerable strength and also covers the joint where the hull meets the deck. One of the latest innovations is to incorporate a rubbing stráke into the rail extrusion, which clearly increases the toerail's versatility. Another idea is to make the stanchion base an integral part of the toerail, but because stanchions must often be located a little inboard from the extreme edge of the deck, this may be more of a cruising than a racing development.

Offsetting its many advantages, the toerail also has some possible drawbacks. One is the need for some form of scupper cut through the bottom flange. Another is the effect a toerail has on the circulation in a crewman's legs when he sits to weather for any length of time. To make sitting more comfortable, and also to reduce windage, many boats have discarded toerails completely. But this practice may be quite dangerous. A compromise solution is to eliminate the toerail only where crewmen sit, that is along a short stretch at the widest part of the deck. Instead of a toerail here, a wire can be run about one or two inches above deck level. This arrangement will effectively stop a foot from slipping over the side, but the wire is still flexible enough to sit on.

## Boom Vang Tracks

Quite often a boom is fitted as low as possible to help gain some end-plate effect from the deck, but with a very low boom the leech of the mainsail becomes more difficult to control. If a hydraulic vang were used with such a low boom, it would probably compress the boom against the mast with such force that the gooseneck fitting would shear before the leech of the sail straightened! Nor is the mainsheet track a totally effective control, for it does not run far enough outboard to tension the leech when broad reaching or running. Consequently, some other solution is needed and this is often provided by a boom vang track.

Like a mainsheet track, a boom vang track is semi-circular, but it is far enough forward so that it can control the leech of the sail throughout the boom's 180 degree arc. For the vang track to be most effective, it must be absolutely horizontal. Any slope will change the shape of the sail as the mainsheet is eased out or tightened, thus requiring a corresponding change in vang tension.

To position the boom vang track, consider the gooseneck pivot point to be the centre of a circle and draw the largest semicircle possible, as shown in Figure 4-10. Locating the vang track may necessitate some modification to the position of the genoa sheet track, but layouts differ from boat to boat. Finalizing the placement of all tracks is best left to a good designer.

## Mainsheet Tracks

There was a time when people thought that the best

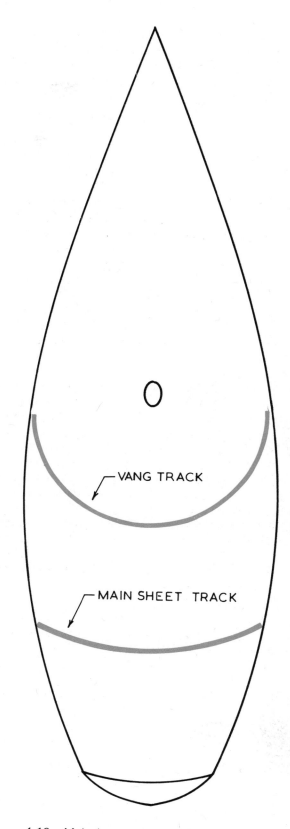

*Figure 4-10.* Mainsheet and vang track positions.

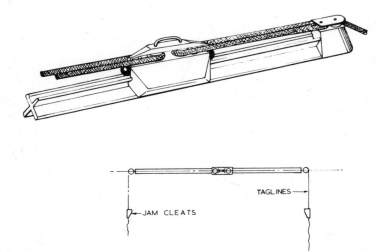

*Figure 4-11.* A typical mainsheet arrangement showing taglines.

mainsheet track was one that went from one side of the boat to the other. The reason for this old-fashioned long track was that at the time boom kickers or vangs were not very effective. With the advent of six-part tackles and efficient winches or hydraulics, however, the performance of the vang has increased tremendously. So nowadays you rarely see a mainsheet track extending very far outboard. Since it is the vang that controls leech shape on a modern racing boat, only short mainsheet tracks are required, and these are mostly for moving the traveller to windward in order to set the boom on the centreline in light air. Taglines, which are arranged as shown in Figure 4-11, are used to move the traveller.

### Mizzen Sheet Tracks

If a boat has a mizzen, a track similar to the mainsheet track is required. One of the primary differences between main and mizzen sheet tracks is that the mizzen boom often overhangs the transom, necessitating either some structure to hold the track or a midboom sheeting arrangement.

## Cleats

### Cleat Size and Positioning

One of the questions most commonly asked about cleats is what is their ideal size. There is no single answer, of course. The best size for a particular cleat

depends on the overall length and displacement of the boat, as well as the uses to which the cleat will be put. Figure 4-12 plots cleat sizes against waterline length for a medium displacement boat. Adjustments in size should be made for heavy or light displacements. As far as the relationship between the purpose of the cleat and its size is concerned, remember that bow cleats are usually a little on the large side to permit larger lines to be used for mooring, towing, or rafting alongside another boat. To size cleats for halyards and sheets, divide the diameter of the rope by $\frac{1}{16}$; the result equals the length of the cleat in inches. For example, a $\frac{1}{2}$ inch diameter rope divided by $\frac{1}{16}$ equals 8, so the cleat should be 8 inches long.

Other frequently asked questions about cleats are where should they be positioned and what is the proper method of fitting them. When a cleat is used with a winch, it should, if possible, be mounted about 12 to 18 inches away from the winch, and at an angle of 10 to 15 degrees to the winch centreline, as shown in Figure 4-13. Because cleats must often withstand loads far in excess of those intended at the design stage, they should be through-bolted, and some form of backing plate should be fitted under the deck. This is particularly important for bow cleats if the boat is to be left on a mooring for long periods of time. Also, because bow cleats are located in such a vulnerable position, they should also have some kind of guard, such as the simple one shown in Figure 4-14.

### Cam Cleats and Jam Cleats

To simplify handling on smaller boats, cam cleats or jam cleats can be used. These cleats come in many different variations; careful thought should be given to the cleat's purpose and the potential loading before making a final selection. Both cam and jam cleats have advantages and disadvantages. On the positive side, they enable lines to be cleated and uncleated in an instant. This is extremely useful in situations where quick or one-handed operations are required—on the mainsheet or spinnaker foreguy, for example. On the negative side, a kick or a knock can inadvertently release the rope. And the jam cleat has the additional drawback of eventually allowing the rope to slip when the load exerted on it increases to a certain point. After this happens, the cleat must usually be replaced, since the grips on the edge have probably been burned off by the friction of the rope against the plastic.

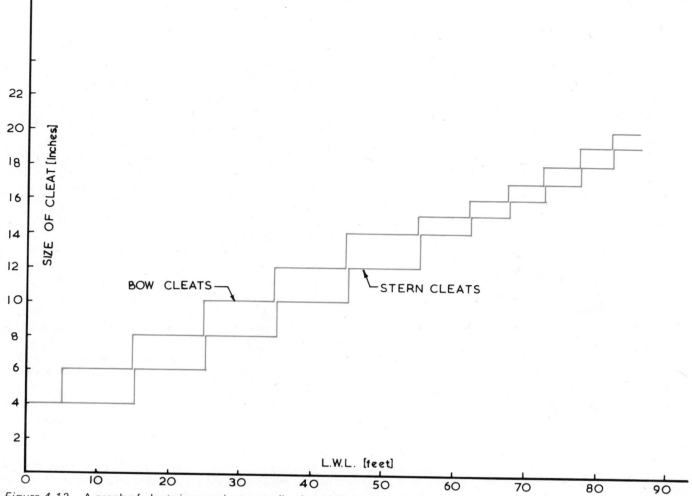

Figure 4-12.   A graph of cleat sizes against waterline length for a medium displacement boat.

## Fairleads, Padeyes, and Sheet Stoppers

### Mooring Fairleads

It is often impossible to lead a line directly to a cleat or winch without causing unnecessary chafing or friction. This is true of mooring lines. The problem is solved by the use of mooring fairleads, through which a mooring line can be passed before it is taken to a cleat.

Mooring fairleads, or chocks, come in several different styles. The best is probably the closed type, shown in Figure 4-15a, because it holds the rope completely captive. This device is often an integral part of the toerail. Of the open types, the style known as the Skene chock, shown in Figure 4-15b, is the most effective, but care must be taken to mount it in such a way that the rope cannot jump out. When straight chocks must be used, a simple latch can prevent the rope from jumping out.

As far as the number and placement of mooring fairleads are concerned, there should be two at the bow, two amidships for spring lines, and two aft for stern lines. As with cleats, mooring fairleads should be through-bolted.

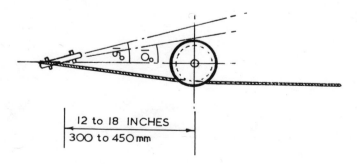

12 to 18 INCHES
300 to 450 mm

Figure 4-13.   The angle a cleat should make to the winch.

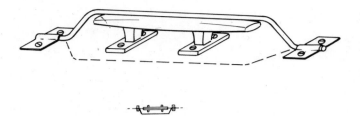

*Figure 4-14.* A typical cleat guard.

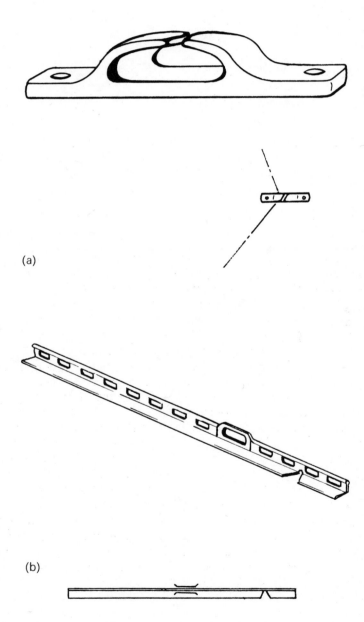

(a)

(b)

*Figure 4-15.* (a) A closed fairlead as part of a toerail. (b) A skene chock or bow fairlead.

## Anchor Roller Fairleads

Although not often seen on around-the-buoy racing boats, many offshore designs have a good set of roller fairleads over which the anchor chain or warp runs. On these boats the anchor size usually exceeds the rule requirements. The main consideration in fitting roller fairleads is the diameter of the roller. This is governed primarily by the thickness of the anchor chain.

## Genoa Fairleads and Turning Blocks

Genoa fairleads, also called cars or sliders, are sited on the genoa tracks and must be moved along the tracks to suit the sheet leads. These adjustments are made by pulling the pin on the car and sliding the car forward or aft. On larger boats, where it is impossible to move the car under load, the pin is sawn off and two stoppers, each with its own pin, are placed on the track fore and aft of the car. When an adjustment is needed, the load on the aft stopper is taken up by a line led forward, the aft stopper is moved to the desired position, and the car is carefully eased back against the stopper. The forward stopper is then slid aft to lock the car firmly in its new position.

There is a difference of opinion as to whether the genoa sheet should be taken directly from the fairlead to a winch or from the fairlead to a turning block and then to a winch. Some designers say that the turning block simply introduces more friction into the system and is unnecessary, but others argue that the turning block ensures a fair lead to the winch no matter what sail is up and is therefore worthwhile. If a turning block is used, it should not be placed too near the winch to which it will lead. Eighteen inches is the minimum distance. Any closer and the turns coming off the winch will not straighten before they foul in the block. Another detail to remember when fitting turning blocks is that the load on the block is almost twice that on the sheet, so both the turning block and the deck must be strong enough to take the force.

Some boats are fitted with double turning blocks, so that the genoa sheet passes through the bottom part and the spinnaker guy through the top. One way to get a fair lead on the spinnaker guy is to shackle a snatch block to the rail a few feet forward of the turning block, and lead the spinnaker guy through it to the turning block and then to the winch. Another method, seen on some custom designs, is to mount the spinnaker afterguy at the point of maximum beam and, using a snatch block as a fairlead, take it directly to the winch. Both arrangements are shown in Figure 4-16.

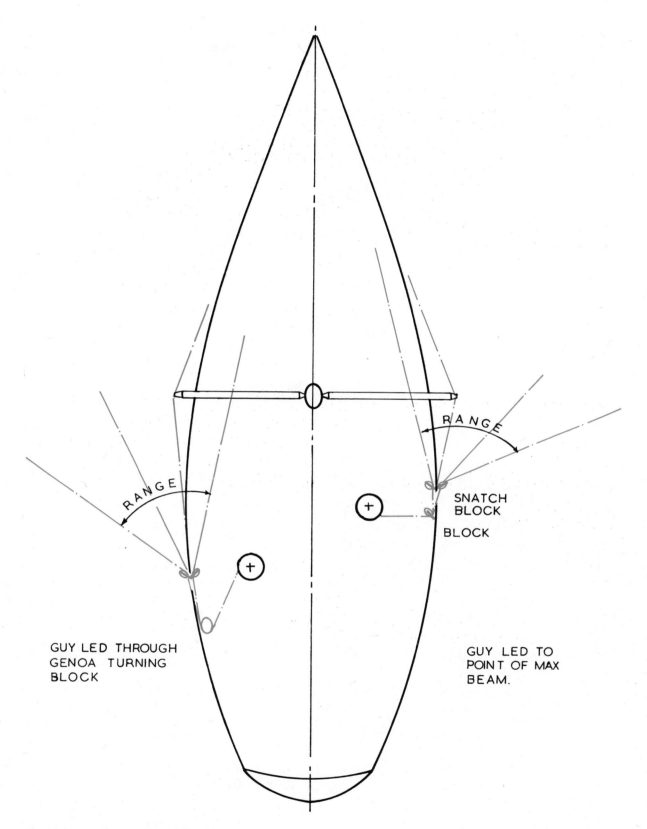

RANGE

RANGE

SNATCH
BLOCK

BLOCK

GUY LED THROUGH
GENOA  TURNING
BLOCK

GUY LED TO
POINT OF MAX
BEAM.

*Figure 4-16.*   Positioning the spinnaker guy for best results.

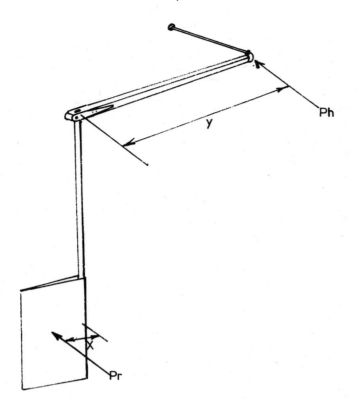

*Figure 4-17.* Diagram of the forces acting on the rudder and tiller.

*Figure 4-18.* Fore and aft bars for the helmsman's feet on a C & C Half Tonner. *(author)*

## Runner and Mast Padeyes

Because runners help steady the mast, much of their load is exerted in a vertical direction against the padeyes. This fact must be considered when choosing or designing runner padeyes and the deck reinforced accordingly. The same is true for padeyes at the base of the mast through which halyards are led. Here the deck must be tied to the keel with one or two tie rods or else the force exerted on padeyes may lift the deck off the hull.

## Storm Jib Padeyes

In order to eliminate the weight of extra genoa track and its reinforcement, padeyes, rather than tracks, are usually used to get a fair lead for the storm jib. To locate the storm jib padeye, bisect the jib angle and project the line until it hits the deck. Note that, once again, reinforcement is needed under the deck.

## Sheet Stoppers

Because it is often essential to move a sheet from one winch to another without releasing the sail, some form of sheet stopper or lock off is needed. One device is the portable sheet stopper which can be clamped onto the rope or wire next to the fairlead. It is most frequently used when the spinnaker sheet or guy is being transferred to another winch so that the genoa can be hoisted, or when the genoa is being transferred in preparation for a spinnaker hoist. Alternatively, a lock-off incorporated into the turning block serves the same purpose. But if the lock-off is closed on the sheave, its effectiveness may be limited because the sheet tends to ease out as the sheave revolves. Still another type of sheet stopper, often found on boats with a limited number of winches, is one that is fixed to the deck between the fairlead and the winch. A halyard can be tensioned on the winch, locked off, and the winch freed for another use. Yet no matter how effective a particular system may be, it should be noted that lock-offs and stoppers are intended only for temporary use. As soon as the sheet has been moved, the load should be taken up again on the new winch.

## Steering Gear

The earliest boats were steered with an oar held over the transom. This simple system was later modified to a rudder with a tiller. As boats increased in size, relieving tackles were used on the end of the tiller so that more manpower could be harnessed to operate the steering mechanism. Eventually, however, boats became so big that the tophamper completely blocked the helmsman's vision. To overcome this new difficulty, a whipstaff was first developed, and then wheel steering. On today's larger racing boats, those over about 30 feet LWL, wheel steering is the preferred system; tillers are better on smaller boats.

## Tiller Steering

The design requirements of tiller steering can be briefly outlined. First, the tiller should be long enough to give the helmsman plenty of leverage. But exactly how does one determine ideal tiller length? Figure 4-17 shows that the force on the rudder ($P_r$) multiplied by the distance from the rudder stock to the centre of pressure on the rudder ($x$) equals the tiller length ($y$) times the helmsman's hand pressure ($P_h$). In light airs, of course, $P_r$ will be small, but as wind strength increases, so does boat speed and the force on the rudder. Naturally, $P_h$ times $y$ must still equal $P_r$ times $x$ regardless of increased speed, and since $P_h$ is limited by the strength of the helmsman, the only way to balance the equation is to increase $y$, the tiller length. Thus if the tiller is too short, the boat may be uncontrollable at higher wind speeds.

In addition to considerations of length, the tiller should also be designed with the helmsman's visibility in mind. This usually means a tiller extension to enable the helmsman to sit as far outboard as possible in order to see the jib luff and wave patterns. The helmsman's balance is important too. If the cockpit is fairly wide, he will probably need fore and aft bars to brace his feet against, as illustrated in Figure 4-18.

## Wheel Steering

Because a tiller is usually directly connected to the top of the rudder stock, the helmsman on a tiller-steered boat must be positioned within a fairly restricted area. This is not the case on a wheel-steered boat where the helm can easily be moved forward, provided, of course, that the boat is sufficiently large. But boats become beamier as one moves forward from the stern, thus requiring either a larger diameter steering wheel or two smaller wheels to enable the helmsman to position himself far enough outboard to see the sails. Note, however, that very large diameter wheels require a trough in the bottom of the cockpit, and this may cause a drainage problem.

The mechanism that connects the wheel to the rudder stock can be simple or complex depending upon the sensitivity or 'feel' desired of the steering system, as well as the desired efficiency. One type of connecting mechanism is the linked rod. It has certain limitations in that the number of links governs the amount of slop in the system, and although there may be no give initially, slop increases with wear. This can be extremely annoying when the helmsman wants to turn the wheel only slightly. Other wheel steering mechanisms are the rack and pinion and the worm gear, to name just two. It is up to the individual designer to decide exactly what type of mechanism is best for a particular boat, and, of course, for the owner's wallet.

The most commonly chosen mechanism is also the simplest—chain and wire moving a quadrant, as shown in Figure 4-19a. When two wheels are fitted, the system becomes more complex, as illustrated in Figure 4-19b. And Figure 4-19c pictures the ultimate, a twin steering wheel system with a trim tab and brake on the wheels.

When designing a wire, chain, and quadrant steering system, there are several points to remember.

1. Use large diameter sheaves.

2. The wire should be strong enough to take the load without excessive stretch.

3. Do not rely on splines or friction to hold the quadrant on the shaft. The quadrant should be firmly keyed on, or the shaft should be squared to not less than 80 per cent of the diameter.

4. With careful design, the steering wires can be mounted around engines, spaces, or tanks, thus allowing the pedestal to be sited in the most efficient position possible.

Also note that a large diameter quadrant reduces the load on the wire, so the quadrant should be as large as space permits. But how does the size of the quadrant relate to the rest of the steering system? From Figure 4-17 we know that on a tiller-steered boat $P_h$ times $y$ must equal $P_r$ times $x$. This basic equation also applies to wheel steering, except that it is complicated somewhat by an indirect linkage (in this case a wire) between the tiller and the rudder.

On the wheel side of the equation, the factor $P_h$ times $y$ becomes hand pressure ($P_h$) times wheel radius ($R_w$) divided by the radius of the sprocket ($R_s$). This is the force acting on the wire which turns the rudder quadrant. On the rudder end of the system, the force exerted on the wire by the rudder is the pressure on the rudder ($P_r$) times the distance from the centreline of the rudder stock to the centre of pressure on the rudder ($x$) divided by the radius of the quadrant ($R_q$).

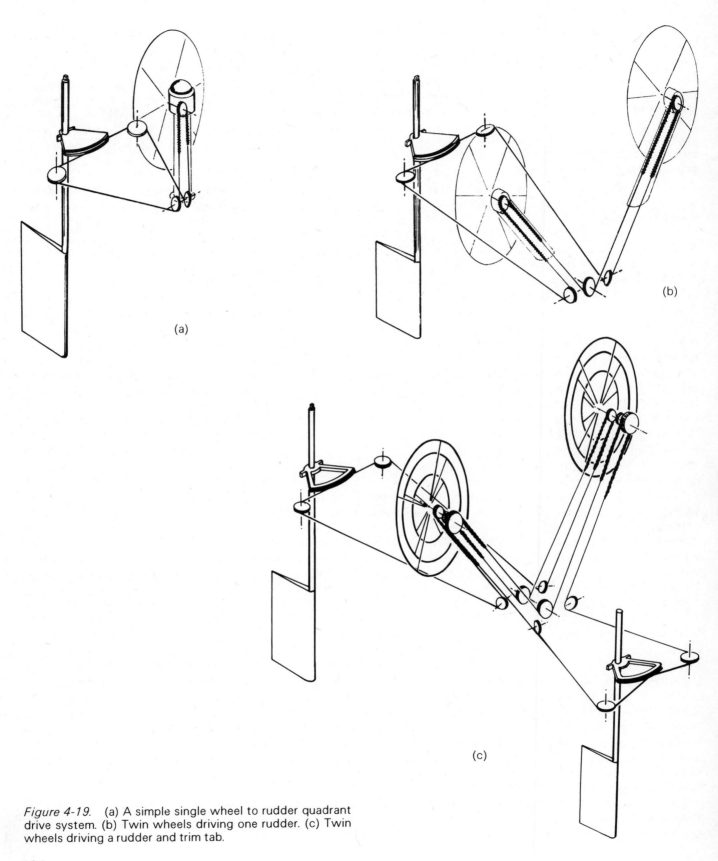

(a)

(b)

(c)

*Figure 4-19.* (a) A simple single wheel to rudder quadrant drive system. (b) Twin wheels driving one rudder. (c) Twin wheels driving a rudder and trim tab.

By putting the two sides of the equation together,

$$\frac{P_h \times R_w}{R_s} = \frac{P_r \times x}{R_q},$$

we can then determine both the size of the quadrant and the related size of the steering sprocket for any system.

Once the sizes of the quadrant and sprocket have been determined, the following measures will help improve the performance of the steering system.

1. Make sure that each sheave has a deep score or groove to help keep the wire from jumping off.

2. When the wire is under extreme load, it can slacken considerably even when properly adjusted, thus increasing the likelihood of jumping off the sheave. A guard should be fitted to prevent this from happening.

3. Make sure there are no sharp edges which may cut or chafe the wire or linkages.

4. Make sure that the quadrant or link arms have strong, well-secured stops, because at times (in a broach, for instance) the entire weight of the helmsman will be forcing down on the edge of the wheel and this amounts to quite a large moment.

5. The maximum rudder angle should not be more than 35 to 40 degrees, and ideally, the number of turns to the steering wheel from lock to lock should not be more than two and a half.

6. There should be easy access to all parts of the system to enable both routine adjustments and lubrications as well as emergency repairs.

7. When the wheel is installed and the boat is about to be launched, measure one foot out from the centre of the wheel and hang a one pound weight at that point. If the weight is sufficient to turn the wheel fairly easily, the helm will be easy to steer when sailing. If the wheel is stiff or does not turn at all, the whole system should be freed up.

## Emergency Steering

According to Murphy's Law, if there is any possibility of something going wrong, it undoubtedly will. Steering systems seem particularly prone to Murphy's Law. The most serious problem that can develop is when the rudder blade becomes separated from the stock. To get the boat home in such an emergency, there should always be a small hole in the top of the blade which, although normally filled, can be punched out and a line led through it and up to the deck.

Fortunately, rudder stocks rarely shear. The more frequent problems are a break in the linkage or a wire jumping a sheave. For cases such as these you should

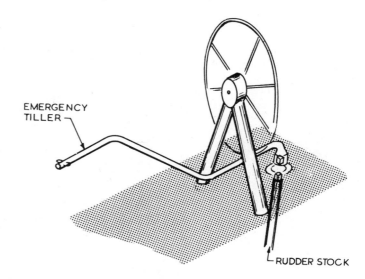

*Figure 4-20.* An emergency steering tiller that fits onto the head of the rudder stock.

have on hand an emergency tiller which can simply drop in place over the head of the rudder stock. Figure 4-20 shows a typical design. Note the welded rings on the end of the handle which can be used to rig relieving tackles if necessary. To gain access to the head of the rudder stock, the stock should be extended to deck level and a deck plate fitted. If this is not possible, the cockpit could be designed so that the head of the stock is accessible by opening a locker.

## Lifelines, Stanchions, and Pulpits

### Lifelines

The offshore regulations require that all boats racing under the IOR have a lifeline around the hull. On larger boats, the top lifeline must be 24 inches high, and the lower line 12 inches. On smaller boats, the single lifeline required must be a minimum of 18 inches off the deck.

The best material for these lifelines is flexible 1 x 19 wire. It should be $\frac{3}{16}$ or $\frac{1}{4}$ inches in diameter for top and single lifelines, and $\frac{1}{8}$ or $\frac{3}{16}$ inches for the lower lines. Although plastic-coated wire looks good and is nice to the touch, it can corrode when the coating gets damaged. Wire with clear plastic tube over it is far safer.

An effective way of fastening lifelines to the pulpit is to use several turns of strong twine. This method gives some measure of shock loading to the system and is easily adjusted. More often, however, bottlescrews or turnbuckles are used. In this case, the turnbuckle should be of the open type, with split pins inserted in

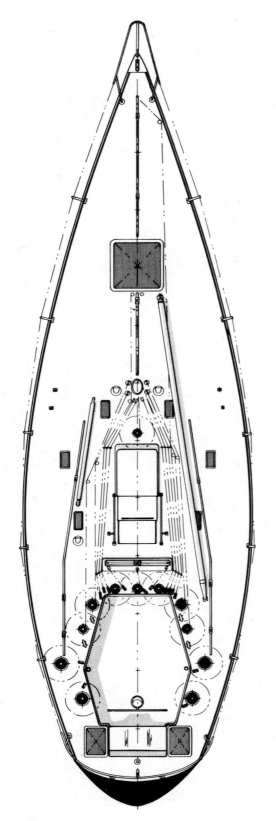

A stock Cuthbertson & Cassian 42.

the screw to prevent the turnbuckle from unwinding.

In addition to the mandatory lifelines around the edge of the hull, deck lifelines for harnesses are also a feature on many racing boats. If such lifelines are positioned carefully, a crewman can move from the cockpit to the bow without unhooking.

## Stanchions

Stanchions must be high enough to hold the lifelines at regulation height and strong enough to support the weight of a man falling against them. Stanchions that obstruct the spinnaker guy may be designed to swing inboard 10 degrees, the maximum amount permitted under the IOR. On some boats, however, it may be more effective to place these particular stanchions as far inboard as the rule allows and then hinge them so they can swing 10 degrees outboard.

## Bow Pulpits

The bow pulpit of a boat is an essential part of the lifeline arrangement, but the pulpit should not be designed simply to tension the lifelines, nor as a mere extension of the bow rake. Pulpits can be planned to serve a number of very useful purposes, thus offsetting their big disadvantage of creating extra windage. Here we will discuss some of the features that can be incorporated into bow pulpits, focusing primarily on those most appropriate for racing boats. There are, of course, many other possibilities in addition to the ones listed here.

### Spinnaker Chute

A recent development on quarter tonners and other small offshore classes is the bow spinnaker chute, an underdeck tube which emerges at the bow. Some form of watertight bow door can be incorporated into the arrangement. If the pulpit is designed as in Figure 1-11 in Chapter 1, it will serve as an extension of this underdeck tube, ensuring that the spinnaker will be carried clear of the headstay on the hoist. Alternatively, if a boat does not have a spinnaker chute, the pulpit can be designed to suit the spinnaker turtle.

### Bow Light Support

In the interest of reducing windage, bow lights are often bolted to the deck. One manufacturer in the United States has gone so far as to make the bow light part of the cove stripe! Unfortunately, when the boat is heeled 25 to 30 degrees, the leeward bow light is almost invisible. Clearly the most effective position for the bow light is 2 feet off the deck, directly under the top of the pulpit rail. This is also true of the stern light. With a little thought, a low-windage light fixture can easily be designed, thus offering much greater safety at night without a significant reduction in boat speed.

*Seat for the Bowman*
For changing sails or gybing, the bowman must often position himself ahead of the forestay. If the pulpit is made shorter than it would ordinarily be if it were an extension of the bow rake, it can provide a handy seat and make the bowman's job just that much easier and quicker.

*Sheet and Halyard Attachment Points*
Halyards cannot be clipped onto the pulpits of most racing boats because the pulpit rail is too thick—usually an inch in diameter. It is an easy job, however, to weld several eyes or rings onto the pulpit, which can serve as sheet or halyard attachment points. An owner who is conscious of windage may argue that he would never carry halyards clipped to the pulpit. But there are times when gybing or changing headsails that such attachment points can prove useful. And they are certainly useful in a marina when you are trying to sleep before a race and the breeze is slapping the halyards against the mast.

*Spinnaker Pole Attachment Point*
The base of the pulpit can be designed to incorporate a ring or cone which can hold the outboard end of the spinnaker pole captive.

## Stern Pulpits

The stern pulpit, too, can have various features incorporated into it: a stern light mounting near the top of the rail, a flag pole socket, an insulated holder for the VHF aerial, and a catch for the lazarette hatch if it rests against the pulpit when opened. Some items, however, should not be attached to the stern pulpit, particularly man-overboard poles and horseshoes, both of which would only create extra windage.

## Lighting, Hatches, and Ventilation

### Deck Lights

To some people, worrying about lighting on the deck of an offshore racing boat is the ultimate in needless concerns. But the matter seems far less trivial when you are out on the race course in the middle of the night and suddenly discover that some inexperienced designer has completely overlooked even the most minimal lighting requirements on your new boat. Obviously, if you are intending to sail offshore, lighting is important, both navigational and deck lights. We have already mentioned bow and stern lights when discussing pulpits, and other mandatory navigational lights will be treated in Chapter 5. Here we will concentrate primarily on lighting the sails.

Elaborate deck lights are hardly ever found on top-class racing boats. Sail changes are typically made in the dark, with crewmen using only torches or flashlights to aid the operation. What is required, though, is a good, steady light on the telltales. In my opinion, this light should be located in a locker below deck just forward of the weather shrouds, and should shine through a clear acrylic panel. So that the light will always illuminate the window in the sail, all sail windows should be located at the same height. A simple remote mercury switch can be used to turn the leeward unit off as the boat tacks. Alternative sail lighting systems have also been tried. A 'black' (ultra violet) light with specially treated telltales is one of the more exotic ideas. Yet another is an arrangement whereby the underdeck lights shine up the luff of the headsail.

A second deck area of a racing boat that requires lighting is the masthead. Here there should be a small light to illuminate the windex. Instruments and compasses, of course, have their own lights and need no further comment, except to say that when selecting them, make sure these lights can all be dimmed.

### Hatches

Hatches and companionways are the traffic centres of the boat, and as such they must be easily accessible and free of any projections that may snag sailbags or crewmen. There are two basic types of hatches, sliding and lifting, and each has its own value and place on the boat. Thought should always be given to the kind of hatch that will work best in a particular area. It would be useless, for instance, to put a lifting hatch under a low boom, just as it would make no sense to try to design a sliding lazarette hatch.

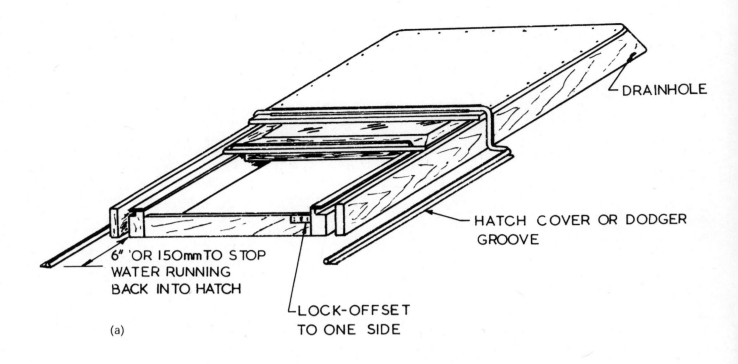

DRAINHOLE

HATCH COVER OR DODGER GROOVE

6" 'OR 150mm TO STOP WATER RUNNING BACK INTO HATCH

LOCK-OFFSET TO ONE SIDE

(a)

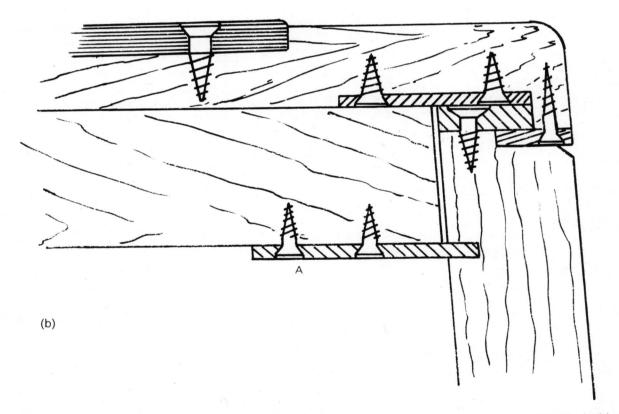

A

(b)

*Figure 4-21.* (a) A wooden sliding hatch. Note clear or smoked plastic top, the drain hole and the fact that the inside flange of the dodger groove is continuous at the corners. The lock and its hasp are to one side of the hatch where they cannot hit a person using the hatch. (b) A section through a wooden sliding hatch. The brass strip labelled A is only on the front of the hatch to serve as a guide.

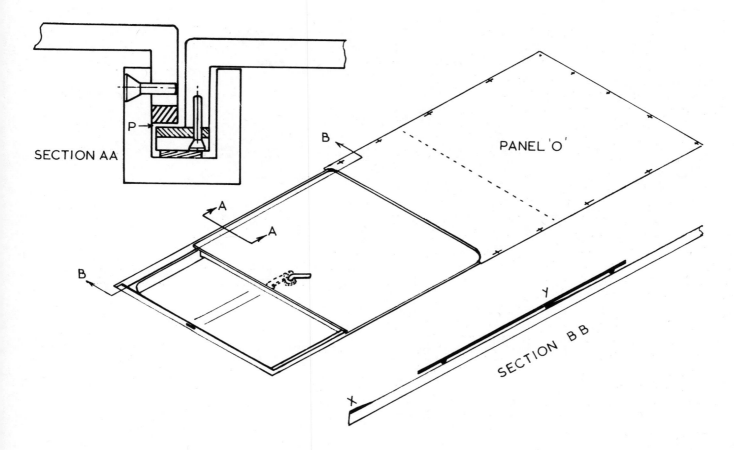

SECTION AA

P

B

A

A

B

PANEL 'O'

Y

X

SECTION BB

*Figure 4-22.* A flush alloy hatch. When the hatch is pulled closed, wedges at X and Y force it up against point P in the sectional view. The handle hooks into the end plate and pulls the hatch up tight against the hard rubber on the end plate. Note also that panel O can be removed to remove the hatch.

The most critical part of a sliding hatch is the slide mechanism itself, which is usually made of brass or some form of phenolic plastic and must work efficiently without binding or leaking. Sliding hatches differ in construction depending upon the material the boat is made of. Figure 4-21 shows a wooden hatch and section. Note how athwartship play is minimized, as are the number of edges that may be broken or damaged. Most sliding hatches, like this one, are built so that the sliding part is above deck. It is possible, of course, to design a flush-mounted hatch, such as the alloy one shown in Figure 4-22, but because of the additional construction expense, these are most frequently seen on custom boats. In all cases, whether the hatch is flush or above deck, the arrangement must allow for some form of access plate; and if winches are intended to be mounted on the hatch, it must be reinforced.

The development of alloy framed hatches, like the one in Figure 4-23, has made lifting hatches much more common than sliding ones. If you use an alloy lifting hatch as a sail or crew hatch, however, be sure to cut off or put a guard over the projections that are cast into the frame. Otherwise they tend to catch sail bags and can be painful to fall against. Lifting hatches can also be constructed of wood; a good design is shown in Figure 4-24. When positioning lifting hatches, remember that the hinged side should be forward so that sea water washing over the foredeck will slam the hatch shut rather than open it.

The sizes of sail hatches, whether of the lifting or sliding type, vary with the size of the boat, although they must always be large enough for the sails and crew to pass through easily. The absolute minimum dimensions are 18 inches × 14 inches. Figure 4-25 is a graph that plots sail area against hatch size. Hatch size can also be plotted against LWL, but the I dimension is better because the sizes of a boat's sail bags are directly related to the height of its sails.

Several safety features should also be kept in mind when designing deck hatches. Properly constructed dodgers can prevent a great deal of water from finding

109

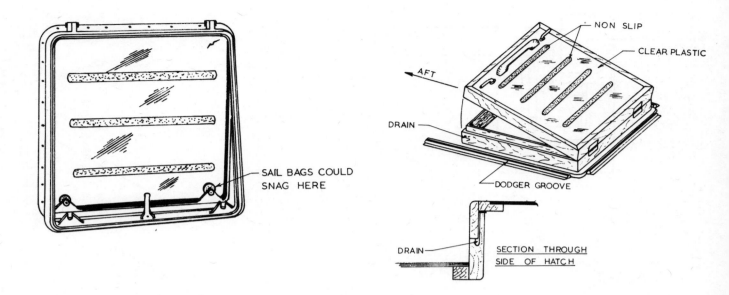

*Figure 4-23.* An alloy framed hatch with the bars that lock it open sawn off to reduce snags. A wedge under the tightening screws can also reduce snagging.

*Figure 4-24.* A wooden lifting hatch and section. The high coaming allows water to wash over the deck without going below. When fully open the hatch top lies flat on the deck, with the locking handles operable from either side.

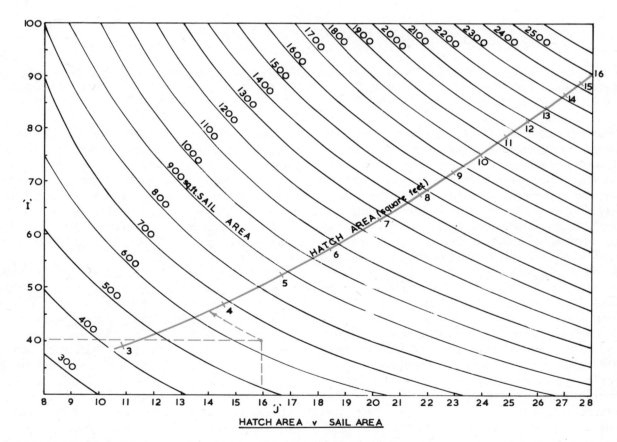

*Figure 4-25.* A graph of hatch area against headsail areas, headsails usually being the largest sails on the boat.

its way below deck when a hatch is left open for ventilation. The dodger grooves should extend at least 6 inches beyond the aft side of the hatch, and the inner face of the grooves should be continuous around three sides of the hatch. Another reminder is that some form of nonslip is needed on hatches with acrylic or smoked glass panels. The best are the 1 inch wide strips, which should be spaced 6 inches apart and run all the way across the hatch.

Finally, we come to the topic of special hatches, primarily those that lead to stowage compartments rather than below deck. On most boats, for example, there is a hatch to the lazarette, the space between the stern and the beginning of the accommodation which is used for stowing fenders and warps. This hatch is usually set flush into the deck, or, alternatively, it is designed as an integral part of the helmsman's seat. The design of other stowage hatches would probably vary depending upon their purpose and location on the boat.

## Ports and Deck Prisms

Boats have always been dark down below, but a judiciously placed prism or small opening port can do much to alleviate the feeling of confinement that ill-lighted interiors create. When siting prisms avoid locating them in such a way that people will routinely hit their heads on one of the sharp glass corners. Over tables and counters where there is plenty of headroom makes the most sense—definitely not over the front end of a berth! Small ports, in contrast, are most useful over the galley or head, where they can be opened to let out heat and odours. But again, careful thought should be given to their exact placement. One boat I sailed on had the main halyard running directly over the top of one of the opening deck ports, thus making it useless except when the boat was in dock.

## Ventilation

Ventilation is important on offshore racing boats. Without good air circulation below decks, crewmen will not get the kind of sleep they need and will be unable to work at peak performance. How much ventilation is enough? More than you might expect. A sleeping man requires approximately 140 cubic feet of fresh air per hour, which means almost 2½ cubic feet per minute!

Natural air flow through a boat varies with wind strength and the angle of the wind to the air ducts. For instance, suppose an air duct six inches in diameter is facing directly into the wind. The area of the duct is 0.2 square feet ($\pi \times 0.25^2$) and the wind speed is 5 mph. 5 mph. = 440ft/min. Thus the amount of air that will enter the duct per minute is 88 cubic feet (440 ft/min × 0.2 sq ft).

This figure, of course, is a maximum, which will seldom be realized in practice. For one thing, it assumes a system with no losses and, unfortunately, the losses through a dorade vent can be as high as 50 per cent. This factor alone could therefore cut the total amount of incoming air to 44 cubic feet per minute. Then there is the angle of the wind to consider. If the wind is hitting the air duct at a 45 degree angle rather than head on, the flow-through of air will again be cut in half—from 44 to 22 cubic feet per minute. And finally, back pressure from various sources can also affect the efficiency of ventilation. Obviously, then, calculating the amount of air that will circulate through a boat is a very tricky business. A rough rule of thumb is to allow one 6 inch dorade type vent for every off-watch crewman.

Where should dorades be sited? If the boat is large enough, avoid placing them directly over the berths, since there is always a possibility that water will come

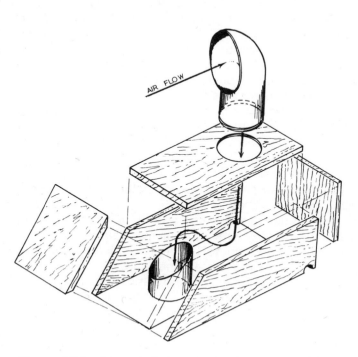

*Figure 4-26.* An exploded view of a dorade vent box: if desired the top is sometimes made of clear plastic for extra light inside the boat.

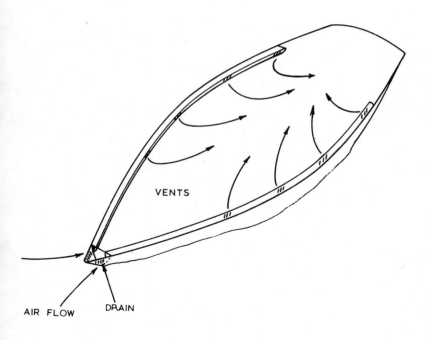

VENTS

AIR FLOW    DRAIN

*Figure 4-27.* A bow ventilation system, which could also be mechanically powered.

through the vent. On fibreglass boats, the dorades can be part of the coaming or coachroof, while on wooden boats they can be designed as shown in Figure 4-26. In either case, to avoid extra windage on day races when no one is sleeping below deck, the dorade vent cowls can be removed and replaced with flat caps.

There are other popular and efficient types of vents in addition to dorades. One is the tannoy or mushroom vent. Because these are made of clear plastic which can easily be broken, be sure to use the chrome or steel covers that come with them. Another, entirely different kind of natural ventilation system is shown in Figure 4-27. The air flows in at the bow and out again through vents located over each berth; water is channelled off by means of a drain at the bow.

Ventilation systems can also be mechanized, using waterproof fans with a minimum output of 150 cubic feet of air per minute to force circulation. Fans are often located in the head and the galley. In addition, they are needed in the battery compartment to remove the explosive hydrogen which accumulates when the battery is being charged, and in the engine compartment since combustion uses air and even the best engines give off fumes. All these areas are best vented to the deck or the transom. For battery and engine compartments, clamshells are the usual method of venting the trunking to the after deck.

112

Yet another vent is required to allow air to escape from the fuel tank. It should lead from the tank to the deck, as near as possible to the centreline. The opening on deck is usually positioned under a winch base where it is protected from any stray water. Quite often, the pipe can be led up inside a stanchion so that it does not have to bend around the interior layout.

## Instruments

Few boats, if any, ever go to sea without instruments of some kind. Even the skipper who sails 'by the seat of his pants' uses crude instruments such as the telltales attached to the shrouds, the luff of the headsail, and the leech of the main, or the wind indicator fitted to the top of the masthead. On racing boats, of course, more sophisticated instruments are used because not every helmsman is an expert 'seat-of-the-pants' sailor. Consequently, the accuracy of instruments can often make the difference between winning and losing.

### Compasses

Of all the instruments on the deck of an offshore racing boat, the compass is the only major one that is not electronic. On a wheel-steered boat, the compass has traditionally been mounted on top of the binnacle, but this position requires that the helmsman move his head in order to take bearings. A better place to site the compass is on the centreline about 6 feet in front of the helmsman either on top of the coachroof or slightly raised off the deck to improve visibility. On a boat with tiller steering, the main navigational compass is also best positioned on the centreline. In addition, however, it is often helpful to have two smaller compasses on either side of the deck. These are not intended to be used as steering compasses, but rather to enable the helmsman to detect wind shifts. Another important factor to consider when positioning the compass on any boat is where the crew will be located. Care should always be taken to ensure that crewmen do not obstruct the helmsman's view of the instrument.

As far as what features to look for when selecting a compass, the best ones have an easily readable card and a bent-over lubber line which enables easy reading from above. A compass light that can be dimmed is also desirable. One of the best compasses on the market, which incorporates all these features, is the Danforth Constellation.

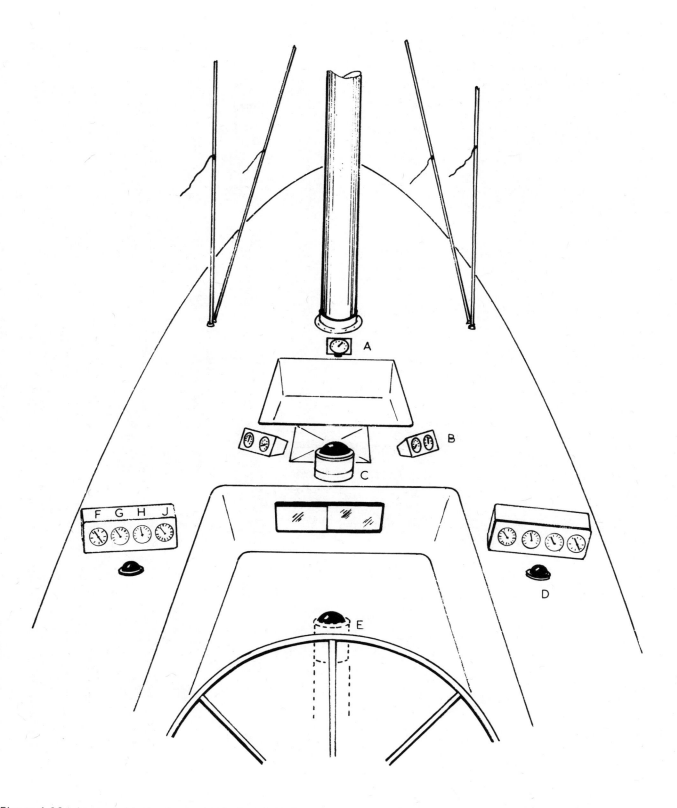

*Figure 4-28.* Layout of instruments. A Wind angle indicator for crew. B Wind direction and amplified speed for sheet trimmer, there could also be a wind speed indicator here. C Compass—best visibility is obtained here, providing crew do not stand in the way. D Wing compass, port and starboard: for checking windshifts. Beware of siting too close to the instruments. E Compass could be here. F Close-hauled indicator. G Wind speed indicator. H Wind direction indicator. J Hull speed indicator.

## Depth Sounder

Like all electronic instruments on a boat, the main component of the depth sounder can be located in the navigator's area, with a repeater sited at the helm. The more sophisticated systems use a pen recorder to give the navigator a continual picture of the bottom of the sea, but on most boats the navigator, like the helmsman above deck, takes readings off a simple dial.

Although not part of the deck layout, the transducers of a depth sounding system are critical elements. On a sailing boat the best location for the transducers is approximately level with the top of the leading edge of the keel, each one positioned a little out from either side of the centreline. Both transducers can be remotely operated by a mercury switch which automatically selects the leeward unit.

Different depth sounders are capable of reading different ranges of depth, so a boat owner should consider the area in which he will be sailing before making a final purchase. After all, it is hardly worth spending a large sum of money for equipment that can read depths over 500 metres if the boat will be sailing only in waters not more than 50 metres deep.

Regardless of range, however, depth sounding equipment should always be highly accurate, or else the boat runs the risk of going aground. It is also useful for an owner to know exactly how much his boat draws fully loaded. To do this, measure the freeboards at the bow and stern with all the crew and stores aboard, and scale them off on the lines plan of the boat. The alarm on the echo sounder can then be set for, say, one foot more than the fully loaded draft. This precaution will help ensure the safety of the boat for close inshore sailing.

## Speedometer/Log

A speedometer is essential for all offshore sailing. Because it consumes less power, the dial type, with a needle pointing to the hull speed, may be preferable over the digital readout type. Again, the major part of the unit can be located in the navigator's area, with a repeater on deck. The Brookes and Gatehouse system has a unit known as the Hound amplifier which shows speed changes of as little as 0.01 knots. It is excellent for fine tuning the sail trim. But when referring to this or any other speedometer for sail trimming, one must also watch the wind speed fluctuations to make sure that a change in hull speed is not due simply to a change in wind velocity. Consequently, on the helmsman's console, these two instruments should be

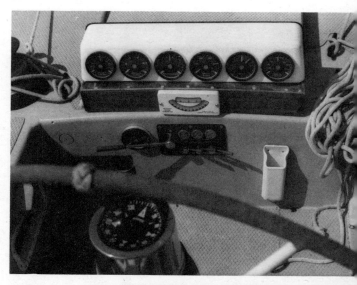

Figure 4-29. *Left* Two different instrument positions. *(author)* *Above* A wind-direction indicator on the foredeck of Mr Syd Fischer's *Ragamuffin. (author)*

mounted adjacent to one another.

A log is usually incorporated into the speedometer. It should have an easily adjusted reset button to enable the navigator to record accurately the distance travelled during each race.

### Wind-speed and Wind-direction Indicators

The wind-speed indicator is usually included as part of the masthead unit. The dial on deck gives the helmsman an immediate reading of any temporary or permanent changes in wind strength, and this helps him to determine whether a trim or sail change is required.

The wind-direction indicator is also located at the top of the mast. It is most useful at night or other times when the windex is not easily visible, or in very heavy winds when it can be damped down to get a fairly constant reading, whereas the windex may be fluctuating wildly due to the movement of the boat. Because the heel angle of the boat and the upwash from the sails can influence the accuracy of the wind-direction indicator, it should be mounted on a long arm well out in front of the masthead.

The close-hauled indicator is simply an amplification of the first 50 degrees of the wind-direction scale. It helps the helmsman locate the precise groove the boat should be in when sailing close hauled. By constant reference to the sails, wind, and instrument, he can hopefully stay in that groove.

All the important instruments on the deck should be positioned so that they can be easily read at a glance, and they should be grouped in a way that makes practical sense from the crew's point of view. Figure 4-28 shows how a set of instruments might be laid out to provide good visibility for the crewmen who must refer to them. The helmsman's console, working from the outside toward the centreline, includes the close-hauled, hull-speed, wind-speed, and wind-direction indicators. The amplified speed is sited further forward where it is visible to the genoa trimmer. The depth sounder is also incorporated into this same unit so that it can be read by a crewman other than the helmsman, who should be concentrating instead on his own job. On larger boats, it is often extremely useful to have a wind-direction indicator positioned on the deck where the spinnaker trimmer can see it; this avoids his constantly having to ask the helmsman where the wind is coming from. Figure 4-29 shows some other possible instrument layouts.

## Deck Covering and Deck Reinforcement

### Deck Covering

Although not really gear or equipment, deck covering is still an important part of any deck. There are three basic types of deck covering: laid wood planking (primarily teak), paint-applied coverings, and coverings that are glued on. Each has its advantages and disadvantages.

Teak is the traditional deck material. Nothing feels or looks better than a beautifully laid teak deck. It is often applied in thin, $\frac{3}{8}$ inch veneers over a fibreglass, plywood, or alloy base. One of the biggest disadvantages of a teak deck is weight. Teak is heavy, weighing about 48 pounds per cubic foot, which means the entire deck will add several hundred pounds to the boat. Teak decks are also relatively high in initial cost and they require regular maintenance.

Compared with teak planking, paint-type coverings are easy to apply. Non-slip deck paint is simply brushed onto the deck; and similar kinds of coverings, such as alloy shavings, ground walnut shells, or sand, are sprinkled onto the freshly painted deck and then painted over. These materials are also very light. On the negative side, however, they virtually make the deck into a sheet of sandpaper, which quickly wears away anything that comes in contact with it, especially oilskins and hands!

Weightwise, glued-on coverings are not as heavy as teak but not as light as deck paint. There are several popular makes on the market. Treadmaster M by James

115

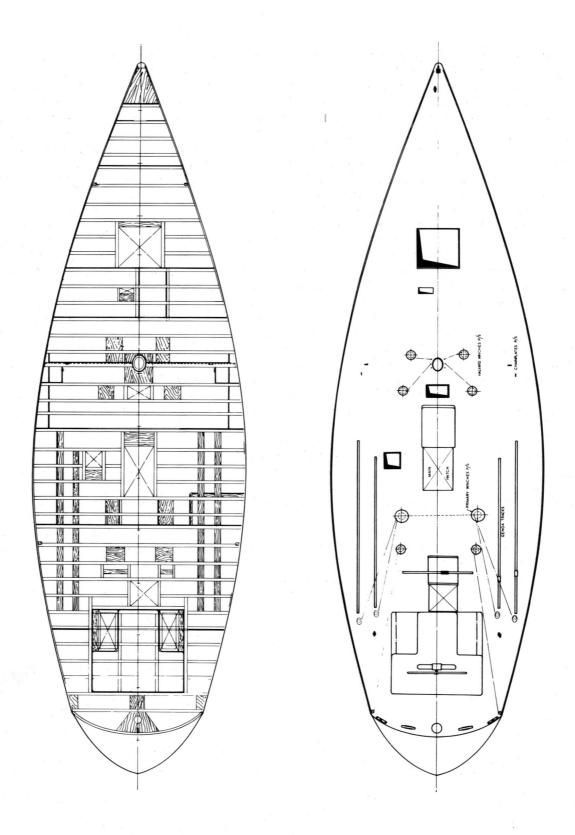

*Figure 4-30.* A Sparkman & Stephens design by the author showing the deck layout and deck beam plan with reinforcement. (Other details have been omitted for simplification.)

Walker Group is a diamond pattern, compressed cork material available in six colours. It weighs about 8½ ounces per square foot (2.5 kg/m²) and is resilient and comfortable. Trakmark by Dunlop is another well-known brand. It is lighter than Treadmaster but seems to lose its non-slip quality sooner. Its other possible disadvantages are that it can be peeled off and tends to collect dirt around the edges. A third material is Safety Walk by 3M. Because it is available only in 1, 2, or 4 inch widths, it is most often seen on hatch coverings or companionway steps. An important advantage shared by all glued-on deck coverings is that they need be applied only to heavily used areas. This means that no more than about 75 per cent of the deck is covered, with consequent reductions in cost and weight.

## Deck Reinforcement

Deck reinforcement is not deck gear either, but it is closely related to it. Much of the deck gear discussed in this and the preceding two chapters is placed under tremendous load, and the thin deck surface fitted on most boats is not intended to withstand this kind of force. Consequently, decks are locally reinforced, the amount of reinforcement in a particular area depending upon the equipment located there and the estimated force that equipment exerts on the deck.

Figure 4-30 is the deck beam plan for a wooden boat. (The beam sizes and the thickness of the deck, which are not indicated here, would be specified in the construction plan.) To provide structurally strong bases for the various pieces of deck gear, wooden blocks are added between the beams. Note that the blocks are large enough to allow equipment to be moved a few inches if necessary. The blocks at the mast are connected to the keel with tie rods, which prevent the deck from lifting up.

Deck reinforcement on an alloy boat is also positioned according to where various gear is located, but the materials used and the method of construction differ from those on a wooden boat. On an alloy boat, reinforcement is provided by flat alloy plates of extra thickness fitted between the deck beams. These plates, which become an integral part of the final deck skin, are recessed into the beams to give a flat deck.

The deck of a fibreglass boat is constructed of a foam or balsa core, sandwiched between two layers of glass laminate. Before laying up the balsa core, the builder must have a deck plan showing where gear will be positioned. He can then either use hardwood core material to reinforce those areas, or connect the two

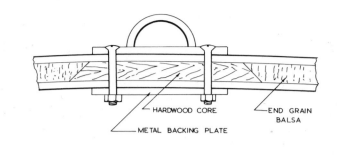

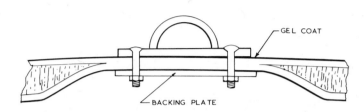

*Figure 4-31.* Two methods of reinforcing a fibreglass deck.

layers of laminate to form a more structurally sound base. As illustrated in Figure 4-31, fittings on a fibreglass boat are bolted to metal plates fitted beneath the deck.

\* \* \* \* \* \*

The items discussed in this chapter are not the only pieces of deck gear that might be found on a modern offshore racing boat. There are other kinds of equipment we have not mentioned, and some of the gear we have talked about is available in other variations. This lack of complete comprehensiveness, however, is intentional. The purpose of this and the preceding two chapters has simply been to outline the basics of deck gear, with a critical eye to efficiency and safety. Similarly, in the following chapter, we turn to another basic topic that must be reviewed before beginning the actual work of laying out a deck–the topic of racing rules and regulations.

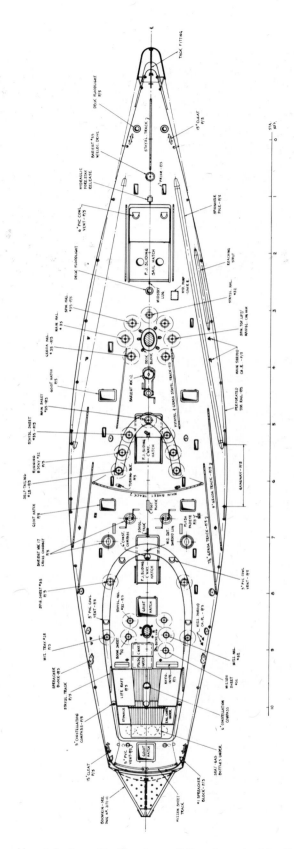

*Kialoa*, a maxi boat designed by Sparkman & Stephens for Mr Jim Kilroy.

# Rules and Regulations

Sailing is replete with rules and regulations. We have safety rules to protect boats and crews from numerous hazards–sometimes even themselves. We have rules to handicap boats, and rules to regulate the gear that racing boats can carry aboard. Yachtsmen often grumble that these regulations take some of the fun out of sailing. Yet, however much we complain about them, rules are as essential to our sport as they are to any other.

But what do all these complex restrictions have to do with deck layout? A great deal. The IOR, for example, imposes direct limitations on several features of the deck, and it indirectly encourages other deck arrangements. Similarly, the ORC Special Regulations specify minimum standards for racing boats, including structural features, equipment carried, and interior accommodations. These, too, have a significant impact on deck layout. In this chapter we will review both these important sets of racing rules and also take a brief look at the Rules for World Championships of Level Rating Classes, as well as the Twelve Metre Rule. Throughout, we will focus on those aspects of the rules that have the greatest impact on deck design.

## International Offshore Rule

The IOR is the international handicapping rule of offshore racing. Fortunately for most readers of this book, relatively few of the IOR's many regulations and measurement procedures affect deck layout. Still, deck design is not immune to their influence.

One aspect of the IOR that clearly affects deck arrangements is the way in which the edge of the working deck is defined. The rule states that at any measurement station, the edge of the working deck, or sheer point, is the lowest point on the topsides of the hull where a line drawn at an angle of 45 degrees to horizontal will be tangent to the hull. (Bulwarks, toerails, or rubbing strakes are ignored when determining the sheer point.) There is, however, one exception to this general rule, which applies when the sheer point determined by the 45 degree line ends up being more than 5 per cent of B max inboard from a vertical line tangent to the hull. In this case, the sheer point is a point on the hull 5 per cent of B max inboard from the vertical line tangent to the hull at that station. The drawings in Figure 5-1 show how a sheer point is located for boats with different deck and hull shapes. By defining sheer points at various stations around the hull, one establishes the height of the sheer line, which in turn gives the edge of the working deck around the entire perimeter of the hull.

How does the sheer line defined by the IOR affect deck layout? The primary way is in the limitation it imposes on the placement of stanchions. The Offshore Racing Council Special Regulations require that stanchions cannot be any further inboard from the edge of the working deck than 5 per cent of B max or 6 inches, whichever is greater. This means that on boats with decks and hulls of certain shapes, the measured sheer line would make safe positioning of stanchions virtually impossible. Consider, for example, the section in Figure 5-2a. If a stanchion was placed 5 per cent of B max inboard, the deck near the stanchion would be extremely dangerous to walk on, particularly when the boat was heeled. The same kind of hazardous positioning of stanchions would be unavoidable on a boat with the section shown in Figure 5-2b. The only solution in either case is to redesign the shape of the deck.

Another aspect of the IOR that affects deck layout is the maximum height of the boom above the deck, which cannot exceed 0.05 P + 4.0 feet without incurring a penalty. But on a boat with a high coachroof, this requirement may leave very little space between the top of the coachroof and the bottom of the boom. If so, severe limitations are imposed on the placement of gear on the cabin top. And there may even be problems

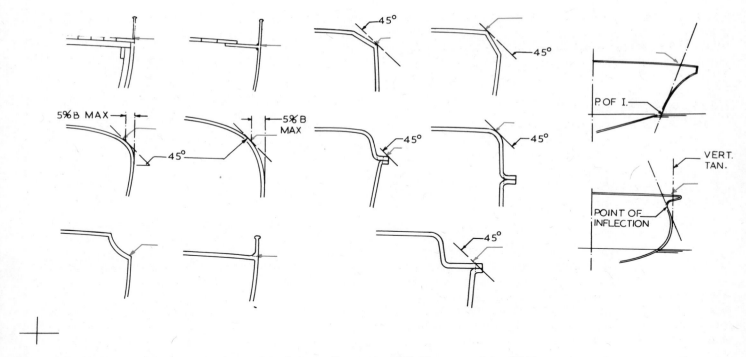

*Figure 5-1.* Locations of the edge of deck according to the IOR. *(Courtesy of the ORC)*

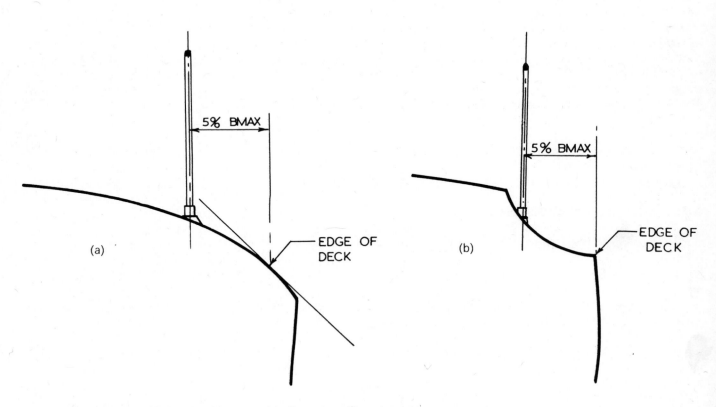

*Figure 5-2.* How the IOR edge of deck could affect stanchion placement.

120

of clearance over grinders mounted on deck. One boat I sailed on had a boom that actually bounced on the top of the pedestals when the boat tacked. Add to this the fact that many booms today are allowed to 'droop' in order to gain extra unmeasured sail area, and what was originally a very narrow margin of space beneath the boom may disappear completely.

The IOR regulations concerning sheeting positions for headsails can also affect deck layout. Genoas, jibs, and staysails can be sheeted anywhere on the foredeck, provided that when they are pulled tightly aft on a line parallel to the centreline not more than 50 per cent of the sail is allowed to come aft of the forward side of the mast. This limitation must be remembered when siting staysail tack points.

So far we have reviewed several of the ways in which IOR requirements can directly influence deck design. But the IOR also influences deck arrangement in more indirect manners. For one thing, it encourages designers and owners to stow equipment in areas that will give the boat a performance advantage over its potential in measurement condition. This means that several items not aboard when the boat is measured are often stowed aft on the race course in order to reduce bow down trim. A major item in this category is the liferaft, which weighs up to 100 pounds or even more and therefore can help considerably to offset bow down trim. But because the liferaft must also be stowed on deck, finding a place for it aft in the crowded main cockpit area is sometimes difficult. Other things that can be stowed aft to help reduce bow down trim are the sails not required aboard when the boat is measured. As will be discussed in Chapter 7, this means

aft sail lockers and sometimes aft sail handling hatches as well. When placing all this gear aft, however, one must be careful not to put it so far back from the centre of the boat that the tendency to pitch increases.

A second way in which the IOR indirectly influences deck design has to do with crew positioning and its effect on trim and stability. On a Quarter Tonner, for example, it is extremely advantageous to site all of the crew aft because of the offsetting impact this has on bow down trim. Consequently, when laying out the deck of a racing boat, designers almost always give thought to how the placement of crewmen and the gear they operate might improve the performance of the boat over its potential in measurement condition.

## Offshore Racing Council Special Regulations

The Offshore Racing Council Special Regulations establish uniform standards for equipment, accommodations, and structural elements on boats competing in various kinds of offshore events. Thus, the ORC rules affect deck layout both by specifying the minimum design features that the deck of a racing boat must have and by setting the lower limits to the amount of gear that must be stowed or fitted on deck. The ORC recommends that its special regulations be adopted by all organizations sponsoring events under the IOR. When these regulations are in use, a boat entering a race may be inspected for compliance at any time, without prior notice.

The Offshore Racing Council divides sailing events into four categories, depending upon the distance to

*a great reason not to use IOR boats for potential cruisers*

*that's not so at all! What this says is that the sail design of the staysail must not be over 150% of the J measure at whatever tack position is chosen.*

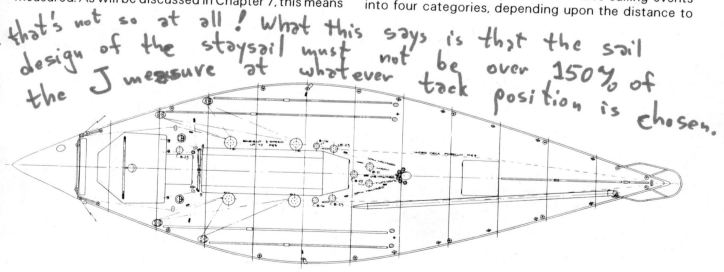

*Gonnagitcha*, a Two Tonner for Mr O. J. Young designed by Gary Mull.

The deck of the round-the-world race winner *Flyer*, owned by Mr Cornelius Van Reitschoten and designed by Sparkman & Stephens. Two days after the boat was launched in 1977 she set out on a transatlantic shake-down cruise which included winning the Transatlantic Race! Note in the first photo the hydraulic vangs, the spaghetti junction at the mast, the use of self-tailing winches, and the alloy hatch dodger. The second photo shows the grinders and how they have been positioned to avoid the mizzen stay. Also shown is the plentiful use of handrails and ventilators. *(Courtesy of Lewmar Marine)*

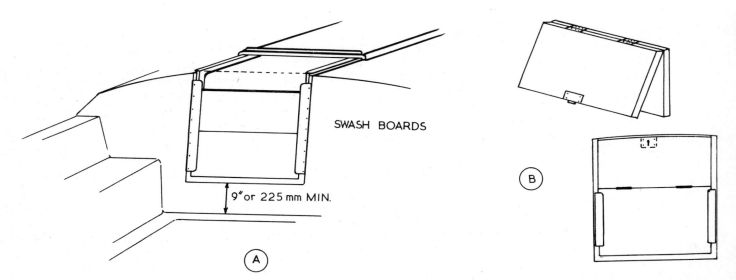

SWASH BOARDS

9" or 225 mm MIN.

(A)

(B)

*Figure 5-3.* (A) Shows the boards inserted—note the small top board which serves as an air gap in bad weather. 9 inches (175 mm) is the minimum distance the bottom of the opening should be above the cockpit sole. A better idea is to make it the same height as the seat.
(B) A board of poor design. The only way it can be closed is by locking it, and when inserted and left open it will bang every time the boat pitches.

be raced and the waters in which the race is to be held. Each category requires different standards of safety and accommodation for competing boats. Category 1 events are long-distance races far off shore, such as the Fastnet, the Newport–Bermuda, or the Sydney–Hobart. Boats entering these races must be self-sufficient for extended periods, capable of weathering heavy storms, and able to handle serious emergencies with little or no outside assistance. Category 2 events are also fairly long races, but they are generally held near shorelines or on large bays of lakes. Offshore events in the English Channel or on the Great Lakes, for example, probably fall into category 2. Like boats competing in category 1 events, boats in category 2 races must be highly self-sufficient, but some of the equipment required for these two subdivisions differs. This is because when a boat in a category 2 event finds itself in serious trouble, the crew can expect to receive help from shore facilities in a reasonable amount of time, unlike boats in category 1 races. The ORC's category 3 events are races held in open but relatively protected waters, always close to shore. Category 4 events, on the other hand, are short races, held within sight of land, and in very protected or warm waters.

In order to be eligible for a race of any distance, in any waters, most offshore boats are designed and equipped for category 1 events. The rules for each category, however, are not unique; many of the category 1 regulations apply to categories 2, 3, and 4 as well. Unless stated otherwise, all the ORC require-

ments discussed in the following sections apply to boats competing in any type of offshore event.

### Regulations for Hatches, Companionways, and Ports

*that's nice!*

The ORC requires that hatches, companionways, and ports be watertight. But outside those on navy submarines, how many really are? Still, the tightness of most hatches can usually be improved. Figure 4-24 in Chapter 4 shows a good wooden lifting hatch, one that could be used on the foredeck. The coaming is high enough to prevent swirls of water from running below deck. And because the hatch opens aft, a wash of water over the bow will slam the lid shut, rather than depositing a waterfall of sea into the accommodation. The other drawings in this same section of Chapter 4 illustrate different kinds of well-designed deck hatches, and the accompanying text and captions point out some of their most important safety features.

The ORC sets additional guidelines for what is perhaps the most common of all sliding hatches, the companionway which leads below from the cockpit. In stormy weather there must be some way of blocking off a companionway hatch to the level of the main deck at the sheer line abreast of the opening. This is usually done by swash boards; Figure 5-3 shows a typical arrangement.

The ORC also requires that on boats with cockpits

opening aft to the sea, the lower edge of the companionway must not be below the main deck level. Unfortunately, for boats with enclosed cockpits the rules do not specify the minimum height the bottom of the companionway should be above the cockpit sole. So some manufacturers simply make it level with the sole. Unavoidably, any waves that fill the cockpit will go straight below. A sill about nine or ten inches above the cockpit sole, like the one shown in Figure 5-3, is a far better arrangement, or there can be a bridge deck between the cockpit and the hatchway.

Most hatches have some form of shatterable glass in them, and even laminated ports can be broken. Consequently, the ORC regulations state that for boats in categories 1, 2, and 3, storm boards must be carried for all windows over two square feet in area. This requirement, of course, is a minimum. It is good practice to carry coverings for all ports, and at the beginning of every season try each one on for fit. If there is no way of bolting the board to the port or hatch, drill some holes in the frame for this purpose. Also, label the boards to indicate where they should go. Remember, you won't be trying to put a board in on a warm sunny afternoon; it will more likely be in the middle of a full gale when the boat is pitching violently.

## Regulations for Cockpits

The ORC regulations state that a cockpit must be a structurally sound, permanent part of the hull, that it must quickly self-drain at all angles of heel, and that it must be watertight up to the main deck level. Bow wells, mid-deck crew pits, and stern wells are all considered cockpits, in addition, of course, to main cockpits. The ORC also specifies maximum cockpit volume. For boats competing in category 1 events, this maximum is 6 per cent of L × B × FA; for boats in category 2, 3, and 4 races, cockpit volumes must not exceed 9 per cent of L × B × FA. And for all boats, regardless of the category of offshore events in which they sail, the height of the cockpit sole must be at least 2 per cent of L above the LWL.

In addition, there are ORC requirements for cockpit drains. These vary depending mostly upon the size of the boat and its age, not strictly the category of race in which that boat competes. On newer boats rating 21 feet and over, the combined area of cockpit drains, after allowing for screens, must be no less than the equivalent of four ¾-inch diameter drains. On boats rating under 21 feet (and on larger boats racing in categories 3 and 4 if built before 1977, or on any larger boat built before 1972), the combined drain area must be at least equal to two drains 1 inch in diameter. All drains should lead to sea cocks or valves which, according to the regulations, must have some means of closing when necessary (except on boats built before 1976 racing in category 4). And in case a sea cock falls out, all boats must carry a selection of soft-wood plugs in assorted sizes to block the opening.

## Regulations for Lifelines, Stanchions, and Pulpits

ORC regulations for lifelines also vary according to boat size. Boats rating 21 feet and over must have double-wire lifelines, with the top line not less than 24 inches above the deck. Boats rating under 21 feet require single-wire lifelines, not less than 18 inches above the deck. If the height of the line is greater than 22 inches at any point, then a second, lower lifeline

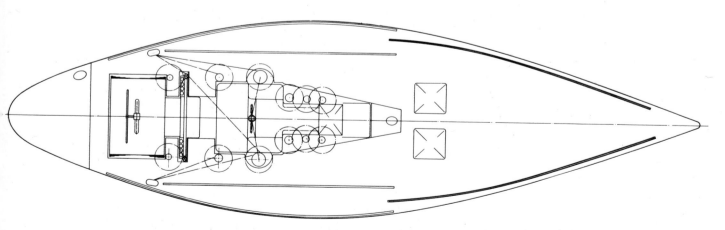

Deck plan of *Morning Cloud* designed by Ron Holland.

must be fitted. All lines, double or single on boats of any size, must be supported at intervals not over 7 feet. Stanchions supporting the lifelines must be through-bolted or welded, and they cannot be angled more than 10 degrees from vertical. The base of each stanchion cannot be further outboard than the edge of the working deck, nor further inboard than 5 per cent of B max or 6 inches, whichever is greater.

According to the ORC, every boat competing in category 1, 2, or 3 events, regardless of its size, must have a through-bolted or securely welded bow pulpit, as well as a fixed stern pulpit unless the lifelines around the stern are arranged in a way that adequately substitutes for a pulpit. A boat entering category 4 races, although it must have a bow pulpit, need not also have a stern pulpit as long as a lifeline at regulation height is extended aft at least to the mid point of the cockpit. The rules for positioning of bow pulpits differ depending upon the size of the boat. On boats rating 21 feet and over, the pulpit must be forward of the headstay, while on boats rating under 21 feet the pulpit can be aft of the headstay but not by more than 16 inches.

Otherwise, all pulpit regulations are similar for boats of every size. The upper rails of all pulpits must be at least as high off the deck as the uppermost lifeline, and the upper rails of bow pulpits must be fastened securely when the boat is racing. If double lifelines are fitted, the lower wire is not required to extend through the bow pulpit. Nor is an upper wire or a single line as long as they are attached to or pass through securely braced stanchions set inside the bow pulpit and overlapping it. The gap between the lifeline and the pulpit, however, must not be more than 6 inches.

## Requirements for Navigational Equipment

Under the ORC regulations, a minimum amount of navigational equipment must be carried on all offshore racers. Not surprising, the requirements vary depending upon how far from land a boat will sail. The only universal requirements are a lead line or an echo sounder, plus a properly fitted and adjusted marine compass. All boats must have these, regardless of the category of race in which they compete. In addition, those participating in category 1, 2, or 3 events must have a spare compass, a speedometer or a distance measuring instrument, charts, a light list, and piloting equipment. Boats entering either category 1 or category 2 races must have a radio direction finder, while only boats in category 1 regattas need have a sextant, navigation tables, and an accurate time piece aboard.

The ORC also specifies rules for navigation lights. These must be in accordance with the International Regulations for Preventing Collisions at Sea, and mounted so as not to be hidden by sails or because of heel angle. The 1972 code (in force 1977) regulations are summarized in Figure 5-4. The United States uses a slightly modified version of these rules, the major difference being that they have not yet adopted the tri-colour masthead light. Also, for inland sailing in the United States, side lights must usually be visible for one mile and stern lights for two. There are, however, two regional variations on these requirements. Boats sailing on rivers in the western part of the country must have side lights visible for 3 miles, and sailing boats on the Great Lakes must show a white light (in lieu of a stern light) on that portion of the boat being approached by another vessel.

When deciding what size lights to use, remember to consider factors such as wire size, voltage drop, and electrolytic corrosion. Using too small a section wire, for instance, can reduce the power and range of a masthead light tremendously; and if that wire is grounded to the mast in any way, severe corrosion can result in a very short time. Glare and reflection are two other points to take into account when fitting navigation lights. Both factors can impair a helmsman's or crewman's night vision. Consequently, to reduce unwanted scatter, it may be helpful to apply matt black paint on the parts of the pulpit forward of the bow light, or even on nonreflective areas inside the lantern. It also helps to have navigation lights as far away from the helm area as possible and also out of the helmsman's line of vision. The bow lights should be visible only for an arc of 112.5 degrees on each side of the bow, so if the helmsman can see them something is wrong.

## Requirements for Emergency Equipment

Emergency navigation lights are one of the regulations the ORC lists under the general heading of emergency equipment. These, however, are required only on a boat competing in category 1 or 2 races. Also required on a boat racing in category 1 or 2 are special storm sails capable of taking the boat to windward in very heavy winds. A boat entering category 3 or 4 races, on the other hand, must have a heavy weather jib and a reefing device for the mainsail. And on all boats with luff-groove devices, there must also be some other method of fastening heavy weather jibs to the headstay.

In addition, the ORC special regulations require that a boat participating in category 1, 2, or 3 events has some form of emergency steering equipment. As

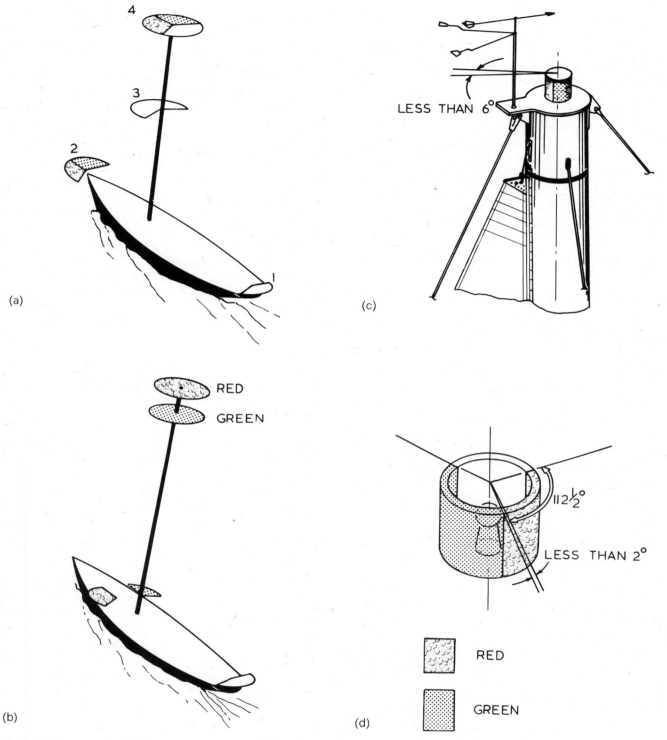

*Figure 5-4.* Navigation lights for yachts. (a) The various requirements for offshore sailing on boats under 12 metres are to use 1, 2, and 3 when under power, and 4 alone or 1 and 2 under sail. (b) Boats larger than 12 metres can have extra red over green all-round lights in addition to the bow and stern lights. (c) A tri-colour masthead light must not be obscured for more than 6 degrees of its arc. (d) Where a vertical filament bulb is used and the screens are edge-glued, there is less than 2 degrees of merging confusion. Depending on the type of screen (glass, for example, is better than plastic), a 25 W bulb gives more than two miles visibility, while a 10 W bulb gives approximately the minimum required visibility of one mile.

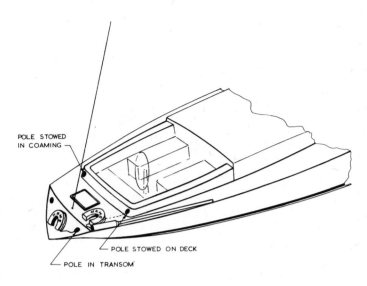

POLE STOWED IN COAMING

POLE STOWED ON DECK

POLE IN TRANSOM

*Figure 5-5.* Various positions for man-overboard poles.

discussed in Chapter 4, the simplest arrangement on a wheel-steered boat is an emergency tiller that fits directly over the head of the rudder stock. The rudder stock, of course, should be accessible from the deck. Another aspect of emergency steering equipment, which is often forgotten, is a small hole in the after edge of the rudder blade through which a line can be reeved if the rudder stock is sheered off the blade.

And finally, we come to the ORC regulations on marine radio equipment. A boat racing in category 1 events must have both a transmitter (with a minimum power of 25 watts) and a receiver, plus an emergency antenna that is not part of the mast structure. A boat racing in category 2, 3, or 4 events, in contrast, need only have a radio receiver capable of picking up weather bulletins.

## Requirements for Safety Equipment

The ORC specifications for safety equipment are as important as any set of rules in offshore racing. Although most of this gear may never be used, its proper maintenance and positioning on the boat can literally make the difference between life and death when an accident happens or a serious emergency strikes.

First on the list of safety equipment are harnesses. A boat racing in category 1, 2, or 3 events must have a safety harness for each crew member; and although not specifically required by the ORC regulations, there should also be convenient and safe places to which a

person can clip his harness. Quite often, though, the only thing to hook onto is the toerail, or the lifeline, or a shroud. And if the mast goes overboard, it will take the lifeline and maybe part of the toerail with it—as well as whoever is clipped onto them. For safe offshore racing, therefore, it is far better to run a deck line for harnesses from the cockpit all the way to within easy reach of the bow. This line, plus one or two padeyes in the cockpit for the helmsman and afterguard to clip onto, is all that is needed to help ensure that safety harnesses will be used effectively by the entire crew.

In the event that a crewman does go over the side, however, a horseshoe lifering with a light and drogue must be positioned within easy reach of the helmsman on any boat regardless of the category of race in which it competes. To reduce windage, horseshoes are often stowed in recessed wells where they are unobtrusive but readily accessible. A boat entering category 1 or 2 events is also required to have a second horseshoe aboard, with a whistle, a dye marker, a drogue, a self-igniting high intensity water light, and a pole with a flag attached. The flag must be able to fly at least 8 feet above the water, and the pole must be fastened to the horseshoe with 25 feet of floating line. Because man-overboard poles are such unwieldy things, stowing them can pose a problem. A widely used solution is to place the poles in tubes set into the transom. Figure 5-5 shows some other possible positions.

When a serious emergency arises, necessitating that the crew abandon the boat, a well-equipped liferaft may be their only chance of survival. The ORC requires that every boat racing in category 1, 2, or 3 events must have a liferaft capable of carrying the entire crew. It cannot be used for any other purpose than saving life at sea. The raft must be stowed directly on deck, or in a special, easily accessible compartment opening to the deck and containing only the liferaft. This means that no blocks, winch handles, or lines can be stowed in the same locker. The most common position for the liferaft compartment is under one of the cockpit seats, usually the helmsman's. The ORC rules specifically state that the raft cannot be carried under a dinghy.

To meet ORC regulations, a liferaft must have certain features. Two separate automatically inflatable buoyancy compartments are required, and the raft must be able to carry its maximum number of occupants even when one compartment is empty. Every liferaft must also be fitted with a full canopy and each must have various pieces of gear attached—a sea anchor, bellows or an air pump, a signalling light, flares, a repair kit, a baler, two paddles, and a knife. By regulation liferafts must be inspected every two years either by the manufacturer or some competent authority.

128

The ORC lists additional safety equipment that must be carried on all racing boats. This includes life jackets for all crew members, at least 50 feet of floating-type heaving line readily accessible to the cockpit, and various kinds of flares and distress signals stowed in a waterproof container. These flares and signals should probably be kept near the liferaft so that in an emergency they can be quickly put aboard.

## Requirements for General Equipment

Finally, we come to some ORC requirements for general equipment. First, winches. On all boats, regardless of the category of events in which they race, sheet winches must be mounted so that the operator will not be located below deck. Second, requirements for anchors. They are mandatory on all boats, although the number varies. Boats rating 21 feet and over that participate in category 1, 2, or 3 races must have two anchors, both with cables. Boats rating under 21 feet, on the other hand, and boats of any size that participate only in category 4 events need carry only one anchor and cable. And third, the ORC rules for bilge pumps. On boats entering category 1 or 2 races there must be at least two manually-operated bilge pumps, and on boats entering category 3 races at least one. In both of these cases, moreover, one bilge pump must be capable of being operated when all hatches, cockpit seats, lockers, and companionways are closed. On boats competing in category 4 races, there need be only one bilge pump, with no further restrictions on its operating capability.

## Rules for World Championships of Level Rating Classes

Another set of rules we should briefly consider is the one for world championships of level rating classes. Because these regulations impose certain restrictions on headroom below deck, on sails, and on the number of crew members, they can often critically affect deck layout.

Minimum interior volumes for each of the five level rating classes are shown in Table 5-6. Note that cabin headroom requirements refer to measured headroom under the deck, and not under deck beams and stringers. In each case, this minimum headroom must be maintained for the full fore and aft and athwartships dimensions given, and it must also span the prescribed amount of cabin sole surface. Any hatch that falls within these designated areas must be permanently fitted and able to be closed immediately. This, of course, rules out hatches of the lift-off variety.

Just as the rules for world championships of level rating classes specify minimums for interior volumes, so they also specify maximums for numbers and sizes of certain sails, as well as for numbers of crewmen. These limitations sometimes make it possible to cut down on the amount of deck gear. For instance, because of sail restrictions, most Quarter Tonners and Half Tonners carry only one staysail, so staysail track can be kept to a minimum. Another sail restriction limits the size of the storm jib to no more than $0.05 I^2$ in area and $0.65 I$ on the luff. Consequently, a padeye is sufficient for a sheet lead.

## Minimum Interior Volume Requirements: World Championships of Level Rating Classes

| | Two Tonners and One Tonners | Three-Quarter Tonners | Half Tonners | Quarter Tonners and Mini Tonners |
|---|---|---|---|---|
| Headroom not less than: | 1.83 m (6' 0") | 1.75 m (5' 9") | 1.7 m (5' 7") | 1.3 m (4' 3") (Quarter Tonners) 1.25 m (4' 1¼") (Mini Tonners) |
| Extending fore and aft for at least: | 1.8 m (5' 11") | 1.8 m (5' 11") | 1.2 m (3' 11¼") | 1.2 m (3' 11¼") |
| Extending athwartships for at least: | 0.45 m (1' 5¾") | 0.4 m (1' 3¾") | 0.35 m (1' 1¾") | 0.35 m (1' 1¾") |
| Above a surface area of cabin sole not less than: | 1.5 sq m (16.14 sq ft) | 1.3 sq m (13.988 sq ft) | 0.5 sq m (5.38 sq ft) | 0.4 sq m (4.304 sq ft) |

Note: Mini Tonners should have a sitting area of 0.5 sq m (5.38 sq ft), with a minimum of 0.9 m (2' 11½") above the seat.

*Table 5-6*

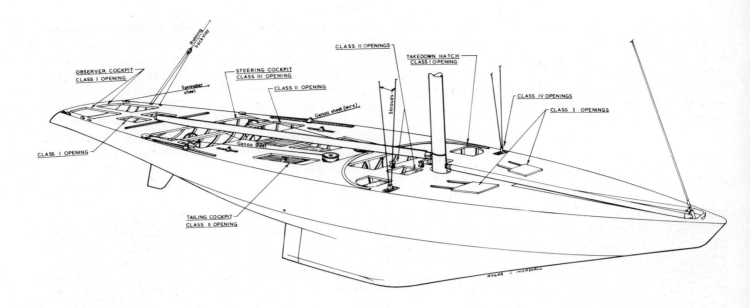

*Figure 5-7. Courageous* as she looked in 1974 before cockpits were required to be watertight.

## The International Twelve Metre Rule

Because twelve metres are so special, it is unlikely that many readers of this book will ever be involved in designing one of their decks. Still, the twelve metre rule is of interest to all racing sailors, if for no other reason than the simple fact that America's Cup racing is the grand prix of sailing events. So here we will take a quick look at one aspect of the rule that critically affects deck layout—the restrictions placed on the size, number, and location of deck openings.

Can a twelve metre sink? Evidently officials at the International Yacht Racing Union thought so when they changed the rule after the 1974 America's Cup series to make the boats more seaworthy. For one thing, they increased freeboards to help prevent water from coming aboard. But more relevant to our purposes, they also tried to eliminate the old-style gaping holes in the deck in favour of IOR-type self-draining cockpits.

Until 1975, the holes in a twelve metre's deck could be almost anywhere and any size. The former rule specified four classes of deck openings. Class I, usually sail hatches, had fitted covers which had to be carried on board and above deck while racing. These openings were unrestricted in area and location provided that they conformed with certain minor provisions. Under the new regulations, however, each Class I opening cannot be more than 0.5 m² (approximately 5½ square

feet); they cannot be closer to the deck edge than 300 mm (approximately 1 foot); and there may not be more than two such openings forward of the mast and two aft of it.

Under the old rule, Class II openings had fitted covers which could be removed while racing, and Class III openings were cockpits. Under the new rule, the former Class II category is eliminated entirely and many more restrictions are imposed on cockpits (now Class II openings). As far as their placement is concerned, cockpits must be located aft of the mast, and as for their size, they may not be greater than 9.0 m² (about 97 square feet) nor less than 4.6 m² (about 49½ square feet). Depth, too, has been restricted both by the stipulation that cockpit soles cannot be lower than 380 mm (about 1¼ feet) above the LWL plane, and by the requirement that cockpit volume cannot exceed 7.5 m³ (about 265 cubic feet). Other regulations affect the minimum distance between the edge of a cockpit and the edge of the deck, the combined area of cockpit drains, and the design of companionway openings.

Even the minor Class III (formerly Class IV) openings on a twelve metre—the small holes for running rigging, lanyards, or similar lines and attachments—have new limitations. Under the current rule, these cannot be larger than 25 mm (approximately 1 inch) without requiring a gaiter boot or some other means of closing the opening.

The illustration of *Courageous* as she looked in 1974 (Figure 5-7) shows just how much of the deck was cut away under the old twelve metre rule. Compare this with the picture of *Enterprise*'s deck, taken while the boat was being built (Figure 5-8). It provides a good idea of how the new breed of twelve metre deck is currently designed.

\* \* \* \* \* \*

We have covered the highlights of the four major sets of yacht racing rules and how they affect the layout of a deck. But as in every other sport, the rules of sailing simply set the broad outlines of what constitutes fair and safe competition. Rules, then, are only a beginning. Like all the other topics covered in the first part of this book, they are basic information a designer must have before starting actually to lay out a deck. From here on the designer's job becomes one of working within whatever limits the rules or the availability of equipment may impose in order to produce the most efficient deck arrangement possible.

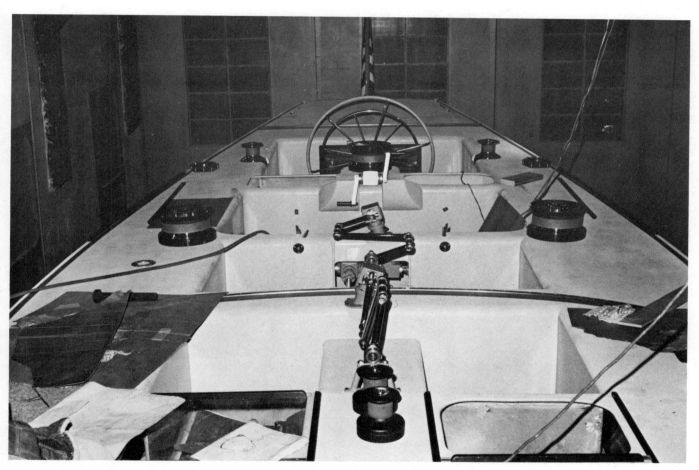

*Figure 5-8.* The deck of *Enterprise* looking aft from the mast when the boat was being constructed. *(author)*

131

# PART II

# The Deck Design Process

With a good knowledge of the techniques and equipment used on a modern racing deck, one can begin to think about the design of particular boats. The second part of this book looks at the many factors that influence deck layout, and how they interact with one another. If yacht design is a series of compromises, it is the designer that manages to make the best trade-offs who will produce the most efficient deck plan possible.

Chapter 6 introduces the reader to some of the problems encountered when trying to design a deck for maximum efficiency. Chapter 7 considers the important relationship between deck layout and interior design. And finally, in Chapter 8, some deck plans of different boats are actually laid out, and their efficiency on various points of sail evaluated.

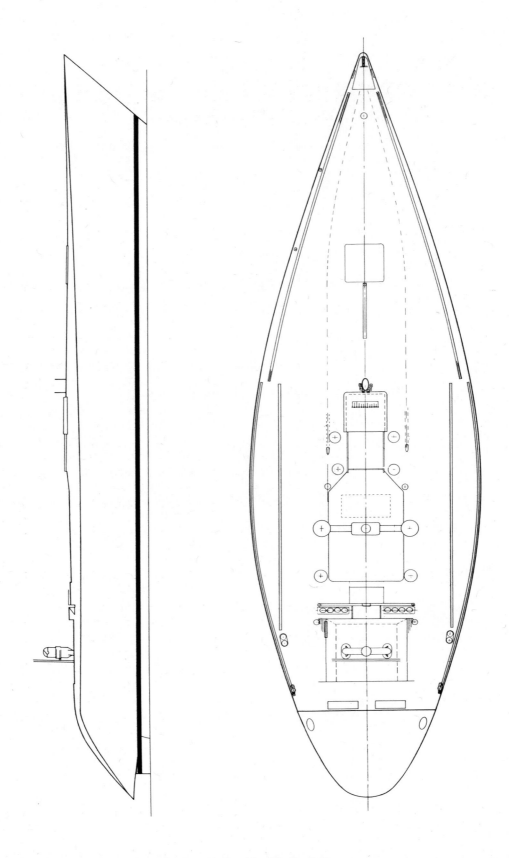

*Big Apple,* a 44 foot Admiral's Cup design by Ron Holland for Mr Hugh Coveney.

134

# Designing for Efficiency

The deck of an ocean racer is first and foremost a working platform. Although this may sound obvious, it is surprising how often the primary aim of work efficiency is seemingly neglected in the deck layout of a racing boat. There are probably two reasons. One is choice. Some owners simply do not want a strictly racing design. They are willing to compromise the goal of work efficiency to a greater or lesser extent in order to have a boat that will better meet their cruising needs. But another quite unfortunate reason is lack of knowledge. Many owners never maximize the efficiency of their deck layouts because they do not know how to identify possible problems. The purpose of this chapter is to discuss some of the major factors that must be considered in designing or redesigning for work efficiency, and how these factors apply to specific areas of the deck.

## Basic Considerations for Efficient Deck Layout

This chapter will not attempt to consider every aspect of racing deck design and provide stock answers. That would be impossible, because every boat and its crew are in some ways unique. There can never be simple, universal solutions. What this chapter does, however, is to provide a first look at some of the most important factors related to layout efficiency. In particular, it discusses five critical considerations in designing a good, working deck—ergonomics, space, comfort, vision, and safety—and points out how these considerations influence major design decisions. Bear in mind, though, that these factors are not separate and distinct, but instead closely interrelate. Although for our purposes it may be useful to consider each somewhat apart from the others, in reality they all affect one another, and trade-offs between them are often required. When laying out a deck, as in any other aspect

of yacht design, one is always faced with hard choices about how much efficiency to sacrifice in one area in order to gain greater efficiency in another.

## Ergonomic Considerations

One critical factor to consider in designing for work efficiency is the need to get the most out of a crewman's physical efforts. This is the domain of ergonomics—the science of designing mechanical equipment so as to extract the maximum amount of work from a given input of human energy. (The term ergonomics comes from the word erg, a unit of energy.)

To design decks with ergonomic considerations in mind, we start by looking at the body size and physical capabilities of the crew. Figure 6-1 shows the dimensions of the average European adult male. These dimensions, of course, are not universal, for average human size varies around the world. The average American, for example, is slightly taller and heavier than his European counterpart, while the average Japanese is shorter and lighter than both. Such variations must be taken into account when designing a boat to be sailed in a particular country. For our purposes, however, we will use average European dimensions.

Note especially the reach of our average crewman, a forward reach of 2 feet 8½ inches, and an overhead reach of 7 feet 5½ inches. By leaning outward or stretching upward on his toes, reach increases a bit further. These maximum dimensions are extremely important in many design decisions. Consider, for example, the placement of gear that involves reaching and pulling movements, such as the location of a halyard exit box. This decision should be made with a thought toward using a crewman's maximum reach, thus enabling him to pull with long, smooth movements rather than short, jerky ones. If a halyard exits from the mast at, say, 6 or 7 feet above the deck, the crewman's

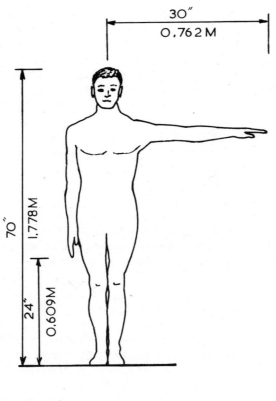

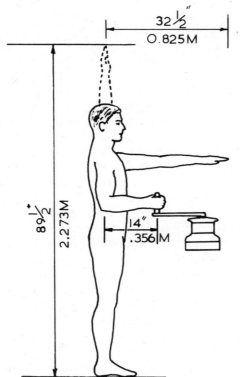

*Figure 6-1.* The dimensions of the average European crewman.

hoisting power will be reduced because the average man can reach higher than that, even when standing flat on his feet. And if he stands on his toes, or jumps a little, he can reach as much as 8 feet or more. To get the most hoist out of each pulling motion, therefore, the exit box for a halyard should be positioned 8 to 9 feet above the deck. Later in this chapter we will review some of the various ergonomic principles that apply to sailing operations, and how they govern deck design.

## Space Requirements

From these examples we can begin to see how the need to get the most out of physical movements constantly influences the placement of equipment on a boat. Unfortunately, however, designing an efficient deck involves much more than simply placing a winch or halyard exit box in the best possible location given the average crewman's reach. Many other factors, and their interrelationships, must be considered. Space requirements, for example, are very important. Anyone who has ever bumped into the steering pedestal when tailing a winch, or had to duck under a spinnaker sheet that crossed the cockpit, already knows how critical space can be.

One aspect of designing for adequate space is that of providing enough room for equipment to be operated without causing snarl-ups. This means keeping an eye out for gear that is located too close together—not leaving enough space between a winch and a lifeline, for instance, or positioning two winches that are used in the same operation so close to one another that their handles collide. It also means being alert to such potential difficulties as a sheet that will foul another line when led to a winch, or a forehatch that is not quite large enough to accommodate your largest sail bag without a minor battle. Although you may think that such problems would be easy to spot at the design stage, they are not always so obvious.

Nor is it always obvious at the design stage how much space a crewman will actually need to work in. To calculate what the work space requirements on your boat are, you must consider both the body dimensions of the average crewman and the kinds of tasks he will be doing in different areas of the deck. For instance, you should provide more work space for hauling on a line, a job that involves a forward and backward movement of the entire body as illustrated in Figure 6-2, than for tailing a sheet, a job that usually involves arm movements alone. Of course, work space requirements are complicated somewhat by the extent to which the boat is pitching and its angle of heel. Spaces that are restricted in any way also impose special problems. People tire easily in confined spaces and therefore need extra room to stretch and relax their muscles than one might ordinarily allow.

## Comfort Considerations

Comfort may strike you as an unnecessary topic to include in a discussion of major factors contributing to work efficiency. But comfort is inversely related to fatigue, and fatigue obviously has an important bearing on how well a crewman can perform. Comfort, therefore, is as essential a consideration on a racing boat as it is on a cruising boat, although in different ways and for far different reasons.

On an ocean racer, comfort is most important to jobs that require sitting for relatively long periods of time—trimming a genoa on an upwind leg, for example, or helming. Figure 6-3 shows the posture and dimensions of the average man when sitting erect. Actually, this kind of straightback sitting position is rarely seen on a racing boat, or anywhere else for that matter. After a short time, a seated person naturally tends to slouch forward. Analysing how a crewman is likely to sit in any given situation is part of designing for maximum work efficiency. The problem is compounded, however, by the fact that a boat heels up to 30 degrees on each tack, and as a result comfortable seating postures change significantly.

## Vision Requirements

When a man's vision of critical items is impeded, he can seldom work as quickly or accurately as possible. This is why good visibility is a part of efficient deck layout. Designing for good visibility first requires an understanding of some of the factors that affect a person's ability to see objects clearly. One, of course, is simply the positioning of equipment that must be scanned or studied so that it falls within the viewer's optimum range of vision. Figure 6-4 shows the horizontal and vertical arcs of vision for a normal human eye. Any object that must be viewed frequently should be located well within this area to eliminate constant head movements. The distance a piece of equipment should ideally be placed from the viewer depends quite naturally on the size of the object, its function, and the degree of concentration needed to read or check it.

With a little thought and planning, you can usually

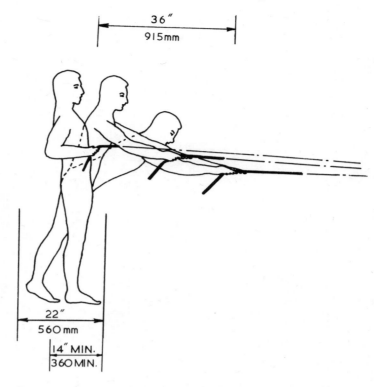

*Figure 6-2.* The minimum space required for a man to pull a line. More space at his feet will allow the man to step forward to get a good pull.

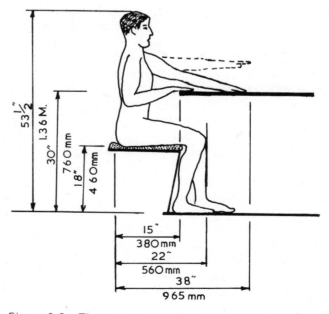

*Figure 6-3.* The posture and dimensions of a man sitting.

137

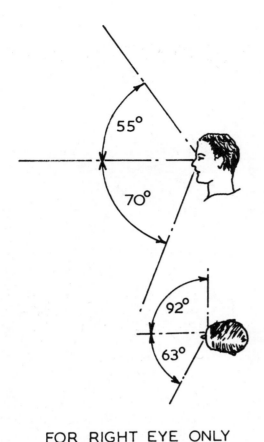

FOR RIGHT EYE ONLY

*Figure 6-4.* The range of eye vision for an average person.

enhance the visibility of any important piece of equipment on your boat. You can increase the readability of key instruments, such as the compass or wind-speed and wind-direction indicators, simply by enlarging them. Or you can aid visibility by contrasting the colour of an item with those of surrounding objects—colour-coding ropes and guys, for instance. And finally, you can take steps to minimize glare. The glare off chromium winches, for example, can be reduced by painting their tops matt black.

## Safety Considerations

People at times think of safety as something that is obtained at the expense of efficiency—as if safety and efficiency were involved in a kind of mutual trade-off. This, however, is an unfortunate misconception, for safety is an integral aspect of designing for work efficiency. Consider, for example, a boat on which the exit box for the spinnaker halyard is placed less than

138

6 feet above the deck. We already know that such a height would be inefficient for ergonomic reasons, but it would be inefficient for safety reasons as well. If a crewman cannot get a good downward pull on the halyard because it exits from the mast too low, he may resort to pulling it upward from the turning block. This would mean that the tailer is not able to carry a safety turn around the winch. If the spinnaker fills early, the man hauling on the halyard may suddenly find his hand pulled into the turning block. The inefficiency of the improperly positioned halyard exit box, then, is as much a matter of neglected attention to safety as it is neglected attention to the ergonomics of hoisting a sail.

## Laying Out a Working Deck

Ergonomic considerations as well as adequate workspace, comfort, vision, and safety are five key factors in the general problem of designing for work efficiency. To understand how these factors interact to influence the actual layout of a deck, we will consider the major areas of the deck and the major design problems in each area. As our basic example we will use a boat of approximately Two Ton size, looking at larger or smaller boats only when they pose unique problems.

### The Cockpit

Most of the work on a boat is done in the cockpit. Although trimming sails and helming, the principal tasks performed in the cockpit, may not be as physically strenuous as hoisting and taking down sails, they are just as difficult because they require such continuous effort. To win races, concentration in the cockpit must be keen and steady; even momentary lapses can cause a boat to lose places.

How can work efficiency in the cockpit be maximized? We will begin to answer this question by looking at some of the problems involved in designing an efficient helm area, and then we will turn to the matter of selecting the best possible locations for primary and secondary winches.

*Designing the Helm Area*
Because the helmsman is the person who controls the boat, everything possible should be done to lessen his fatigue. This is why comfort is such an important consideration in designing the helm area. Unfortunately, however, the helmsman's seat is sometimes the

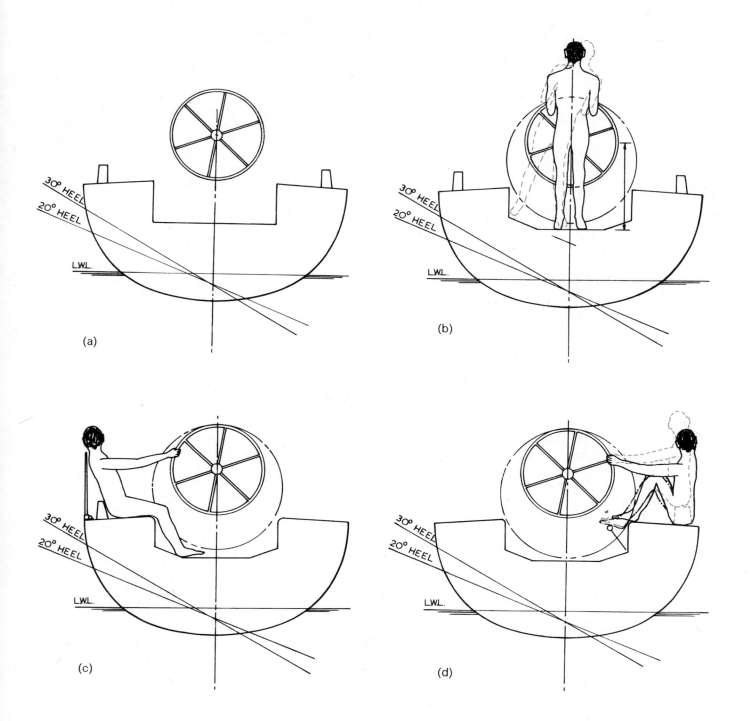

*Figure 6-5.* (a) A typical cross-section through the cockpit of a modern boat. (b) The helmsman standing when the boat is vertical and when the boat is heeled 20 degrees (dashed line). (c) The helmsman sitting to leeward. The coaming can either be modified to enable the helmsman to lean outboard (port side) or left off altogether (starboard side). Note also the rounding of all the corners in the cockpit. (d) The helmsman sitting to weather on the coaming (dashed line) or on the deck where there is no coaming. The hinged footbar can drop out from the cockpit side to provide a good footrest.

139

most uncomfortable one on the boat. The reason is simply lack of forethought. Although care is often taken to make the helmsman comfortable when the boat is fairly upright, little regard may be given to his comfort at a heel angle of 25 degrees. To see the sails from leeward on an upwind leg, the helmsman ends up lying on his side with his ear rubbed raw by the guard rail and the coaming digging into his side, while a cleat happens to be just where he wants to put his hand.

Given the various positions a helmsman must adopt on different legs of the course, how can he be made reasonably comfortable most of the time? Figure 6-5 shows various ways the problem might be solved on a boat with wheel steering. Drawing (a) is a section through the cockpit of a fibreglass boat as it might be designed if little thought had been given to the helmsman's comfort. Now suppose the boat is sailing downwind and heeling at an angle of 20 degrees. (Tip this book so that the 20 degree line is horizontal.) You can see immediately why the helmsman would have to redistribute his weight greatly to maintain his balance, but he would have nowhere to comfortably place his feet. The arrangement in drawing (b) is a good solution. The addition of a sloping cockpit sole gives the helmsman a flat surface for one foot which allows him to stand upright quite naturally.

Next, imagine that the helmsman is sitting to leeward and watching the sail. How can he be given a fairly comfortable seat? One way, shown in drawing (c), is to move the coaming outboard a little and slope its inner side, while at the same time rounding the edge of the cockpit. This gives the helmsman a comfortable back rest and eliminates a sharp corner that might dig into his legs. Further improvements could be made for a helmsman sitting to weather, as in drawing (d). If there is a coaming, it should be made wide enough for the helmsman to sit on easily, or the coaming could be removed altogether. Also note the addition of a convenient foot bar which can be pulled out from the cockpit wall.

Another way of designing for the helmsman's comfort is to mould the slope of the deck around the helm area so that it conforms relatively well to the shape of a man's body, regardless of whether he is sitting upright or leaning far outboard. How this might be done is shown in Figure 6-6. The deck is slightly recessed on either side of the cockpit for the comfort of the helmsman sitting to leeward or to weather. Aft of the cockpit the deck slopes gradually upward, levelling off toward the centreline to form a seat to be used when the boat is sailing downwind.

In addition to well-designed standing and sitting areas, the size and location of the steering wheel is

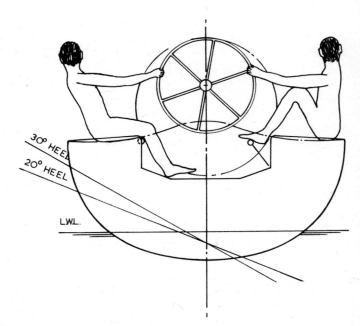

*Figure 6-6.* The final arrangement with no coamings and all the corners rounded. Note the seat profile, which fairs into the deck.

also important to a helmsman's comfort. A wheel must be large enough for the helmsman to reach easily, but not so large that it gets in the way of crewmen moving aft. About 42 inches is the maximum wheel diameter that is comfortable for steering. On a boat with a particularly beamy stern, two wheels are a possible way of preventing the helmsman from having to stretch too far.

Nowadays, many boats up to One Ton size, and even some Two Tonners, have tillers rather than wheel steering. On a boat with a tiller, the helmsman usually sits to weather to enhance stability. He can maintain a comfortable position quite easily in the lighter going, when the boat is only a few degrees from vertical. But once the boat heels to any extent, the helmsman must have foot blocks and some form of tiller extension to enable him to sit outboard comfortably. Figure 6-7 shows just how important these features are.

On a tiller-steered boat, as on a boat with wheel steering, one of the biggest influences on the helmsman's comfort is the contour of the deck he sits on. Again, a few simple modifications can make a great difference—for example, moulding the deck surface slightly to conform to body shape, rounding the top corner of the cockpit, and making sure the genoa foot block is not precisely where the helmsman wants to place his rear end. By removing all such obstacles to the helmsman's comfort, his steering performance can be significantly improved.

Good visibility is also essential to top performance at the helm. Most of the time a helmsman is concentrating on the sails. Upwind, his major concern is the luff of the genoa, which he can view from either the weather or the leeward side; downwind, he focuses on the luff of the spinnaker. From a design point of view, the need to see the sails clearly may necessitate a long tiller with a sizeable extension, or a fairly large diameter wheel or two wheels to allow the helmsman to position himself well outboard.

It is equally essential that the helmsman be able to view the compass and other instruments clearly, and without major head movements if possible. Tips on enhancing instrument readability have already been mentioned earlier in this chapter. Another possible aid to visibility is fitting two compasses, or perhaps two sets of certain other instruments, each set being used on a different tack.

A final factor that should be considered when designing a deck layout to maximize the helmsman's field of vision is the position of each crewman on the boat who might possibly block the helmsman's view of dials, compasses, and so forth. A common mistake, for example, is siting the compass in such a way that a winch tailer obstructs the helmsman's view of it. Thus, when locating all important instruments, first check to see where crewmen will usually be positioned.

And last, a note on safety in the helm area. Like everyone else on the boat, the helmsman must have a place to hook his safety harness, and this attachment point must be strong enough to hold his full weight when he is thrown off-balance. For wheel steering the harness attachment point should be sited away from the wheel, about hip high, on the inside of the cockpit. Just slightly aft of the helmsman when he is standing, not more than six feet away from him, is best. Remember, too, that an attachment point should be fitted on each side of the wheel so that a change of

*Figure 6-7.* This cockpit is spacious and comfortable when the boat is upright, but notice how uncomfortable the helmsman is when the boat is heeled. He must hold the stanchion to keep from sliding to leeward and there is a cleat immediately under his right leg even though it cannot be seen in this picture. *(author)*

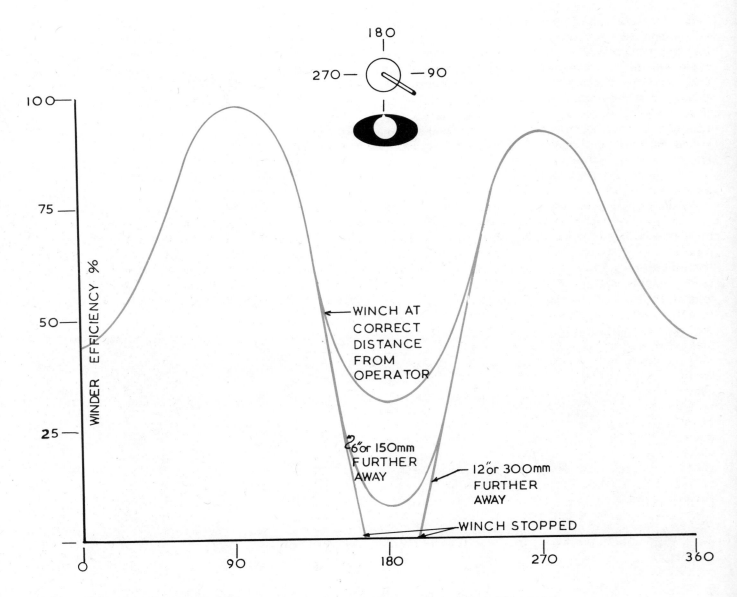

*Figure 6-8.* A graph plotting efficiency against the distance between a winch and the operator.

helmsmen can be made without the first man having to unclip before leaving the wheel, or the second having to clip on while steering the boat. On a boat with tiller steering, on the other hand, a reasonably good location for the harness padeye is on the centreline in front of the tiller so that the helmsman does not have to unclip every time the boat tacks. Alternatively, one padeye can be sited on either side of the cockpit, but this arrangement is somewhat less convenient.

*Siting Primary and Secondary Winches*
When siting primary and secondary winches, ergo-

nomic requirements are always high on anyone's list of priorities. Many people think that winding a winch is all brawn and no brains. But it is not. While brawn is certainly important, knowing where to place a winch for maximum operator efficiency is just as critical. Even the strongest crewman cannot operate a winch to best advantage if that winch is badly sited.

First, there is the problem of siting top-action winches. The circle your hands and arms make when winding a winch has peaks and lows of efficiency. The weakest points in a complete turn are at the top and bottom—the split seconds at which the operator is changing from a pushing to a pulling motion, or vice versa. If a winch is positioned too far from or too close to its operator, winding efficiency falls off rapidly because the weak points of the turn are that much more difficult to overcome. As shown in Figure 6-8, a few inches in any direction can make a substantial difference in the power the operator can exert. A similar drop in efficiency occurs when a winch is positioned too high or too low. Ideally, the centre of a winch should be 16 inches from the operator's belt buckle and 30 inches above his feet—that is, about in the middle of the man's area of reach and just slightly below his hips.

A linked winch system with a remote drive pedestal also necessitates good planning to maximize the power of the operators. Consider the problem of how to position the pedestal. If the pedestal is placed so that the operators are facing athwartships, winding efficiency will be seriously reduced when the boat is heeled; the man on the leeward side, particularly, will be able to exert virtually no power at all. Consequently, a remote drive pedestal is most efficient when it is placed so that the operators face fore and aft.

As for where in the cockpit the pedestal should be located, it is often best to place it a little forward of the centre of the cockpit to allow room for the man trimming and tailing; but remember that efficiency falls off sharply when the angle from the drum to the pedestal is greater than 10 degrees. Another way to make room for the trimmer/tailer is to stand him on a platform located in the hatch on either side of the cockpit. This layout is shown in Figure 6-9. It has the advantage of making the cockpit less crowded, and it also allows the tailer to pull the sheet at approximately the same level as the winch, thus helping to ensure that the line will not come off the top of the drum. But this arrangement does require careful interior planning.

Although the problem of siting a remote-drive pedestal is closely related to ergonomic considerations, we have seen that space requirements are also involved. In fact, general spacing needs have a great deal to do with efficient placement of winches. Consider, for example, the space required to provide the winch operator with a good, firm footing. For top-action winches, the operator must be able to spread his feet a minimum of 24 inches when the boat is upright, and more when it is heeled. If the cockpit is particularly wide, it is a good idea to position a foot block about 30 inches from the side of the cockpit and 4 to 6 inches off the deck. The operator can then brace himself as he leans over the winch.

On a larger boat that has a middeck cockpit with a remote drive pedestal, there is another way to provide firm footing for the operators. The cockpit sole can be

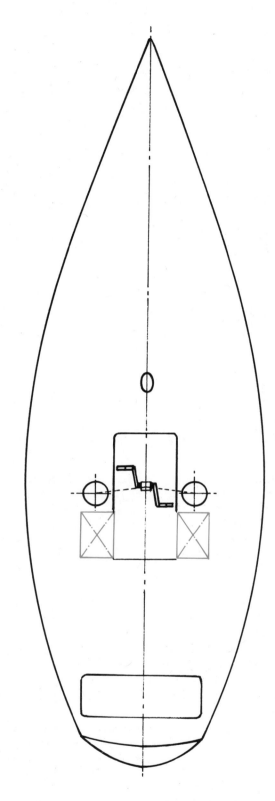

*Figure 6-9.* A method of using twin hatches to enable a winch tailer to operate winches efficiently. The tailer stands in the hatch giving the winders plenty of space in the cockpit.

143

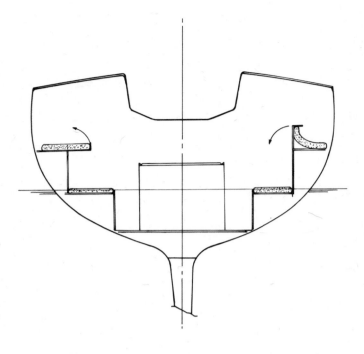

*Figure 6-10.* How extra space can be obtained in a middeck cockpit.

approximately 24 inches wide, allowing adequate foot space for operators when the boat is upright. But instead of the sides of the cockpit being at right angles to the sole, they can slope at 20 to 25 degrees so that the cockpit measures 34 or 36 inches across at deck level. This design is shown in Figure 6-10. It offers both ample foot space for winch operators when the boat is heeled, and a little bit of extra room below deck.

Another spacing consideration important to the positioning of winches has to do with the proximity of equipment. When winches are spaced too closely together—say, about 20 inches or less—their handles are in danger of hitting. This is only a problem, of course, when the winches are likely to be used simultaneously. A spinnaker halyard winch could be located close to a genoa halyard winch with no negative results because the two would rarely be used at the same time. But a spinnaker sheet winch should not be close to the winch for a genoa sheet because a staysail might be led to the genoa winch when a spinnaker is set.

There are times, though, when placing winches fairly close together is an aid to work efficiency. This is the case with self-tailing foreguy and afterguy winches. When placed close enough to one another, both winches can be operated by a single person. But remember not to make the mistake of locating them so close together that the handle of the smaller foreguy

winch (which is lower to the deck) hits the larger afterguy winch. And also be sure that the operator is allowed enough space to give a good hard pull on either line, as is often required.

Another problem related to space considerations when locating winches is that of obtaining fair leads. Every yachtsman is aware that a line leading to a winch must be far enough away from other winches, and also from cleats or the cockpit coaming, so that it will not cause friction or chafe. You may think that unfair leads will always be obvious in the deck plan of a boat, but there are problems caused by badly positioned sheets that may be quite difficult to detect at the drawing stage. Suppose the boat shown in Figure 6-11 is going downwind with the spinnaker trimmed from the weather side. Given the winch layout, the spinnaker sheet will cross the cockpit and the mainsheet, while the main will foul the genoa halyard winch. A bit more thought as to how each winch will actually be used in different operations could avoid such problems. For example, the spinnaker winch could be moved well forward, as shown by the dotted line in Figure 6-12, so that the sheet will not get in the way of the crew in the cockpit. Of course, if the boat has a high deck camber, you will have to raise the winch so that the sheet can clear the deck.

It is also possible for an unfair lead to get in a winch operator's own way, hampering his ability to wind efficiently. One common error is illustrated in Figure 6-12. If the operator stands behind the winch platform as he should, the lead interferes with his movements and there is even a chance that his sleeve or some other part of his clothing could be drawn into the turns on the drum. To be certain to prevent mishap, the crewman would have to stand in front of the winch facing astern, where he could not see the sail.

The needs of the crewman operating a winch clearly have a critical influence on where that winch will be located. A winch must be situated so as to allow the operator maximum power when winding, and the operator must also have enough surrounding work space. But anyone who has been the genoa trimmer in variable wind conditions on a long beat knows how important the factor of comfort is as well. To lessen the trimmer's fatigue and increase his efficiency, one possible solution is a simple drop seat designed into an aft cockpit. Notice how the seat in Figure 6-13 can be adjusted to a fairly horizontal position when the boat is heeled. Including a remote drive pedestal in the winch system would probably improve the trimmer's performance since he would be relieved of the physical work of winding and could concentrate on calling the trim as he tails the winch.

144

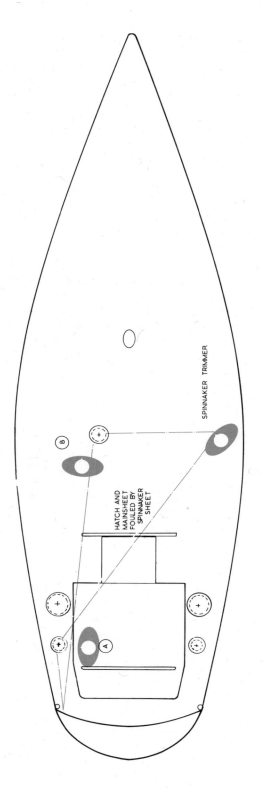

Figure 6-11. Designing the ideal spinnaker sheet winch position. With the winch positioned at A, the winder has to face outboard and cannot see the sail. But with the winch at B, both the winder and trimmer can see the spinnaker.

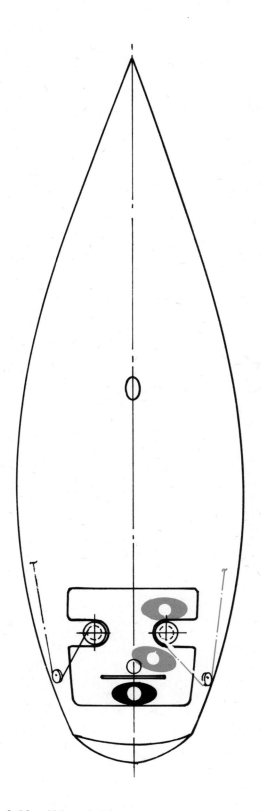

Figure 6-12. Although this arrangement may seem efficient, the winchman could get his clothing caught in the winch.

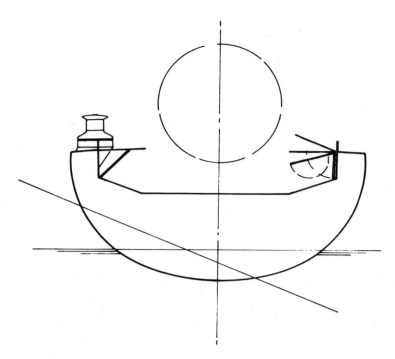

*Figure 6-13.* A hinged drop seat in the cockpit to lessen the trimmer's fatigue. It folds away when not in use and can be fixed in three positions.

Finally, when siting primary and secondary winches, one must also be sure that the operators can position themselves for full visibility of the sails. On boats with aft cockpits, genoa and spinnaker sheet winches were traditionally placed on the edge of the coaming. This, however, was not an ideal location, because there was no way that a crewman could wind a winch powerfully and still face forward to see the sail he was trimming. Today, this traditional placement of primary and secondary winches has been largely abandoned. On most boats with aft cockpits, genoa and spinnaker winches are located more toward the forward end of the cockpit so an operator can stand behind a winch and look forward toward the sails. If deck space at the forward end of the cockpit is at a premium, primary and secondary winches can alternatively be located on platforms within the cockpit, again allowing room for the operators to stand behind them and look forward when winding.

Similar visibility considerations are involved when siting winches on a boat with a middeck cockpit. Suppose a middeck cockpit is fitted with a typical linked winch system using molehills, as shown in Figure 6-14. Given this layout, the crewman tailing the winch must face outboard if he is to stand in the crewpit. But with a slight alteration in the shape of the cockpit,

the addition of two 'wings' as indicated by the dotted lines, the tailer can easily see the sails and call the trim. Below deck, these cockpit 'wings' can be hidden by lockers designed around them. Careful athwartship and fore and aft winch positioning is also critical to visibility on a boat with a middeck cockpit. Generally, a genoa winch should be placed about halfway between the centreline and the clew of the sail, while on a line about even with the clew in a fore and aft direction. A little aft of this position is probably even better, because it allows the trimmer to see the head of the sail without too much head movement.

## The Mast Area

Unlike the cockpit, where work goes on continually, the mast area of a boat sees relatively little activity. Crewmen work around the mast only to change genoas and spinnakers, or to reef the mainsail. The rest of the time they should be sitting on the weather rail. Given our present focus on how to lay out a deck for maximum efficiency, we will turn our attention to two of the most important design problems in this area of the boat: siting the halyard winches and designing the coachroof.

### Siting Halyard Winches

An essential factor to keep in mind when siting halyard winches is the operator's need for adequate work space while sails are being changed. If a boat has a middeck cockpit, the halyard winches are usually sited at the forward end of it, provided the cockpit is large enough to hold both the halyard operator and the winch grinders. If cockpit space is limited, the halyard operator can be positioned in a hatch at the forward end. This arrangement is shown in Figure 6-15. Note that everyone is low enough so that the boom will clear them when gybing.

On boats without a middeck cockpit, the halyard winches can be led back to the main cockpit. In this case, too, space is an important consideration, for the cockpit must be large enough to comfortably fit the various crewmen involved in a sail change. Usually, the extra cockpit space is gained at the expense of below-deck accommodation. Some advantages to this aft positioning of halyard winches are reduced windage and increased stability, both due to the fact that the weight of the crew is below deck level.

An alternative and probably more common halyard winch arrangement is grouping the winches in a semicircle around the base of the mast. The order in

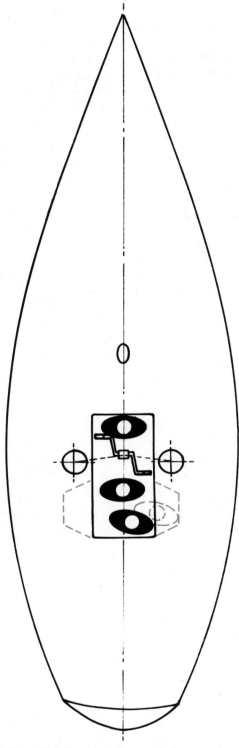

*Figure 6-14.* Visibility is an important factor when tailing a winch. This figure shows how the cockpit could be extended to move the tailer outboard for better vision. The extensions would have to be carefully integrated with the below deck accommodation for this layout to be successful.

which the winches are positioned is governed by the order in which halyards enter and exit from the mast. This avoids halyard crossovers. Here again, space is a key concern. For one thing, there must be enough space under the boom for the halyard operator to work. Putting the main halyard winch on the centreline, for example, may look fine in a deck drawing, but a boat is typically head-to-wind when the mainsail is being raised, so the boom moves constantly. Therefore, if the boom is low, say under 3½ feet above the deck, the halyard operator will have difficulty sweating up the last few inches.

Spacing considerations between the halyard winches and other deck gear are also important with this around-the-mast type of winch configuration. Consider first the distance between the winches and the mast itself. If the winches are too close to the mast, the halyard lead may be unfair, causing riding turns. The problem might be partially solved by fitting a block under the winch in order to slope it aft, but this will probably render the winch virtually useless for any other job. In addition, it might also make smooth operation of the winch impossible due to interference from the boom vang. Remember that the vang is considerably larger than the thin pencil line on a deck drawing suggests. On larger boats, hydraulic vangs may be up to 3 inches in diameter, plus tubing. So, even if a halyard winch is not elevated by a block under its base, care must still be taken to observe where the vang will be when the boom is in different positions. This kind of attention to possible obstructions of halyard winches is necessary not only regarding the vang, but also regarding any other protuberance from the boom, such as a reefing winch.

A final possible location for certain halyard winches is on the mast. If this position is chosen, attention must be given to both space and ergonomic factors. Concerning spacing, a winch and cleat arrangement drawing (like the one described in Chapter 2) should probably be made to ensure fair leads and no cross-overs. And as for ergonomic efficiency, the winches should be sited no higher than chest level, but no lower than the knees. This will increase the ease with which one man can pull the halyard off the winch while another winds.

*Designing the Coachroof*

A second major design problem in the mast area of a boat is the coachroof. First, consideration must be given to the width of the coachroof. For instance, if a crewman stands 18 inches away from the mast to pull a halyard, and the half breadth of the cabin trunk is

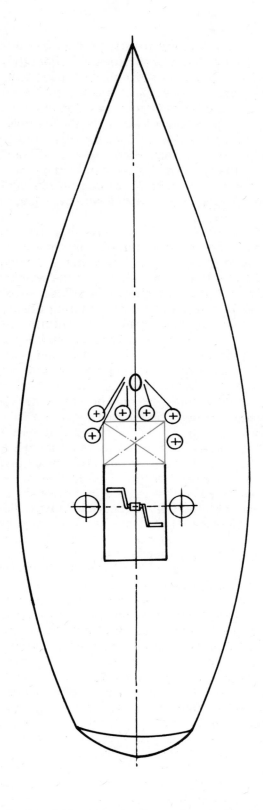

*Figure 6-15*. A hatch at the forward end of a middeck cockpit provides a place from which a crewman can operate the halyard winches. Note the ideal work height.

only 20 inches at that point, he may easily slip off the cabin top. Or, if the boat is heeled, he may have to stand on the deck below the cabin, thus reducing his reach and the efficiency of his movements.

The slope of the coachroof is also a primary design concern, particularly for safety reasons. If the front of the coachroof is gradually sloped, say at an angle between 35 and 50 degrees, the resulting profile may be aesthetically pleasing, and even appear to be a reasonably efficient working platform. In actual practice, however, a surface with this kind of slope is rather difficult to get a firm footing on, and it can be especially slippery when constructed of fibreglass and a crewman is wearing wet sea-boots.

Finally, the length of a coachroof and its height may also present certain obstacles to efficient deck layout. If a coachroof is designed so that it ends before reaching the mast, it is difficult to lead halyards to winches mounted on top. Consequently, the halyards must be led either around the coachroof, which requires extra turning blocks and thus more friction, or to the sidedecks, which provides a possible tripline for crewmen working at night. Consider, too, the potential problems of having a high coachroof and a low boom. Crewmen moving across the boat would have to go either forward of the mast or back aft of the boom, and this, of course, would only add to the confusion during a tack.

## The Foredeck

Finally, we come to the foredeck, an area of the boat that presents relatively few problems in designing for work efficiency. The most efficient thing that can be done with a foredeck is to make it as clean and open as possible. This both reduces windage and facilitates sail packing.

### Designing a Clean and Open Deck

Space is a foredeck hand's main requirement, and sometimes it can be in short supply. When dip-pole spinnaker gybes are made, for instance, a crewman must stand on the point of the bow ahead of the forestay while the pole swings through the foretriangle. This space problem is most extreme on a twelve metre where, in some cases, the foredeckman has to pivot on the ball of one foot because room in front of the forestay is so tight.

Fortunately, we do not all sail regularly on twelve metres, and the area around the forestay can be increased if required. Pulpits can also be designed to allow the foredeckman a good, comfortable position, holding him close to the forestay, but not too close. Also, if the sails have hanks, it may be worthwhile to design the pulpit so as to allow a man to sit in it while he unhanks the headsail during a sail change. Usually, though, a modern racing boat will have a luff groove device and the foredeckman will work in an area just abaft the headstay. In this case, consideration must be given to a safety factor: the toerail must be carried far enough forward to prevent the crewman's foot from slipping out through the pulpit as the boat pitches.

In the effort to achieve that clean, open look, it is important not to forget other safety requirements on the foredeck. Hatches, spinnaker poles, and staysail tracks provide many natural handholds for crewmen, so there is usually no need for special rails. There is, however, a need for one or two strategically placed padeyes for a man to hook his safety harness onto. The most essential of these is in the bow area, and most especially within range of the tack fitting.

### Designing Foredeck Hatches

Another design consideration in the foredeck area is the hatches. On smaller boats, these should be large enough for a man to pass through with ease. The shoulder dimension of an average person is about 19 inches, which governs the minimum size hatch that can be fitted. On larger boats, the size of the biggest sail bag is the governing factor. On larger boats, too, a sail platform under the hatch makes it easier to get sails and crew in and out.

Remember also that forehatches must often be opened by crewmen with cold, wet hands. Consequently, large handles and clasps should be fitted rather than small, hard to operate ones. But the fittings should not be so large as to interfere with sails or sheets—or, perhaps, misplaced feet.

\* \* \* \* \* \*

We have been discussing some of the ways that the factor of efficiency enters into the deck design equation. But this has been only a first look at the problem. Efficiency is the primary consideration in racing deck layout, and as such it comes up again and again in the process of designing and analysing deck arrangements. In the following chapter, for example, we will look at how certain features of the interior of a boat can sometimes compromise the efficiency of the deck above, as well as some of the ways that an efficient deck layout can limit space and living comfort below deck.

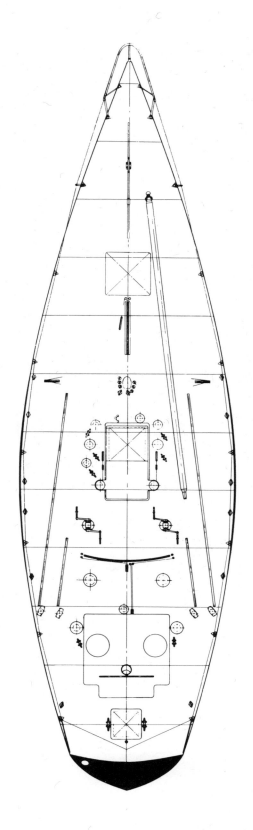

*Scaramouche* (1977), owned by Mr Charles E. Kirsh and designed by German Frers. (See also jacket picture.)

149

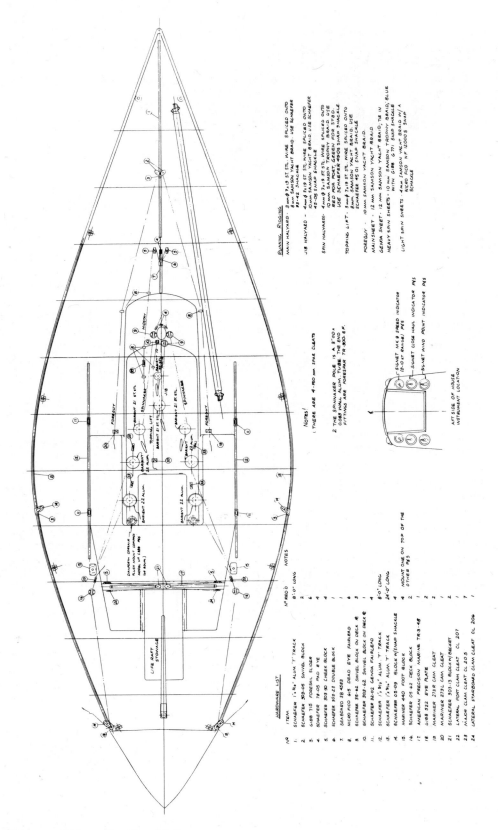

*Perception*, a Half Tonner designed by Gary Mull.

CHAPTER SEVEN
# Considering the Interior

The deck and the interior are not separate, unrelated areas of a boat. Quite the opposite. Because the deck forms the roof of the interior, deck layout and interior design are always closely interrelated. Certain things on the deck–such as cockpits, companionway hatches and ladders, the mast and chainplates–have a significant influence on interior space below. Similarly, requirements below deck–the need for adequate headroom especially–can affect the working arrangement above. One cannot fully discuss the topic of deck layout, therefore, without also discussing interior design.

The extent to which deck layout influences interior design, or interior design deck layout, is really a matter of priorities. On a purely racing boat, the interior is dictated almost entirely by the demand of the deck. This, however, can be carried to extremes. A certain Admiral's Cup boat several years back had tubes for storing the spinnaker poles that were set into the coach roof and ran below deck. This meant that two six-inch diameter tubes approximately 17 feet long extended through the main cabin. In addition, all the halyards were carried from the mast, below deck, and then out to various winches mounted on the bridge deck. Some ten wires crossed the living area. All this deck gear intruding on the interior was particularly inconvenient for the cook who was left with not much more than 10 inches of clearance above the stove!

Few wives would take delight in this interior arrangement. Nor would it be the choice of many owners. Most of us, no matter how committed we are to racing, want to use our boats for cruising once in a while. And if not, then at least we want to be able to resell them to people who may. Consequently, the most practical ocean racer is one that has a well-designed, efficient deck, but also a bit more below than a dark cell cluttered with equipment.

How does a designer strike the right balance between stripped-out efficiency and living comfort?

The first step is to find out the owner's priorities. When the architect knows what things the owner considers most important and what least, he can make design decisions accordingly. But regardless of the particular owner's priorities, there will always be features of the interior that affect the layout of the deck, as well as features of the deck that influence the interior. This chapter considers the interaction between these two areas of the boat, and how the needs of each can be made as compatible as possible.

## Deck Fittings That Influence the Interior

We begin with those deck fittings that affect interior space below. Most notable, of course, are cockpits, companionway hatches, and masts. But other items on deck also influence interior layout, although to a much smaller extent. Because together these comparatively minor factors can have a sizable influence on how living space below deck is arranged, we will consider them in the sections that follow, along with the more major factors.

### Cockpits

Not long ago, when foul weather gear was not as waterproof as it is today, the cockpit was considered a place of refuge from the elements. Quite often, a 'doghouse' was placed in front of the cockpit to afford the helmsman and other crew members some measure of protection from wind and sea. On modern ocean racers, of course, all this has changed. Today's highly effective water- and wind-resistant clothing allows the crew to spend far more time on deck, usually sitting on the weather rail. The only remaining purposes of the cockpit are a place for the helmsman to stand and a place for the winch operators to work. Consequently,

151

the old deep, protective cockpit lined with seats for the crew has given way to a number of smaller, shallower crewpits sited so as to get maximum efficiency from the largest number of winches.

How does the modern cockpit affect the interior of a boat? Although its influence may not be as great as that of the large, deep cockpit of the past, its influence on interior arrangement is still significant. Depending on its position, even a shallow cockpit can impose severe limitations on the living space below it.

### The Helmsman's Cockpit

On boats with tiller steering, the helmsman's cockpit need only be a foot well for use when steering downwind. On wheel-steered boats, on the other hand, the helmsman's cockpit can be quite large, depending upon the size of the wheel.

Typically, the helmsman's cockpit on a wheel-steered boat is so far aft that it does not really intrude on the interior living area. If the boat has an unusually beamy stern, however, a quarter berth might be pushed all the way aft, and the depth of the helmsman's cockpit would then dictate the room above the berth. But it is not easy to fit a quarter berth in this position. Unless it has twin wheels, a wide-sterned boat tends to have a large diameter steering wheel which must be recessed into the cockpit sole, thus leaving even less space below deck. Also, the sheaves and wires of the steering mechanism hang down under the cockpit, tending to interfere with clearance above a berth.

Above deck, there is one primary drawback to locating the helmsman's cockpit as far aft as it can go.

This is the absence of space behind the cockpit for a lazarette. With such a layout, therefore, other areas must be found for stowing the gear that would normally be put in the aft lazarette. Of course, some sailors would argue that being forced to stow heavy gear further forward is a good thing because of the benefit in weight distribution it creates.

### The Aft Crew Cockpit

The area directly forward of the helm has traditionally been an important work place for the crew, and on smaller boats, those up to One Ton size, it still is. On some boats, the aft crew cockpit is simply an extension of the helmsman's cockpit, while on others it is an entirely separate area. Consequently, aft crew cockpits vary considerably in size and shape.

A common shape is the T cockpit. The crew is located at the base of the T and the helmsman in the crossbar. The winches are bolted to the deck at the forward end of the crew area, in other words, at the very bottom of the T. When well designed, the T-shaped cockpit has the advantage of keeping volume to a minimum while concentrating the weight of the crew. But it is quite difficult to design a small area that can comfortably fit a winch operator, a tailer, and a crewman to throw off the line, so the T cockpit is not always as effective as it might seem in theory.

A better idea for inshore racing may be the U-shaped aft cockpit. For boats with tiller steering, this is an extremely comfortable arrangement. The helmsman stands or sits in the bottom of the U while the crewmen sit in the wings. This distributes the weight of the crew

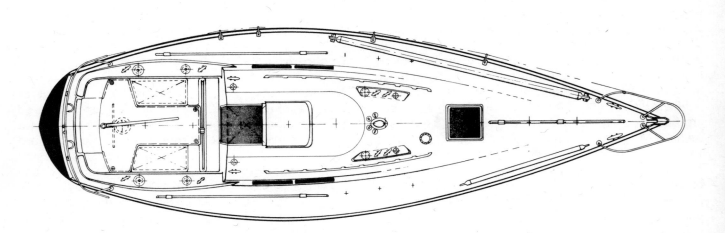

A stock C & C 33.

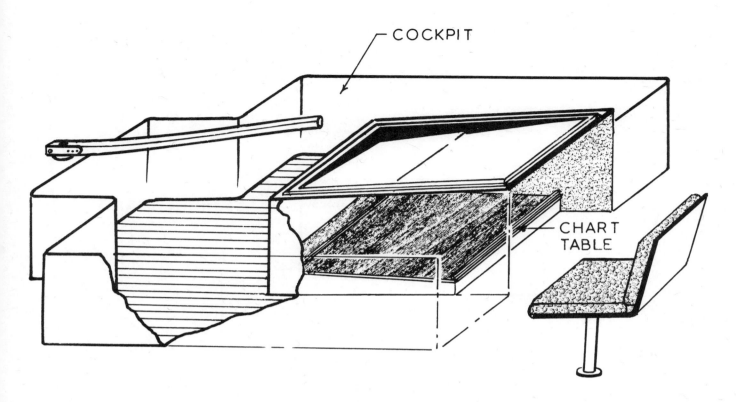

COCKPIT

CHART
TABLE

*Figure 7-1.* A U-shaped aft cockpit with a chart table below it.

as far outboard as possible, but allows the men to face inboard. It also concentrates crew weight on the weather rail if the sheet leads are taken to the high side. The halyard winches can be led to the forward end of the U if the boat has a coachroof; otherwise, the halyard winches can be brought toward the middle of the U. With a U-shaped aft cockpit, it is also covenient to place the chart table in the central console formed by the surrounding well. Figure 7-1 shows a possible arrangement.

Unfortunately, an aft crew cockpit, regardless of its shape, intrudes a great deal on the interior accommodation below. A traditional solution is to site the engine under the cockpit, with a quarter berth on each side. Another idea, advanced by S&S and Nautor, is an aft cabin with two berths. The engine is placed forward of the cabin, and a high bridge deck gives interior headroom.

### The Middeck Cockpit

On larger boats, the search for a more efficient crew work area has led to the development of the middeck cockpit, located about half way between the helmsman's cockpit and the mast. The primary sheet winches are placed slightly outboard of this central crewpit and

are operated from a pedestal sited within it. This arrangement has several benefits. First, it enables the winches to be positioned at the optimum height; and second, it keeps the pedestal winders and tailers low in the boat, thus reducing windage and lowering the centre of gravity.

But for all its advantages on deck, the middeck cockpit imposes severe limitations below, and it takes a skilled designer to avoid a completely chopped up interior accommodation. Several things, of course, can be sited under a middeck cockpit, but in each case there are drawbacks. Figure 7-2a shows a galley located in this space. When the boat is heeled to A–A, the headroom is so low that the cook cannot stand upright, and his vision of the work area is also seriously impaired. Figure 7-2b shows berths under the cockpit. Sleeping here, however, with crewmen stomping directly up above, is a sure way to get very little rest. And finally, the engine could also be positioned in this location, as illustrated in Figure 7-2c. But having the engine so close to the centre of the boat is likely to result in a high engine and propeller factor, and thus to a higher rating.

Another disadvantage the middeck cockpit creates below deck is the way in which it distributes the flow of traffic to the sides of the hull. Unfortunately, this is

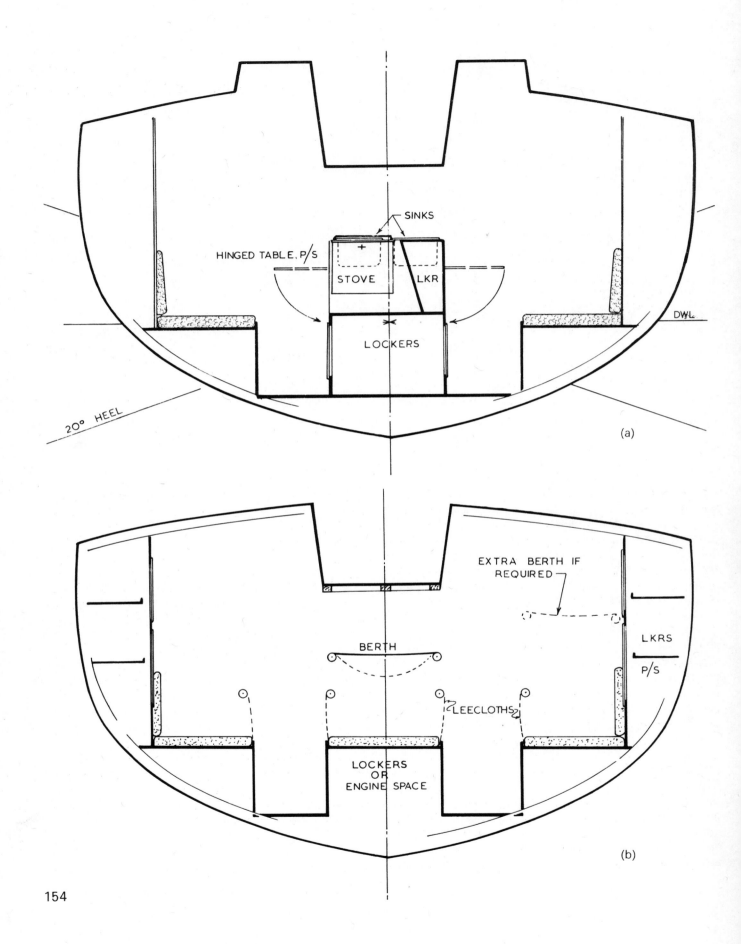

SINKS

HINGED TABLE, P/S

STOVE          LKR

LOCKERS

DWL

20° HEEL

(a)

EXTRA BERTH IF
REQUIRED

BERTH

LKRS

P/S

LEECLOTHS

LOCKERS
OR
ENGINE SPACE

(b)

154

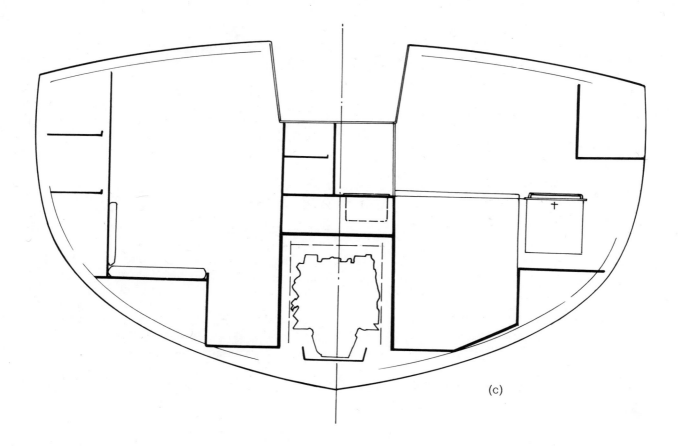

*Figure 7-2.* (a) A galley under the middeck cockpit. (b) Berths under the middeck cockpit. (c) An engine under the middeck cockpit.

precisely where headroom is likely to be lowest. Figure 7–2a shows how a coaming around the cockpit can help gain extra interior headroom. And because this arrangement also raises the level of the winches the cockpit sole can be higher, thus providing more space beneath it.

### Yawl and Ketch Cockpits

Up to now, we have been considering cockpits on sloops, but what about ketches and yawls? On these boats, the helmsman's cockpit is rarely located directly aft of the mizzen because the helmsman's visibility would be seriously impaired. Consequently, the helm is placed forward of the mizzen, imposing predictable restrictions on the accommodation below. The problems in living area are similar to those created by middeck cockpits. On a yawl or ketch, however, the interior space behind the helmsman's cockpit is sometimes used as a separate owner's stateroom with either a walk-through from the main cabin or an aft ladder leading down from the helm area.

### Hatches

Hatches, like cockpits, can have an important effect on interior space below. Here we will consider the two kinds of hatches that probably have the greatest influence on living area—companionway hatches and sail-handling hatches.

### Companionway Hatches

When a racing boat has a separate sail-handling hatch, the main companionway hatch should be small in order to keep lost deck space to a minimum. A companionway hatch, however, must still be large enough to allow a man to pass through comfortably. The absolute minimum width is 20 inches, but this is quite tight. Up to 24 inches in width is more usual. The length of the hatch can be calculated by measuring the horizontal extension of the ladder beneath it. The hatch should be about 6 to 8 inches longer than the point where the base of the ladder ends, or else an ascending crewman might hit his head. Figure 7-3 shows these dimensions.

155

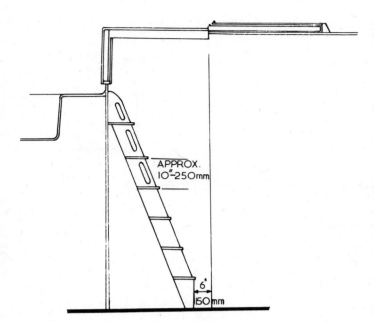

APPROX.
10"-250mm

6"
150mm

LADDER SLOPE NOT MORE THAN 72°

*Figure 7-3.* Dimensions of a hatch over a ladder.

The ladder leading from the companionway hatch to the interior should also meet certain design requirements. One is optimum slope, which is greatly influenced by available space under the hatchway. As a basic rule, a ladder should be positioned at an angle that allows crewmen to ascend and descend easily. The most comfortable slope is 60 degrees to the horizontal, but a ladder may be as steep as 72 degrees if space in the cabin is at a premium. If, for reasons of fit, a ladder must be any steeper than this, it should be completely vertical. The width of a companionway ladder is also important. The minimum width is 14 inches and the maximum is 18; beyond this dimension, the ladder takes up too much cabin space. And finally, the measurement between the rungs of a ladder must be considered too. The ideal step distance is 10 inches.

Ladders for companionway hatches can be constructed of either alloy or wood, and each has slightly different design requirements. If lightness is the main consideration, alloy tubing is by far the best material to use. One of the most important design features to remember to incorporate into an alloy tubing ladder is a series of flats covered in nonslip which are welded onto the rungs. Wooden ladders are more commonly found on boats used for both racing and cruising. It is customary to make the steps of a wooden ladder 6 inches wide, and to place nonslip material on the forward side of each step.

Quite often a hatchway may be used as a cockpit when a boat is racing in protected waters near shore. A good arrangement is a vertical alloy ladder with a platform that can be securely attached to it and later removed. Such a system, with its effects on cabin space below, is shown in Figure 7-4. When the platform is in use, it is advisable to have a canvas hatch screen to protect the interior from rain and spray.

*Sail Hatches*

A major focus of interaction between the deck and the interior of a boat is the sail-handling hatch. Ideally, a sail hatch should be immediately over the sail stowage bins, so that it will not be necessary to drag the sails through the interior accommodation before passing them up on deck. And because most sail handling is done on the foredeck, the sail hatch has traditionally been located forward. The current rating rule, however, has made this traditional position a matter of some dispute. When a boat is measured, sails must be stowed aft of the mainmast, so on the race course, any sails stowed in the forepeak increase undesirable bow down trim. It did not take designers long to realize this fact. As a result, the sail hatches on a few boats are now being located aft—in spite of the obvious problems involved in moving sails quickly forward over various deck obstructions when the boat is pitching heavily on a dark night.

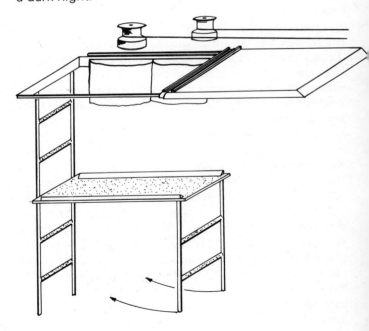

*Figure 7-4.* A crew platform under a hatch which can be removed when not in use.

But wherever its location on a boat, the sail hatch, and its accompanying sail bins beneath, lay claim to a great deal of interior living space. For instance, on a strictly racing boat, separate bins for each sail may be used instead of sail bags. On a boat of, say, 45 feet overall, this would mean perhaps ten or twelve individual canvas sail bins, each measuring approximately 2 feet by 3 feet. Thus, the total sail stowage space would necessarily be quite large, and on many boats it would even take up the entire area forward of the mast.

## Masts and Tie Rods

The mast of a boat is another factor that has a great deal of influence on the living space below deck. Like certain kinds of cockpits and hatches, a mast is positioned where it must be, and the designer is left with the problem of planning the accommodation around it. Tie rods, which prevent the forces exerted by the rigging from lifting the deck, also have an affect on interior arrangement, although to a far lesser extent than the mast. The degree to which both these deck factors influence interior space is discussed in the following sections.

### Masts and Mast Reinforcement

Masts can be mounted in two different ways, either stepped on deck or stepped on the keel. Most racing boats have keel-stepped masts because they allow a smaller mast section.

Regardless of how they are mounted, masts require structural reinforcement. Figure 7-5, which shows the loads on a mast and the area around it, gives a good idea of the kinds of reinforcement that are needed. Note how the tension at the chainplates is transmitted to the hull, and how the deck between the chainplates and the mast is under compression. If reinforcement in key areas is inadequate, the mast will be lost.

Methods of mast reinforcement vary depending upon the material the boat is made of. Alloy boats generally have at least one web frame in the same hull section as the mast. Usually, though, there are additional frames to take the load off the chainplates. When chainplates happen to fall between two frames, a longitudinal plate is welded to the frames at the depth the designer calls for, but he must always avoid requesting critical welding in areas that are difficult to reach. Otherwise, the job may be done improperly and the plate will be structurally weak; or the welding may simply not be done at all, and if the weld was included

in the design calculations you may end up waving goodbye to the rig!

How are masts on wooden and fibreglass boats reinforced? On wood boats, the methods of structural support differ depending upon which rules are followed. Lloyd's rules call for three frames of extra strength positioned fore and aft of the mast. But quite often, some form of stainless steel or alloy web frame is used as well. Masts on fibreglass boats are often reinforced by a 'top hat' web frame. The frame is bolted at the bottom to the mast step and extends around the hull

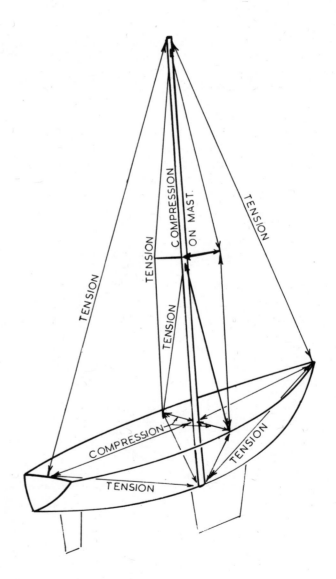

*Figure 7-5.*   The forces a mast can exert on a boat.

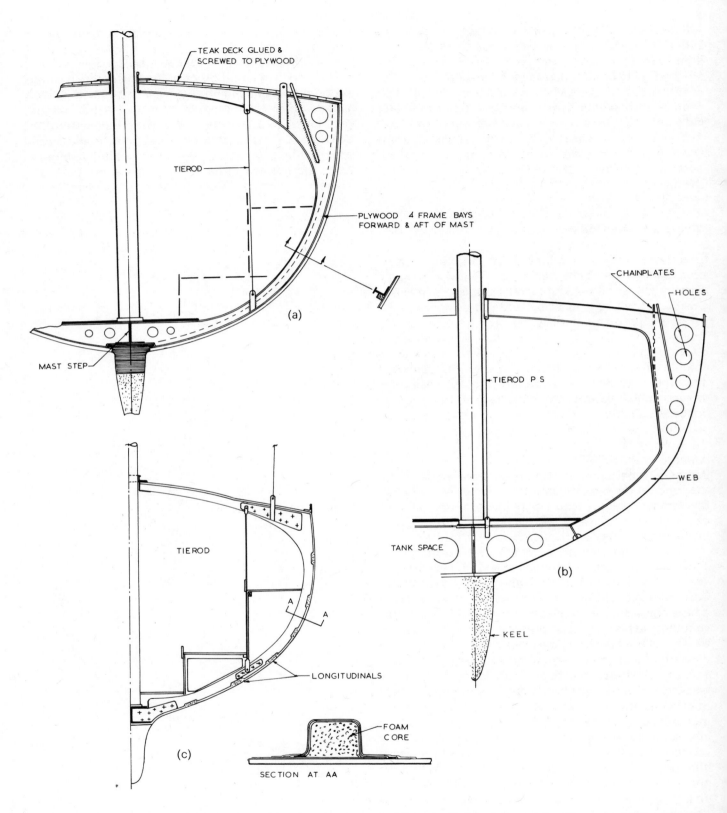

*Figure 7-6.* (a) A stainless steel web frame construction in a wooden boat. (b) A web frame in an alloy boat. (c) A web frame in a fibreglass boat.

158

and across the deck, forming a continuous web which incorporates the mast partners. Figure 7-6a, b, and c shows the methods of reinforcing the mast on a 42 foot boat constructed of different materials.

When the mast and its reinforcement protrude into the interior accommodation, they have an enormous affect on living space. Traditionally, designers attempted to solve this problem by making the mast and its structural bulkhead the forward end of the main cabin. On modern sailing boats, however, the main cabin typically extends much farther forward than on older boats, so the mast becomes a major interior obstruction. To hold wasted space to a minimum, a table is usually fitted around the mast. Berths are also positioned far enough inboard to clear the web frame supporting the mast and the chainplates attaching the shrouds. Overhead lockers can then be designed to help cover these structural reinforcements.

### Tie Rods

Looking back at Figure 7-5, you can see how the compressive forces exterted horizontally from the chainplates toward the mast are coupled with the upward pull of the halyards. If the boat was improperly constructed, the deck could lift up amidships and possibly break. A tie rod running from a strong point on the deck down to the mast step prevents this from happening. Large boats may have two tie rods for this purpose, one about 6 inches forward of the mast and the other about 6 inches aft of it. Tie rods positioned this close to the mast are relatively unobtrusive below deck. Often, they can be disguised completely by fitting stanchions around them.

On some boats, additional tie rods are required. They should be used whenever there is a heavy upward pull on the deck and no structural reinforcement beneath. For example, if there is no bulkhead under the fitting where the babystay attaches to the deck, a tie rod should be installed to transmit the load to the keel. A tie rod used for this purpose could be either rod or wire, usually 1 × 19 and the same diameter as the stay.

They can also be used on a beamy boat to allow berths to be positioned far outboard without obstruction from the web frame. Figure 7-6a or c shows how this is done. The frame is made shallower and the chainplate is ended at the bottom of the deck beam. A tie rod is then run from the deck beam, inboard of the berth, to the lower frame of the web. This arrangement provides room for a berth while the load of the chainplate is still transmitted to the keel.

## Winches

On many boats, winches have very little if any effect on interior living space. There are, however, a few exceptions. One is a boat with a centreboard winch which operates a wire or rope pennant leading from the deck to the centreboard box; the pennant is usually contained in a tube which runs through the interior cabin. Another exception is a boat with a modular linked winch system, where the bevel gears and linkages are below deck and consequently potential head knockers. We will discuss the influence that each of these factors has on interior design, as well as the special problems that winches may impose on the interior of a fibreglass boat.

### Centreboard Winches and Pennant Tubes

As shown in Figure 7-7, a pennant tube is usually designed so that if the centreboard sticks when being

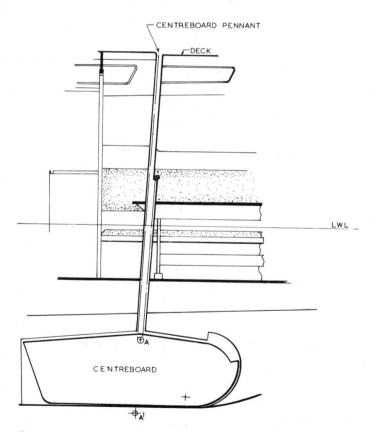

*Figure 7-7.* A centreboard pennant tube. Note how pin A is just exposed at A' when the board is fully lowered.

lowered, a boat hook handle can be pushed down the tube to free it. On the other hand, if the winch jams when the centreboard is being raised, the lazy end of the pennant can be used to pull the board all the way up.

How can a pennant tube be positioned below deck so that it will be as unobstructive as possible? One answer is to design the tube so that it serves some secondary function—a stanchion, for instance, or a table support. Another is to make sure that the pennant tube does not get in the way of the main companionway hatch, since on many boats these two are potentially very close together.

*Modular Linked Winch Systems*
How many times have you banged your head on some piece of equipment below deck? No doubt many times. Modular linked winch systems create one more overhead obstacle that a crewman can potentially bump into. Yet lumps on the head need not be one of the sailor's standard insignia. With good design of overhead protrusions such as winch linkages, head-knocking problems can be virtually eliminated—unless, of course, they are of the 'against-a-brick-wall' variety.

The overhead obstruction caused by winch linkages cannot be reduced by repositioning, since correctly siting sheet winches, particularly the genoa winch, is a critical part of efficient deck layout. The extent to which bevel gears and link rods protrude into the interior, however, can be minimized by raising the winches on low pedestals. On alloy or wooden boats, which have fairly thick deck beams, a slight raising of

the winches may be all that is needed to prevent the gears and rods from showing at all. Often, a locker can be fitted around the equipment, and on larger boats, the overhead liner can be lowered a little, as well as the cabin sole if required to maintain adequate headroom.

But when all possible design solutions fail, and the winch gears and linkages must unavoidably protrude into the cabin, it is best to cover the equipment with flexible plywood, making the obstruction as gently sloping as possible. The arrangement shown in Figure 7-8, for example, will certainly cause less damage to a crewman's head should he happen to walk into it than would some more sharp-cornered object.

*Winches on Fibreglass Boats*
On smaller fibreglass boats that have no overhead liner in the interior, winch bolts simply protrude through the deck head and are capped with domed nuts. As tiny and harmless looking as these nuts may appear, they have an unfortunate penchant for scraping the heads and snagging the hair of passing crewmen. A good solution to the problem is to mount the winches on small, raised bases, which below deck allow the areas around the bolts to be recessed. This is quite easy for a manufacturer to do at the time the deck mold is constructed. The recesses can then be either left open or filled with wooden plugs. The same solution, of course, can be used for making other overhead bolts on small fibreglass boats less obstructive—such as the bolts that hold the genoa tracks and turning block, for instance, or those that secure cleats.

**Instruments and Wiring**

Instruments on deck are rarely sited so that they protrude into the interior. Instead, most are fitted on cockpit bulkheads or in special watertight boxes. The main design problem from inside the boat, therefore, is simply to make sure that if instruments do go through a bulkhead, the backs are easily accessible for adjustment and repair.

Although instruments themselves generally have very little influence on interior arrangement, instrument wiring may pose somewhat more of a problem. This is true primarily when a boat has no overhead liner behind which both instrument and interior wiring can be hidden. In this case, care should be taken to run the wiring in areas where it cannot be grabbed as an emergency handrail. Also, if wiring is to be run though holes in deck beams, some form of conduit tube is recommended to prevent chafe.

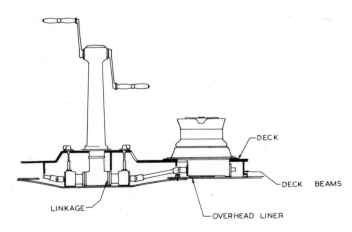

*Figure 7-8.* A method of 'hiding' a winch linkage so that crewmen will not bang their heads below deck.

## Hydraulics

Like instruments, hydraulic control panels must be accessible from the rear, so the panel is often mounted in a hole cut through a bulkhead. Similarly, the pressure tubing, which exits from the back of the panel, must pass through holes cut in the deck, a bulkhead, or the hull in order to reach the hydraulic rams. To keep the interior of the boat as dry as possible, all these holes must be watertight. It is also a good idea to avoid positioning the hydraulic control panel or a ram over bunks or sail bins, where leaking hydraulic fluid might cause substantial damage.

Hydraulic pressure tubes should be led through the interior so as to intrude as little as possible on living space, and so as not to become convenient head knockers or grab rails. Remember, too, that hydraulic tubes contain steel and should be carefully positioned away from compasses. For this reason, it is often useful to draw a hydraulic diagram for a boat, as shown in Figure 7-9.

## Interior Features that Influence the Deck

On the average racing boat, the deck has a far greater effect on the interior than the interior has on the deck. Still, features of the accommodation do have an influence above deck. This is particularly true of provisions made for adequate headroom, although other factors—vents and ports, for example—also have a minor impact on deck layout. We will consider these and other topics in the sections that follow.

### Interior Headroom

A fundamental interior design problem, especially on smaller boats, is providing adequate headroom. Extra headroom can be gained in several ways, and each affects the deck arrangement to varying degrees. Coachroofs or trunk cabins undoubtedly have the greatest impact above deck. But because a coachroof usually reduces the efficiency of the deck layout and always creates additional windage, many modern ocean racers have completely flush decks. The coachroof, however, is still far from extinct, especially on boats used for both racing and cruising.

*Coachroofs or Trunk Cabins*
One of the first rules of designing a coachroof is that it should be as small as possible, no larger than is called

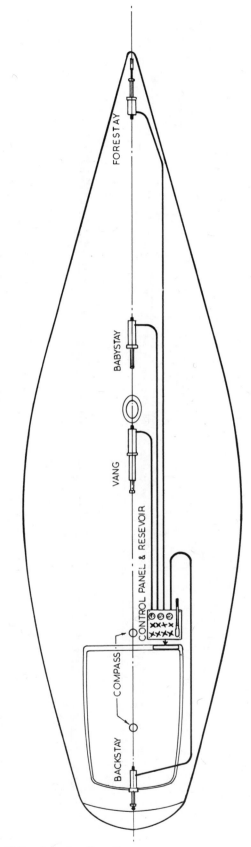

*Figure 7-9.* A hydraulics diagram.

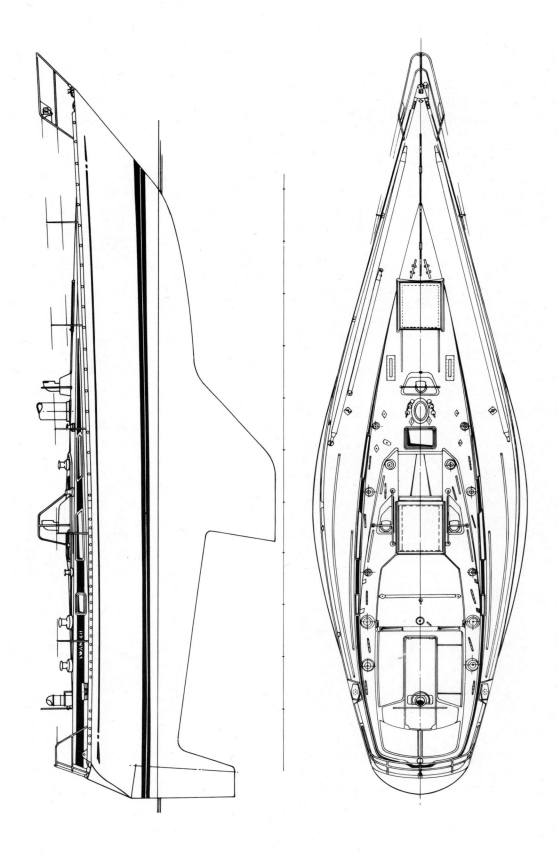

*Figure 7-10.* A Nautor coachroof.

162

for to give the headroom required. Coachroof width is especially important. There should be enough room between the coachroof and the sides of the deck for the crew to sit safely and comfortably. This means at least 10 inches, but 18 inches is preferable because the extra space allows someone to walk easily past a person sitting on the weather rail.

A second rule of coachroof design concerns safety. The front and sides of a coachroof should be almost vertical, or slope at less than 60° from horizontal. Otherwise it could be dangerous for walking on when the boat is underway. The coachroofs on Nautor boats, such as the one shown in Figure 7-10, meet both these design requirements: they provide the interior headroom needed without being excessively large, and they are safe to walk on while sailing.

Nautor coachroofs are also aesthetically pleasing, another design aim particularly important on cruiser-racers. A cockpit coaming, although discarded on many custom racing boats in the interest of efficiency, can nevertheless help to fair the coachroof into a streamlined profile. Rather than appearing to be chopped off bluntly at the aft end, the coachroof appears longer and smoother because it is extended by the lines of the coaming.

Coachroofs, no matter how well designed, can impose special problems on deck efficiency. Consider, for example, Figure 7-11a. Any halyards led to the winch must extend from the mast at the height of the cabin top in order to provide a fair lead. But a number of exit boxes in the same area could seriously weaken the mast. Consequently, a bale of some sort must be fitted at the required height to take the turning blocks. But this would mean that the angle of the boom vang would have to be smaller and therefore not as efficient. Also, given the height of this coachroof, it might be difficult to wind the winch when the boom is directly over it because the vang could interfere with the handle.

Figure 7-11b shows a possible solution. By extending the coachroof farther forward so that the mast passes through it, more interior headroom is gained and the problem of getting a fair lead to the halyard winch is solved with no extra strain on the mast. The vang, however, is still not as efficient as it could be, and the larger coachroof creates slight additional windage. But overall, the advantages achieved are well worth the costs. The alternative arrangement shown in Figure 7-11c would be preferable if the halyard winches are to be operated from the aft cockpit.

In addition to problems with halyard leads and vangs, coachroofs can also limit the efficiency of sails. The sheet lead for a staysail, for instance, may have to be

mounted on the top of a coachroof, and this means a loss in sail area because the clew of the staysail is higher than normal. Similarly, the effective area of a genoa is reduced if the genoa track runs along the deck on the side of a coachroof.

Finally, coachroofs can also have an impact on the ease with which crewmen can move from one side of the boat to the other. On a small boat with a low boom and a high coachroof, the men on the rail may have difficulty getting across the boat during a tack. As a result, they may be forced to climb through the cockpit or to go around the front of the mast, and either route reduces tacking efficiency.

*Deck Camber*

Clearly, coachroofs require some compromise in deck layout. So before planning for a cabin top, it is always advisable to check if the extra headroom needed below

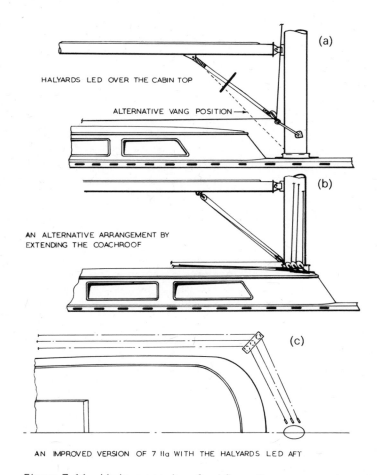

HALYARDS LED OVER THE CABIN TOP

ALTERNATIVE VANG POSITION →

(a)

(b)

AN ALTERNATIVE ARRANGEMENT BY EXTENDING THE COACHROOF

(c)

AN IMPROVED VERSION OF 7 11a WITH THE HALYARDS LED AFT

*Figure 7-11.* Various coachroof configurations.

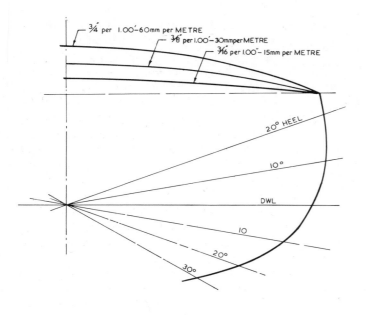

Figure 7-12. Sections through various deck camber curves.

deck could be gained simply with a little more deck camber.

The ideal deck camber is $\frac{3}{8}$ inch per 1 foot of deck beam, although up to $\frac{3}{4}$ inch per foot is permissible. Any more than this has serious drawbacks. First, the leeward side becomes too steep to work on when the boat heels a few degrees; and second, the crown in the middle of the deck is too high for a sheet to be led to weather, unless the winch is mounted on a block. Deck camber less than $\frac{1}{8}$ inch per foot also has disadvantages. Perhaps most important, the rigidity of the deck is reduced and the entire structure is somewhat weakened. Moreover, camber this slight makes the deck look flat or dished, which is aesthetically unattractive. The differences in appearance between these three possible deck cambers is shown in Figure 7-12. By tilting the page until the 20 degree line is horizontal, you can see how the $\frac{3}{4}$ inch per foot curve becomes dangerously steep on the leeward side when the boat is heeled. If this much deck camber is essential to provide adequate headroom below deck, the only alternatives would be either a raised crown in the middle of the deck, as illustrated in figure 7-13, or a coachroof.

To design a deck with a $\frac{3}{8}$ inch per foot camber, begin by dividing the deck into eight equal parts, four on each side of the centreline. If the maximum beam of the boat is 12 feet, the height of the deck above the hull will be $4\frac{1}{2}$ inches at the centreline–12 × $\frac{3}{8}''$ = $4\frac{1}{2}''$. From

here, the camber of the deck at each of the eight dividing points can be easily calculated. At one quarter of the distance outboard on either side of the centreline, the camber is $(0.25)^2 \times 4.5'' = 0.2813''$ or just over $\frac{1}{4}$ inch. At one half the distance outboard, the camber is $(0.5)^2 \times 4.5'' = 1.125''$ or $1\frac{1}{8}$ inches. And at three quarters the distance out, it is $(0.75)^2 \times 4.5'' = 2.53''$ or about $2\frac{1}{2}$ inches. By drawing a fair line from the edges of the deck to the centreline through these points, you arrive at the curve of the deck, as shown in Figure 7-14. If the deck is to have a high crown at the centre, then another camber curve must be worked out and superimposed over the first one.

## Fittings for Natural Lighting and Ventilation

To provide natural lighting in the interior, most boats have either clear acrylic panels fitted into the deck or small opening hatches. Because these fittings have among the lowest priority of all items on the deck of a racing boat, they should always be positioned after the major pieces of deck gear.

The same holds true when siting the vents that circulate fresh air below deck. But although vents are one of the last things added to a deck plan, they should not be carelessly positioned. Avoid, for example, placing vents directly over berths, where a wash of sea above deck could prove extremely annoying to sleeping crewmen. And avoid compromising a good location for the essential galley vent. Also, make sure that vents are not positioned so close to winches that they interfere

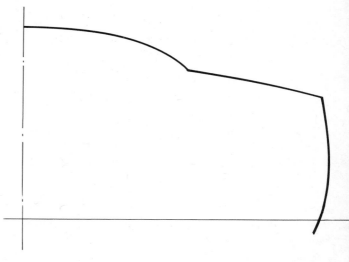

Figure 7-13. A section through a raised crown in the middle of the deck. This will fair into the deck at about the mast.

164

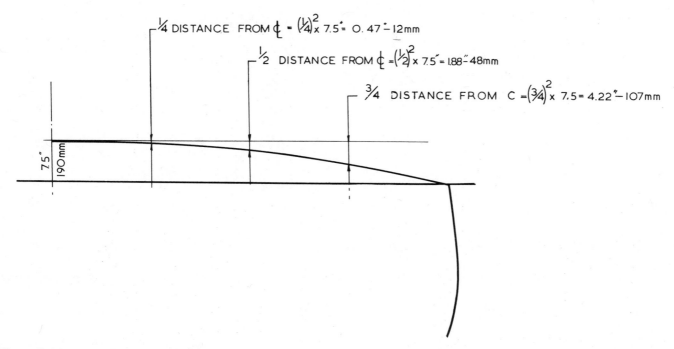

MAX BEAM AT DECK = 12.00 ft − 3.66 M.
CAMBER = ⅝" −16 mm PER FOOT− 0.3 M = ⅝ × 12' = 7.5"−190 mm

¼ DISTANCE FROM ₵ = (¼)² × 7.5 = 0.47"−12 mm

½ DISTANCE FROM ₵ = (½)² × 7.5 = 1.88"−48 mm

¾ DISTANCE FROM C = (¾)² × 7.5 = 4.22"−107 mm

7.5"
190 mm

*Figure 7-14.* How to design a deck camber curve.

with handle action, or so close to the edge of the deck that they fill with water as soon as the boat heels, or perhaps so directly in the centre of a walkway that they are constantly tripped over on dark nights.

### Tank Filling Pipes and Air Vents

The filling pipes and air vents for fuel and water tanks also have an influence on the arrangement of a deck, although certainly a very minor one. A filling pipe should ideally be straight and vertical so that a calibrated dip stick can be inserted into it, but this is not always possible. One thing, however, to always avoid when positioning fuel and water filling pipes is getting them so close together that fuel may accidentally find its way into your fresh water supply. Below deck, provided that tanks are carefully sited, both fuel and water filling pipes can second as stanchions.

Stanchions might also be used to cover the air vent tubing from tanks. Above deck, these vents can usually be concealed under the base of a winch, as shown in Figure 7-15.

### Minimum Accommodation: How Much to Compromise?

Most of the topics we have covered in this chapter have been items on deck that affect the interior, rather than features of the interior that influence the deck. This reflects the high priority given to the deck of an ocean racer. But there are limits to how far the accommodation of a boat can be compromised. These limits are the minimum standards essential for adequate living space.

How much can a designer actually squeeze into the interior of a boat? Often, not as much as he would like. For example, the smallest dimensions for a berth are 20 inches wide at a person's shoulders, 12 inches wide at his feet, and 6 feet 1 inch long. But these are absolute minimums. A more comfortable berth would be 24 inches at the shoulders, 14 inches at the feet, and 6 feet 6 inches long. Also, regardless of a berth's length and width, the space above it should never be less than 20 inches.

Headroom below deck also has its minimums. If a man is to be able to stand up in a cabin with his head

165

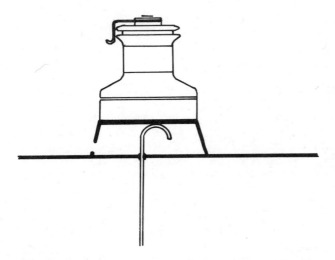

*Figure 7-15.* A fuel or water tank vent concealed under a winch base near the centreline of the boat.

Here are the minimum sizes for a number of other interior features. The absolute minimum width for an enclosed head is 26 inches. The minimum size of a galley varies, but it must always be large enough to fit a stove, an ice box, and at least three lockers for dishes, utensils, and food. A chart table can be no smaller than one fourth the size of the largest chart. The minimum depth of a hanging locker is sometimes overlooked in the interest of trying to squeeze it into a small space. But a hanging locker must always be at least 2 inches deeper than the length of the average coat hanger, which is about 17 inches. Finally, the bare minimum width for a doorway is 16 inches, although 18 inches is more suitable. Remember, too, that these minimums do not apply to doorways through which sails will be passed; these must be as wide as the longest dimension on the main sail-handling hatch.

All these dimensions, of course, are minimums. Many owners will want more spacious and comfortable accommodation even if they do intend to use their boats primarily for racing. Again, the question is one of priorities, for nearly any extra that is added to the interior of a boat will almost invariably have some influence, however minor, on the deck above. This is one of the basic trade-offs of yacht design.

slightly bowed, he must have at least 5 feet 9 inches of space. Six feet or 6 feet 3 inches of space is, of course, even better. But remember, headroom is required only where a person is going to stand. There is no need for 6 feet of headroom over a berth!

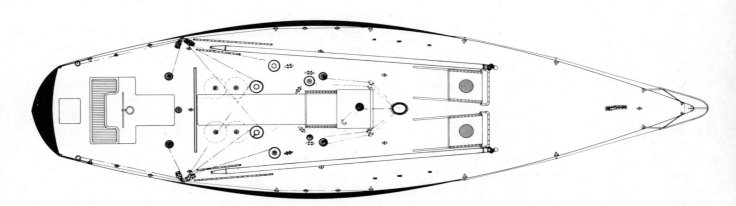

*Recluta*, designed by German Frers and owned by Mr Walter Hanson.

# CHAPTER EIGHT
# Laying Out some Decks

In previous chapters we have reviewed the many different factors that influence the layout of a racing deck. In doing this, we naturally restricted our focus to particular aspects of the design process. But now we are ready to look at the deck as a whole. Using the information discussed so far, how can the various pieces of equipment found on the deck of a modern ocean racer be arranged in a clean, efficient way? The answer, of course, varies depending upon the size and purpose of the boat. In this chapter we look at several possibilities: a Quarter Tonner based on a light-weight dinghy concept, a stock boat designed for the cruiser/racer market, an Admiral's Cup boat rating 34 feet and a singlehanded ketch 56 feet overall. Remember, though, that there is no final answer to the question of deck layout. Each designer, each owner, each crewman has his own preferences. The design ideas that follow, then, are just some of many workable solutions.

## The Planning Stage of Deck Layout

Before putting pen to paper, a designer should consider a number of factors that significantly influence deck layout. First, how will the boat be used? It may be, for example, that the owner wants to race in the major regattas with a full crew, but he also wants to cruise at other times with his wife and children. Whatever the owner's plans may be, the designer should carefully think through any special features of the deck arrangement that will be required. Second, what sail changing techniques will be employed? Obviously, these, too, must be considered in any deck layout. And third, what equipment do the owner, skipper, and crewmen want? A few meetings with the key people involved at an early stage in the design process can save the designer many hours at the drawing board.

It is a common tendency, of course, for an owner to want more than is necessary on a deck layout, or more than he can afford. So in compiling a list of deck equipment, it is always a good idea for someone to repeatedly question the usefulness of each item. Is it really essential? Is there some less expensive fitting that may work just as well? Can one piece of gear be made to do the job of two? Thoughtful answers to questions such as these can avoid both an overly complex deck arrangement and a cost that is far higher than the owner originally intended.

It is now time to do a rough sketch of the deck plan. At this point, a few basic aims should be kept in mind. First, remember that mere men will be operating the equipment, not super-humans with 8 foot arm spans or the ability to work effectively while balanced on one foot. Always consider the positioning of winches carefully, especially the foreguy and afterguy winches. Try to visualise the arrangement in use when the boat is well heeled and anticipate what the possible problems will be. Second, and equally important, keep the design clean and uncomplicated. The key to efficiency is simplicity. If a designer forgets this and tries to do too much with deck gear, he often ends up with a layout that is both extremely heavy and very complex to use.

Most deck plans go through several revisions before the final arrangement is agreed upon. The owner and his crew usually want to make some modifications to the designer's preliminary sketch, and the designer usually wants to refine and improve the owner's alterations. In the end, when everyone is satisfied, the result should be a simple, efficient layout, well suited to the purpose for which it was designed.

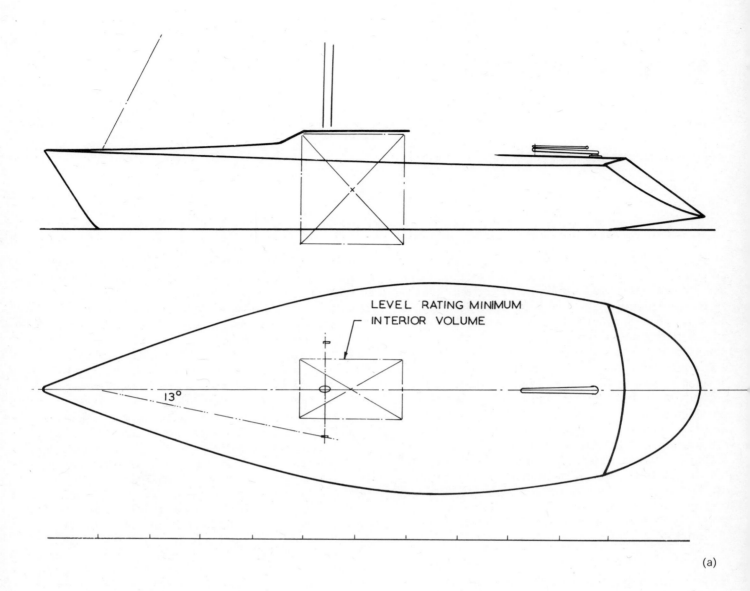

LEVEL RATING MINIMUM
INTERIOR VOLUME

13°

(a)

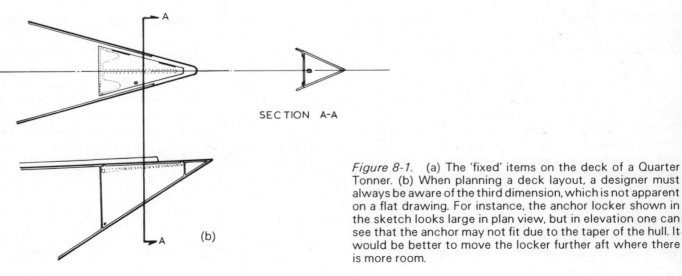

A

SECTION A-A

A

(b)

*Figure 8-1.* (a) The 'fixed' items on the deck of a Quarter Tonner. (b) When planning a deck layout, a designer must always be aware of the third dimension, which is not apparent on a flat drawing. For instance, the anchor locker shown in the sketch looks large in plan view, but in elevation one can see that the anchor may not fit due to the taper of the hull. It would be better to move the locker further aft where there is more room.

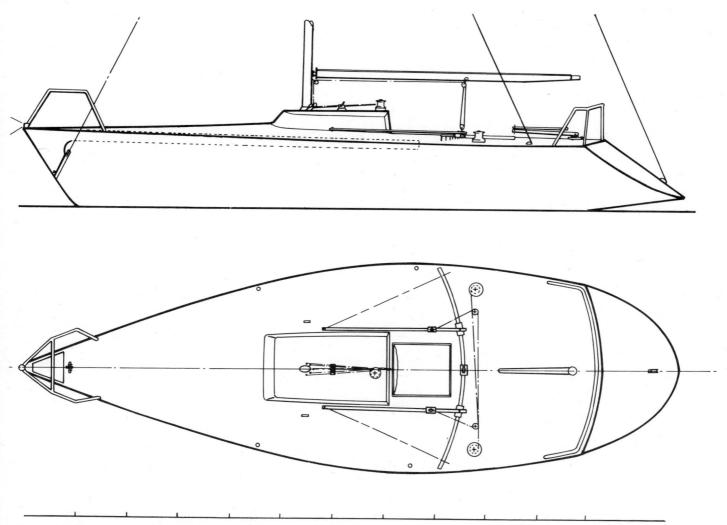

*Figure 8-2.* A first look at the deck plan of the Quarter Tonner. Note how the genoa tracks can slide outboard if required.

## Designing the Decks of Various Boats

### A Quarter Tonner

With today's intense competition in the Quarter Ton class, every aspect of a boat, not simply the deck layout, must be carefully planned for maximum performance potential. One way to lower the rating, and so increase sail area, is to trim the boat by the bow in measurement condition and then use crew weight aft to restore level trim while racing. We will assume that this design technique is planned for our hypothetical Quarter Tonner.

A quick calculation will give a good idea of how much bow down trim is desirable for the boat. Assume there are four crewmen weighing 160 pounds each.

Work out their distance from the longitudinal centre of flotation (LCF) while they are sailing the boat. Let's say that this is 6 feet. Now 4 crewmen × 160 lb × 6 ft = 3840 ft lb of trimming moment. A typical Quarter Tonner has a moment to change trim 1 inch of 600 ft lb. Thus, 3840/600 = 6.4 inches. Six inches of bow trim, then, is the maximum that should be incorporated into this design. In practice, of course, you can find this figure by putting the crew in their working positions and then trimming the boat level. When the crew is removed from the boat, the resulting bow down trim is the maximum desired for inclining.

But how does bow down trim affect deck layout? As mentioned earlier, when a boat is designed for the maximum bow down trim, the deck should be arranged in such a way as to keep the crew weight aft. Upwind

169

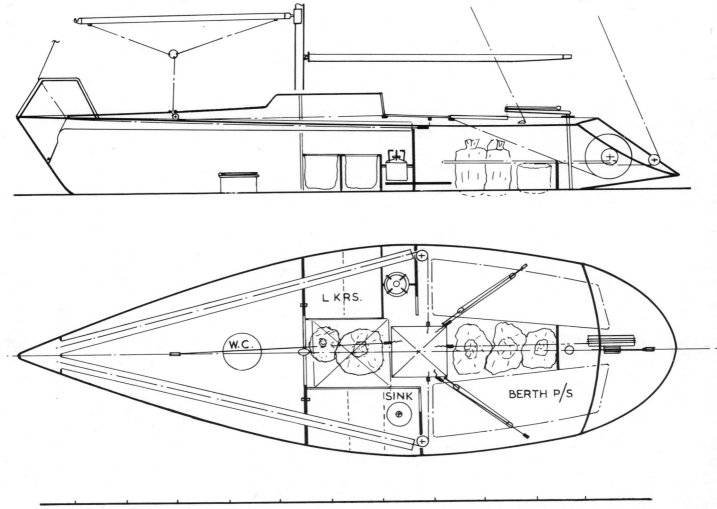

*Figure 8-3*.  The interior of the Quarter Tonner. Most of the weight is concentrated aft, with many of the 'strings' being operable from the main hatch. Note the windlass arrangement on the backstay.

the crewmen should be at the point of maximum beam—around station 6 to 7 on the deck plan. Off the wind, because the spinnaker tends to depress the bow, the crew should be even further aft. If this crew placement is neglected, boat performance invariably suffers.

Besides crew positioning aft, there are a number of other deck design features that the owner and his crew desire. All of them have been chosen with the primary aims of boat speed and work efficiency in mind.

1.  The sail plan will feature ¾ rig. Consequently, underdeck spinnaker tubes and a suitably designed pulpit are called for.

2.  The tack fitting will be a horn type, designed to avoid catching on the spinnaker.

3.  The smallest sized Stearn twin stay will be fitted.

4.  The spinnaker pole will be on the centreline, there

will be no foredeck hatch, and all the controls will be led to an aft cockpit.

5.  There will be a minimum number of winches with leads to the weather side where possible.

6.  There will be no hydraulics because they are too heavy.

7.  There will be some form of barber haul system.

8.  There will be a minimum freeboard and a minimum height coachroof with the boom as low as possible. Can a vang be fitted?

9.  The chart table will be positioned aft so that it can be viewed from the cockpit.

The next step is to prepare a preliminary sketch of the deck plan. First, the designer draws in all the 'fixed' items, such as the mast, the tiller, and the coachroof if any. This is shown in Figure 8-1. Next, he refines the

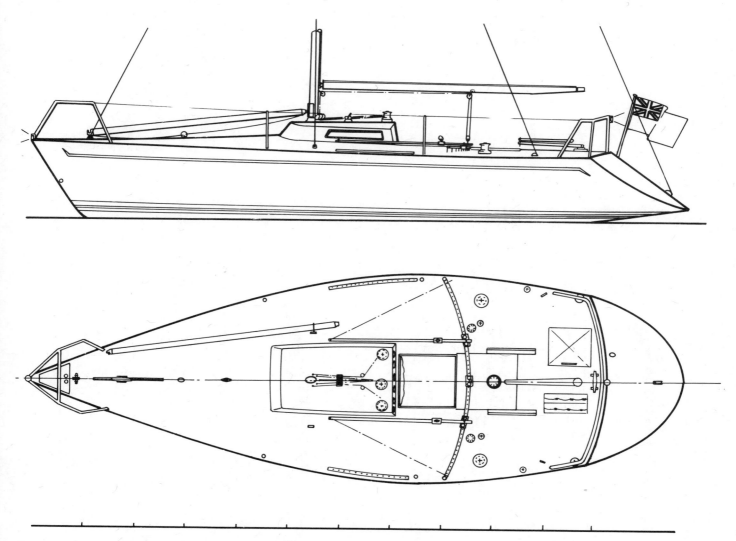

*Figure 8-4.* The final deck plan of our Quarter Tonner.

layout to suit the mainsheet and genoa tracks. Because of the $\frac{3}{4}$ rig and low boom, he specifies a full width mainsheet track. And rather than have extra fittings to move the genoa tracks athwartships, he allows the aft end of each genoa track to move on a car that runs along the mainsheet track. Taglines are used to pull the track inboard or outboard as required. This arrangement enables the main hatch to be situated aft of the small coachroof, and so it can serve as a cockpit. All the halyards and sail adjusters are led to a single winch on the coachroof, with lockoffs just in front of it. The primary winches are taken as far outboard as possible and are positioned far enough forward to avoid interference with the helmsman. Figure 8-2 shows the deck plan at this stage.

Figure 8-3 gives a view of the interior. Two quarter berths are sited well aft. The designer and owner agree that these berths will not be used much during a race, and so they are not worried about extra weight this far aft, which could be detrimental to performance. After all, it is difficult to sleep in a Quarter Tonner while a race is underway, and crewmen are likely to spend more time on the weather rail than in berths. For cooking, a gimballed gas burner is fitted, and there are canvas stowage lockers for crew belongings and other gear. The chart table is designed to be normally positioned over these lockers, but can be pulled out during a race so that a man in the hatch can use it. Some of the sails are also stowed under the chart table, and the rest are stowed on the cabin sole behind the mast. The only things forward of the mast are the head and the anchor stowage. The reasoning behind posi-

171

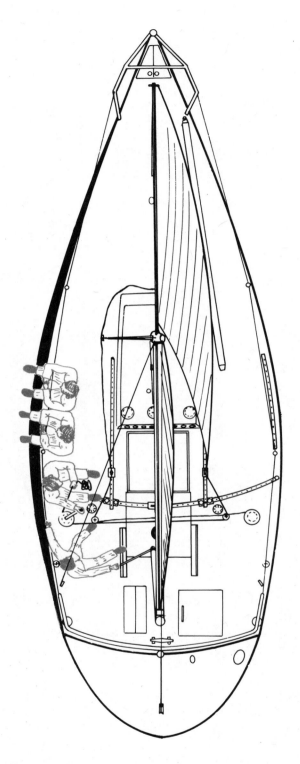

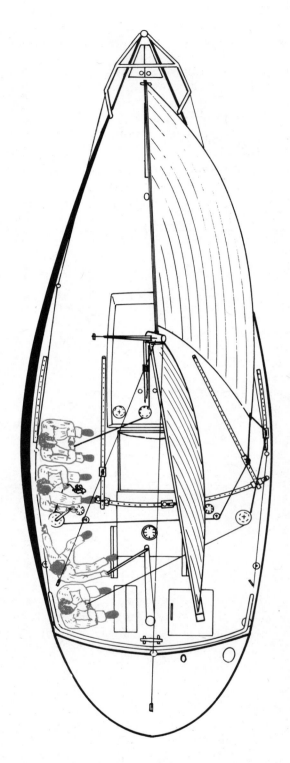

*Figure 8-5.* Quarter Tonner crew positions when sailing to windward. Note that the genoa track is all the way inboard. The helmsman could be playing the mainsheet, or one of the crew could turn around and play it. Although all the crewmen are shown on the windward rail, often one man will want to sit to leeward to watch the genoa.

*Figure 8-6.* Reaching on the Quarter Tonner. The genoa can be barberhauled further outboard after the track is all the way out.

172

tioning most gear aft is largely to eliminate the excessive bow down trim designed to reduce the boat's rating in measurement condition. One final feature of the interior to note are the underdeck leads, which helps considerably to keep the deck surface clear.

Now all that remains to do is to finalize the deck plan. A completed version is illustrated in Figure 8-4. In the plan view, the spinnaker pole is shown stowed, while in the profile view, the pole is in sailing position. Note that extra reaching tracks have been added to allow the genoa sheet to be barber hauled outboard if necessary. There are three compasses: one main steering compass on the centreline, and two smaller compasses on either side for the helmsman to detect wind shifts. Liferafts and horseshoes are stowed aft in wells set in the deck. Note, too, the single, removable bow cleat fitted on a track, and the single stern cleat. Apart from the lockoffs at the mast there are no sheet cleats because it is assumed that lines will be constantly trimmed.

Although we have a finished deck plan, we may not be absolutely certain that the crew can work efficiently under various sailing conditions. Figures 8-5 to 8-8 help detect any problems that might have been overlooked. They show the boat and its crew sailing under four typical conditions: (1) beating to windward, (2) close reaching with two sails, (3) reaching with a spinnaker, and (3) running with a spinnaker and blooper.

Several things become immediately apparent when considering Figure 8-5. First, the runner looks as if it will cut the helmsman's head, but in fact, a profile view shows that it will just clear him. Second, when the genoa tracks are hauled all the way inboard, the genoa is sheeted on a 7 degree line, and this is ideal. The designer, however, must carefully consider spreader lengths and chainplate positions when laying out a mast drawing.

In Figure 8-6, the genoa track has been pulled fully outboard, and a second sheet, slightly further forward than the first, has been lead to an outboard track. This allows the genoa to be eased even further outboard if desired. The second sheet is played by a crewman located behind the helmsman, and this extra weight aft helps offset the slight bow down trim from the increased power of the headsail. In heavier winds, it also increased rudder effectiveness.

In Figures 8-7 and 8-8, which show the boat under spinnaker, indicate that the original plan of using only three winches was inadequate. Two more winches, one on either side of the coachroof, are therefore incorporated into the deck plan. An extra bonus is achieved by adding two small cheek blocks on the coachroof. Any

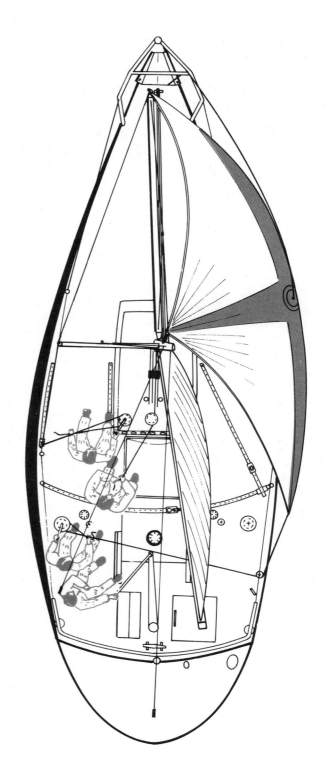

*Figure 8-7.* Quarter Tonner crew trimming the starcut on a close reach.

173

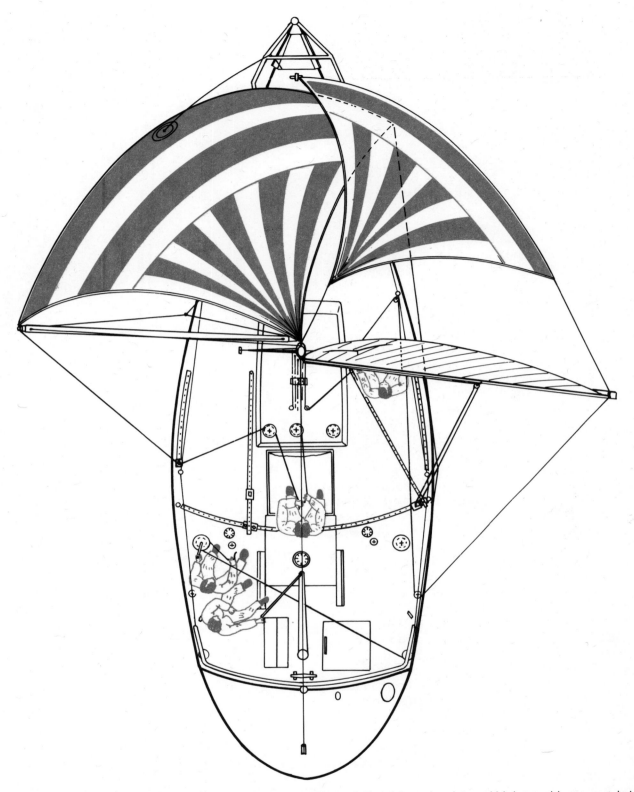

*Figure 8-8.*    Quarter Tonner running downwind in light to medium winds with a spinnaker and bigboy or blooper set. In heavy winds, the crew would be positioned on the transom or well aft. The mainsail may or may not be reefed depending upon the conditions.

of the mast lines can now be led to any of the three winches on the coachroof without being removed from the lockoffs.

In Figure 8-8, the boat is heading downwind with everything set. The man in front of the helmsman is operating the spinnaker sheet from a position where he can see the luff easily. Note that the spinnaker sheet passes under the tiller. Without a three-dimensional mock-up of the layout, it is impossible to judge heights with complete accuracy, so it is not certain if the spinnaker sheet avoids fouling the tiller. If any difficulty arose, however, the spinnaker sheet could always be led through the leeward genoa turning block and then to the winch. The man in the hatch in Figure 8-8 is available to play any of the underdeck leads (which have their own jam cleats), to trim the spinnaker pole, or to trim the mainsheet. The mainsheet preventer must be operated by the man under the main boom, who is playing the bigboy sheet and halyard. All the leads look as fair as possible.

With a series of drawings such as these, a designer can try to anticipate any problems that may arise when a boat is actually being sailed under various conditions. In this way he not only increases the efficiency of a particular deck plan, but also saves the owner costly changes to the layout at a later date. Space does not permit the other designs in this chapter to be analysed in such detail. When there is any doubt about how well an arrangement will work in practice, however, these kinds of sketches are recommended before the plan leaves the drawing board.

## A 32 Foot Stock Boat

The primary goal in developing a stock boat is to sell as many of them as possible. The design, consequently, must attempt to be all things to all people. A good performance record is needed to appeal to racing families, but the equipment cannot be so complex that the owner's teenage children are unable to handle it. An attractive exterior is essential to those who are interested in maintaining a good resale value, while a smart interior helps convince the owner's wife that this is a boat she can sail in comfortably. The designer and builder who want to produce a successful stock boat, then, must take all these and many other requirements into account. Often the various demands are difficult to reconcile and trade-offs must be made.

If there is one feature that cannot be compromised, however, it is an attractive look. In many families, the wife makes a convincing argument for design X because of its sleek profile and appealing arrangement

below deck. The superior efficiency of design Y's rig does little to change her preference. To the designer, this means that the interior plan exerts a strong influence on the deck layout, and not vice versa. If, for instance, a 6 inch movement of the companionway ladder makes access to the galley a little easier, the companionway hatch may end up in a somewhat less than ideal position on deck.

With these priorities in mind, the designer can begin to make a list of the features in his basic plan. Here are some likely possibilities.

1. A comfortable interior arrangement, using attractive colour schemes.
2. An attractive exterior, both in the hull profile and the deck arrangement.
3. A deck layout that can be operated by the owner's wife and children when cruising, and also by a full crew of men when racing.
4. A moulded deck which allows many items to be built in, thus reducing assembly costs.
5. No custom fittings.
6. Good headroom below deck—5 ft 10 in to 6 ft.
7. Deck fittings that do not intrude into the main cabin, or if they do intrude are hidden from sight.
8. Underdeck foreguys that run through overhead grab rails in the interior arrangement.
9. Some form of anchor well and chain lockers.
10. A stock alloy-framed forehatch.

The complete list, of course, should consider every major item on the boat. It will probably be bounced back and forth between the builder and the designer until a final plan is agreed upon. At this stage, the actual drawings can be started.

The first drawing, Figure 8-9, is of the interior. The sails are stowed aft, opposite a quarter berth, on which the navigator can sit when working at the chart table. Across from the chart table is a fairly simple galley with an ice box, stove, and sink. Note that the galley is near the hatch to allow good ventilation for heat and cooking odours without having to fit numerous vent boxes. The galley table folds down and the starboard settee slides out to form a berth. Forward of the mast is an enclosed head, essential on a family boat, and opposite it is a hanging locker. A berth big enough to comfortably sleep two children or one adult is located in the forepeak. All the way in the bow is an anchor well with a drainage hole.

The profile of the boat can be varied, of course, as long as adequate headroom is maintained. To get a good idea of the attractiveness of alternative designs, it often helps to draw up several different versions of the profile plan in smaller scale. Two possibilities are shown in Figure 8-10. The straight sheerline and thick

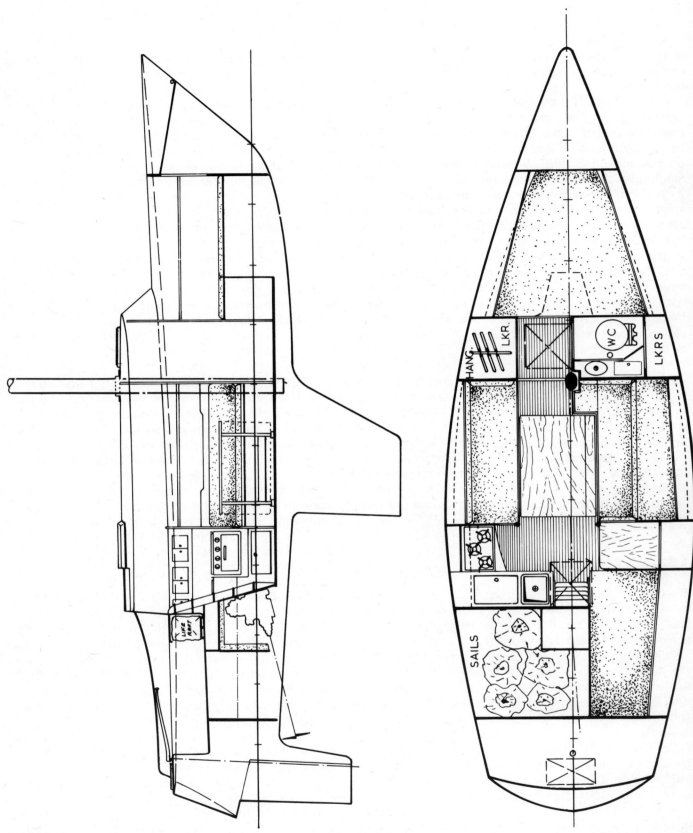

*Figure 8-9.* The interior plan and profile of a stock boat for family cruising and racing. Although not shown, each berth has leecloths, and items such as a cook's harness are called for in the specifications.

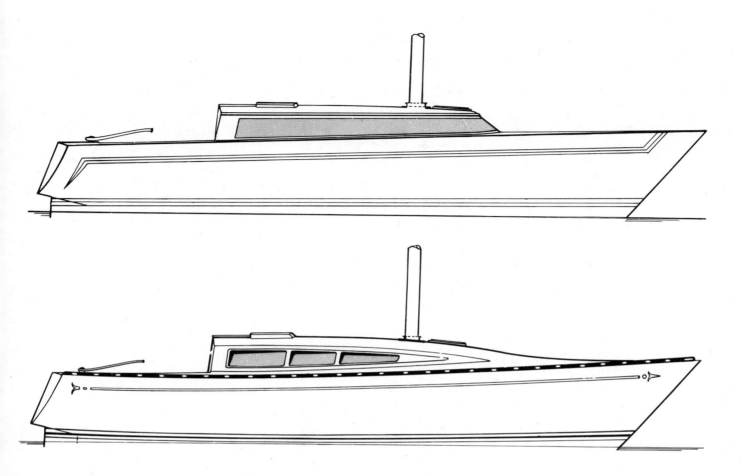

*Figure 8-10.* Two possible profiles for the same stock boat.

cove stripe on the upper profile give the boat a long, sleek appearance. The continuous window covering helps accentuate this look. Beneath this covering, however, the actual window cut-outs would not extend to the mast or else they could seriously weaken the mast support at the coachroof. Another problem with this profile is that when the boat is heeled, the curve of the deck would tend to make the straight sheerline look as if it had a reverse curve. In the lower profile, in contrast, the deckhouse is faired into the foredeck, as on a C & C or Nautor boat. For the sake of continuity, we will assume that we are rejecting both these alternative profile plans and keeping the one shown in the interior arrangement drawing.

Figure 8-11 shows the items on deck that are fixed by the interior. Notice that this boat has more fixed items than the previous Quarter Tonner because the influence of the interior arrangement is so much greater. An easy way to work up these parts of the deck plan is to place a drawing of the interior under an outline of the deck. This gives the precise location of all interior items without having to scale them off.

The more detailed deck plan, shown in Figure 8-12, is fairly conventional although certain features are worth noting. The primary winches have been set inboard a little to allow the trimmer to see the genoa, and they have also been raised sufficiently so that the handle will clear the coachroof. Although not apparent from this drawing, care would have to be taken to make sure that the genoa sheet does not foul the coaming. Notice, too, the positioning of the other winches. The spinnaker sheet winches are located forward, on the cabin top, for less congestion in the cockpit and easier trimming. And the halyard winches are sited so that they can be operated by a crewman standing on deck beside the coachroof, thus enabling him to work more efficiently. A few other aspects of the layout should also be mentioned briefly. The genoa tracks have been run almost parallel to the centreline because the coachroof prevents them from being carried further inboard. The width of the cockpit is such that the helmsman can comfortably sit with his legs braced across the well. And the sail hatches are of maximum size to allow quick and easy access.

177

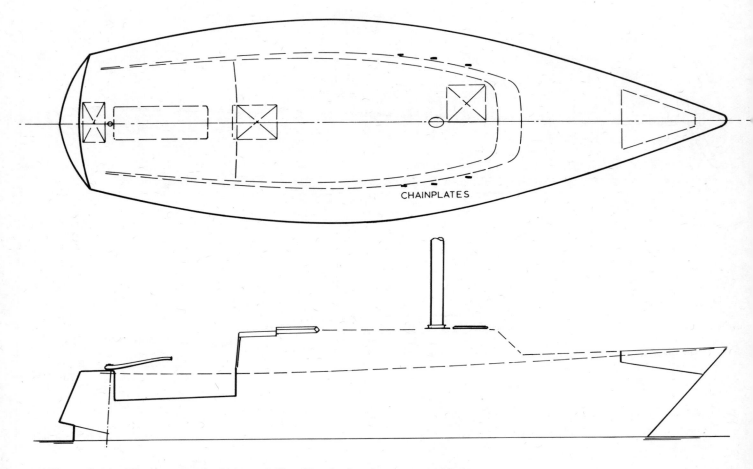

*Figure 8-11.* The items on deck that are 'fixed' by the interior accommodation.

## A 34 Foot Rating Admiral's Cup Boat

One of the primary aims when designing a 34 foot rating Admiral's Cup boat (45 feet LOA) is to get the most out of every item fitted on deck. In this respect, the problems of laying out an Admiral's Cup boat are somewhat similar to those of laying out the deck of a Quarter Tonner. In terms of their interior arrangements, however, the two boats differ considerably. Whereas not much is done with the interior of a typical Quarter Tonner, a good deal of thought should be given to the interior of the typical Admiral's Cup boat because a damp, uncomfortable accommodation usually means sleepless nights and a tired, inefficient crew.

Consequently, the owner's list of requirements will usually include features above and below deck. Here is a typical sample.

1. A centre crewpit and aft helmsman's cockpit, both with hatches.

2. A single spinnaker pole permanently attached to the mast, with a breakdown pole in two pieces and a jockey pole stowed below deck.

3. Twin foredeck hatches designed for hoisting sails directly out of them.

4. A three-halyard masthead.

5. Chainplates that can swing inboard.

6. The question of spinnaker tubes on a boat of this size was raised by the owner, but the sailmaker recommended takedown patches.

7. As 'clean' a mast as possible to reduce windage.

8. Good natural lighting through opening ports in cockpits where possible. Good ventilation through bow vents and dorades where possible.

9. The chart table located in the aft cabin because the owner will navigate.

10. A long passageway below deck to enable a spinnaker to be easily flaked and stopped.

Figure 8-13 shows the deck layout that was ultimately decided upon, as well as the interior arrangement. Both plans were worked up simultaneously to ensure total design integration.

Looking first at the interior, you can see that there is

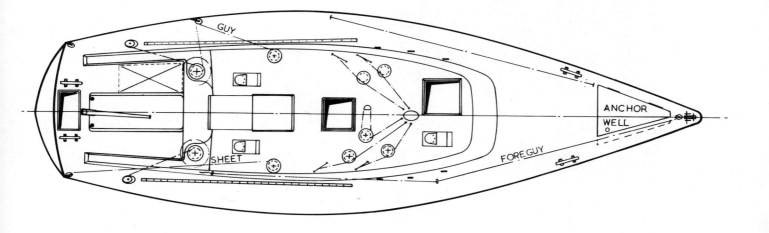

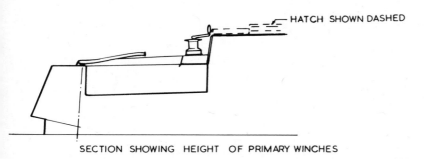

SECTION SHOWING HEIGHT OF PRIMARY WINCHES

*Figure 8-12.* The final deck plan of the stock boat, and a section through the aft cockpit showing the primary winch positions.

space for stowing stormsails under the berths; the rest of the sails when racing are stowed on the floor. At the dock, of course, all sails are stowed forward. A clip-on removable platform is designed for under the forward hatch to allow the halyards to be worked easily when racing inshore. This platform is not used offshore. Stowage space and lockers have been kept to a minimum to encourage the crew to bring less clothing and gear with them. There are six lockers under the central crewpit, and oilskins are stowed on the aft head wall in a canvas locker. Since both the head and the galley are located to port, various batteries and tanks are to be sited to starboard to balance any athwart-ship trim.

On deck, all the owner's requirements are met. One of the more novel features is a crank which crosses the middeck cockpit and terminates in bevel boxes under the winches. It cuts down on the equipment needed for a pedestal winch arrangement and also increases winding efficiency by about 8 to 10 per cent. Notice that the spinnaker sheet winches are sited well forward

to ensure that these sheets do not cross the mainsheet track or the crewpit. During a gybe, the spinnaker sheets would be handled by the man in the hatch. On the foredeck there are two staysail tracks and two babystay chainplates which can be used with the spinnaker pole on either side of the bow. Note also that the main halyard is located below deck to reduce windage and deck clutter. Another point worth mentioning is that the forward dorade boxes are under the deck and drain over the side, with only the removable cowls visible from above. Usually, these vents will not be required when racing.

With the deck plan completed, the next step is to anticipate how everything will work on the race course. A very expensive way of doing this, used on the twelve metre *Courageous*, is to build a mock-up of the deck, put the crew on it, and make whatever adjustments are needed. A cheaper method, of course, although not quite so accurate, is simply to sketch out where the crewmen will be during the various steps of a sail change or gybe.

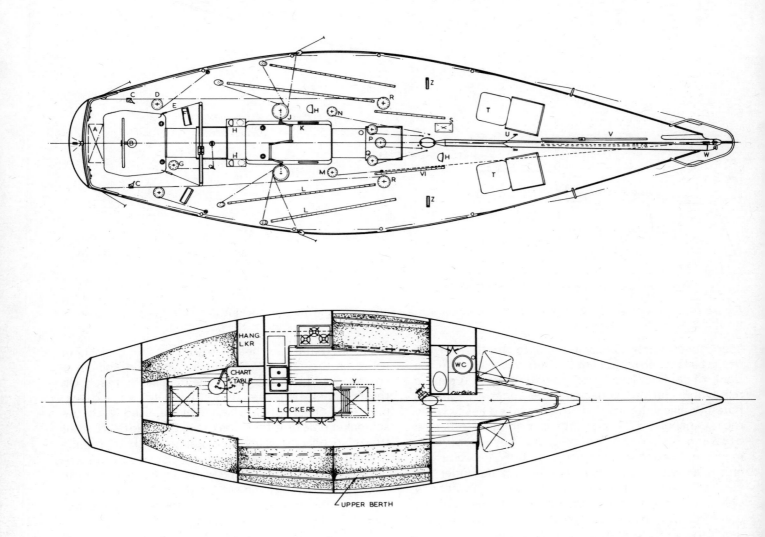

*Figure 8-13.* The interior and deck plan of an Admiral's Cup design. A Liferaft stowage. B Compass. C Sheet stopper. D Runner winches. E Taglines. F Instrument boxes. G Mainsheet winch. H Dorade vents. J Primary genoa winches. K Opening ports. L Genoa tracks. M Foreguy winch. N Topping lift winch. O Port halyard. P Centre halyard. Q Starboard halyard. R Spinnaker sheet winch. S Alloy hatch. T Forehatch. U Babystay chainplates. V Staysail tack track. Note that the foredeck cleats slide on the staysail track and can be removed. V1 Staysail sheet track. W Bow vent system. X Main halyard. Y Removable platform for halyard winchman. Z Chainplates.

*High Roler* sailing off Miami. Note how the helmsman has braced himself to see to weather and how the genoa trimmer is sitting where he can operate the winch and see the sails. By analyzing pictures of this sort, crew positions can be improved to lessen fatigue and enhance efficiency. *(Alastair Black)*

*Figure 8-14.* Crew positions on the Admiral's Cup boat for a bear-away spinnaker set. At position A, the boat is approaching the mark. The pole is raised and the spinnaker has been started. The foredeckman (under the genoa) is watching the buoy and calling its position for the helmsman.

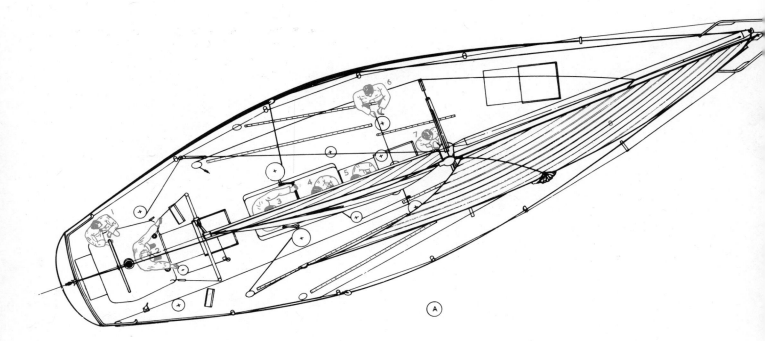

Position A
1 Helmsman.
2 Mainsail trimmer eases the traveller and then the sheet.
3 Winch grinder pulls guy aft on self-tailing winch.
4 Man in forward end of the cockpit eases foreguy and genoa sheet.
5 Man in hatch raises spinnaker then lowers genoa.
6 Spinnaker sheet trimmer.
7 Mast man raises pole, helps pull on spinnaker halyard and then puts jockey pole up if required.
8 Foredeck man (under genoa) ensures the spinnaker leaves the bag clean and stands by to gather genoa.

182

Position A in Figure 8-14 shows this particular Admiral's Cup boat beating to the mark with the crew ready to hoist the spinnaker. Immediately you see that the man with the spinnaker sheet must hold it up reasonably high to avoid fouling the halyard operator. But this is probably preferable to having the spinnaker sheet pass either under the mainsheet or across the crewpit. If necessary the spinnaker sheet could be locked off back near the helmsman and put on the runner winch; or the sail could be initially sheeted at the runner winch and changed to the forward winch later. Position B in Figure 8-14 shows where the crew will be moments after the hoist, when the genoa is on deck and the spinnaker is up and drawing. At this stage, the foredeckman is about to set a staysail, and the rest of the crew is busy making sure that the sails are trimmed to their optimum setting.

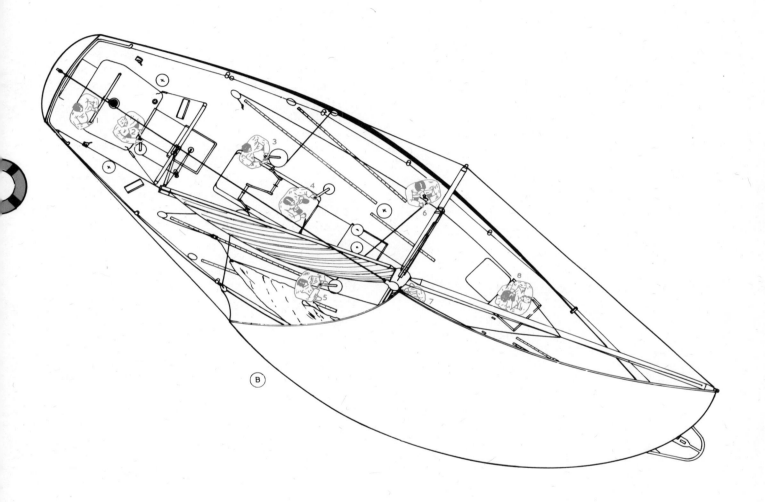

Position B
1 Helmsman.
2 Mainsail trimmer also works hydraulics to rake rig forward and tension vang.
3 Guy trimmer fine trims pole with handle in winch.
4 Foreguy and spinnaker topping lift trimmer (this exercise shows that the afterguy, foreguy and topping lift winches should be moved closer together).
5 Sheet winch winder.
6 Spinnaker sheet trimmer.
7 Mast man gets staysail halyard ready.
8 Foredeck man gets staysail ready for hoisting.

Of course, for the experienced designer, drawings such as these are usually unnecessary because he is able to visualise in his mind's eye how efficient a deck will be in most circumstances. But for the beginning designer, or for the owner designing his own deck, such sketches can be extremely helpful. Although they lack a third dimension, they nevertheless make it easier to spot potential problems with a given layout, so that these weaknesses can be corrected while the plan is still on the drawing board.

Looking back over the three decks we have designed so far, it is clear how different goals and priorities critically affect deck layout. On the Quarter Tonner, the deck design and the crew weight positioning were of enormous importance, while the interior arrangement was relatively unimportant. On the stock boat, in contrast, these priorities were essentially reversed. The interior received the greatest attention, and the deck layout, although designed to be efficient, was subservient to the demands of the below-deck accommodation. And finally, on this Admiral's Cup boat, these two aspects of design—deck and interior—have been carefully integrated to enable the crew to work efficiently for long periods of time and also to get the best possible rest off watch.

## A 56 Foot Single-Handed Ketch

The final deck we are going to consider is that of a single-handed ketch for the Transatlantic Race. Here, although work efficiency on deck is of course important, the primary accent is on safety for the sole occupant. Not surprising, the owner's list of requirements for such a boat is completely different from anything else we have seen in this chapter. But it suggests that, with careful thought, a boat of almost any size can be handled by one person.

1.  All sheets should be double-ended, with one end leading to an aft cockpit and the other to a middeck cockpit.

2.  Whenever possible the winches should be organized so that a given sheet is in the same position in both cockpits.

3.  The aft cockpit should be deep and well-drained.

4.  Vane steering is a must, but there should also be a separate system to drive the rudder if the vane breaks—for example, a tab on the rudder. (Do we want a trim tab on the keel?)

5.  All halyard winches should be sited on the mast, and there should be bars on deck for the operator to lean against.

6.  There should be an easy reefing system on the main and mizzen.

7.  The boat should be able to be steered from above or below deck. (An observation dome?)

8.  A forward well for sail changing or a roller reefing system?

9.  There should be self-tending staysails.

10.  The winches should be slightly oversized for ease of operation.

11.  Good compasses and instruments are essential.

12.  The below deck accommodation should be comfortable, with plenty of stowage and good drainage.

13.  Wherever possible, arrangements should be designed to minimize chafe.

For the deck layout of any single-handed boat, the designer is called upon to incorporate novel features in a way that works well for the individual owner/sailor. He is also called upon to anticipate safety hazards, and he will want to imagine the worst conditions possible and create methods for the single crewman to handle them effectively.

Figure 8-15 shows one plan that meets the objectives just listed. Each of the two cockpits has access from below, and any sheet, except the reacher, can be thrown off or trimmed from either cockpit. The hatches have their own dodgers to keep spray out, and there are also breakwaters just forward of the cockpits. Note, too, how the sail area has been broken up into easily handled portions. This arrangement, of course, requires many sheet leads, but these can run through tubes below deck if necessary.

## Checking the Details of a Deck Layout

On all the drawings in this chapter, many of the details were purposely left out in an effort to emphasize the general concept of the deck, not the exact placement of every single item. But in the final stages of a deck design, details are, of course, important. Table 8-16 is a checklist of all the major areas of a deck and pieces of deck equipment commonly fitted. It can be used to help make sure that nothing is inadvertently overlooked.

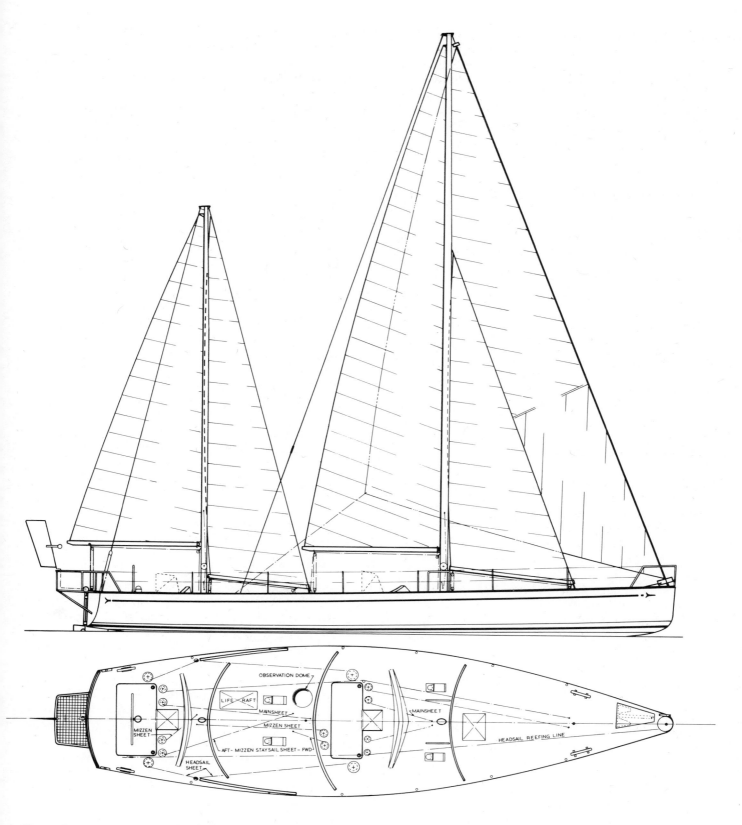

*Figure 8-15.*   A 56 foot LOA (46 foot LWL) ketch for the single-handed Transatlantic Race.

Table 8-16

# Deck Plan Check List

Masts
Chainplates
   headstay
   backstay
   lowers (D1's)
   verticals (V1's)
   runner padeyes
   midstay attachment
   babystay attachment
Mizzen Chainplates
Tracks
   genoa sheet tracks
   staysail sheet tracks
   staysail tack track
   toerail
   boom vang track
   mainsheet track (indicate taglines)
   mizzen sheet track or block
Fairleads, Padeyes, and Sheet Stoppers
   mooring fairleads/chocks (bow; midships; stern)
   mooring cleats (bow; midships; stern)
   anchor roller fairlead
   genoa fairlead/turning blocks
   foreguy padeye
   mast padeyes
   staysail padeyes (also tracks)
   mizzen staysail padeyes
   spinnaker sheet and guy padeyes and blocks
   jib topsail padeye
   storm jib padeyes
   sheet stoppers
Steering Gear
   tiller steering (extension)
   wheel steering (single or twin; indicate diameter)
   pedestal(s)
   emergency steering
Safety Equipment
   stanchions and folding stanchions
   lifelines around boat and decklines
   handrails
   bow pulpit
   anchors
   stern pulpit
   liferaft stowage
   navigation lights (bow; stern)
Lighting, Hatches, and Vents
   deck lights (to light sails)
   deck prisms
   small alloy hatches for ventilation
   sail hatches
   crew hatches and companionways
   dodger grooves
   ventilators and guards (indicate type, i.e. dorade)
   fresh water tank fills and vents
   fuel tank fills and vents
   engine compartment vents
   exhaust pipe from engine

Instruments
   compasses
   depth sounder
   speedometer/log
   wind-speed indicator
   wind-direction indicator
   hull-speed indicator
Halyard Winches
   staysail
   topping lift
   spinnaker
   genoa
   main
   mizzen
   mizzen staysail
Sheet Winches
   genoa
   spinnaker
   staysail
   runner
   pedestals and linkages
   grinders
Cleats for Winches
Cleats for Taglines
Hydraulics
   backstay
   headstay
   vang
   babystay/midstay
   control panel and pump
Cockpits and Cabins
   cockpit coamings
   winch bases
   helmsman's seat
   cockpit scuppers
   deckhouse or cabin
Other Items
   tack fitting
   foreguy (underdeck tube)
   stove gas stowage and drain overside
   spinnaker poles
   jockey poles
   boathook
   deck scuppers
   flagpole socket
   dinghy stowage
   gangway
   spinnaker launching tubes
   spreader outlines (optional)

In spite of its comprehensiveness, however, certain types of details are not included on this list. Take, for example, the heights of winches. Are closely positioned winches raised to different heights so that the handle of one is in danger of hitting the other? Do the winch handles clear the coachroof or other potential obstacles easily? (If you look back at Figure 8-12, you can see how the winch handle just misses the coachroof. Perhaps the winch should be raised a little more—a possible problem which can be checked on the deck plug.) Another detail to check is whether the genoa sheet bears on the coaming. If it does, it will either fray and eventually snap or score a groove in the coaming. And also check, as far as possible, to see that the spinnaker pole, jockey pole stowages, dorade vents, winches, and so forth will not catch the genoa sheet as the boat is tacked.

There are other details to remember, too. Be sure, for instance, to show rounded corners wherever they are desired and not leave this feature to the builder's discretion. Also, if coamings or cabins are intended to serve as backrests, be sure to indicate a comfortable slope (about 1 inch in 10 inches is good). And careful thought should be given to the slope of each cockpit for proper drainage. The cockpit sole should slope slightly downward toward the forward end where the drains should be located, unless, of course, this arrangement interferes with the accommodation beneath. In addition, one should always note where winch handles can be stowed and where instruments can be conveniently placed. These may seem like minor points, but often it is lack of attention to small details that spoils an otherwise efficient deck layout.

## The Continuing Process of Deck Design

Hopefully, this book has helped to further your understanding of what constitutes effective deck design. But it is always up to the individual to assess what makes a deck arrangement work for him—or fail to work.

This is most easily done when you are out on the race course. If you find something on a particular boat that works exceptionally well, wait until you are off watch, measure it, and sketch it up. It may be an extra comfortable helmsman's seat which seems to feel right at all angles of heel. Or it may be a hatchway that has some special feature to make it easy to open perhaps, or that allows sail bags and people to pass through smoothly without snagging. But whatever it is, always make a drawing of it for future reference.

Similarly, always record those items on a deck that do not work well. Take a careful look and analyze why you think they fall short. In some cases it may be useful to go back and redefine the purpose of the item to help rethink it. You may find that a simple, very inexpensive change may greatly improve its efficiency. Or you may be led to design an entirely new arrangement to replace the old one. As long as the cost is not too high, the new solution may be well worth trying. Note, too, that one way of spotting possible problem areas on a deck is to pay attention to breakage. Find out why something snapped, for example, and determine if the difficulty can be eliminated either by a new design or by a redefinition of an old item's function.

Eventually, with a watchful eye and the patience to collect as many drawings and measurements as possible, you will develop a file which is a valuable design tool in its own right and also the potential source of new ideas and innovations. All this may give your deck layout any edge over those of competing boats and help make the final difference between winning and losing.

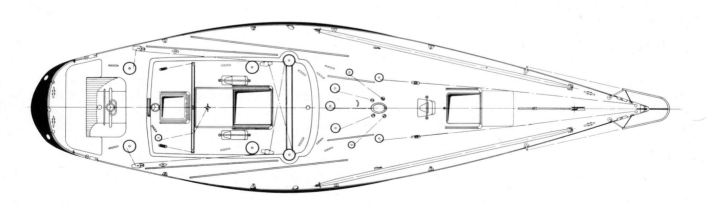

*Tantara*, designed by Sparkman & Stephens for Mr Earl Birdzell.

CONCLUSION
# Some Future Trends

By and large, major new developments in racing hull shapes are greatly restricted by the present handicapping rules. Even if the method for rating boats changed substantially, it would probably not be long before designers discovered how to optimize their lines plans under the new set of parameters, and hull shapes would become fairly predictable once again. Where, then, will the design advantages of the future come from? There are several areas of potential innovation that have still not yet been fully tapped. One is sail technology; another rig design; and a third very important factor is deck gear and deck layout. Here we will mention some of the possible developments that might be seen on the decks of ocean racers in the not-to-distant future.

Winches are one aspect of deck design that will probably experience continuing improvement. One of the next innovations is likely to be a variable-speed winch. The operator turns the handle in one direction, and as the load on the sheet increases, the drum speed automatically slows so that the ideal power ratio is always maintained. This model might even be fitted with hydraulics using a high-pressure system, although there is currently some question as to how long high-pressure hydraulics would last on a boat. If the problem of durability could be solved, however, one way that a hydraulic-operated winch might work would be for the system to be pressurized by winding the winch, say off watch, and the power stored for later use during a tack.

Another innovation in winch technology now under consideration is the development of pedal-powered winches. Whereas the average man can exert a force of about $\frac{1}{5}$ of a horsepower using his arms, this force can be raised to about $\frac{1}{3}$ of a horsepower if the same man uses his legs instead. Thus the pedal-powered winch has obvious speed advantages.

The concepts of both the 'bicycle' winch and the variable-speed winch are currently being worked on by winch manufacturers, but it is not known how long

it will be before either idea reaches the production and marketing stage. Perhaps they are best thought of as long-run developments. One other possible change in winch technology that may emerge in the long run is the introduction of multiple-drummed winches. These would be geared to move several parts of the rig together—such as the genoa lead and tension and the backstay/headstay tension. The ideal setting for the entire system might be controlled by a computerized 'black box'.

Deck hardware, in addition to winches, can be expected to evolve too. In the near future, most deck fittings will be made lighter and more efficient, and quite a few may be removable after they have served their specific purposes. In the more distant future, decks may be streamlined to a greater extent than ever imagined today. In fact, extensive wind tunnel testing of deck plans may be used by designers to ensure that a layout is as 'clean' as possible before it even leaves the drawing board.

Changes in the use of cockpits might be predicted as well. Many designers already feel that large, deep cockpits are a throwback to the days of high doghouses to afford shelter to the crew. Large cockpits, therefore, may very well disappear completely. The only remnant of the old cockpit may be a shallow pit designed to position a crewman at the ideal height for operating a winch.

And finally, in the area of mast and rigging technology, a few trends seem likely to occur. Multiple spreader rigs have already appeared on the scene. The next significant development may be a 100 per cent carbon fibre spar, after a drop in the cost of carbon fibre and a removal of the exotic materials penalty currently in the rating rule. Such spars are already being developed by Vickers-Slingsby, although they are not in general use because of the IOR penalty. Beyond this development, the masts of tomorrow may become highly flexible structures, rakeable to the limits of the then-existing rule.

# Bibliography

All these changes, of course, are only possibilities. In sailing, as in any other sport, the future cannot always be predicted. Hopefully, though, in thinking about where ocean racing design is going, we may be able to stimulate ideas that will help the present breed of boat go faster. And that, after all, is what the pleasure of yacht racing is all about. With this in mind, good luck and good sailing.

Not many up-to-date sources are available on the topic of deck layout. In writing this book, I was fortunate to have access to the design data of the Sparkman & Stephens office. I also found the catalogues and brochures of various manufacturers particularly helpful, namely Lewmar Marine, Ltd., Barient, Inc., Barlow, Pty. Ltd., Merriman-Holbrook, Inc., Costruzioni Barbarossa, Goiot, Aldo, M. S. Gibb, Ltd., Hood Yacht Systems, North Sails, Stearn Sailing Systems, South Coast Rod Rigging, and H. R. Spencer.

As for published books and articles by other authors, the following were especially valuable:

Peter Johnson, *Ocean Racing & Offshore Yachts*. Lymington: Nautical Publishing Company.

The editors of *Sail* magazine, *The Best of Sail Trim*. New York: W. W. Norton & Company, Inc.; London: Adlard Coles Ltd.

Ian Godfrey, *Winches—A Combination of Speed, Power, and Layout*. Seahorse.

Ian Godfrey, *Advanced Deck Layouts*. Seahorse, September, 1973.

Peter Johnson, *Making the Winch Do the Work*. Yachting World, May, 1974.

Rob Humphreys, *Offshore Deck Layouts*. Yachts & Yachting, March–April, 1976.

Tim Stearn, *The Hydraulic Edge*. Yacht Racing, May, 1976.

# Index